Stories of Ourselves

Volume 3

Cambridge International Education
Anthology of Stories in English

Shaftesbury Road, Cambridge CB2 8EA, United Kingdom

One Liberty Plaza, 20th Floor, New York, NY 10006, USA

477 Williamstown Road, Port Melbourne, VIC 3207, Australia

314–321, 3rd Floor, Plot 3, Splendor Forum, Jasola District Centre, New Delhi – 110025, India

103 Penang Road, #05–06/07, Visioncrest Commercial, Singapore 238467

Cambridge University Press & Assessment is a department of the University of Cambridge.

We share the University's mission to contribute to society through the pursuit of education, learning and research at the highest international levels of excellence.

www.cambridge.org
Information on this title: www.cambridge.org/9781009467681 (Paperback)

© Cambridge University Press & Assessment 2025

This publication is in copyright. Subject to statutory exception and to the provisions of relevant collective licensing agreements, no reproduction of any part may take place without the written permission of Cambridge University Press & Assessment.

First published 2025

20 19 18 17 16 15 14 13 12 11 10 9 8 7 6 5 4 3 2 1

Printed in Malaysia by Vivar Printing

A catalogue record for this publication is available from the British Library

ISBN 978-1-009-46768-1 Paperback
ISBN 978-1-009-46770-4 Digital Access (1 Year)
ISBN 978-1-009-46769-8 eBook

Cambridge University Press & Assessment has no responsibility for the persistence or accuracy of URLs for external or third-party internet websites referred to in this publication, and does not guarantee that any content on such websites is, or will remain, accurate or appropriate. Information regarding prices, travel timetables, and other factual information given in this work is correct at the time of first printing but Cambridge University Press & Assessment does not guarantee the accuracy of such information thereafter.

NOTICE TO TEACHERS

It is illegal to reproduce any part of this work in material form (including photocopying and electronic storage) except under the following circumstances:

(i) where you are abiding by a licence granted to your school or institution by the Copyright Licensing Agency;

(ii) where no such licence exists, or where you wish to exceed the terms of a licence, and you have gained the written permission of Cambridge University Press & Assessment;

(iii) where you are allowed to reproduce without permission under the provisions of Chapter 3 of the Copyright, Designs and Patents Act 1988, which covers, for example, the reproduction of short passages within certain types of educational anthology and reproduction for the purposes of setting examination questions.

....

Every effort has been made to trace the owners of copyright material included in this book. The publishers would be grateful for any omissions to be brought to their notice for acknowledgement in future editions of the book.

Our **Cambridge Dedicated Teacher Awards** are an opportunity to show appreciation for the incredible work teachers do every day.

Thank you to everyone who nominated this year; we have been inspired and moved by all of your stories. Well done to all of our nominees for your dedication to learning and for inspiring the next generation of thinkers, leaders and innovators.

Congratulations to our winners!

Global Winner
South East Asia & Pacific
Sydney Engelbert
Keningau Vocational College, Malaysia

East Asia
Pengfei Jiang
Zhuji Ronghuai Foreign Language School, China

Pakistan
Saeeda Salim
SISA - School of International Studies in Sciences & Arts, Pakistan

South Asia
Meena Mishra
Dr Sarvepalli Radhakrishnan International School, India

Middle East and North Africa
Gina Justus
Our Own English High school- Sharjah- Girls, United Arab Emirates

Sub-Saharan Africa
Tajudeen Odufeso
Isara Secondary School, Isara Remo, Nigeria

Europe
Aynur Bayazit
Menekşe Ahmet Yalçınkaya Kindergarten, Türkiye

Latin America & the Caribbean
Ramon Majé Floriano
Montessori sede San Francisco, Colombia

North America
Marisa Santos
Seminole Ridge Community High School, United States

For more information about our dedicated teachers and their stories, go to **dedicatedteacher.cambridge.org**

Contents

Introduction ix

1 *The Invisible Girl* 1
   MARY SHELLEY

2 *The Black Veil* 10
   CHARLES DICKENS

3 *The Nightingale* 19
   HANS CHRISTIAN ANDERSEN

4 *The Tell-Tale Heart* 26
   EDGAR ALLAN POE

5 *The Necklace* 30
   GUY DE MAUPASSANT

6 *The Model Millionaire* 37
   OSCAR WILDE

7 *Tony Kytes, the Arch-Deceiver* 41
   THOMAS HARDY

8 *The Sea Raiders* 48
   H G WELLS

9 *A Pair of Silk Stockings* 55
   KATE CHOPIN

10 *A Wagner Matinée* 59
    WILLA CATHER

11 *The Mission of Mr Scatters* 65
    PAUL LAURENCE DUNBAR

12 *Sultana's Dream* 75
    BEGUM ROKEYA SAKHAWAT HOSSAIN

Contents

13	*The Preliminaries* CORNELIA A P COMER	84
14	*Araby* JAMES JOYCE	96
15	*The Mark on the Wall* VIRGINIA WOOLF	101
16	*The Interlopers* SAKI (HECTOR HUGH MUNRO)	106
17	*The Nightmare Room* ARTHUR CONAN DOYLE	111
18	*The Return* ELIZABETH BOWEN	116
19	*The Woman at the Store* KATHERINE MANSFIELD	123
20	*Never* H E BATES	132
21	*Atrophy* EDITH WHARTON	135
22	*A Lady's Beaded Bag* TENNESSEE WILLIAMS	144
23	*Excursion* HERMAN BOSMAN	147
24	*Like Mother Used to Make* SHIRLEY JACKSON	151
25	*The Lagoon* JANET FRAME	158
26	*The Flying Machine* RAY BRADBURY	161
27	*The Cricket Match* SAM SELVON	165

28	*The Blush* ELIZABETH TAYLOR	169
29	*The Sacrificial Egg* CHINUA ACHEBE	175
30	*Action Will Be Taken* (An Action-Packed Story) HEINRICH BÖLL	179
31	*Woman from America* BESSIE HEAD	183
32	*The Man Who Wouldn't Get Up* DAVID LODGE	185
33	*A Very Desirable Residence* P D JAMES	190
34	*Sale* ANITA DESAI	198
35	*Land Deal* GERALD MURNANE	203
36	*The Teddy-bears' Picnic* WILLIAM TREVOR	207
37	*My Father Writes to My Mother* ASSIA DJEBAR	220
38	*Smoke* ILA MEHTA	223
39	*Fishing* PATRICIA GRACE	229
40	*The Fire Eater's Return* EARL LOVELACE	232
41	*The Secret of My Youth* MIMOZA AHMETI	238
42	*The Light on the Sea* JOHN WICKHAM	241

Contents

43	*New York Day Women* EDWIDGE DANTICAT	245
44	*A Village after Dark* KAZUO ISHIGURO	249
45	*The Clean Slate* HILARY MANTEL	258
46	*The American Embassy* CHIMAMANDA NGOZI ADICHIE	264
47	*Nietverloren* J M COETZEE	272
48	*The Universal Story* ALI SMITH	277
49	*Golden Boys* SHIH-LI KOW	283
50	*Staying Behind* KEN LIU	292
51	*My Father's Head* OKWIRI ODUOR	304
52	*The Nominee* CURTIS SITTENFELD	311
53	*Hard to Say* SHARON MORSE	318
54	*Reflection* SILMY ABDULLAH	329
55	*Kind Stranger* MERON HADERO	334
56	*Widows* MARGARET ATWOOD	341

Acknowledgements   345

Introduction

Following the successful Cambridge anthologies *Stories of Ourselves Volume 1* and *Volume 2*, this third volume continues a series which pulls together a range of stories which will be set for a number of Cambridge examination syllabuses. At the same time, it presents a collection of stories, mostly written in English, from across the world and which will provide much material for the general reader to explore.

While some writers have specialised in the short story – such as Katherine Mansfield, Hans Christian Andersen and Saki – others we would more readily class as novelists have also published more compressed stories – like Charles Dickens, J M Coetzee and Chimamanda Ngozi Adichie – showing equal adeptness with the shorter form. All these writers are represented in this anthology, alongside many other well-known authors. Others may be less familiar, and the anthology may be introducing readers to these writers for the first time.

A short story may seem a slight thing next to a major novel, but the form carries its own particular challenges. Indeed, the renowned writer Isaac Bashevis Singer argued that the short story 'constitutes the utmost challenge to the creative writer'. With far fewer words to play with, short-story writers must achieve their effects with economy and precision, making deft choices then editing and revising in order to create their impact in a limited space. As Irish author Frank O'Connor once said, the short story is 'the nearest thing I know to lyric poetry'.

Short stories give the reader a condensed snapshot of another world, another place of being, which can be a character's mind, a particular time period, a location or a culture. The stories in this collection have time settings ranging from the nineteenth century to many years in the future, geographical settings from the ocean to the inner city, and cultural settings from pioneer New Zealand to an Algeria in the midst of social change.

While general guides to short stories tend to stress a firm focus on character, conflict, setting and plot, the stories here include these elements but go beyond, offering a much wider range. You will find stories which are about the setting, and others which focus almost exclusively on character. There is conflict in most, but not all the stories. Some stories are dominated by dialogue, as the reader eavesdrops on the characters' conversations. There are stories about stories.

The collected stories also vary widely in genre, with gothic mystery, science fiction, social observation, satire, crime writing, myth, horror, comedy and epistolary fiction all represented. As the stories come from more than twenty different countries, such a range should not cause surprise; this is very much a global collection, fully intended to represent and celebrate the diversity of the Cambridge learner community.

Though the range is broad and varied, there are ways of reading and studying the stories that are common to all. A short story is designed to be read in a single sitting,

Introduction

so it has to create its effects economically. A high proportion of short stories use a first-person narrator who is involved in the story in some way, though not always as a central character. Consideration of narrative perspective and voice is often a useful way to begin to think about how the writer composes the story, and how the reader responds to the narrator. Readers might also consider how the author creates character in so few words, perhaps looking at the combination of description and dialogue. Structure is always important – has the author arranged the events chronologically, or does the story move backwards and forwards in time? What methods does the writer use to create tension, suspense and interest as the story develops?

As readers explore the collection, they may find connections between them, and comparison can be fruitful. Most importantly, we hope that readers will enjoy the range of writing and perspectives which this collection contains. As Joseph Conrad wrote, the writer's desire is 'by the power of the written word to make you hear, to make you feel […] to make you see'.

Editor's Acknowledgements

Special thanks are due to Tiffany Duck for her contributions to the anthology, as well as to friends and colleagues who have offered suggestions, given directions and lent books, especially Justine Ehlers, Greg Hacksley, Alistair Jolly, Harry Perrin and Kevin Squibb.

Note on Selections

The stories in this collection were chosen primarily by Noel Cassidy alongside Tiffany Duck and Peter Johnston, with additional recommendations from those acknowledged above, as well as from colleagues at Cambridge International (including Sonia Attwell, David Blaikie, Tricia Harriss and Kevin O'Grady) and a range of contributors from our wider global Cambridge community.

1

The Invisible Girl

(1833)

Mary Shelley

This slender narrative has no pretensions to the regularity of a story, or the development of situations and feelings; it is but a slight sketch, delivered nearly as it was narrated to me by one of the humblest of the actors concerned: nor will I spin out a circumstance interesting principally from its singularity and truth, but narrate, as concisely as I can, how I was surprised on visiting what seemed a ruined tower, crowning a bleak promontory overhanging the sea, that flows between Wales and Ireland, to find that though the exterior preserved all the savage rudeness that betokened many a war with the elements, the interior was fitted up somewhat in the guise of a summer-house, for it was too small to deserve any other name. It consisted but of the ground-floor, which served as an entrance, and one room above, which was reached by a staircase made out of the thickness of the wall. This chamber was floored and carpeted, decorated with elegant furniture; and, above all, to attract the attention and excite curiosity, there hung over the chimney-piece – for to preserve the apartment from damp a fire-place had been built evidently since it had assumed a guise so dissimilar to the object of its construction – a picture simply painted in water-colours, which seemed more than any part of the adornments of the room to be at war with the rudeness of the building, the solitude in which it was placed, and the desolation of the surrounding scenery. This drawing represented a lovely girl in the very pride and bloom of youth; her dress was simple, in the fashion of the day – (remember, reader, I write at the beginning of the eighteenth century), her countenance was embellished by a look of mingled innocence and intelligence, to which was added the imprint of serenity of soul and natural cheerfulness. She was reading one of those folio romances which have so long been the delight of the enthusiastic and young; her mandoline was at her feet – her parroquet perched on a huge mirror near her; the arrangement of furniture and hangings gave token of a luxurious dwelling, and her attire also evidently that of home and privacy, yet bore with it an appearance of ease and girlish ornament, as if she wished to please. Beneath this picture was inscribed in golden letters, 'The Invisible Girl.'

1 The Invisible Girl

Rambling about a country nearly uninhabited, having lost my way, and being overtaken by a shower, I had lighted on this dreary looking tenement, which seemed to rock in the blast, and to be hung up there as the very symbol of desolation. I was gazing wistfully and cursing inwardly my stars which led me to a ruin that could afford no shelter, though the storm began to pelt more seriously than before, when I saw an old woman's head popped out from a kind of loophole, and as suddenly withdrawn: – a minute after a feminine voice called to me from within, and penetrating a little brambly maze that skreened a door, which I had not before observed, so skilfully had the planter succeeded in concealing art with nature, I found the good dame standing on the threshold and inviting me to take refuge within. 'I had just come up from our cot hard by,' she said, 'to look after the things, as I do every day, when the rain came on – will ye walk up till it is over?' I was about to observe that the cot hard by, at the venture of a few rain drops, was better than a ruined tower, and to ask my kind hostess whether 'the things' were pigeons or crows that she was come to look after, when the matting of the floor and the carpeting of the staircase struck my eye. I was still more surprised when I saw the room above; and beyond all, the picture and its singular inscription, naming her invisible, whom the painter had coloured forth into very agreeable visibility, awakened my most lively curiosity: the result of this, of my exceeding politeness towards the old woman, and her own natural garrulity, was a kind of garbled narrative which my imagination eked out, and future inquiries rectified, till it assumed the following form.

Some years before in the afternoon of a September day, which, though tolerably fair, gave many tokens of a tempestuous evening, a gentleman arrived at a little coast town about ten miles from this place; he expressed his desire to hire a boat to carry him to the town of —— about fifteen miles further on the coast. The menaces which the sky held forth made the fishermen loathe to venture, till at length two, one the father of a numerous family, bribed by the bountiful reward the stranger promised – the other, the son of my hostess, induced by youthful daring, agreed to undertake the voyage. The wind was fair, and they hoped to make good way before nightfall, and to get into port ere the rising of the storm. They pushed off with good cheer, at least the fishermen did; as for the stranger, the deep mourning which he wore was not half so black as the melancholy that wrapt his mind. He looked as if he had never smiled – as if some unutterable thought, dark as night and bitter as death, had built its nest within his bosom, and brooded therein eternally; he did not mention his name; but one of the villagers recognised him as Henry Vernon, the son of a baronet who possessed a mansion about three miles distant from the town for which he was bound. This mansion was almost abandoned by the family; but Henry had, in a romantic fit, visited it about three years before, and Sir Peter had been down there during the previous spring for about a couple of months.

The boat did not make so much way as was expected; the breeze failed them as they got out to sea, and they were fain with oar as well as sail, to try to weather the promontory that jutted out between them and the spot they desired to reach. They were yet far distant when the shifting wind began to exert its strength, and to blow with violent though unequal puffs. Night came on pitchy dark, and the howling waves rose and broke with frightful violence, menacing to overwhelm the tiny bark that dared resist their fury. They were forced to lower every sail, and take to their oars; one man was obliged to bale out the water, and Vernon himself took an oar, and rowing with desperate energy, equalled the force of the more practised boatmen. There had been much talk between the sailors before the tempest came on; now, except a brief command, all were silent. One thought of his wife and children, and silently cursed the caprice of the stranger that endangered in its effects, not only his life, but their welfare; the other feared less, for he was a daring lad, but he worked hard, and had no time for speech; while Vernon bitterly regretting the thoughtlessness which had made him cause others to share a peril, unimportant as far as he himself was concerned, now tried to cheer them with a voice full of animation and courage, and now pulled yet more strongly at the oar he held. The only person who did not seem wholly intent on the work he was about, was the man who baled; every now and then he gazed intently round, as if the sea held afar off, on its tumultuous waste, some object that he strained his eyes to discern. But all was blank, except as the crests of the high waves showed themselves, or far out on the verge of the horizon, a kind of lifting of the clouds betokened greater violence for the blast. At length he exclaimed – 'Yes, I see it! – the larboard oar! – now! if we can make yonder light, we are saved!' Both the rowers instinctively turned their heads, – but cheerless darkness answered their gaze.

'You cannot see it,' cried their companion, 'but we are nearing it; and, please God, we shall outlive this night.' Soon he took the oar from Vernon's hand, who, quite exhausted, was failing in his strokes. He rose and looked for the beacon which promised them safety; – it glimmered with so faint a ray, that now he said, 'I see it;' and again, 'it is nothing:' still, as they made way, it dawned upon his sight, growing more steady and distinct as it beamed across the lurid waters, which themselves became smoother, so that safety seemed to arise from the bosom of the ocean under the influence of that flickering gleam.

'What beacon is it that helps us at our need?' asked Vernon, as the men, now able to manage their oars with greater ease, found breath to answer his question.

'A fairy one, I believe,' replied the elder sailor, 'yet no less a true: it burns in an old tumble-down tower, built on the top of a rock which looks over the sea. We never saw it before this summer; and now each night it is to be seen, – at least when it is looked for, for we cannot see it from our village; – and it is such an out of the way place that no one has need to go near it, except through a chance like this. Some say it is burnt by witches, some say by smugglers; but this I know, two parties have been to search, and found nothing but the bare walls of the tower. All is deserted by day, and dark by night; for no light was to be seen while we were there, though it burned sprightly enough when we were out at sea.'

'I have heard say,' observed the younger sailor, 'it is burnt by the ghost of a maiden who lost her sweetheart in these parts; he being wrecked, and his body found at the foot of the tower: she goes by the name among us of the "Invisible Girl"'.

The voyagers had now reached the landing-place at the foot of the tower. Vernon cast a glance upward, – the light was still burning. With some difficulty, struggling with the breakers, and blinded by night, they contrived to get their little bark to shore, and to draw her up on the beach: they then scrambled up the precipitous pathway, overgrown by weeds and underwood, and, guided by the more experienced fisherman, they found the entrance to the tower, door or gate there was none, and all was dark as the tomb, and silent and almost as cold as death.

1   The Invisible Girl

'This will never do,' said Vernon; 'surely our hostess will show her light, if not herself, and guide our darkling steps by some sign of life and comfort.'

'We will get to the upper chamber,' said the sailor, 'if I can but hit upon the broken down steps: but you will find no trace of the Invisible Girl nor her light either, I warrant.'

'Truly a romantic adventure of the most disagreeable kind,' muttered Vernon, as he stumbled over the unequal ground: 'she of the beacon-light must be both ugly and old, or she would not be so peevish and inhospitable.'

With considerable difficulty, and, after divers knocks and bruises, the adventurers at length succeeded in reaching the upper story; but all was blank and bare, and they were fain to stretch themselves on the hard floor, when weariness, both of mind and body, conduced to steep their senses in sleep.

Long and sound were the slumbers of the mariners. Vernon but forgot himself for an hour; then, throwing off drowsiness, and finding his rough couch uncongenial to repose, he got up and placed himself at the hole that served for a window, for glass there was none, and there being not even a rough bench, he leant his back against the embrasure, as the only rest he could find. He had forgotten his danger, the mysterious beacon, and its invisible guardian: his thoughts were occupied on the horrors of his own fate, and the unspeakable wretchedness that sat like a night-mare on his heart.

It would require a good-sized volume to relate the causes which had changed the once happy Vernon into the most woful mourner that ever clung to the outer trappings of grief, as slight though cherished symbols of the wretchedness within. Henry was the only child of Sir Peter Vernon, and as much spoiled by his father's idolatry as the old baronet's violent and tyrannical temper would permit. A young orphan was educated in his father's house, who in the same way was treated with generosity and kindness, and yet who lived in deep awe of Sir Peter's authority, who was a widower; and these two children were all he had to exert his power over, or to whom to extend his affection. Rosina was a cheerful-tempered girl, a little timid, and careful to avoid displeasing her protector; but so docile, so kind-hearted, and so affectionate, that she felt even less than Henry the discordant spirit of his parent. It is a tale often told; they were play-mates and companions in childhood, and lovers in after days. Rosina was frightened to imagine that this secret affection, and the vows they pledged, might be disapproved of by Sir Peter. But sometimes she consoled herself by thinking that perhaps she was in reality her Henry's destined bride, brought up with him under the design of their future union; and Henry, while he felt that this was not the case, resolved to wait only until he was of age to declare and accomplish his wishes in making the sweet Rosina his wife. Meanwhile he was careful to avoid premature discovery of his intentions, so to secure his beloved girl from persecution and insult. The old gentleman was very conveniently blind; he lived always in the country, and the lovers spent their lives together, unrebuked and uncontrolled. It was enough that Rosina played on her mandoline, and sang Sir Peter to sleep every day after dinner; she was the sole female in the house above the rank of a servant, and had her own way in the disposal of her time. Even when Sir Peter frowned, her innocent caresses and sweet voice were powerful to smooth the rough current of his temper. If ever human spirit lived in an earthly paradise, Rosina did at this time: her pure love was made happy by Henry's constant presence; and the confidence they felt in each other, and the security with which they looked forward to the future, rendered their path one of roses under a cloudless sky. Sir Peter was the slight drawback that only rendered their *tête-à-tête* more delightful, and gave value to the sympathy they each bestowed on the other. All at once an ominous personage made its appearance in Vernon-Place, in the shape of a widow sister of Sir Peter, who, having succeeded in killing her husband and children with the effects of her vile temper, came, like a harpy, greedy for new prey, under her brother's roof. She too soon detected the attachment of the unsuspicious pair. She made all speed to impart her discovery to her brother, and at once to restrain and inflame his rage. Through her contrivance Henry was suddenly despatched on his travels abroad, that the coast might be clear for the persecution of Rosina; and then the richest of the lovely girl's many admirers, whom, under Sir Peter's single reign, she was allowed, nay, almost commanded, to dismiss, so desirous was he of keeping her for his own comfort, was selected, and she was ordered to marry him. The scenes of violence to which she was now exposed, the bitter taunts of the odious Mrs Bainbridge, and the reckless fury of Sir Peter, were the more frightful and overwhelming from their novelty. To all she could only oppose a silent, tearful, but immutable steadiness of purpose: no threats, no rage could extort from her more than a touching prayer that they would not hate her, because she could not obey.

'There must be something we don't see under all this,' said Mrs Bainbridge, 'take my word for it, brother, – she corresponds secretly with Henry. Let us take her down to your seat in Wales, where she will have no pensioned beggars to assist her; and we shall see if her spirit be not bent to our purpose.'

Sir Peter consented, and they all three posted down to ——shire, and took up their abode in the solitary and dreary looking house before alluded to as belonging to the family. Here poor Rosina's sufferings grew intolerable: – before, surrounded by well-known scenes, and in perpetual intercourse with kind and familiar faces, she had not despaired in the end of conquering by her patience the cruelty of her persecutors; – nor had she written to Henry, for his name had not been mentioned by his relatives, nor their attachment alluded to, and she felt an instinctive wish to escape the dangers about her without his being annoyed, or the sacred secret of her love being laid bare, and wronged by the vulgar abuse of his aunt or the bitter curses of his father. But when she was taken to Wales, and made a prisoner in her apartment, when the flinty mountains about her seemed feebly to imitate the stony hearts she had to deal with, her courage began to fail. The only attendant permitted to approach her was Mrs Bainbridge's maid; and under the tutelage of her fiend-like mistress, this woman was used as a decoy to entice the poor prisoner into confidence, and then to be betrayed. The simple, kind-hearted Rosina was a facile dupe, and at last, in the excess of her despair, wrote to Henry, and gave the letter to this woman to be forwarded. The letter in itself would have softened marble; it did not speak of their mutual vows, it but asked him to intercede with his father, that he would restore her to the kind place she had formerly held in his affections, and cease from a cruelty that would destroy her. 'For I may die,' wrote the hapless girl, 'but marry another – never!' That single word, indeed, had sufficed to betray her secret, had it not been already discovered; as it was, it gave increased fury to Sir Peter, as his

1 The Invisible Girl

sister triumphantly pointed it out to him, for it need hardly be said that while the ink of the address was yet wet, and the seal still warm, Rosina's letter was carried to this lady. The culprit was summoned before them; what ensued none could tell; for their own sakes the cruel pair tried to palliate their part. Voices were high, and the soft murmur of Rosina's tone was lost in the howling of Sir Peter and the snarling of his sister. 'Out of doors you shall go,' roared the old man; 'under my roof you shall not spend another night.' And the words infamous seductress, and worse, such as had never met the poor girl's ear before, were caught by listening servants; and to each angry speech of the baronet, Mrs Bainbridge added an envenomed point worse than all.

More dead than alive, Rosina was at last dismissed. Whether guided by despair, whether she took Sir Peter's threats literally, or whether his sister's orders were more decisive, none knew, but Rosina left the house; a servant saw her cross the park, weeping, and wringing her hands as she went. What became of her none could tell; her disappearance was not disclosed to Sir Peter till the following day, and then he showed by his anxiety to trace her steps and to find her, that his words had been but idle threats. The truth was, that though Sir Peter went to frightful lengths to prevent the marriage of the heir of his house with the portionless orphan, the object of his charity, yet in his heart he loved Rosina, and half his violence to her rose from anger at himself for treating her so ill. Now remorse began to sting him, as messenger after messenger came back without tidings of his victim; he dared not confess his worst fears to himself; and when his inhuman sister, trying to harden her conscience by angry words, cried, 'The vile hussy has too surely made away with herself out of revenge to us;' an oath, the most tremendous, and a look sufficient to make even her tremble, commanded her silence. Her conjecture, however, appeared too true: a dark and rushing stream that flowed at the extremity of the park had doubtless received the lovely form, and quenched the life of this unfortunate girl. Sir Peter, when his endeavours to find her proved fruitless, returned to town, haunted by the image of his victim, and forced to acknowledge in his own heart that he would willingly lay down his life, could he see her again, even though it were as the bride of his son – his son, before whose questioning he quailed like the veriest coward; for when Henry was told of the death of Rosina, he suddenly returned from abroad to ask the cause – to visit her grave, and mourn her loss in the groves and valleys which had been the scenes of their mutual happiness. He made a thousand inquiries, and an ominous silence alone replied. Growing more earnest and more anxious, at length he drew from servants and dependants, and his odious aunt herself, the whole dreadful truth. From that moment despair struck his heart, and misery named him her own. He fled from his father's presence; and the recollection that one whom he ought to revere was guilty of so dark a crime, haunted him, as of old the Eumenides tormented the souls of men given up to their torturings. His first, his only wish, was to visit Wales, and to learn if any new discovery had been made, and whether it were possible to recover the mortal remains of the lost Rosina, so to satisfy the unquiet longings of his miserable heart. On this expedition was he bound, when he made his appearance at the village before named; and now in the deserted tower, his thoughts were busy with images of despair and death, and what his beloved one had suffered before her gentle nature had been goaded to such a deed of woe.

While immersed in gloomy reverie, to which the monotonous roaring of the sea made fit accompaniment, hours flew on, and Vernon was at last aware that the light of morning was creeping from out its eastern retreat, and dawning over the wild ocean, which still broke in furious tumult on the rocky beach. His companions now roused themselves, and prepared to depart. The food they had brought with them was damaged by sea water, and their hunger, after hard labour and many hours fasting, had become ravenous. It was impossible to put to sea in their shattered boat; but there stood a fisher's cot about two miles off, in a recess in the bay, of which the promontory on which the tower stood formed one side, and to this they hastened to repair; they did not spend a second thought on the light which had saved them, nor its cause, but left the ruin in search of a more hospitable asylum. Vernon cast his eyes round as he quitted it, but no vestige of an inhabitant met his eye, and he began to persuade himself that the beacon had been a creation of fancy merely. Arriving at the cottage in question, which was inhabited by a fisherman and his family, they made an homely breakfast, and then prepared to return to the tower, to refit their boat, and if possible bring her round. Vernon accompanied them, together with their host and his son. Several questions were asked concerning the Invisible Girl and her light, each agreeing that the apparition was novel, and not one being able to give even an explanation of how the name had become affixed to the unknown cause of this singular appearance; though both of the men of the cottage affirmed that once or twice they had seen a female figure in the adjacent wood, and that now and then a stranger girl made her appearance at another cot a mile off, on the other side of the promontory, and bought bread; they suspected both these to be the same, but could not tell. The inhabitants of the cot, indeed, appeared too stupid even to feel curiosity, and had never made any attempt at discovery. The whole day was spent by the sailors in repairing the boat; and the sound of hammers, and the voices of the men at work, resounded along the coast, mingled with the dashing of the waves. This was no time to explore the ruin for one who whether human or supernatural so evidently withdrew herself from intercourse with every living being. Vernon, however, went over the tower, and searched every nook in vain; the dingy bare walls bore no token of serving as a shelter; and even a little recess in the wall of the staircase, which he had not before observed, was equally empty and desolate. Quitting the tower, he wandered in the pine wood that surrounded it, and giving up all thought of solving the mystery, was soon engrossed by thoughts that touched his heart more nearly, when suddenly there appeared on the ground at his feet the vision of a slipper. Since Cinderella so tiny a slipper had never been seen; as plain as shoe could speak, it told a tale of elegance, loveliness, and youth. Vernon picked it up; he had often admired Rosina's singularly small foot, and his first thought was a question whether this little slipper would have fitted it. It was very strange! – it must belong to the Invisible Girl. Then there was a fairy form that kindled that light, a form of such material substance, that its foot needed to be shod; and yet how shod? – with kid so fine, and of shape so exquisite, that it exactly resembled such as Rosina wore! Again the recurrence of the image of the beloved dead came forcibly across him; and a thousand home-felt associations, childish yet sweet, and lover-like though trifling, so filled Vernon's heart, that he threw himself his length on the ground, and wept more bitterly than ever the miserable fate of the sweet orphan.

1   The Invisible Girl

In the evening the men quitted their work, and Vernon returned with them to the cot where they were to sleep, intending to pursue their voyage, weather permitting, the following morning. Vernon said nothing of his slipper, but returned with his rough associates. Often he looked back; but the tower rose darkly over the dim waves, and no light appeared. Preparations had been made in the cot for their accommodation, and the only bed in it was offered Vernon; but he refused to deprive his hostess, and spreading his cloak on a heap of dry leaves, endeavoured to give himself up to repose. He slept for some hours; and when he awoke, all was still, save that the hard breathing of the sleepers in the same room with him interrupted the silence. He rose, and going to the window, looked out over the now placid sea towards the mystic tower; the light was burning there, sending its slender rays across the waves. Congratulating himself on a circumstance he had not anticipated, Vernon softly left the cottage, and, wrapping his cloak round him, walked with a swift pace round the bay towards the tower. He reached it; still the light was burning. To enter and restore the maiden her shoe, would be but an act of courtesy; and Vernon intended to do this with such caution, as to come unaware, before its wearer could, with her accustomed arts, withdraw herself from his eyes; but, unluckily, while yet making his way up the narrow pathway, his foot dislodged a loose fragment, that fell with crash and sound down the precipice. He sprung forward, on this, to retrieve by speed the advantage he had lost by this unlucky accident. He reached the door; he entered: all was silent, but also all was dark. He paused in the room below; he felt sure that a slight sound met his ear. He ascended the steps, and entered the upper chamber; but blank obscurity met his penetrating gaze, the starless night admitted not even a twilight glimmer through the only aperture. He closed his eyes, to try, on opening them again, to be able to catch some faint, wandering ray on the visual nerve; but it was in vain. He groped round the room: he stood still, and held his breath; and then, listening intently, he felt sure that another occupied the chamber with him, and that its atmosphere was slightly agitated by another's respiration. He remembered the recess in the staircase; but, before he approached it, he spoke: – he hesitated a moment what to say. 'I must believe,' he said, 'that misfortune alone can cause your seclusion; and if the assistance of a man – of a gentleman ...'

An exclamation interrupted him; a voice from the grave spoke his name – the accents of Rosina syllabled, 'Henry! – is it indeed Henry whom I hear?'

He rushed forward, directed by the sound, and clasped in his arms the living form of his own lamented girl – his own Invisible Girl he called her; for even yet, as he felt her heart beat near his, and as he entwined her waist with his arm, supporting her as she almost sank to the ground with agitation, he could not see her; and, as her sobs prevented her speech, no sense, but the instinctive one that filled his heart with tumultuous gladness, told him that the slender, wasted form he pressed so fondly was the living shadow of the Hebe beauty he had adored.

The morning saw this pair thus strangely restored to each other on the tranquil sea, sailing with a fair wind for L——, whence they were to proceed to Sir Peter's seat, which, three months before, Rosina had quitted in such agony and terror. The morning light dispelled the shadows that had veiled her, and disclosed the fair person of the Invisible

Girl. Altered indeed she was by suffering and woe, but still the same sweet smile played on her lips, and the tender light of her soft blue eyes were all her own. Vernon drew out the slipper, and showed the cause that had occasioned him to resolve to discover the guardian of the mystic beacon; even now he dared not inquire how she had existed in that desolate spot, or wherefore she had so sedulously avoided observation, when the right thing to have been done was, to have sought him immediately, under whose care, protected by whose love, no danger need be feared. But Rosina shrunk from him as he spoke, and a death-like pallor came over her cheek, as she faintly whispered, 'Your father's curse – your father's dreadful threats!' It appeared, indeed, that Sir Peter's violence, and the cruelty of Mrs Bainbridge, had succeeded in impressing Rosina with wild and unvanquishable terror. She had fled from their house without plan or forethought – driven by frantic horror and overwhelming fear, she had left it with scarcely any money, and there seemed to her no possibility of either returning or proceeding onward. She had no friend except Henry in the wide world; whither could she go? – to have sought Henry would have sealed their fates to misery; for, with an oath, Sir Peter had declared he would rather see them both in their coffins than married. After wandering about, hiding by day, and only venturing forth at night, she had come to this deserted tower, which seemed a place of refuge. How she had lived since then she could hardly tell; – she had lingered in the woods by day, or slept in the vault of the tower, an asylum none were acquainted with or had discovered: by night she burned the pine-cones of the wood, and night was her dearest time; for it seemed to her as if security came with darkness. She was unaware that Sir Peter had left that part of the country, and was terrified lest her hiding-place should be revealed to him. Her only hope was that Henry would return – that Henry would never rest till he had found her. She confessed that the long interval and the approach of winter had visited her with dismay; she feared that, as her strength was failing, and her form wasting to a skeleton, that she might die, and never see her own Henry more.

An illness, indeed, in spite of all his care, followed her restoration to security and the comforts of civilized life; many months went by before the bloom revisiting her cheeks, and her limbs regaining their roundness, she resembled once more the picture drawn of her in her days of bliss, before any visitation of sorrow. It was a copy of this portrait that decorated the tower, the scene of her suffering, in which I had found shelter. Sir Peter, overjoyed to be relieved from the pangs of remorse, and delighted again to see his orphan-ward, whom he really loved, was now as eager as before he had been averse to bless her union with his son: Mrs Bainbridge they never saw again. But each year they spent a few months in their Welch mansion, the scene of their early wedded happiness, and the spot where again poor Rosina had awoke to life and joy after her cruel persecutions. Henry's fond care had fitted up the tower, and decorated it as I saw; and often did he come over, with his 'Invisible Girl,' to renew, in the very scene of its occurrence, the remembrance of all the incidents which had led to their meeting again, during the shades of night, in that sequestered ruin.

2

The Black Veil

(1836)

Charles Dickens

One winter's evening towards the close of the year 1800, or within a year or two of that time, a young medical practitioner, recently established in business, was seated by a cheerful fire in his little parlour, listening to the wind which was beating the rain in pattering drops against the window, and rumbling dismally in the chimney. The night was wet and cold; he had been walking through mud and water the whole day, and was now comfortably reposing in his dressing-gown and slippers, more than half asleep and less than half awake, revolving a thousand matters in his wandering imagination. First he thought how hard the wind was blowing, and how the cold, sharp rain would be at that moment beating in his face if he were not comfortably housed at home. Then his mind reverted to his annual Christmas visit to his native place and dearest friends; he thought how glad they would all be to see him, and how happy it would make Rose if he could only tell her that he had got a patient at last, and hoped to have more, and to come down again in a few months' time and marry her, and take her home to gladden his lonely fireside, and stimulate him to fresh exertions. Then he began to wonder when his first patient would appear, or whether he was destined by special dispensation of Providence never to have any patients at all; and then he thought about Rose again, and dropped to sleep and dreamed about her, till the very tones of her sweet merry voice sounded in his ears, and her soft tiny hand rested on his shoulder.

There *was* a hand upon his shoulder, but it was neither soft nor tiny; its owner being a corpulent round-headed boy, who, in consideration of the sum of one shilling per week and his food, was let out by the parish to carry medicine and messages. As there was no demand for the one, however, and no necessity for the other, he usually occupied his unemployed hours – averaging fourteen a day – in abstracting peppermint drops, taking animal nourishment, and going to sleep.

'A lady, Sir – a lady!' whispered the boy, rousing his master with a shake.

'What lady?' cried our friend, starting up, not quite certain that his dream was an illusion, and half expecting that it might be Rose herself. – 'What lady? Where?'

'*There*, Sir,' replied the boy, pointing to the glass door leading into the surgery, with an expression of alarm which the very unusual apparition of a customer might have tended to excite.

The surgeon looked towards the door, and started himself for an instant on beholding the appearance of his unlooked-for visitor.

It was a singularly tall female, dressed in deep mourning, and standing so close to the door that her face almost touched the glass. The upper part of her person was carefully muffled in a black shawl, as if for the purpose of concealment, and her face was shrouded by a thick black veil. She stood perfectly erect; her figure was drawn up to its full height, and though the surgeon *felt* that the eyes beneath the veil were fixed on him, she stood perfectly motionless, and evinced, by no gesture whatever, the slightest consciousness of his having turned towards her.

'Do you wish to consult me?' he inquired, with some hesitation, holding open the door. It opened inwards, and therefore the action did not alter the position of the figure, which still remained motionless on the same spot.

The female slightly inclined her head, in token of acquiescence.

'Pray walk in,' said the surgeon.

The figure moved a step forward; and then turning its head in the direction of the boy – to his infinite horror – appeared to hesitate.

'Leave the room, Tom,' said the young man, addressing the boy, whose large round eyes had been extended to their utmost width during this brief interview. – 'Draw the curtain, and shut the door.'

The boy drew a green curtain across the glass part of the door, retired into the surgery, closed the door after him, and immediately applied one of his large eyes to the keyhole on the other side.

The surgeon drew a chair to the fire, and motioned the visitor to a seat. The mysterious figure slowly moved towards it, and as the blaze shone upon the black dress, the surgeon observed that the bottom of it was saturated with mud and rain.

'You are very wet,' he said.

'I am,' said the stranger, in a low deep voice.

'And you are ill?' added the surgeon, compassionately, for the tone was that of a person in severe pain.

'I am,' was the reply – 'very ill: not bodily, but mentally. It is not for myself, or on my own behalf,' continued the stranger, 'that I come to you. If I laboured under bodily disease, I should not be out alone at such an hour, or on such a night as this; and if I were afflicted with it twenty-four hours hence, God knows how gladly I would lie down and pray to die. It is for another that I beseech your aid, Sir. I may be mad to ask it for him – I think I am; but, night after night through the long dreary hours of watching and weeping, the thought has been ever present to my mind; and though even *I* see the hopelessness of human assistance availing him, the bare thought of laying him in his grave without it makes my blood run cold!' And a shudder, such as the surgeon well knew art could not produce, trembled through the speaker's frame.

There was a desperate earnestness in this woman's manner that went to the young man's heart. He was young in his profession, and had not yet witnessed enough of the miseries which are daily presented before the eyes of its members, to have grown comparatively callous to human suffering.

'If,' he said, rising hastily, 'the person of whom you speak be in so hopeless a condition as you describe, not a moment is to be lost. I will go with you instantly. Why did you not obtain medical advice before?'

'Because it would have been useless before – because it is useless even now,' replied the woman, clasping her hands passionately.

The surgeon gazed for a moment on the black veil, as if to ascertain the expression of the features beneath it; its thickness, however, rendered such a result impossible.

'You *are* ill,' he said, gently, 'although you do not know it. The fever which has enabled you to bear without feeling it the fatigue you have evidently undergone, is burning within you now. Put that to your lips,' he continued, pouring out a glass of water – 'compose yourself for a few moments, and then tell me, as calmly as you can, what the disease of the patient is, and how long he has been ill. The moment I know what it is necessary I should know, to render my visit serviceable to him, I am ready to accompany you.'

The stranger lifted the glass of water to her mouth without raising the veil, put it down again untasted, and burst into tears.

'I know,' she said, sobbing aloud, 'that what I say to you now, seems like the ravings of fever. I have been told so before, less kindly than by you. I am not a young woman, Sir; and they do say, that as life steals on towards its final close, the last short remnant, worthless as it may seem to all beside, is dearer to its possessor than all the years that have gone before, connected though they be with the recollection of old friends long since dead, and young ones – children perhaps – who have fallen off from, and forgotten one as completely as if they had died too. My natural term of life cannot be many years longer, and should be dear on that account; but I would lay it down without a sigh – with cheerfulness – with joy – if what I tell you now were only false, or imaginary. To-morrow morning he of whom I speak will be, I *know*, though I would fain think otherwise, beyond the reach of human aid; and yet, to-night, though he is in deadly peril, you must not see, and could not serve him.'

'I am unwilling to increase your distress,' said the surgeon, after a short pause, 'by making any comment on what you have just said, or appearing desirous to investigate a subject you seem so anxious to conceal; but there is an inconsistency in your statement which I cannot reconcile with probability. This person is dying to-night, and I cannot see him when my assistance might possibly avail; you apprehend it will be useless to-morrow, and yet you would have me see him then. If he be, indeed, as dear to you, as your words and manner would imply, why not try to save his life before delay and the progress of his disease render it impracticable?'

'God help me!' exclaimed the woman, weeping bitterly, 'how can I hope strangers will believe what appears incredible, even to myself? You will *not* see him then, Sir?' she added, rising suddenly.

'I did not say that I declined to see him,' replied the surgeon: 'but I warn you, that if you persist in this extraordinary procrastination, and the individual dies, a fearful responsibility rests with you.'

'The responsibility will rest heavily somewhere,' replied the stranger bitterly. 'Whatever responsibility rests with me, I am content to bear and ready to answer.'

'As I incur none,' continued the surgeon, 'by acceding to your request, I will see him in the morning, if you leave me the address. At what hour can he be seen?'

'*Nine*,' replied the stranger.

'You must excuse my pressing these inquiries,' said the surgeon. 'But is he in your charge now?'

'He is not,' was the rejoinder.

'Then if I gave you instructions for his treatment through the night, you could not assist him?'

The woman wept bitterly, as she replied, 'I could not.'

Finding that there was but little prospect of obtaining further information by prolonging the interview; and anxious to spare the woman's feelings, which, subdued at first by a violent effort, were now irrepressible and most painful to witness, the surgeon repeated his promise of calling in the morning at the appointed hour; and his visitor, after giving him a direction to an obscure part of Walworth, left the house in the same mysterious manner as she had entered it.

It will be readily believed that so extraordinary a visit produced a considerable impression on the mind of the young surgeon, and that he speculated a great deal and to very little purpose on the possible circumstances of the case. In common with the generality of people, he had often heard and read of singular instances, in which a presentiment of death at a particular day or even minute had been entertained and realized. At one moment he was inclined to think that the present might be such a case, but then it occurred to him that all the anecdotes of the kind he had ever heard, were of persons who had been troubled with a foreboding of their own death. This woman, however, spoke of another person – a man; and it was impossible to suppose that a mere dream or delusion of fancy would induce her to speak of his approaching dissolution with such terrible certainty as she had done. It could not be that the man was to be murdered in the morning, and that the woman, originally a consenting party and bound to secrecy by an oath, had relented, and, though unable to prevent the commission of some outrage on the victim, had determined to prevent his death if possible by the timely interference of medical aid. The idea of such things happening within two miles of the metropolis appeared too wild and preposterous to be entertained beyond the instant. Then his original impression that the woman's intellects were disordered, recurred; and as it was the only mode of solving the difficulty with any degree of satisfaction, he obstinately made up his mind to believe she was mad. Certain misgivings upon this point, however, stole upon his thoughts at the time, and presented themselves again and again through the long dull course of a sleepless night, during which, in spite of all his efforts to the contrary, he was unable to banish the black veil from his disturbed imagination.

The back part of Walworth, at its greatest distance from town, is a straggling, miserable place enough, even in these days; but five-and-thirty years ago the greater portion of it was little better than a dreary waste, inhabited by a few scattered people of most questionable character, whose poverty prevented their living in any better neighbourhood, or whose pursuits and mode of life rendered its solitude peculiarly desirable. Very many of the houses which have since sprung up on all sides, were not built until some years afterwards; and the great majority even of those which were sprinkled about at irregular intervals, were of the rudest and most miserable description.

The appearance of the place through which he walked was not calculated to raise the spirits of the young surgeon, or to dispel any feeling of anxiety or depression which the singular kind of visit he was about to make, had awakened. Striking off from the high road, his way lay across a marshy common, through irregular lanes, with here and there a ruinous and dismantled cottage fast falling to pieces with decay and neglect. A stunted tree, or pool of stagnant water, roused into a creeping sluggish action by the heavy rain of the preceding night, skirted the path occasionally; and now and then a miserable patch of garden-ground, with a few old boards knocked together for a summer-house, and old palings imperfectly mended with stakes pilfered from the neighbouring hedges, bore testimony at once to the poverty of the inhabitants, and the little scruple they entertained in appropriating the property of other people to their own use. Occasionally, a filthy-looking woman would make her appearance from the door of a dirty house, to empty the contents of some cooking utensil into the gutter in front, or to scream after a little slipshod girl, who had contrived to stagger a few yards from the door under the weight of a sallow infant almost as big as herself; but scarcely anything was stirring around, and so much of the prospect as could be faintly traced through the cold damp mist which hung heavily over it, presented a lonely and dreary appearance perfectly in keeping with the objects we have described.

After plodding wearily through the mud and mire; making many inquiries for the place to which he had been directed; and receiving as many contradictory and unsatisfactory replies in return, the young man at length arrived before the house which had been pointed out to him as the object of his destination. It was a small low building, one story above the ground, with a more desolate and unpromising exterior than any he had yet passed. An old yellow curtain was closely drawn across the window up stairs, and the parlour shutters were closed, but not fastened. The house was detached from any other, and, as it stood at an angle of a narrow lane, there was no other habitation in sight.

When we say that the surgeon hesitated, and walked a few paces beyond the house before he could prevail upon himself to lift the knocker, we say nothing that need raise a smile upon the face of the boldest reader. The police of London were a very different body in that day to what they are now: the isolated position of the suburbs, when the rage for building and the progress of improvement had not yet begun to connect them with the main body of the city and its environs, rendered many of them (and this in particular) a place of resort for the worst and most depraved characters. Even the streets in the gayest parts of London were imperfectly lighted at that time, and such places as these were left entirely to the mercy of the moon and stars. The chances of detecting desperate characters, or of tracing them to their haunts, were thus rendered very few, and their offences naturally increased in boldness, as the consciousness of comparative security became the more impressed upon them by daily experience. Added to these considerations, it must be remembered that the young man had spent some time in the public hospitals of the metropolis; and although neither Burke nor Bishop had then gained a horrible notoriety, still his own observation might have suggested to him how easily the atrocities to which the former has since given his name, might be committed. Be this as it may, whatever reflection made him hesitate, he *did* hesitate; but, being a young man of strong mind and great personal daring, it was only for an instant; – he stepped briskly back, and knocked gently at the door.

A low whispering was audible immediately afterwards, as if some person at the end of the passage were conversing stealthily with another on the landing above. It was succeeded by the noise of a pair of heavy boots upon the bare floor. The door-chain was softly unfastened; the door opened, and a tall, ill-favoured man, with black hair, and a face, as the surgeon often declared afterwards, as pale and haggard, as the countenance of any dead man he ever saw, presented himself.

'Walk in, Sir,' he said in a low tone.

The surgeon did so, and the man having secured the door again by the chain, led the way to a small back parlour at the extremity of the passage.

'Am I in time?'

'Too soon,' replied the man. The surgeon turned hastily round, with a gesture of astonishment not unmixed with alarm, which he found it impossible to repress, though he would gladly have recalled it.

'If you'll step in here, Sir,' said the man, who had evidently noticed the action – 'if you'll step in here, Sir, you won't be detained five minutes, I assure you.'

The surgeon at once walked into the room. The man closed the door, and left him alone.

It was a little cold room, with no other furniture than two deal chairs and a table of the same material. A handful of fire unguarded by any fender, was burning in the grate, which brought out the damp if it served no more comfortable purpose; for the unwholesome moisture was stealing down the walls in long slug-like tracks. The window, which was broken and patched in many places, looked into a small enclosed piece of ground almost covered with water. Not a sound was to be heard, either within the house or without. The young surgeon sat down by the fireplace, to await the result of his first professional visit.

He had not remained in this position many minutes when the noise of some approaching vehicle struck his ear. It stopped; the street-door was opened; a low talking succeeded, accompanied with a shuffling noise of footsteps along the passage and on the stairs, as if two or three men were engaged in carrying some heavy body to the room above. The creaking of the stairs a few seconds afterwards, announced that the new comers having completed their task, whatever it was, were leaving the house. The door was again closed, and the former silence was restored.

Another five minutes elapsed, and the surgeon had just resolved to explore the house in search of some one to whom he might make his errand known, when the room-door opened, and his last night's visitor, dressed in exactly the same manner, with the veil lowered as before, motioned him to advance. The singular height of her form, coupled with the circumstance of her not speaking, caused the idea to pass across his brain for an instant that it might be a man disguised in woman's attire. The hysteric sobs which issued from beneath the veil, and the convulsive attitude of grief of the whole figure, however, at once exposed the absurdity of the suspicion, and he hastily followed.

The woman led the way up stairs to the front room, and paused at the door to let him enter first. It was scantily furnished with an old deal box, a few chairs, and a tent bedstead without hangings or cross-rails, which was covered with a patchwork counterpane. The dim light admitted through the curtain which he had noticed from the outside, rendered the objects in the room so indistinct, and communicated to all of them so uniform a hue, that he did not at first perceive the object on which his eye at once rested when the woman rushed frantically past him, and flung herself on her knees by the bedside.

Stretched upon the bed, closely enveloped in a linen wrapper, and covered with blankets, lay a human form stiff and motionless. The head and face, which were those of a man, were uncovered, save by a bandage which passed over the head and under the chin. The eyes were closed. The left arm lay heavily across the bed, and the woman held the passive hand.

The surgeon gently pushed the woman aside, and took the hand in his.

'My God!' he exclaimed, letting it fall involuntarily – 'the man is dead!'

The woman started to her feet and beat her hands together. – 'Oh! don't say so, Sir,' she exclaimed, with a burst of passion, amounting almost to frenzy – 'Oh! don't say so, Sir! I can't bear it, indeed I can't! Men have been brought to life before when unskilful people have given them up for lost; and men have died who might have been restored, if proper means had been resorted to. Don't let him lie here, Sir, without one effort to save him. This very moment life may be passing away. Do try, Sir, – do, for God's sake!' – And while speaking, she hurriedly chafed, first the forehead and then the breast of the senseless form before her, and then wildly beat the cold hands, which, when she ceased to hold them, fell listlessly and heavily back on the coverlet.

'It is of no use, my good woman,' said the surgeon, soothingly, as he withdrew his hand from the man's breast. 'Stay – undo that curtain.'

'Why?' said the woman, starting up.

'Undo that curtain,' repeated the surgeon, in an agitated tone.

'*I* darkened the room on purpose,' said the woman, throwing herself before him as he rose to undraw it. – 'Oh! Sir, have pity on me! If it can be of no use, and he is really dead, do not – do not expose that corpse to other eyes than mine!'

'This man died no natural or easy death,' said the surgeon. 'I *must* see the body!' And with a motion so sudden, that the woman hardly knew that he had slipped from beside her, he tore open the curtain, admitted the full light of day, and returned to the bedside.

'There has been violence here,' he said, pointing towards the body, and gazing intently on the face, from which the black veil was now for the first time removed. In the excitement of a minute before, the female had dashed off the bonnet and veil, and now stood with her eyes fixed upon him. Her features were those of a woman of about fifty, who had once been handsome. Sorrow and weeping had left traces upon them which not time itself would ever have produced without their aid: her face was deadly pale, and there was a nervous contortion of the lip, and an unnatural fire in her eye, which showed too plainly that her bodily and mental powers had nearly sunk beneath an accumulation of misery.

'There has been violence here,' said the surgeon, preserving his searching glance.

'There has!' replied the woman.

'This man has been murdered.'

'That I call God to witness he has,' said the woman, passionately; 'pitilessly, inhumanly murdered!'

'By whom?' said the surgeon, seizing the woman by the arm.

'Look at the butchers' marks, and then ask me,' she replied.

The surgeon turned his face towards the bed, and bent over the body which lay full in the light of the window. The throat was swollen, and a blue livid mark encircled it. The truth flashed suddenly upon him.

'This is one of the men who were hanged this morning!' he exclaimed, turning away with a shudder.

'It is,' replied the woman, with a cold, unmeaning stare.

'Who was he?' inquired the surgeon.

'*My son*,' rejoined the woman; and fell senseless at his feet.

It was true. A companion, equally guilty with himself, had been acquitted for want of evidence; and this man had been left for death, and executed. To recount the circumstances of the case at this distant period, must be unnecessary, and might give pain to some persons still alive. The history was an every-day one. The mother was a widow without friends or money, and had denied herself necessaries to bestow them on her orphan boy. That boy, unmindful of her prayers, and forgetful of the sufferings she had endured for him – incessant anxiety of mind, and voluntary starvation of body – had plunged into a career of dissipation and crime. And this was the result: his own death by the hangman's hands, and his mother's shame, and incurable insanity.

For many years after this occurrence, and when profitable and arduous avocations would have led many men to forget that such a miserable being existed, the young surgeon was a daily visitor at the side of the harmless mad woman; not only soothing her by his presence and kindness, but alleviating the rigour of her condition by pecuniary donations for her comfort and support, bestowed with no sparing hand. In the transient gleam of recollection and consciousness which preceded her death, a prayer for his welfare and protection as fervent as mortal ever breathed, rose from the lips of this poor friendless creature. That prayer flew to Heaven, and was heard. The blessings he was instrumental in conferring have been repaid to him a thousand-fold; but, amid all the honours of rank and station which have since been heaped upon him, and which he has so well earned, he can have no one reminiscence more gratifying to his feelings than that connected with – The Black Veil.

3

The Nightingale

(1843)

Hans Christian Andersen

In China, you must know, the Emperor is a Chinaman, and all whom he has about him are Chinamen too. It happened a good many years ago, but that's just why it's worth while to hear the story, before it is forgotten! The Emperor's palace was the most splendid in the world; it was made entirely of porcelain, very costly, but so delicate and brittle that one had to take care how one touched it. In the garden were to be seen the most wonderful flowers, and to the costliest of them silver bells were tied, which sounded, so that nobody should pass by without noticing the flowers. Yes, everything in the Emperor's garden was admirably arranged. And it extended so far, that the gardener himself did not know where the end was. If a man went on and on, he came into a glorious forest with high trees and deep lakes. The wood extended straight down to the sea, which was blue and deep; great vessels could sail beneath the branches of the trees, and in the trees lived a nightingale, which sang so splendidly that even the poor fisherman, who had many other things to do, stopped still and listened, when he had gone out at night, to throw out his nets, and heard the nightingale. 'How beautiful that is!' he said; but he was obliged to attend to his property, and thus forgot the bird. But when in the next night, the bird sang again and the fisherman heard it, he exclaimed again, 'How beautiful that is!'

From all the countries of the world travellers came to the city of the Emperor and admired it, and the palace and the garden, but when they heard the nightingale, they said: 'That is the best of all!'

And the travellers told of it when they came home; and the learned men wrote many books about the town, the palace, and the garden. But they did not forget the nightingale; that was placed highest of all; and those who were poets wrote most magnificent poems about the nightingale in the wood, by the deep lake.

The books went through all the world; and a few of them once came to the Emperor. He sat in his golden chair, and read, and read; every moment he nodded his head, for it pleased him to peruse the masterly descriptions of the city, the palace, and the garden. 'But the nightingale is the best of all,' it stood written there.

3 The Nightingale

'What's that?' exclaimed the Emperor. 'I don't know the nightingale at all! Is there such a bird in my empire, and even in my garden? I've never heard of that: – To learn such a thing for the first time from books!'

And hereupon he called his cavalier. This cavalier was so grand that if any one lower in rank than himself dared to speak to him, or to ask him any question, he answered nothing but 'P!' – and that meant nothing.

'There is said to be a wonderful bird here called a nightingale!' said the Emperor. 'They say, it is the best thing in all my great empire. Why have I never heard anything about it?'

'I have never heard him named,' replied the cavalier. 'He has never been introduced at court.'

'I command that he shall appear this evening, and sing before me,' said the Emperor. 'All the world knows what I possess, and I do not know it myself!'

'I have never heard him mentioned,' said the cavalier. 'I will seek for him. I will find him.'

But where was he to be found? The cavalier ran up and down all the staircases, through halls and passages, but no one among all those whom he met had heard talk of the nightingale. And the cavalier ran back to the Emperor, and said that it must be a fable invented by the writers of books. 'Your Imperial Majesty cannot believe how much is written that is fiction, and something that they call the black art.'

'But the book in which I read this,' said the Emperor, 'was sent to me by the high and mighty Emperor of Japan, and therefore it cannot be a falsehood. I will hear the nightingale! It must be here this evening! It has my imperial favour! And if it does not come, all the court shall be trampled upon after the court has supped!'

'Tsing-pe,' said the cavalier; and again he ran up and down all the staircases, and through all the halls and corridors; and half the court ran with him, for the courtiers did not like being trampled upon.

Then there was a great inquiry after the wonderful nightingale, which all the world knew, excepting the people at court.

At last they met with a poor little girl in the kitchen, who said, 'The nightingale? I know it well; yes, it can sing gloriously. Every evening I get leave to carry my poor sick mother the scraps from the table. She lives down by the strand, and when I get back and am tired, and rest in the wood, then I hear the nightingale sing! And then the water comes into my eyes, and it is just as if my mother kissed me!'

'Little kitchen-girl,' said the cavalier, 'I will get you a place in the kitchen, with permission to see the Emperor dine, if you will lead us to the nightingale, for it is announced for this evening.'

So they all went out into the wood where the nightingale was accustomed to sing; half the court went forth. When they were in the midst of their journey a cow began to low.

'Oh!' cried the court pages, 'now we have it! That shows a wonderful power in so small a creature! I have certainly heard it before.'

'No; those are cows lowing!' said the little kitchen-girl. 'We are a long way from the place yet!'

Now the frogs began to quack in the marsh. 'Glorious!' said the Chinese court preacher. 'Now I hear it – it sounds just like little church bells.' 'No; those are frogs!' said the little kitchen-maid. 'But now I think we shall soon hear it.' And then the nightingale began to sing.

'That is it!' exclaimed the little girl. 'Listen, listen! and yonder it sits,' and she pointed to a little grey bird up in the boughs.

'Is it possible?' cried the cavalier. 'I should never have thought it looked like that! How simple it looks! It must certainly have lost its colour at seeing such grand people around.'

'Little nightingale!' called the little kitchen-girl, quite loudly, 'our gracious Emperor wishes you to sing before him!' 'With the greatest pleasure!' replied the nightingale, and began to sing most delightfully.

'It sounds just like glass bells!' said the cavalier. 'And look at the little throat, how it's working! It's wonderful that we should never have heard it before. That bird will be a great success at court.'

'Shall I sing once more before the Emperor?' asked the nightingale, for it thought the Emperor was present.

'My excellent little nightingale!' said the cavalier, 'I have great pleasure in inviting you to a court festival this evening, when you shall charm his Imperial Majesty with your beautiful singing.'

'My song sounds best in the green wood!' replied the nightingale; still it came willingly when it heard what the Emperor wished.

The palace was festively adorned. The walls and the flooring, which were of porcelain, gleamed in the rays of thousands of golden lamps. The most glorious flowers, which could ring clearly, had been placed in the passages. There was a running to and fro, and a thorough draught, and all the bells rang so loudly that one could not hear oneself speak.

In the midst of the great hall, where the Emperor sat, a golden perch had been placed, on which the nightingale was to sit. The whole court was there, and the little cook maid had got leave to stand behind the door, as she had now received the title of a real court cook. All were in full dress, and all looked at the little grey bird, to which the Emperor nodded.

And the nightingale sang so gloriously that the tears came into the Emperor's eyes. The tears ran down over his cheeks, and then the nightingale sang still more sweetly, that went straight to the heart. The Emperor was so much pleased that he said the nightingale should have his golden slipper to wear round its neck. But the nightingale declined this with thanks, saying it had already received a sufficient reward.

'I have seen tears in the Emperor's eyes, that is the real treasure to me! An Emperor's tears have a peculiar power. I am rewarded enough.' And then it sang again with a sweet glorious voice.

3 The Nightingale

'That's the most amiable coquetry I ever saw!' said the ladies who stood round about, and then they took water in their mouths to gurgle when any one spoke to them. They thought they should be nightingales too. And the lackeys and chambermaids reported that they were satisfied too; and that was saying a good deal, for they are the most difficult to please. In short, the nightingale achieved a real success.

It was now to remain at court, to have its own cage, with liberty to go out twice every day and once at night. Twelve servants were appointed when the nightingale went out, each of whom had a silken string fastened to the bird's leg, and which they held very tight. There was really no pleasure in an excursion of that kind.

The whole city spoke of the wonderful bird, and when two people met, one said nothing but 'nightin,' and the other said 'gale;' and then they sighed, and understood one another. Eleven pedlars' children were named after the bird, but not one of them could sing a note.

One day the Emperor received a large parcel, on which was written 'The Nightingale!'

'There we have a new book about this celebrated bird,' said the Emperor. But it was not a book, but a little work of art, contained in a box, an artificial nightingale, which was to be like a natural one, but was brilliantly ornamented with diamonds, rubies, and sapphires. So soon as the artificial bird was wound up, he could sing one of the pieces that he really sang, and then his tail moved up and down, and shone with silver and gold. Round his neck hung a little riband, and on that was written, 'The Emperor of Japan's nightingale is poor, compared to that of the Emperor of China.'

'That is capital!' said they all, and he who had brought the artificial bird, immediately received the title, Imperial Head-Nightingale-Bringer.

'Now they must sing together; what a duet that will be!' And so they had to sing together; but it did not go very well, for the real nightingale sang in its own way, and the artificial bird sang waltzes. 'That's not his fault,' said the playmaster, 'he's quite perfect, and very much in my style.' Now the artificial bird was to sing alone. He had just as much success as the real one, and then it was much handsomer to look at; it shone like bracelets and breast-pins.

Three-and-thirty times over did it sing the same piece, and yet was not tired. The people would gladly have heard it again, but the Emperor said that the living nightingale ought to sing something now. But where was it? No one had noticed that it had flown away out of the open window, back to her green wood.

'But what is that?' said the Emperor. And all the courtiers abused the nightingale, and declared that it was a very ungrateful creature. 'We have the best bird after all,' said they, and so the artificial bird had to sing again, and that was the thirty-fourth time that they listened to the same piece. For all that they did not know it quite by heart, for it was so very difficult, and the playmaster praised the bird particularly; yes, he declared that it was better than a nightingale, not only with regard to its plumage, and the many beautiful diamonds, but inside as well.

'For you see, ladies and gentlemen, and above all, your Imperial Majesty, with a real nightingale one can never calculate what is coming, but in this artificial bird everything is settled. One can explain it; one can open it and make people understand where the waltzes come from, how they go, and how one follows upon another.'

'Those are quite our own ideas,' they all said, and the speaker received permission to show the bird to the people on the next Sunday. The people were to hear it sing too, the Emperor commanded, and they did hear it, and were as much pleased as if they had all got tipsy upon tea, for that's quite the Chinese fashion; and they all said, 'Oh!' and held up their forefingers and nodded. But the poor fisherman, who had heard the real nightingale, said, 'It sounds pretty enough, and the melodies resemble each other, but there's something wanting, I know not what!'

The real nightingale was banished from the country and empire. The artificial bird had its place on a silken cushion, close to the Emperor's bed; all the presents it had received, gold and precious stones, were ranged about it; in title it had advanced to be the High Imperial After-Dinner-Singer, and in rank to number one on the left hand; for the Emperor considered that side the most important on which the heart is placed, and even in an Emperor the heart is on the left side; and the playmaster wrote a work of five-and-twenty volumes about the artificial bird; it was very learned and very long, full of the most difficult Chinese words; but yet all the people declared that they had read it, and understood it, for fear of being considered stupid, and having their bodies trampled on.

So a whole year went by. The Emperor, the court, and all the other Chinese knew every little twitter in the artificial bird's song, by heart. But just for that reason it pleased them best; they could sing with it themselves, and they did so. The street boys sang 'Tsi-tsi-tsi-glug-glug,' and the Emperor himself sung it too. Yes! That was certainly famous.

But one evening, when the artificial bird was singing its best, and the Emperor lay in bed listening to it, something inside the bird said, 'Whizz!' Something cracked. 'Whirr!' All the wheels ran around, and then the music stopped.

The Emperor immediately sprang out of bed, and caused his body physician to be called; but what could *he* do? Then they sent for a watchmaker, and after a good deal of talking and investigation, the bird was put into something like order; but the watchmaker said that the bird must be carefully treated, for the barrels were worn, and it would be impossible to put new ones in, in such a manner that the music would go. There was a great lamentation; only once in a year was it permitted to let the bird sing, and that was almost too much. But then the playmaster made a little speech, full of heavy words, and said this was just as good as before, and so of course it was as good as before.

Now five years had gone by, and a real grief came upon the whole nation. The Chinese really were fond of their Emperor, and now he was ill, and could not, it was said, live much longer. Already a new Emperor had been chosen, and the people stood out in the street and asked the cavalier how their old Emperor did.

'P!' said he, and shook his head.

Cold and pale lay the Emperor in his great gorgeous bed; the whole court thought him dead, and each one ran to pay homage to the new ruler. The chamberlains ran out to talk it over, and the ladies' maids had a great coffee party. All about, in all the halls and passages, cloth had been laid down so that no footstep could be heard, and therefore

3 The Nightingale

it was quiet there, quite quiet. But the Emperor was not dead yet; stiff and pale he lay on the gorgeous bed with the long velvet curtains and the heavy gold tassels; high up, a window stood open, and the moon shone in upon the Emperor and the artificial bird.

The poor Emperor could scarcely breathe; it was just as if something lay upon his chest; he opened his eyes, and then he saw that it was Death who sat upon his chest, and had put on his golden crown and held in one hand the Emperor's sword and in the other his beautiful banner. And all around, from among the folds of the splendid velvet curtains, strange heads peered forth; a few very ugly, the rest quite lovely and mild. These were all the Emperor's bad and good deeds, that stood before him now that Death sat upon his heart.

'Do you remember this?' whispered one to the other. 'Do you remember that?' and then they told him so much that the perspiration ran from his forehead.

'I did not know that!' said the Emperor. 'Music! Music! The great Chinese drum!' he cried, 'so that I need not hear all they say!' and they continued speaking, and Death nodded like a Chinaman to all they said.

'Music, music!' cried the Emperor. 'You little precious golden bird, sing, sing! I have given you gold and costly presents; I have even hung my golden slipper around your neck – sing now, sing!' But the bird stood still; no one was there to wind him up, and he could not sing without that; but Death continued to stare at the Emperor with his great hollow eyes, and it was quiet, fearfully quiet!

Then there sounded from the window, suddenly, the most lovely song. It was the little live nightingale, that sat outside on a spray. It had heard of the Emperor's sad plight and had come to sing to him of comfort and hope. And as it sung the spectres grew paler and paler; the blood ran quicker and more quickly through the Emperor's weak limbs, and even Death listened, and said, 'Go on, little nightingale, go on!'

'But will you give me that splendid golden sword? Will you give me that rich banner? Will you give me the Emperor's crown?' And Death gave up each of these treasures for a song. And the nightingale sang on and on; and it sung of the quiet churchyard where the white roses grow, where the elder blossom smells sweet, and where the fresh grass is moistened by the tears of survivors. Then Death felt a longing to see his garden, and floated out at the window in the form of a cold white mist.

'Thanks, thanks!' said the Emperor. 'You heavenly little bird! I know you well! I banished you from my country and empire, and yet you have charmed away the evil faces from my couch, and banished Death from my heart! How can I reward you?'

'You have rewarded me!' replied the nightingale. 'I have drawn tears from your eyes, when I sang the first time, I shall never forget that. These are the jewels that rejoice a singer's heart; but now sleep and grow fresh and strong again; I will sing you something.'

And it sang, and the Emperor fell into a sweet slumber. Ah! How mild and refreshing that sleep was. The sun shone upon him through the windows, when he awoke refreshed and restored; not one of his servants had yet returned, for they all thought he was dead; only the nightingale still sat beside him and sang.

'You must always stay with me!' said the Emperor. 'You shall sing as you please; and I'll break the artificial bird into a thousand pieces.'

'Not so,' replied the nightingale. 'It did well so long as it could! Keep it as you have done till now. I cannot build my nest in the palace to dwell in it, but let me come when I feel the wish; then I will sit in the evening on the spray yonder by the window, and sing you something so that you may be glad and thoughtful at once.'

'I will sing of those who are happy, and of those who suffer. I will sing of good and of evil that remains hidden round about you. The little singing-bird flies far around, to the poor fisherman, to the peasant's roof, to everyone who dwells far away from you and from your court. I love your heart more than your crown, and yet the crown has an air of sanctity about it – I come, I shall sing to you – but one thing you must promise me.'

'Everything!' said the Emperor; and he stood there in his imperial robes, which he had put on himself, and pressed the sword which was heavy with gold to his heart.

'One thing I beg of you; tell no one that you have a little bird who tells you everything. Then it will go all the better.' And the nightingale flew away.

The servants came in, to look to their dead Emperor – and – yes, there they stood, and the Emperor said, 'Good-morning.'

4

The Tell-Tale Heart

(1843)

Edgar Allan Poe

True! – nervous – very, very dreadfully nervous I had been and am; but why *will* you say that I am mad? The disease had sharpened my senses – not destroyed – not dulled them. Above all was the sense of hearing acute. I heard all things in the heaven and in the earth. I heard many things in hell. How, then, am I mad? Hearken! and observe how healthily – how calmly I can tell you the whole story.

It is impossible to say how first the idea entered my brain; but once conceived, it haunted me day and night. Object there was none. Passion there was none. I loved the old man. He had never wronged me. He had never given me insult. For his gold I had no desire. I think it was his eye! yes, it was this! One of his eyes resembled that of a vulture – a pale blue eye, with a film over it. Whenever it fell upon me, my blood ran cold; and so by degrees – very gradually – I made up my mind to take the life of the old man, and thus rid myself of the eye for ever.

Now this is the point. You fancy me mad. Madmen know nothing. But you should have seen *me*. You should have seen how wisely I proceeded – with what caution – with what foresight – with what dissimulation I went to work! I was never kinder to the old man than during the whole week before I killed him. And every night, about midnight, I turned the latch of his door and opened it – oh, so gently! And then, when I had made an opening sufficient for my head, I put in a dark lantern, all closed, closed, so that no light shone out, and then I thrust in my head. Oh, you would have laughed to see how cunningly I thrust it in! I moved it slowly – very, very slowly, so that I might not disturb the old man's sleep. It took me an hour to place my whole head within the opening so far that I could see him as he lay upon his bed. Ha! – would a madman have been so wise as this? And then, when my head was well in the room, I undid the lantern cautiously – oh, so cautiously – cautiously (for the hinges creaked) – I undid it just so much that a single thin ray fell upon the vulture eye. And this I did for seven long nights – every night just at midnight – but I found the eye always closed; and so it was impossible to do the work; for it was not the old man who vexed me, but his Evil Eye. And every morning, when the day broke, I went boldly into the chamber, and spoke courageously to him, calling him by name in a hearty tone, and inquiring how he had passed the night. So you see he would have been a very profound old man, indeed, to suspect that every night, just at twelve, I looked in upon him while he slept.

Upon the eighth night I was more than usually cautious in opening the door. A watch's minute hand moves more quickly than did mine. Never before that night had I *felt* the extent of my own powers – of my sagacity. I could scarcely contain my feelings of triumph. To think that there I was, opening the door, little by little, and he not even to dream of my secret deeds or thoughts. I fairly chuckled at the idea; and perhaps he heard me; for he moved on the bed suddenly, as if startled. Now you may think that I drew back – but no. His room was as black as pitch with the thick darkness (for the shutters were close fastened, through fear of robbers), and so I knew that he could not see the opening of the door, and I kept pushing it on steadily, steadily.

I had my head in, and was about to open the lantern, when my thumb slipped upon the tin fastening, and the old man sprang up in the bed, crying out – 'Who's there?'

I kept quite still and said nothing. For a whole hour I did not move a muscle, and in the meantime I did not hear him lie down. He was still sitting up in the bed listening; – just as I have done, night after night, hearkening to the death watches in the wall.

Presently I heard a slight groan, and I knew it was the groan of mortal terror. It was not a groan of pain or of grief – oh, no! – it was the low stifled sound that arises from the bottom of the soul when overcharged with awe. I knew the sound well. Many a night, just at midnight, when all the world slept, it has welled up from my own bosom, deepening, with its dreadful echo, the terrors that distracted me. I say I knew it well. I knew what the old man felt, and pitied him, although I chuckled at heart. I knew that he had been lying awake ever since the first slight noise, when he had turned in the bed. His fears had been ever since growing upon him. He had been trying to fancy them causeless, but could not. He had been saying to himself – 'It is nothing but the wind in the chimney – it is only a mouse crossing the floor,' or 'it is merely a cricket which has made a single chirp'. Yes, he had been trying to comfort himself with these suppositions; but he had found all in vain. *All in vain*; because Death, in approaching him, had stalked with his black shadow before him, and enveloped the victim. And it was the mournful influence of the unperceived shadow that caused him to feel – although he neither saw nor heard – to *feel* the presence of my head within the room.

When I had waited a long time, very patiently, without hearing him lie down, I resolved to open a little – a very, very little crevice in the lantern. So I opened it – you cannot imagine how stealthily, stealthily – until, at length, a single dim ray, like the thread of the spider, shot from out the crevice and full upon the vulture eye.

It was open – wide, wide open – and I grew furious as I gazed upon it. I saw it with perfect distinctness – all a dull blue, with a hideous veil over it that chilled the very marrow in my bones; but I could see nothing else of the old man's face or person: for I had directed the ray as if by instinct, precisely upon the damned spot.

And now have I not told you that what you mistake for madness is but over-acuteness of the senses? – now, I say there came to my ears a low, dull, quick sound, such as a watch makes when enveloped in cotton. I knew *that* sound well too. It was the beating of the old man's heart. It increased my fury, as the beating of a drum stimulates the soldier into courage.

But even yet I refrained and kept still. I scarcely breathed. I held the lantern motionless. I tried how steadily I could maintain the ray upon the eye. Meantime the hellish tattoo of the heart increased. It grew quicker and quicker, and louder and louder every instant. The old man's terror *must* have been extreme! It grew louder, I say, louder every moment! – do you mark me well? I have told you that I am nervous: so I am. And now at the dead hour of the night, amid the dreadful silence of that old house, so strange a noise as this excited me to uncontrollable terror. Yet, for some minutes longer I refrained and stood still. But the beating grew louder, louder! I thought the heart must burst. And now a new anxiety seized me – the sound would be heard by a neighbour! The old man's hour had come! With a loud yell, I threw open the lantern and leaped into the room. He shrieked once – once only. In an instant I dragged him to the floor, and pulled the heavy bed over him. I then smiled gaily, to find the deed so far done. But, for many minutes, the heart beat on with a muffled sound. This, however, did not vex me; it would not be heard through the wall. At length it ceased. The old man was dead. I removed the bed and examined the corpse. Yes, he was stone, stone dead. I placed my hand upon the heart and held it there many minutes. There was no pulsation. He was stone dead. His eye would trouble me no more.

If still you think me mad, you will think so no longer when I describe the wise precautions I took for the concealment of the body. The night waned, and I worked hastily, but in silence. First of all I dismembered the corpse. I cut off the head and the arms and the legs.

I then took up three planks from the flooring of the chamber, and deposited all between the scantlings. I then replaced the boards so cleverly, so cunningly, that no human eye – not even *his* – could have detected any thing wrong. There was nothing to wash out – no stain of any kind – no blood-spot whatever. I had been too wary for that. A tub had caught all – ha! ha!

When I had made an end of these labours, it was four o'clock – still dark as midnight. As the bell sounded the hour, there came a knocking at the street door. I went down to open it with a light heart, – for what had I *now* to fear? There entered three men, who introduced themselves, with perfect suavity, as officers of the police. A shriek had been heard by a neighbour during the night; suspicion of foul play had been aroused; information had been lodged at the police office, and they (the officers) had been deputed to search the premises.

I smiled, – for *what* had I to fear? I bade the gentlemen welcome. The shriek, I said, was my own in a dream. The old man, I mentioned, was absent in the country. I took my visitors all over the house. I bade them search – search *well*. I led them, at length, to *his* chamber. I showed them his treasures, secure, undisturbed. In the enthusiasm of my confidence, I brought chairs into the room, and desired them *here* to rest from their fatigues, while I myself, in the wild audacity of my perfect triumph, placed my own seat upon the very spot beneath which reposed the corpse of the victim.

The officers were satisfied. My *manner* had convinced them. I was singularly at ease. They sat, and while I answered cheerily, they chatted familiar things. But, ere long, I felt myself getting pale and wished them gone. My head ached, and I fancied a ringing in my ears: but still they sat and still chatted. The ringing became more distinct: – it continued and became more distinct: I talked more freely to get rid of the feeling: but it continued and gained definitiveness – until, at length, I found that the noise was *not* within my ears.

No doubt I now grew *very* pale; – but I talked more fluently, and with a heightened voice. Yet the sound increased – and what could I do? It was *a low, dull, quick sound – much such a sound as a watch makes when enveloped in cotton*. I gasped for breath – and yet the officers heard it not. I talked more quickly – more vehemently; but the noise steadily increased. I arose and argued about trifles, in a high key and with violent gesticulations, but the noise steadily increased. Why *would* they not be gone? I paced the floor to and fro with heavy strides, as if excited to fury by the observation of the men – but the noise steadily increased. Oh God! what *could* I do? I foamed – I raved – I swore! I swung the chair upon which I had been sitting, and grated it upon the boards, but the noise arose over all and continually increased. It grew louder – louder – *louder*! And still the men chatted pleasantly, and smiled. Was it possible they heard not? Almighty God! – no, no! They heard! – they suspected! – they *knew*! – they were making a mockery of my horror! – this I thought, and this I think. But any thing was better than this agony! Any thing was more tolerable than this derision! I could bear those hypocritical smiles no longer! I felt that I must scream or die! – and now – again! – hark! louder! louder! louder! *louder*! –

'Villains!' I shrieked, 'dissemble no more! I admit the deed! – tear up the planks! – here, here! – it is the beating of his hideous heart!'

5

The Necklace

(1884)

Guy de Maupassant

She was one of those pretty and charming girls who, by some freak of destiny, are born into families that have always held subordinate appointments. Possessing neither dowry nor expectations, she had no hope of meeting some man of wealth and distinction, who would understand her, fall in love with her, and wed her. So she consented to marry a small clerk in the Ministry of Public Instruction.

She dressed plainly, because she could not afford to be elegant, but she felt as unhappy as if she had married beneath her. Women are dependent on neither caste nor ancestry. With them, beauty, grace, and charm take the place of birth and breeding. In their case, natural delicacy, instinctive refinement, and adaptability constitute their claims to aristocracy and raise girls of the lower classes to an equality with the greatest of great ladies. She was eternally restive under the conviction that she had been born to enjoy every refinement and luxury. Depressed by her humble surroundings, the sordid walls of her dwelling, its worn furniture and shabby fabrics were a torment to her. Details which another woman of her class would scarcely have noticed, tortured her and filled her with resentment. The sight of her little Breton maid-of-all-work roused in her forlorn repinings and frantic yearnings. She pictured to herself silent antechambers, upholstered with oriental tapestry, lighted by great bronze standard lamps, where two tall footmen in knee-breeches slumbered in huge arm-chairs, overcome by the oppressive heat from the stove. She dreamed of spacious drawing-rooms with hangings of antique silk, and beautiful tables laden with priceless ornaments: of fragrant and coquettish boudoirs, exquisitely adapted for afternoon chats with intimate friends, men of note and distinction, whose attentions are coveted by every woman.

She would sit down to dinner at the round table, its cloth already three days old, while her husband, seated opposite to her, removed the lid from the soup tureen and exclaimed, '*Pot-au-feu*! How splendid! My favourite soup!' But her own thoughts were dallying with the idea of exquisite dinners and shining silver, in rooms whose tapestried walls were gay with antique figures and grotesque birds in fairy forests. She would dream of delicious dishes served on wonderful plate, of soft, whispered nothings, which evoke a sphinx-like smile, while one trifles with the pink flesh of a trout or the wing of a plump pullet.

She had no pretty gowns, no jewels, nothing – and yet she cared for nothing else. She felt that it was for such things as these that she had been born. What joy it would have given her to attract, to charm, to be envied by women, courted by men! She had a wealthy friend, who had been at school at the same convent, but after a time she refused to go and see her, because she suffered so acutely after each visit. She spent whole days in tears of grief, regret, despair, and misery.

One evening her husband returned home in triumph with a large envelope in his hand.

'Here is something for you,' he cried.

Hastily she tore open the envelope and drew out a printed card with the following inscription:

'The Minister of Public Instruction and Madame Georges Ramponneau have the honour to request the company of Monsieur and Madame Loisel at an At Home at the Education Office on Monday, 18th January.'

Instead of being delighted as her husband had hoped, she flung the invitation irritably on the table, exclaiming:

'What good is that to me?'

'Why, my dear, I thought you would be pleased. You never go anywhere, and this is a really splendid chance for you. I had no end of trouble in getting it. Everybody is trying to get an invitation. It's very select, and only a few invitations are issued to the clerks. You will see all the officials there.'

She looked at him in exasperation, and exclaimed petulantly:

'What do you expect me to wear at a reception like that?'

He had not considered the matter, but he replied hesitatingly:

'Why, that dress you always wear to the theatre seems to me very nice indeed …'

He broke off. To his horror and consternation he saw that his wife was in tears. Two large drops were rolling slowly down her cheeks.

'What on earth is the matter?' he gasped.

With a violent effort she controlled her emotion, and drying her wet cheeks said in a calm voice:

'Nothing. Only I haven't a frock, and so I can't go to the reception. Give your invitation to some friend in your office, whose wife is better dressed than I am.'

He was greatly distressed.

'Let us talk it over, Mathilde. How much do you think a proper frock would cost, something quite simple that would come in useful for other occasions afterwards?'

She considered the matter for a few moments, busy with her calculations, and wondering how large a sum she might venture to name without shocking the little clerk's instincts of economy and provoking a prompt refusal.

5 The Necklace

'I hardly know,' she said at last, doubtfully, 'But I think I could manage with four hundred francs.'

He turned a little pale. She had named the exact sum that he had saved for buying a gun and treating himself to some Sunday shooting parties the following summer with some friends, who were going to shoot larks in the plain of Nanterre.

But he replied:

'Very well, I'll give you four hundred francs. But mind you buy a really handsome gown.'

The day of the party drew near. But although her gown was finished Madame Loisel seemed depressed and dissatisfied.

'What is the matter?' asked her husband one evening. 'You haven't been at all yourself the last three days.'

She answered: 'It vexes me to think that I haven't any jewellery to wear, not even a brooch. I shall feel like a perfect pauper. I would almost rather not go to the party.'

'You can wear some fresh flowers. They are very fashionable this year. For ten francs you can get two or three splendid roses.'

She was not convinced.

'No, there is nothing more humiliating than to have an air of poverty among a crowd of rich women.'

'How silly you are!' exclaimed her husband. 'Why don't you ask your friend, Madame Forestier, to lend you some jewellery. You know her quite well enough for that.'

She uttered a cry of joy.

'Yes, of course, it never occurred to me.'

The next day she paid her friend a visit and explained her predicament.

Madame Forestier went to her wardrobe, took out a large jewel case and placed it open before her friend.

'Help yourself, my dear,' she said.

Madame Loisel saw some bracelets, a pearl necklace, a Venetian cross exquisitely worked in gold and jewels. She tried on these ornaments in front of the mirror and hesitated, reluctant to take them off and give them back.

'Have you nothing else?' she kept asking.

'Oh, yes, look for yourself. I don't know what you would prefer.'

At length, she discovered a black satin case containing a superb diamond necklace, and her heart began to beat with frantic desire. With trembling hands she took it out, fastened it over her high-necked gown, and stood gazing at herself in rapture.

Then, in an agony of doubt, she said:

'Will you lend me this? I shouldn't want anything else.'

'Yes, certainly.'

She threw her arms round her friend's neck, kissed her effusively, and then fled with her treasure.

It was the night of the reception. Madame Loisel's triumph was complete. All smiles and graciousness, in her exquisite gown, she was the prettiest woman in the room. Her head was in a whirl of joy. All the men stared at her and inquired her name and begged for an introduction; all the junior staff asked her for waltzes. She even attracted the attention of the minister himself.

Carried away by her enjoyment, glorying in her beauty and her success, she threw herself ecstatically into the dance. She moved as in a beatific dream, wherein were mingled all the homage and admiration she had evoked, all the desires she had kindled, all that complete and perfect triumph, so dear to a woman's heart.

It was close on four before she could tear herself away. Ever since midnight her husband had been dozing in a little, deserted drawing-room together with three other men whose wives were enjoying themselves immensely.

He threw her outdoor wraps round her shoulders, unpretentious, every-day garments, whose shabbiness contrasted strangely with the elegance of her ball dress. Conscious of the incongruity, she was eager to be gone, in order to escape the notice of the other women in their luxurious furs. Loisel tried to restrain her.

'Wait here while I fetch a cab. You will catch cold outside.'

But she would not listen to him and hurried down the staircase. They went out into the street, but there was no cab to be seen. They continued their search, vainly hailing drivers whom they caught sight of in the distance. Shivering with cold and in desperation they made their way towards the Seine. At last, on the quay, they found one of those old vehicles which are only seen in Paris after nightfall, as if ashamed to display their shabbiness by daylight.

The cab took them to their door in the Rue des Martyrs and they gloomily climbed the stairs to their dwelling. All was over for her. As for him, he was thinking that he would have to be in the office by ten o'clock.

She took off her wraps in front of the mirror, for the sake of one last glance at herself in all her glory. But suddenly she uttered a cry. The diamonds were no longer round her neck.

'What is the matter?' asked her husband, who was already half undressed.

She turned to him in horror. 'I ... I've ... lost Madame Forestier's necklace.'

He started in dismay. 'What? Lost the necklace? Impossible!'

They searched the pleats of the gown, the folds of the cloak, and all the pockets, but in vain.

'You are sure you had it on when you came away from the ball?'

'Yes, I remember feeling it in the lobby at the Education Office.'

5 The Necklace

'But if you had lost it in the street we should have heard it drop. It must be in the cab.'

'Yes. I expect it is. Did you take the number?'

'No. Did you?'

'No.'

They gazed at each other, utterly appalled. In the end Loisel put on his clothes again.

'I will go over the ground that we covered on foot and see if I cannot find it.'

He left the house. Lacking the strength to go to bed, unable to think, she collapsed into a chair and remained there in her evening gown, without a fire.

About seven o'clock her husband returned. He had not found the diamonds.

He applied to the police, advertised a reward in the newspapers, made inquiries of all the hackney cab offices; he visited every place that seemed to hold out a vestige of hope.

His wife waited all day long in the same distracted condition, overwhelmed by this appalling calamity.

Loisel returned home in the evening, pale and hollow-cheeked. His efforts had been in vain.

'You must write to your friend,' he said, 'and tell her that you have broken the catch of the necklace and that you are having it mended. That will give us time to think things over.'

She wrote a letter to his dictation.

After a week had elapsed, they gave up all hope. Loisel, who looked five years older, said:

'We must take steps to replace the diamonds.'

On the following day they took the empty case to the jeweller whose name was inside the lid. He consulted his books.

'The necklace was not bought here, madam; I can only have supplied the case.'

They went from jeweller to jeweller, in an endeavour to find a necklace exactly like the one they had lost, comparing their recollections. Both of them were ill with grief and despair.

At last in a shop in the Palais-Royal they found a diamond necklace, which seemed to them exactly like the other. Its price was forty thousand francs. The jeweller agreed to sell it to them for thirty-six. They begged him not to dispose of it for three days, and they stipulated for the right to sell it back for thirty-four thousand francs, if the original necklace was found before the end of February.

Loisel had eighteen thousand francs left to him by his father. The balance of the sum he proposed to borrow. He raised loans in all quarters, a thousand francs from one man, five hundred from another, five louis here, three louis there. He gave promissory notes, agreed to exorbitant terms, had dealings with usurers, and with all the money-lending hordes. He compromised his whole future, and had to risk his signature, hardly knowing if he would be able to honour it. Overwhelmed by the prospect of future suffering, the black misery which was about to come upon him, the physical privations and moral torments, he went to fetch the new necklace, and laid his thirty-six thousand francs down on the jeweller's counter.

When Madame Loisel brought back the necklace, Madame Forestier said reproachfully:

'You ought to have returned it sooner; I might have wanted to wear it.'

To Madame Loisel's relief she did not open the case. Supposing she had noticed the exchange, what would she have thought? What would she have said? Perhaps she would have taken her for a thief.

Madame Loisel now became acquainted with the horrors of extreme poverty. She made up her mind to it, and played her part heroically. This appalling debt had to be paid, and pay it she would. The maid was dismissed; the flat was given up, and they moved to a garret. She undertook all the rough household work and the odious duties of the kitchen. She washed up after meals and ruined her pink finger-nails scrubbing greasy dishes and saucepans. She washed the linen, the shirts, and the dusters, and hung them out on the line to dry. Every morning she carried down the sweepings to the street, and brought up the water, pausing for breath at each landing. Dressed like a working woman, she went with her basket on her arm to the greengrocer, the grocer, and the butcher, bargaining, wrangling, and fighting for every farthing.

Each month some of the promissory notes had to be redeemed, and others renewed, in order to gain time.

Her husband spent his evenings working at some tradesman's accounts, and at night he would often copy papers at five sous a page.

This existence went on for ten years.

At the end of that time they had paid off everything to the last penny, including the usurious rates and the accumulations of interest.

Madame Loisel now looked an old woman. She had become the typical poor man's wife, rough, coarse, hardbitten. Her hair was neglected, her skirts hung awry, and her hands were red. Her voice was no longer gentle, and she washed down the floors vigorously. But now and then, when her husband was at the office, she would sit by the window and her thoughts would wander back to that far-away evening, the evening of her beauty and her triumph.

What would have been the end of it if she had not lost the necklace? Who could say? Who could say? How strange, how variable are the chances of life! How small a thing can serve to save or ruin you!

One Sunday she went for a stroll in the Champs-Élysées, for the sake of relaxation after the week's work, and she caught sight of a lady with a child. She recognized Madame Forestier, who looked as young, as pretty, and as attractive as ever. Madame Loisel felt a thrill of emotion. Should she speak to her? Why not? Now that the debt was paid, why should she not tell her the whole story? She went up to her.

'Good morning, Jeanne.'

Her friend did not recognize her and was surprised at being addressed so familiarly by this homely person.

'I am afraid I do not know you – you must have made a mistake,' she said hesitatingly.

'No. I am Mathilde Loisel.'

Her friend uttered a cry.

'Oh, my poor, dear Mathilde, how you have changed!'

'Yes, I have been through a very hard time since I saw you last, no end of trouble, and all through you.'

'Through me? What do you mean?'

'You remember the diamond necklace you lent me to wear at the reception at the Education Office?'

'Yes. Well?'

'Well, I lost it.'

'I don't understand; you brought it back to me.'

'What I brought you back was another one, exactly like it. And for the last ten years we have been paying for it. You will understand that it was not an easy matter for people like us, who hadn't a penny. However, it's all over now. I can't tell you what a relief it is.'

Madame Forestier stopped dead.

'You mean to say that you bought a diamond necklace to replace mine?'

'Yes. And you never noticed it? They were certainly very much alike.'

She smiled with ingenuous pride and satisfaction.

Madame Forestier seized both her hands in great distress.

'Oh, my poor, dear Mathilde! Why, mine was only imitation. At the most it was worth five hundred francs!'

6

The Model Millionaire

(1887)

Oscar Wilde

Unless one is wealthy there is no use in being a charming fellow. Romance is the privilege of the rich, not the profession of the unemployed. The poor should be practical and prosaic. It is better to have a permanent income than to be fascinating. These are the great truths of modern life which Hughie Erskine never realised. Poor Hughie! Intellectually, we must admit, he was not of much importance. He never said a brilliant or even an ill-natured thing in his life. But then he was wonderfully good-looking, with his crisp brown hair, his clear-cut profile, and his grey eyes. He was as popular with men as he was with women and he had every accomplishment except that of making money. His father had bequeathed him his cavalry sword and a History of the Peninsular War in fifteen volumes. Hughie hung the first over his looking-glass, put the second on a shelf between Ruff's Guide and Bailey's Magazine, and lived on two hundred a year that an old aunt allowed him. He had tried everything. He had gone on the Stock Exchange for six months; but what was a butterfly to do among bulls and bears? He had been a tea-merchant for a little longer, but had soon tired of pekoe and souchong. Then he had tried selling dry sherry. That did not answer; the sherry was a little too dry. Ultimately he became nothing, a delightful, ineffectual young man with a perfect profile and no profession.

To make matters worse, he was in love. The girl he loved was Laura Merton, the daughter of a retired Colonel who had lost his temper and his digestion in India, and had never found either of them again. Laura adored him, and he was ready to kiss her shoestrings. They were the handsomest couple in London, and had not a penny-piece between them. The Colonel was very fond of Hughie, but would not hear of any engagement.

'Come to me, my boy, when you have got ten thousand pounds of your own, and we will see about it,' he used to say; and Hughie looked very glum in those days, and had to go to Laura for consolation.

One morning, as he was on his way to Holland Park, where the Mertons lived, he dropped in to see a great friend of his, Alan Trevor. Trevor was a painter. Indeed, few people escape that nowadays. But he was also an artist, and artists are rather rare. Personally he was a strange rough fellow, with a freckled face and a red ragged beard. However, when he took up the brush he was a real master, and his pictures were eagerly sought after. He had been very much attracted by Hughie at first, it must be acknowledged, entirely on account of his personal charm. 'The only people a painter should know,' he used to say, 'are people who are bête and beautiful, people who are an artistic pleasure to look at and an intellectual repose to talk to. Men who are dandies and women who are darlings rule the world, at least they should do so.' However, after he got to know Hughie better, he liked him quite as much for his bright, buoyant spirits and his generous, reckless nature, and had given him the permanent entrée to his studio.

When Hughie came in he found Trevor putting the finishing touches to a wonderful life-size picture of a beggar-man. The beggar himself was standing on a raised platform in a corner of the studio. He was a wizened old man, with a face like wrinkled parchment, and a most piteous expression. Over his shoulders was flung a coarse brown cloak, all tears and tatters; his thick boots were patched and cobbled, and with one hand he leant on a rough stick, while with the other he held out his battered hat for alms.

'What an amazing model!' whispered Hughie, as he shook hands with his friend.

'An amazing model?' shouted Trevor at the top of his voice; 'I should think so! Such beggars as he are not to be met with every day. *A trouvaille, mon cher*; a living Velasquez! My stars! what an etching Rembrandt would have made of him!'

'Poor old chap!' said Hughie, 'how miserable he looks! But I suppose, to you painters, his face is his fortune?'

'Certainly,' replied Trevor, 'you don't want a beggar to look happy, do you?'

'How much does a model get for sitting?' asked Hughie, as he found himself a comfortable seat on a divan.

'A shilling an hour.'

'And how much do you get for your picture, Alan?'

'Oh, for this I get two thousand!'

'Pounds?'

'Guineas. Painters, poets, and physicians always get guineas.'

'Well, I think the model should have a percentage,' cried Hughie, laughing; 'they work quite as hard as you do.'

'Nonsense, nonsense! Why, look at the trouble of laying on the paint alone, and standing all day long at one's easel! It's all very well, Hughie, for you to talk, but I assure you that there are moments when Art almost attains to the dignity of manual labour. But you mustn't chatter; I'm very busy. Smoke a cigarette, and keep quiet.'

After some time the servant came in, and told Trevor that the frame maker wanted to speak to him.

'Don't run away, Hughie,' he said, as he went out, 'I will be back in a moment.'

The old beggar-man took advantage of Trevor's absence to rest for a moment on a wooden bench that was behind him. He looked so forlorn and wretched that Hughie could not help pitying him, and felt in his pockets to see what money he had. All he could find was a sovereign and some coppers. 'Poor old fellow,' he thought to himself, 'he wants it more than I do, but it means no hansoms for a fortnight'; and he walked across the studio and slipped the sovereign into the beggar's hand.

The old man started, and a faint smile flitted across his withered lips. 'Thank you, sir,' he said, 'thank you.'

Then Trevor arrived, and Hughie took his leave, blushing a little at what he had done. He spent the day with Laura, got a charming scolding for his extravagance, and had to walk home.

That night he strolled into the Palette Club about eleven o'clock, and found Trevor sitting by himself in the smoking-room drinking hock and seltzer.

'Well, Alan, did you get the picture finished all right?' he said, as he lit his cigarette.

'Finished and framed, my boy!' answered Trevor; 'and, by the bye, you have made a conquest. That old model you saw is quite devoted to you. I had to tell him all about you – who you are, where you live, what your income is, what prospects you have –'

'My dear Alan,' cried Hughie, 'I shall probably find him waiting for me when I go home. But of course you are only joking. Poor old wretch! I wish I could do something for him. I think it is dreadful that any one should be so miserable. I have got heaps of old clothes at home – do you think he would care for any of them? Why, his rags were falling to bits.'

'But he looks splendid in them,' said Trevor. 'I wouldn't paint him in a frock coat for anything. What you call rags I call romance. What seems poverty to you is picturesqueness to me. However, I'll tell him of your offer.'

'Alan,' said Hughie seriously, 'you painters are a heartless lot.'

'An artist's heart is his head,' replied Trevor; 'and besides, our business is to realise the world as we see it, not to reform it as we know it. *À chacun son métier*. And now tell me how Laura is. The old model was quite interested in her.'

'You don't mean to say you talked to him about her?' said Hughie.

'Certainly I did. He knows all about the relentless colonel, the lovely Laura, and the £10,000.'

'You told that old beggar all my private affairs?' cried Hughie, looking very red and angry.

'My dear boy,' said Trevor, smiling, 'that old beggar, as you call him, is one of the richest men in Europe. He could buy all London to-morrow without overdrawing his account. He has a house in every capital, dines off gold plate, and can prevent Russia going to war when he chooses.'

'What on earth do you mean?' exclaimed Hughie.

'What I say,' said Trevor. 'The old man you saw to-day in the studio was Baron Hausberg. He is a great friend of mine, buys all my pictures and that sort of thing, and gave me a commission a month ago to paint him as a beggar. *Que voulez-vous? La fantaisie d'un millionnaire!* And I must say he made a magnificent figure in his rags, or perhaps I should say in my rags; they are an old suit I got in Spain.'

6 The Model Millionaire

'Baron Hausberg!' cried Hughie. 'Good heavens! I gave him a sovereign!' and he sank into an armchair the picture of dismay.

'Gave him a sovereign!' shouted Trevor, and he burst into a roar of laughter. 'My dear boy, you'll never see it again. *Son affaire c'est l'argent des autres.*'

'I think you might have told me, Alan,' said Hughie sulkily, 'and not have let me make such a fool of myself.'

'Well, to begin with, Hughie,' said Trevor, 'it never entered my mind that you went about distributing alms in that reckless way. I can understand your kissing a pretty model, but your giving a sovereign to an ugly one – by Jove, no! Besides, the fact is that I really was not at home to-day to any one; and when you came in I didn't know whether Hausberg would like his name mentioned. You know he wasn't in full dress.'

'What a duffer he must think me!' said Hughie.

'Not at all. He was in the highest spirits after you left; kept chuckling to himself and rubbing his old wrinkled hands together. I couldn't make out why he was so interested to know all about you; but I see it all now. He'll invest your sovereign for you, Hughie, pay you the interest every six months, and have a capital story to tell after dinner.'

'I am an unlucky devil,' growled Hughie. 'The best thing I can do is to go to bed; and, my dear Alan, you mustn't tell any one. I shouldn't dare show my face in the Row.'

'Nonsense! It reflects the highest credit on your philanthropic spirit, Hughie. And don't run away. Have another cigarette, and you can talk about Laura as much as you like.'

However, Hughie wouldn't stop, but walked home, feeling very unhappy, and leaving Alan Trevor in fits of laughter.

The next morning, as he was at breakfast, the servant brought him up a card on which was written, 'Monsieur Gustave Naudin, *de la part de* M le Baron Hausberg.'

'I suppose he has come for an apology,' said Hughie to himself; and he told the servant to show the visitor up.

An old gentleman with gold spectacles and grey hair came into the room, and said, in a slight French accent, 'Have I the honour of addressing Monsieur Erskine?'

Hughie bowed.

'I have come from Baron Hausberg,' he continued. 'The Baron –'

'I beg, sir, that you will offer him my sincerest apologies,' stammered Hughie.

'The Baron,' said the old gentleman with a smile, 'has commissioned me to bring you this letter'; and he extended a sealed envelope.

On the outside was written, 'A wedding present to Hugh Erskine and Laura Merton, from an old beggar,' and inside was a cheque for £10,000.

When they were married Alan Trevor was the best man, and the Baron made a speech at the wedding breakfast.

'Millionaire models,' remarked Alan, 'are rare enough; but, by Jove, model millionaires are rarer still!'

7

Tony Kytes, the Arch-Deceiver

(1894)

Thomas Hardy

I shall never forget Tony's face. 'Twas a little, round, firm, tight face, with a seam here and there left by the smallpox, but not enough to hurt his looks in a woman's eye, though he'd had it baddish when he was a boy. So very serious-looking and unsmiling 'a was, that young man, that it really seemed as if he couldn't laugh at all without great pain to his conscience. He looked very hard at a small speck in your eye when talking to 'ee. And there was no more sign of a whisker or beard on Tony Kytes' face than on the palm of my hand. He used to sing 'The Tailor's Breeches' with a religious manner, as if it were a hymn:

'O the petticoats went off, and the breeches they went on!' and all the rest of the scandalous stuff. He was quite the women's favourite, and in return for their likings he loved 'em in shoals.

But in course of time Tony got fixed down to one in particular, Milly Richards, a nice, light, small, tender little thing; and it was soon said that they were engaged to be married. One Saturday he had been to market to do business for his father, and was driving home the waggon in the afternoon. When he reached the foot of the very hill we shall be going over in ten minutes who should he see waiting for him at the top but Unity Sallet, a handsome girl, one of the young women he'd been very tender toward before he'd got engaged to Milly.

As soon as Tony came up to her she said, 'My dear Tony, will you give me a lift home?'

'That I will, darling,' said Tony. 'You don't suppose I could refuse 'ee?'

She smiled a smile, and up she hopped, and on drove Tony.

'Tony,' she says, in a sort of tender chide, 'why did ye desert me for that other one? In what is she better than I? I should have made 'ee a finer wife, and a more loving one too. 'Tisn't girls that are so easily won at first that are the best. Think how long we've known each other – ever since we were children almost – now haven't we, Tony?'

'Yes, that we have,' says Tony, a-struck with the truth o't.

7 Tony Kytes, the Arch-Deceiver

'And you've never seen anything in me to complain of, have ye, Tony? Now tell the truth to me?'

'I never have, upon my life,' says Tony.

'And – can you say I'm not pretty, Tony? Now look at me!'

He let his eyes light upon her for a long while. 'I really can't,' says he. 'In fact, I never knowed you was so pretty before!'

'Prettier than she?'

What Tony would have said to that nobody knows, for before he could speak, what should he see ahead, over the hedge past the turning, but a feather he knew well – the feather in Milly's hat – she to whom he had been thinking of putting the question as to giving out the banns that very week.

'Unity,' says he, as mild as he could, 'here's Milly coming. Now I shall catch it mightily if she see 'ee riding here with me; and if you get down she'll be turning the corner in a moment, and, seeing 'ee in the road, she'll know we've been coming on together. Now, dearest Unity, will ye, to avoid all unpleasantness, which I know ye can't bear any more than I, will ye lie down in the back part of the waggon, and let me cover you over with the tarpaulin till Milly has passed? It will all be done in a minute. Do! – and I'll think over what we've said; and perhaps I shall put a loving question to you after all, instead of to Milly. 'Tisn't true that it is all settled between her and me.'

Well, Unity Sallet agreed, and lay down at the back of the waggon, and Tony covered her over, so that the waggon seemed to be empty but for the loose tarpaulin; and then he drove on to meet Milly.

'My dear Tony!' cries Milly, looking up with a little pout at him as he came near. 'How long you've been coming home! Just as if I didn't live at Upper Longpuddle at all! And I've come to meet you as you asked me to do, and to ride back with you, and talk over our future home – since you asked me, and I promised. But I shouldn't have come else, Mr Tony!'

'Ay, my dear, I did ask 'ee – to be sure I did, now I think of it – but I had quite forgot it. To ride back with me, did you say, dear Milly?'

'Well, of course! What can I do else? Surely you don't want me to walk, now I've come all this way?'

'O no, no! I was thinking you might be going on to town to meet your mother. I saw her there – and she looked as if she might be expecting 'ee.'

'O no; she's just home. She came across the fields, and so got back before you.'

'Ah! I didn't know that,' says Tony. And there was no help for it but to take her up beside him.

They talked on very pleasantly, and looked at the trees, and beasts, and birds, and insects, and at the ploughman at work in the fields, till presently who should they see looking out of the upper window of a house that stood beside the road they were following, but Hannah Jolliver, another young beauty of the place at that time, and the very first woman that Tony had fallen in love with – before Milly and before Unity, in fact – the one that he had almost arranged to marry instead of Milly. She was a much more dashing girl than Milly Richards, though he'd not thought much of her of late. The house Hannah was looking from was her aunt's.

'My dear Milly – my coming wife, as I may call 'ee,' says Tony in his modest way, and not so loud that Unity could overhear, 'I see a young woman a-looking out of the window, who I think may accost me. The fact is, Milly, she had a notion that I was wishing to marry her, and since she's discovered I've promised another, and a prettier than she, I'm rather afeared of her temper if she sees us together. Now, Milly, would you do me a favour – my coming wife, as I may say?'

'Certainly, dearest Tony,' says she.

'Then would ye creep under the empty sacks just here in the front of the waggon, and hide there out of sight till we've passed the house? She hasn't seen us yet. You see, we ought to live in peace and goodwill since 'tis almost Christmas, and 'twill prevent angry passions rising, which we always should do.'

'I don't mind, to oblige you, Tony,' Milly said; and though she didn't care much about doing it, she crept under, and crouched down just behind the seat, Unity being snug at the other end. So they drove on till they got near the roadside cottage. Hannah had soon seen him coming, and waited at the window, looking down upon him. She tossed her head a little disdainfully and smiled off-hand.

'Well, aren't you going to be civil enough to ask me to ride home with you!' she says, seeing that he was for driving past with a nod and a smile.

'Ah, to be sure! What was I thinking of?' said Tony, in a flutter. 'But you seem as if you was staying at your aunt's?'

'No, I am not,' she said. 'Don't you see I have my bonnet and jacket on? I have only called to see her on my way home. How can you be so stupid, Tony?'

'In that case – ah – of course you must come along wi' me,' says Tony, feeling a dim sort of sweat rising up inside his clothes. And he reined in the horse, and waited till she'd come downstairs, and then helped her up beside him, her feet outside. He drove on again, his face as long as a face that was a round one by nature well could be.

Hannah looked round sideways into his eyes. 'This is nice, isn't it, Tony?' she said. 'I like riding with you.'

Tony looked back into her eyes. 'And I with you,' he said after a while. In short, having considered her, he warmed up, and the more he looked at her the more he liked her, till he couldn't for the life of him think why he had ever said a word about marriage to Milly or Unity while Hannah Jolliver was in question. So they sat a little closer and closer, their feet upon the foot-board and their shoulders touching, and Tony thought over and over again how handsome Hannah was. He spoke tenderer and tenderer, and called her 'dear Hannah' in a whisper at last.

'You've settled it with Milly by this time, I suppose,' she said.

'No-no, not exactly.'

'What? How low you talk, Tony.'

7   Tony Kytes, the Arch-Deceiver

'Yes – I've a kind of hoarseness. I said, not exactly.'

'I suppose you mean to?'

'Well, as to that – ' His eyes rested on her face, and hers on his. He wondered how he could have been such a fool as not to follow up Hannah. 'My sweet Hannah!' he burst out, taking her hand, not being really able to help it, and forgetting Milly and Unity, and all the world besides. 'Settled it? I don't think I have.'

'Hark!' says Hannah.

'What?' says Tony, letting go her hand.

'Surely I heard a sort of little screaming squeak under those sacks? Why, you've been carrying corn, and there's mice in this waggon, I declare!' She began to haul up the tails of her gown.

'Oh no; 'tis the axle,' said Tony in an assuring way. 'It do go like that sometimes in dry weather.'

'Perhaps it was … Well, now, to be quite honest, dear Tony, do you like her better than me? Because – because, although I've held off so independent, I'll own at last that I do like 'ee, Tony, to tell the truth; and I wouldn't say no if you asked me – you know that.'

Tony was so won over by this pretty offering mood of a girl who had been quite the reverse (Hannah had a backward way with her at times, if you can mind) that he just glanced behind, and then whispered very soft, 'I haven't quite promised her, and I think I can get out of it, and ask you that question you speak of.'

'Throw over Milly? – all to marry me! How delightful!' broke out Hannah, quite loud, clapping her hands.

At this there was a real squeak – an angry, spiteful squeak, and afterward a long moan, as if something had broke its heart, and a movement of the empty sacks.

'Something's there!' said Hannah, starting up.

'It's nothing, really,' says Tony in a soothing voice, and praying inwardly for a way out of this. 'I wouldn't tell 'ee at first, because I wouldn't frighten 'ee. But, Hannah, I've really a couple of ferrets in a bag under there, for rabbiting, and they quarrel sometimes. I don't wish it knowed, as 'twould be called poaching. Oh, they can't get out, bless 'ee – you are quite safe! And – and – what a fine day it is, isn't it, Hannah, for this time of year? Be you going to market next Saturday? How is your aunt now?' And so on, says Tony, to keep her from talking any more about love in Milly's hearing.

But he found his work cut out for him, and wondering again how he should get out of this ticklish business, he looked about for a chance. Nearing home he saw his father in a field not far off, holding up his hand as if he wished to speak to Tony.

'Would you mind taking the reins a moment, Hannah,' he said, much relieved, 'while I go and find out what father wants?'

She consented, and away he hastened into the field, only too glad to get breathing time. He found that his father was looking at him with rather a stern eye.

'Come, come Tony,' says old Mr Kytes, as soon as his son was alongside him, 'this won't do, you know.'

'What?' says Tony.

'Why, if you mean to marry Milly Richards, do it, and there's an end o't. But don't go driving about the country with Jolliver's daughter and making a scandal. I won't have such things done.'

'I only asked her – that is, she asked me, to ride home.'

'She? Why, now, if it had been Milly, 'twould have been quite proper; but you and Hannah Jolliver going about by yourselves – '

'Milly's there too, father.'

'Milly? Where?'

'Under the corn-sacks! Yes, the truth is, father, I've got rather into a nunnywatch, I'm afeared! Unity Sallet is there too – yes, at the other end, under the tarpaulin. All three are in that waggon, and what to do with 'em I know no more than the dead! The best plan is, as I'm thinking, to speak out loud and plain to one of 'em before the rest, and that will settle it; not but what 'twill cause 'em to kick up a bit of a miff, for certain. Now which would you marry, father, if you was in my place?'

'Whichever of 'em did *not* ask to ride with thee.'

'That was Milly, I'm bound to say, as she only mounted by my invitation. But Milly – '

'Then stick to Milly, she's the best … But look at that!'

His father pointed toward the waggon. 'She can't hold that horse in. You shouldn't have left the reins in her hands. Run on and take the horse's head, or there'll be some accident to them maids!'

Tony's horse, in fact, in spite of Hannah's tugging at the reins, had started on his way at a brisk walking pace, being very anxious to get back to the stable, for he had had a long day out. Without another word Tony rushed away from his father to overtake the horse.

Now of all things that could have happened to wean him from Milly there was nothing so powerful as his father recommending her. No; it could not be Milly, after all. Hannah must be the one, since he could not marry all three as he longed to do. This he thought while running after the waggon. But queer things were happening inside it.

It was, of course, Milly who had screamed under the sack-bags, being obliged to let off her bitter rage and shame in that way at what Tony was saying, and never daring to show, for very pride and dread o' being laughed at, that she was in hiding. She became more and more restless, and in twisting herself about, what did she see but another woman's foot and white stocking close to her head. It quite frightened her, not knowing that Unity Sallet was in the waggon likewise. But after the fright was over she determined to get to the bottom of all this, and she crept and crept along the bed of the waggon, under the tarpaulin, like a snake, when lo and behold she came face to face with Unity.

'Well, if this isn't disgraceful!' says Milly in a raging whisper to Unity.

7 Tony Kytes, the Arch-Deceiver

''Tis,' says Unity, 'to see you hiding in a young man's waggon like this, and no great character belonging to either of ye!'

'Mind what you are saying!' replied Milly, getting louder. 'I am engaged to be married to him, and haven't I a right to be here? What right have you, I should like to know? What has he been promising you? A pretty lot of nonsense, I expect! But what Tony says to other women is all mere wind, and no concern to me!'

'Don't you be too sure!' says Unity. 'He's going to have Hannah, and not you, nor me either; I could hear that.'

Now at these strange voices sounding from under the cloth Hannah was thunderstruck almost into a swound; and it was just at the time that the horse moved on. Hannah tugged away wildly, not knowing what she was doing; and as the quarrel rose louder and louder Hannah got so horrified that she let go the reins altogether. The horse went on at his own pace, and coming to the corner where we turn round to drop down the hill to Lower Longpuddle he turned too quick, the off wheels went on the bank, the waggon rose sideways till it was quite on edge upon the near axles, and out rolled the three maidens into the road in a heap. The horse looked round and stood still.

When Tony came up, frightened and breathless, he was relieved enough to see that none of his darlings was hurt, beyond a few scratches from the brambles of the hedge. But he was rather alarmed when he heard how they were going on at one another.

'Don't ye quarrel, my dears – don't ye!' says he, taking off his hat out of respect to 'em. And then he would have kissed them all round, as fair and square as a man could, but they were in too much of a taking to let him, and screeched and sobbed till they were quite spent.

'Now I'll speak out honest, because I ought to,' says Tony as soon as he could get heard. 'And this is the truth,' says he. 'I've asked Hannah to be mine, and she is willing, and we are going to put up the banns next – '

Tony had not noticed that Hannah's father was coming up behind, nor had he noticed that Hannah's face was beginning to bleed from the scratch of a bramble. Hannah had seen her father, and had run to him, crying worse than ever.

'My daughter is *not* willing, sir!' said Mr Jolliver hot and strong. 'Be you willing, Hannah? I ask ye to have spirit enough to refuse him!'

'I have spirit, and I do refuse him!' says Hannah, partly because her father was there, and partly, too, in a tantrum because of the discovery, and the scar that might be left on her face. 'Little did I think when I was so soft with him just now that I was talking to such a false deceiver!'

'What, you won't have me, Hannah?' says Tony, his jaw hanging down like a dead man's.

'Never – I would sooner marry no-nobody at all!' she gasped out, though with her heart in her throat, for she would not have refused Tony if he had asked her quietly, and her father had not been there, and her face had not been scratched by the bramble. And having said that, away she walked upon her father's arm, thinking and hoping he would ask her again.

Tony didn't know what to say next. Milly was sobbing her heart out; but as his father had strongly recommended her he couldn't feel inclined that way. So he turned to Unity.

'Well, will you, Unity dear, be mine?' he says.

'Take her leavings? Not I!' says Unity. 'I'd scorn it!' And away walks Unity Sallet likewise, though she looked back when she'd gone some way, to see if he was following her.

So there at last were left Milly and Tony by themselves, she crying in watery streams, and Tony looking like a tree struck by lightning.

'Well, Milly,' he says at last, going up to her, 'it do seem as if fate had ordained that it should be you and I, or nobody. And what must be must be, I suppose. Hey, Milly?'

'If you like, Tony. You didn't really mean what you said to them?'

'Not a word of it!' declares Tony, bringing down his fist upon his palm.

And then he kissed her, and put the waggon to rights, and they mounted together; and their banns were put up the very next Sunday. I was not able to go to their wedding, but it was a rare party they had, by all account.

8

The Sea Raiders

(1896)

H G Wells

1

Until the extraordinary affair at Sidmouth, the peculiar species *Haploteuthis ferox* was known to science only generically, on the strength of a half-digested tentacle obtained near the Azores, and a decaying body pecked by birds and nibbled by fish, found early in 1896 by Mr Jennings, near Land's End.

In no department of zoological science, indeed, are we quite so much in the dark as with regard to the deep-sea cephalopods. A mere accident, for instance, it was that led to the Prince of Monaco's discovery of nearly a dozen new forms in the summer of 1895, a discovery in which the before-mentioned tentacle was included. It chanced that a cachalot was killed off Terceira by some sperm whalers, and in its last struggles charged almost to the Prince's yacht, missed it, rolled under, and died within twenty yards of his rudder. And in its agony it threw up a number of large objects, which the Prince, dimly perceiving they were strange and important, was, by a happy expedient, able to secure before they sank. He set his screws in motion, and kept them circling in the vortices thus created until a boat could be lowered. And these specimens were whole cephalopods and fragments of cephalopods, some of gigantic proportions, and almost all of them unknown to science!

It would seem, indeed, that these large and agile creatures, living in the middle depths of the sea, must, to a large extent, for ever remain unknown to us, since under water they are too nimble for nets, and it is only by such rare, unlooked-for accidents that specimens can be obtained. In the case of *Haploteuthis ferox*, for instance, we are still altogether ignorant of its habitat, as ignorant as we are of the breeding-ground of the herring or the sea-ways of the salmon. And zoologists are altogether at a loss to account for its sudden appearance on our coast. Possibly it was the stress of a hunger migration that drove it hither out of the deep. But it will be, perhaps, better to avoid necessarily inconclusive discussion, and to proceed at once with our narrative.

The first human being to set eyes upon a living *Haploteuthis* – the first human being to survive, that is, for there can be little doubt now that the wave of bathing fatalities and boating accidents that travelled along the coast of Cornwall and Devon in early May was due to this cause – was a retired tea-dealer of the name of Fison, who was stopping at a Sidmouth boarding-house. It was in the afternoon, and he was walking along the cliff path between Sidmouth and Ladram Bay. The cliffs in this direction are very high, but down the red face of them in one place a kind of ladder staircase has been made. He was near this when his attention was attracted by what at first he thought to be a cluster of birds struggling over a fragment of food that caught the sunlight, and glistened pinkish-white. The tide was right out, and this object was not only far below him, but remote across a broad waste of rock reefs covered with dark seaweed and interspersed with silvery shining tidal pools. And he was, moreover, dazzled by the brightness of the further water.

In a minute, regarding this again, he perceived that his judgment was in fault, for over this struggle circled a number of birds, jackdaws and gulls for the most part, the latter gleaming blindingly when the sunlight smote their wings, and they seemed minute in comparison with it. And his curiosity was, perhaps, aroused all the more strongly because of his first insufficient explanations.

As he had nothing better to do than amuse himself, he decided to make this object, whatever it was, the goal of his afternoon walk, instead of Ladram Bay, conceiving it might perhaps be a great fish of some sort, stranded by some chance, and flapping about in its distress. And so he hurried down the long steep ladder, stopping at intervals of thirty feet or so to take breath and scan the mysterious movement.

At the foot of the cliff he was, of course, nearer his object than he had been; but, on the other hand, it now came up against the incandescent sky, beneath the sun, so as to seem dark and indistinct. Whatever was pinkish of it was now hidden by a skerry of weedy boulders. But he perceived that it was made up of seven rounded bodies distinct or connected, and that the birds kept up a constant croaking and screaming but seemed afraid to approach it too closely.

Mr Fison, torn by curiosity, began picking his way across the wave-worn rocks, and finding the wet seaweed that covered them thickly rendered them extremely slippery, he stopped, removed his shoes and socks, and rolled his trousers above his knees. His object was, of course, merely to avoid stumbling into the rocky pools about him, and perhaps he was rather glad, as all men are, of an excuse to resume, even for a moment, the sensations of his boyhood. At any rate, it is to this, no doubt, that he owes his life.

He approached his mark with all the assurance which the absolute security of this country against all forms of animal life gives its inhabitants. The round bodies moved to and fro, but it was only when he surmounted the skerry of boulders I have mentioned that he realised the horrible nature of the discovery. It came upon him with some suddenness.

The rounded bodies fell apart as he came into sight over the ridge, and displayed the pinkish object to be the partially devoured body of a human being, but whether of a man or woman he was unable to say. And the rounded bodies were new and ghastly-looking creatures, in shape somewhat resembling an octopus, with huge and very long

8   The Sea Raiders

and flexible tentacles, coiled copiously on the ground. The skin had a glistening texture, unpleasant to see, like shiny leather. The downward bend of the tentacle-surrounded mouth, the curious excrescence at the bend, the tentacles, and the large intelligent eyes, gave the creatures a grotesque suggestion of a face. They were the size of a fair-sized swine about the body, and the tentacles seemed to him to be many feet in length. There were, he thinks, seven or eight at least of the creatures. Twenty yards beyond them, amid the surf of the now returning tide, two others were emerging from the sea.

Their bodies lay flatly on the rocks, and their eyes regarded him with evil interest; but it does not appear that Mr Fison was afraid, or that he realised that he was in any danger. Possibly his confidence is to be ascribed to the limpness of their attitudes. But he was horrified, of course, and intensely excited and indignant, at such revolting creatures preying upon human flesh. He thought they had chanced upon a drowned body. He shouted to them, with the idea of driving them off, and finding they did not budge, cast about him, picked up a big rounded lump of rock, and flung it at one.

And then, slowly uncoiling their tentacles, they all began moving towards him – creeping at first deliberately, and making a soft purring sound to each other.

In a moment Mr Fison realised that he was in danger. He shouted again, threw both his boots, and started off, with a leap, forthwith. Twenty yards off he stopped and faced about, judging them slow, and behold! the tentacles of their leader were already pouring over the rocky ridge on which he had just been standing!

At that he shouted again, but this time not threatening, but a cry of dismay, and began jumping, striding, slipping, wading across the uneven expanse between him and the beach. The tall red cliffs seemed suddenly at a vast distance, and he saw, as though they were creatures in another world, two minute workmen engaged in the repair of the ladder-way, and little suspecting the race for life that was beginning below them. At one time he could hear the creatures splashing in the pools not a dozen feet behind him, and once he slipped and almost fell.

They chased him to the very foot of the cliffs, and desisted only when he had been joined by the workmen at the foot of the ladder-way up the cliff. All three of the men pelted them with stones for a time, and then hurried to the cliff top and along the path towards Sidmouth, to secure assistance and a boat, and to rescue the desecrated body from the clutches of these abominable creatures.

2

And, as if he had not already been in sufficient peril that day, Mr Fison went with the boat to point out the exact spot of his adventure.

As the tide was down, it required a considerable detour to reach the spot, and when at last they came off the ladder-way, the mangled body had disappeared. The water was now running in, submerging first one slab of slimy rock and then another, and the four men in the boat – the workmen, that is, the boatman, and Mr Fison – now turned their attention from the bearings off shore to the water beneath the keel.

At first they could see little below them, save a dark jungle of laminaria, with an occasional darting fish. Their minds were set on adventure, and they expressed their disappointment freely. But presently they saw one of the monsters swimming through the water seaward, with a curious rolling motion that suggested to Mr Fison the spinning roll of a captive balloon. Almost immediately after, the waving streamers of laminaria were extraordinarily perturbed, parted for a moment, and three of these beasts became darkly visible, struggling for what was probably some fragment of the drowned man. In a moment the copious olive-green ribbons had poured again over this writhing group.

At that all four men, greatly excited, began beating the water with oars and shouting, and immediately they saw a tumultuous movement among the weeds. They desisted to see more clearly, and as soon as the water was smooth, they saw, as it seemed to them, the whole sea bottom among the weeds set with eyes.

'Ugly swine!' cried one of the men. 'Why, there's dozens!'

And forthwith the things began to rise through the water about them. Mr Fison has since described to the writer this startling eruption out of the waving laminaria meadows. To him it seemed to occupy a considerable time, but it is probable that really it was an affair of a few seconds only. For a time nothing but eyes, and then he speaks of tentacles streaming out and parting the weed fronds this way and that. Then these things, growing larger, until at last the bottom was hidden by their intercoiling forms, and the tips of tentacles rose darkly here and there into the air above the swell of the waters.

One came up boldly to the side of the boat, and clinging to this with three of its sucker-set tentacles, threw four others over the gunwale, as if with an intention either of oversetting the boat or of clambering into it. Mr Fison at once caught up the boat-hook, and, jabbing furiously at the soft tentacles, forced it to desist. He was struck in the back and almost pitched overboard by the boatman, who was using his oar to resist a similar attack on the other side of the boat. But the tentacles on either side at once relaxed their hold, slid out of sight, and splashed into the water.

'We'd better get out of this,' said Mr Fison, who was trembling violently. He went to the tiller, while the boatman and one of the workmen seated themselves and began rowing. The other workman stood up in the fore part of the boat, with the boat-hook, ready to strike any more tentacles that might appear. Nothing else seems to have been said. Mr Fison had expressed the common feeling beyond amendment. In a hushed, scared mood, with faces white and drawn, they set about escaping from the position into which they had so recklessly blundered.

But the oars had scarcely dropped into the water before dark, tapering, serpentine ropes had bound them, and were about the rudder; and creeping up the sides of the boat with a looping motion came the suckers again. The men gripped their oars and pulled, but it was like trying to move a boat in a floating raft of weeds. 'Help here!' cried the boatman, and Mr Fison and the second workman rushed to help lug at the oar.

Then the man with the boat-hook – his name was Ewan, or Ewen – sprang up with a curse and began striking downward over the side, as far as he could reach, at the bank of tentacles that now clustered along the boat's bottom. And, at the same time, the two rowers stood up to get a better purchase for the recovery of their oars. The boatman handed his to Mr Fison, who lugged desperately, and, meanwhile, the boatman opened a big clasp-knife, and leaning over the side of the boat, began hacking at the spiring arms upon the oar shaft.

Mr Fison, staggering with the quivering rocking of the boat, his teeth set, his breath coming short, and the veins starting on his hands as he pulled at his oar, suddenly cast his eyes seaward. And there, not fifty yards off, across the long rollers of the incoming tide, was a large boat standing in towards them, with three women and a little child in it. A boatman was rowing, and a little man in a pink-ribboned straw hat and whites stood in the stern hailing them. For a moment, of course, Mr Fison thought of help, and then he thought of the child. He abandoned his oar forthwith, threw up his arms in a frantic gesture, and screamed to the party in the boat to keep away 'for God's sake!' It says much for the modesty and courage of Mr Fison that he does not seem to be aware that there was any quality of heroism in his action at this juncture. The oar he had abandoned was at once drawn under, and presently reappeared floating about twenty yards away.

At the same moment Mr Fison felt the boat under him lurch violently, and a hoarse scream, a prolonged cry of terror from Hill, the boatman, caused him to forget the party of excursionists altogether. He turned, and saw Hill crouching by the forward row-lock, his face convulsed with terror, and his right arm over the side and drawn tightly down. He gave now a succession of short, sharp cries, 'Oh! oh! oh! – oh!' Mr Fison believes that he must have been hacking at the tentacles below the water-line, and have been grasped by them, but, of course, it is quite impossible to say now certainly what had happened. The boat was heeling over, so that the gunwale was within ten inches of the water, and both Ewan and the other labourer were striking down into the water, with oar and boat-hook, on either side of Hill's arm. Mr Fison instinctively placed himself to counterpoise them.

Then Hill, who was a burly, powerful man, made a strenuous effort, and rose almost to a standing position. He lifted his arm, indeed, clean out of the water. Hanging to it was a complicated tangle of brown ropes, and the eyes of one of the brutes that had hold of him, glaring straight and resolute, showed momentarily above the surface. The boat heeled more and more, and the green-brown water came pouring in a cascade over the side. Then Hill slipped and fell with his ribs across the side, and his arm and the mass of tentacles about it splashed back into the water. He rolled over; his boot kicked Mr Fison's knee as that gentleman rushed forward to seize him, and in another moment fresh tentacles had whipped about his waist and neck, and after a brief, convulsive struggle, in which the boat was nearly capsized, Hill was lugged overboard. The boat righted with a violent jerk that all but sent Mr Fison over the other side, and hid the struggle in the water from his eyes.

He stood staggering to recover his balance for a moment, and as he did so he became aware that the struggle and the inflowing tide had carried them close upon the weedy rocks again. Not four yards off a table of rock still rose in rhythmic movements above the in-wash of the tide. In a moment Mr Fison seized the oar from Ewan, gave one vigorous stroke, then dropping it, ran to the bows and leapt. He felt his feet slide over the rock, and, by a frantic effort, leapt again towards a further mass. He stumbled over this, came to his knees, and rose again.

'Look out!' cried someone, and a large drab body struck him. He was knocked flat into a tidal pool by one of the workmen, and as he went down he heard smothered, choking cries, that he believed at the time came from Hill. Then he found himself marvelling at the shrillness and variety of Hill's voice. Someone jumped over him, and a curving rush of foamy water poured over him, and passed. He scrambled to his feet dripping, and without looking seaward, ran as fast as his terror would let him shoreward. Before him, over the flat space of scattered rocks, stumbled the two workmen – one a dozen yards in front of the other.

He looked over his shoulder at last, and seeing that he was not pursued, faced about. He was astonished. From the moment of the rising of the cephalopods out of the water he had been acting too swiftly to fully comprehend his actions. Now it seemed to him as if he had suddenly jumped out of an evil dream.

For there were the sky, cloudless and blazing with the afternoon sun, the sea weltering under its pitiless brightness, the soft creamy foam of the breaking water, and the low, long, dark ridges of rock. The righted boat floated, rising and falling gently on the swell about a dozen yards from shore. Hill and the monsters, all the stress and tumult of that fierce fight for life, had vanished as though they had never been.

Mr Fison's heart was beating violently; he was throbbing to the finger-tips, and his breath came deep.

There was something missing. For some seconds he could not think clearly enough what this might be. Sun, sky, sea, rocks – what was it? Then he remembered the boat-load of excursionists. It had vanished. He wondered whether he had imagined it. He turned, and saw the two workmen standing side by side under the projecting masses of the tall pink cliffs. He hesitated whether he should make one last attempt to save the man Hill. His physical excitement seemed to desert him suddenly, and leave him aimless and helpless. He turned shoreward, stumbling and wading towards his two companions.

He looked back again, and there were now two boats floating, and the one farthest out at sea pitched clumsily, bottom upward.

3

So it was *Haploteuthis ferox* made its appearance upon the Devonshire coast. So far, this has been its most serious aggression. Mr Fison's account, taken together with the wave of boating and bathing casualties to which I have already alluded, and the absence of fish from the Cornish coasts that year, points clearly to a shoal of these voracious deep-sea monsters prowling slowly along the sub-tidal coast-line. Hunger migration, has, I know, been suggested as the force that drove them hither; but, for my own part, I prefer to believe the alternative theory of Hemsley. Hemsley holds that a pack or shoal of these creatures may have become enamoured of human flesh by the accident of a foundered ship sinking among them, and have wandered in search of it out of their accustomed zone; first waylaying and following ships, and so coming to our shores in the wake of the Atlantic traffic. But to discuss Hemsley's cogent and admirably-stated arguments would be out of place here.

It would seem that the appetites of the shoal were satisfied by the catch of eleven people – for, so far as can be ascertained, there were ten people in the second boat, and certainly these creatures gave no further signs of their presence off Sidmouth that day. The coast between Seaton and Budleigh Salterton was patrolled all that evening and night by four Preventive Service boats, the men in which were armed with harpoons and cutlasses, and as the evening advanced, a number of more or less similarly equipped expeditions, organised by private individuals, joined them. Mr Fison took no part in any of these expeditions.

About midnight excited hails were heard from a boat about a couple of miles out at sea to the south-east of Sidmouth, and a lantern was seen waving in a strange manner to and fro and up and down. The nearer boats at once hurried towards the alarm. The venturesome occupants of the boat – a seaman, a curate, and two schoolboys – had actually seen the monsters passing under their boat. The creatures, it seems, like most deep-sea organisms, were phosphorescent, and they had been floating, five fathoms deep or so, like creatures of moonshine through the blackness of the water, their tentacles retracted and as if asleep, rolling over and over, and moving slowly in a wedge-like formation towards the south-east.

These people told their story in gesticulated fragments, as first one boat drew alongside and then another. At last there was a little fleet of eight or nine boats collected together, and from them a tumult, like the chatter of a market-place, rose into the stillness of the night. There was little or no disposition to pursue the shoal, the people had neither weapons nor experience for such a dubious chase, and presently – even with a certain relief, it may be – the boats turned shoreward.

And now to tell what is perhaps the most astonishing fact in this whole astonishing raid. We have not the slightest knowledge of the subsequent movements of the shoal, although the whole south-west coast was now alert for it. But it may, perhaps, be significant that a cachalot was stranded off Sark on June 3. Two weeks and three days after this Sidmouth affair, a living *Haploteuthis* came ashore on Calais sands. It was alive, because several witnesses saw its tentacles moving in a convulsive way. But it is probable that it was dying. A gentleman named Pouchet obtained a rifle and shot it.

That was the last appearance of a living *Haploteuthis*. No others were seen on the French coast. On the 15th of June a dead carcass, almost complete, was washed ashore near Torquay, and a few days later a boat from the Marine Biological station, engaged in dredging off Plymouth, picked up a rotting specimen, slashed deeply with a cutlass wound. How the former had come by its death it is impossible to say. And on the last day of June, Mr Egbert Caine, an artist, bathing near Newlyn, threw up his arms, shrieked, and was drawn under. A friend bathing with him made no attempt to save him, but swam at once for the shore. This is the last fact to tell of this extraordinary raid from the deeper sea. Whether it is really the last of these horrible creatures it is, as yet, premature to say. But it is believed, and certainly it is to be hoped, that they have returned now, and returned for good, to the sunless depths of the middle seas, out of which they have so strangely and so mysteriously arisen.

9

A Pair of Silk Stockings

(1897)

Kate Chopin

Little Mrs Sommers one day found herself the unexpected possessor of fifteen dollars. It seemed to her a very large amount of money, and the way in which it stuffed and bulged her worn old *porte-monnaie* gave her a feeling of importance such as she had not enjoyed for years.

The question of investment was one that occupied her greatly. For a day or two she walked about apparently in a dreamy state, but really absorbed in speculation and calculation. She did not wish to act hastily, to do anything she might afterward regret. But it was during the still hours of the night when she lay awake revolving plans in her mind that she seemed to see her way clearly toward a proper and judicious use of the money.

A dollar or two should be added to the price usually paid for Janie's shoes, which would insure their lasting an appreciable time longer than they usually did. She would buy so and so many yards of percale for new shirt waists for the boys and Janie and Mag. She had intended to make the old ones do by skilful patching. Mag should have another gown. She had seen some beautiful patterns, veritable bargains in the shop windows. And still there would be left enough for new stockings – two pairs apiece – and what darning that would save for a while! She would get caps for the boys and sailor-hats for the girls. The vision of her little brood looking fresh and dainty and new for once in their lives excited her and made her restless and wakeful with anticipation.

The neighbors sometimes talked of certain 'better days' that little Mrs Sommers had known before she had ever thought of being Mrs Sommers. She herself indulged in no such morbid retrospection. She had no time – no second of time to devote to the past. The needs of the present absorbed her every faculty. A vision of the future like some dim, gaunt monster sometimes appalled her, but luckily to-morrow never comes.

Mrs Sommers was one who knew the value of bargains; who could stand for hours making her way inch by inch toward the desired object that was selling below cost. She could elbow her way if need be; she had learned to clutch a piece of goods and hold it and stick to it with persistence and determination till her turn came to be served, no matter when it came.

But that day she was a little faint and tired. She had swallowed a light luncheon – no! when she came to think of it, between getting the children fed and the place righted, and preparing herself for the shopping bout, she had actually forgotten to eat any luncheon at all!

She sat herself upon a revolving stool before a counter that was comparatively deserted, trying to gather strength and courage to charge through an eager multitude that was besieging breastworks of shirting and figured lawn. An all-gone limp feeling had come over her and she rested her hand aimlessly upon the counter. She wore no gloves. By degrees she grew aware that her hand had encountered something very soothing, very pleasant to touch. She looked down to see that her hand lay upon a pile of silk stockings. A placard near by announced that they had been reduced in price from two dollars and fifty cents to one dollar and ninety-eight cents; and a young girl who stood behind the counter asked her if she wished to examine their line of silk hosiery. She smiled, just as if she had been asked to inspect a tiara of diamonds with the ultimate view of purchasing it. But she went on feeling the soft, sheeny luxurious things – with both hands now, holding them up to see them glisten, and to feel them glide serpent-like through her fingers.

Two hectic blotches came suddenly into her pale cheeks. She looked up at the girl.

'Do you think there are any eights-and-a-half among these?'

There were any number of eights-and-a-half. In fact, there were more of that size than any other. Here was a light-blue pair; there were some lavender, some all black and various shades of tan and gray. Mrs Sommers selected a black pair and looked at them very long and closely. She pretended to be examining their texture, which the clerk assured her was excellent.

'A dollar and ninety-eight cents,' she mused aloud. 'Well, I'll take this pair.' She handed the girl a five-dollar bill and waited for her change and for her parcel. What a very small parcel it was! It seemed lost in the depths of her shabby old shopping-bag.

Mrs Sommers after that did not move in the direction of the bargain counter. She took the elevator, which carried her to an upper floor into the region of the ladies' waiting-rooms. Here, in a retired corner, she exchanged her cotton stockings for the new silk ones which she had just bought. She was not going through any acute mental process or reasoning with herself, nor was she striving to explain to her satisfaction the motive of her action. She was not thinking at all. She seemed for the time to be taking a rest from that laborious and fatiguing function and to have abandoned herself to some mechanical impulse that directed her actions and freed her of responsibility.

How good was the touch of the raw silk to her flesh! She felt like lying back in the cushioned chair and reveling for a while in the luxury of it. She did for a little while. Then she replaced her shoes, rolled the cotton stockings together and thrust them into her bag. After doing this she crossed straight over to the shoe department and took her seat to be fitted.

She was fastidious. The clerk could not make her out; he could not reconcile her shoes with her stockings, and she was not too easily pleased. She held back her skirts and turned her feet one way and her head another way as she glanced down at the polished, pointed-tipped boots. Her foot and ankle looked very pretty. She could not realize that they belonged to her and were a part of herself. She wanted an excellent and stylish fit, she told the young fellow who served her, and she did not mind the difference of a dollar or two more in the price so long as she got what she desired.

It was a long time since Mrs Sommers had been fitted with gloves. On rare occasions when she had bought a pair they were always 'bargains,' so cheap that it would have been preposterous and unreasonable to have expected them to be fitted to the hand.

Now she rested her elbow on the cushion of the glove counter, and a pretty, pleasant young creature, delicate and deft of touch, drew a long-wristed 'kid' over Mrs Sommers's hand. She smoothed it down over the wrist and buttoned it neatly, and both lost themselves for a second or two in admiring contemplation of the little symmetrical gloved hand. But there were other places where money might be spent.

There were books and magazines piled up in the window of a stall a few paces down the street. Mrs Sommers bought two high-priced magazines such as she had been accustomed to read in the days when she had been accustomed to other pleasant things. She carried them without wrapping. As well as she could she lifted her skirts at the crossings. Her stockings and boots and well-fitting gloves had worked marvels in her bearing – had given her a feeling of assurance, a sense of belonging to the well-dressed multitude.

She was very hungry. Another time she would have stilled the cravings for food until reaching her own home, where she would have brewed herself a cup of tea and taken a snack of anything that was available. But the impulse that was guiding her would not suffer her to entertain any such thought.

There was a restaurant at the corner. She had never entered its doors; from the outside she had sometimes caught glimpses of spotless damask and shining crystal, and soft-stepping waiters serving people of fashion.

When she entered her appearance created no surprise, no consternation, as she had half feared it might. She seated herself at a small table alone, and an attentive waiter at once approached to take her order. She did not want a profusion; she craved a nice and tasty bite – a half dozen blue-points, a plump chop with cress, a something sweet – a *crème-frappée*, for instance; a glass of Rhine wine, and after all a small cup of black coffee.

While waiting to be served she removed her gloves very leisurely and laid them beside her. Then she picked up a magazine and glanced through it, cutting the pages with a blunt edge of her knife. It was all very agreeable. The damask was even more spotless than it had seemed through the window, and the crystal more sparkling. There were quiet ladies and gentlemen, who did not notice her, lunching at the small tables like her own. A soft, pleasing strain of music could be heard, and a gentle breeze was blowing through the window. She tasted a bite, and she read a word or two, and she sipped the amber wine and wiggled her toes in the silk stockings. The price of it made no difference.

She counted the money out to the waiter and left an extra coin on his tray, whereupon he bowed before her as before a princess of royal blood.

There was still money in her purse, and her next temptation presented itself in the shape of a matinee poster.

It was a little later when she entered the theatre, the play had begun and the house seemed to her to be packed. But there were vacant seats here and there, and into one of them she was ushered, between brilliantly dressed women who had gone there to kill time and eat candy and display their gaudy attire. There were many others who were there solely for the play and acting. It is safe to say there was no one present who bore quite the attitude which Mrs Sommers did to her surroundings. She gathered in the whole – stage and players and people in one wide impression, and absorbed it and enjoyed it. She laughed at the comedy and wept – she and the gaudy woman next to her wept over the tragedy. And they talked a little together over it. And the gaudy woman wiped her eyes and sniffled on a tiny square of filmy, perfumed lace and passed little Mrs Sommers her box of candy.

The play was over, the music ceased, the crowd filed out. It was like a dream ended. People scattered in all directions. Mrs Sommers went to the corner and waited for the cable car.

A man with keen eyes, who sat opposite to her, seemed to like the study of her small, pale face. It puzzled him to decipher what he saw there. In truth, he saw nothing – unless he were wizard enough to detect a poignant wish, a powerful longing that the cable car would never stop anywhere, but go on and on with her forever.

10

A Wagner Matinée

(1904)

Willa Cather

I received one morning a letter, written in pale ink, on glassy, blue-lined note-paper, and bearing the postmark of a little Nebraska village. This communication, worn and rubbed, looking as though it had been carried for some days in a coat-pocket that was none too clean, was from my Uncle Howard. It informed me that his wife had been left a small legacy by a bachelor relative who had recently died, and that it had become necessary for her to come to Boston to attend to the settling of the estate. He requested me to meet her at the station, and render her whatever services might prove necessary. On examining the date indicated as that of her arrival, I found it no later than to-morrow. He had characteristically delayed writing until, had I been away from home for a day, I must have missed the good woman altogether.

The name of my Aunt Georgiana called up not alone her own figure, at once pathetic and grotesque, but opened before my feet a gulf of recollections so wide and deep that, as the letter dropped from my hand, I felt suddenly a stranger to all the present conditions of my existence, wholly ill at ease and out of place amid the surroundings of my study. I became, in short, the gangling farmer-boy my aunt had known, scourged with chilblains and bashfulness, my hands cracked and raw from the corn husking. I felt the knuckles of my thumb tentatively, as though they were raw again. I sat again before her parlor organ, thumbing the scales with my stiff, red hands, while she beside me made canvas mittens for the huskers.

The next morning, after preparing my landlady somewhat, I set out for the station. When the train arrived I had some difficulty in finding my aunt. She was the last of the passengers to alight, and when I got her into the carriage she looked not unlike one of those charred, smoked bodies that firemen lift from the *débris* of a burned building. She had come all the way in a day coach; her linen duster had become black with soot and her black bonnet gray with dust during the journey. When we arrived at my boarding-house the landlady put her to bed at once, and I did not see her again until the next morning.

Whatever shock Mrs Springer experienced at my aunt's appearance she considerately concealed. Myself, I saw my aunt's misshapened figure with that feeling of awe and respect with which we behold explorers who have left their ears and fingers north of Franz Josef Land, or their health somewhere along the Upper Congo. My Aunt Georgiana had been a music-teacher at the Boston Conservatory, somewhere back in the latter sixties. One summer, which she had spent in the little village in the Green Mountains where her ancestors had dwelt for generations, she had kindled the callow fancy of the most idle and shiftless of all the village lads, and had conceived for this Howard Carpenter one of those absurd and extravagant passions which a handsome country boy of twenty-one sometimes inspires in a plain, angular, spectacled woman of thirty. When she returned to her duties in Boston, Howard followed her; and the upshot of this inexplicable infatuation was that she eloped with him, eluding the reproaches of her family and the criticism of her friends by going with him to the Nebraska frontier. Carpenter, who of course had no money, took a homestead in Red Willow County, fifty miles from the railroad. There they measured off their eighty acres by driving across the prairie in a wagon, to the wheel of which they had tied a red cotton handkerchief, and counting off its revolutions. They built a dugout in the red hillside, one of those cave dwellings whose inmates usually reverted to the conditions of primitive savagery. Their water they got from the lagoons where the buffalo drank, and their slender stock of provisions was always at the mercy of bands of roving Indians. For thirty years my aunt had not been farther than fifty miles from the homestead.

But Mrs Springer knew nothing of all this, and must have been considerably shocked at what was left of my kinswoman. Beneath the soiled linen duster, which on her arrival was the most conspicuous feature of her costume, she wore a black stuff dress whose ornamentation showed that she had surrendered herself unquestioningly into the hands of a country dressmaker. My poor aunt's figure, however, would have presented astonishing difficulties to any dressmaker. Her skin was yellow as a Mongolian's from constant exposure to a pitiless wind, and to the alkaline water, which transforms the most transparent cuticle into a sort of flexible leather. She wore ill-fitting false teeth. The most striking thing about her physiognomy, however, was an incessant twitching of the mouth and eyebrows, a form of nervous disorder resulting from isolation and monotony, and from frequent physical suffering.

In my boyhood this affliction had possessed a sort of horrible fascination for me, of which I was secretly very much ashamed, for in those days I owed to this woman most of the good that ever came my way, and had a reverential affection for her. During the three winters when I was riding herd for my uncle, my aunt, after cooking three meals for half a dozen farm-hands, and putting the six children to bed, would often stand until midnight at her ironing-board, hearing me at the kitchen table beside her recite Latin declensions and conjugations, and gently shaking me when my drowsy head sank down over a page of irregular verbs. It was to her, at her ironing or mending, that I read my first Shakespere; and her old text-book of mythology was the first that ever came into my empty hands. She taught me my scales and exercises, too, on the little parlor organ which her husband had bought her after fifteen years, during which she had not so much as seen any instrument except an accordion, that belonged to one of the Norwegian farm-hands. She would sit beside me by the hour, darning and counting, while I struggled with the 'Harmonious Blacksmith'; but she seldom talked to me about music, and I understood why. She was a pious woman; she had the consolation of religion; and to her at least her martyrdom was not wholly sordid. Once when I had been doggedly beating out some easy passages from an old score of 'Euryanthe' I had found among her music-books, she came up to me and, putting her hands over my eyes, gently drew my head back upon her shoulder, saying tremulously, 'Don't love it so well, Clark, or it may be taken from you. Oh! dear boy, pray that whatever your sacrifice be it is not that.'

When my aunt appeared on the morning after her arrival, she was still in a semi-somnambulant state. She seemed not to realize that she was in the city where she had spent her youth, the place longed for hungrily half a lifetime. She had been so wretchedly train-sick throughout the journey that she had no recollection of anything but her discomfort, and, to all intents and purposes, there were but a few hours of nightmare between the farm in Red Willow County and my study on Newbury Street. I had planned a little pleasure for her that afternoon, to repay her for some of the glorious moments she had given me when we used to milk together in the straw-thatched cow-shed, and she, because I was more than usually tired, or because her husband had spoken sharply to me, would tell me of the splendid performance of Meyerbeer's 'Huguenots' she had seen in Paris in her youth. At two o'clock the Boston Symphony Orchestra was to give a Wagner programme, and I intended to take my aunt, though as I conversed with her I grew doubtful about her enjoyment of it. Indeed, for her own sake, I could only wish her taste for such things quite dead, and the long struggle mercifully ended at last. I suggested our visiting the Conservatory and the Common before lunch, but she seemed altogether too timid to wish to venture out. She questioned me absently about various changes in the city, but she was chiefly concerned that she had forgotten to leave instructions about feeding half-skimmed milk to a certain weakling calf, 'Old Maggie's calf, you know, Clark,' she explained, evidently having forgotten how long I had been away. She was further troubled because she had neglected to tell her daughter about the freshly opened kit of mackerel in the cellar, that would spoil if it were not used directly.

I asked her whether she had ever heard any of the Wagnerian operas, and found that she had not, though she was perfectly familiar with their respective situations and had once possessed the piano score of 'The Flying Dutchman.' I began to think it would have been best to get her back to Red Willow County without waking her, and regretted having suggested the concert.

From the time we entered the concert-hall, however, she was a trifle less passive and inert, and seemed to begin to perceive her surroundings. I had felt some trepidation lest she might become aware of the absurdities of her attire, or might experience some painful embarrassment at stepping suddenly into the world to which she had been dead for a quarter of a century. But again I found how superficially I had judged her. She sat looking about her with eyes as impersonal, almost as stony, as those with which the granite Rameses in a museum watches the froth and fret that ebbs and flows about his pedestal, separated from it by the lonely stretch of centuries. I have seen this same aloofness in old miners who drift into the Brown Hotel at Denver, their pockets full of bullion, their linen soiled, their haggard faces unshorn, and who stand in the thronged corridors as solitary as though they were still in a frozen camp on the Yukon, or in the yellow blaze of the Arizona desert, conscious that certain experiences have isolated them from their fellows by a gulf no haberdasher could conceal.

The audience was made up chiefly of women. One lost the contour of faces and figures, indeed any effect of line whatever, and there was only the color contrast of bodices past counting, the shimmer and shading of fabrics soft and firm, silky and sheer, resisting and yielding: red, mauve, pink, blue, lilac, purple, écru, rose, yellow, cream, and white, all the colors that an impressionist finds in a sunlit landscape, with here and there the dead black shadow of a frock-coat. My Aunt Georgiana regarded them as though they had been so many daubs of tube paint on a palette.

When the musicians came out and took their places, she gave a little stir of anticipation, and looked with quickening interest down over the rail at that invariable grouping; perhaps the first wholly familiar thing that had greeted her eye since she had left old Maggie and her weakling calf. I could feel how all those details sank into her soul, for I had not forgotten how they had sunk into mine when I came fresh from ploughing forever and forever between green aisles of corn, where, as in a treadmill, one might walk from daybreak to dusk without perceiving a shadow of change in one's environment. I reminded myself of the impression made on me by the clean profiles of the musicians, the gloss of their linen, the dull black of their coats, the beloved shapes of the instruments, the patches of yellow light thrown by the green-shaded stand-lamps on the smooth, varnished bellies of the 'cellos and the bass viols in the rear, the restless, wind-tossed forest of fiddle necks and bows; I recalled how, in the first orchestra I had ever heard, those long bow strokes seemed to draw the soul out of me, as a conjurer's stick reels out paper ribbon from a hat.

The first number was the Tannhäuser overture. When the violins drew out the first strain of the Pilgrim's chorus, my Aunt Georgiana clutched my coat-sleeve. Then it was that I first realized that for her this singing of basses and stinging frenzy of lighter strings broke a silence of thirty years, the inconceivable silence of the plains. With the battle between the two motifs, with the bitter frenzy of the Venusberg theme and its ripping of strings, came to me an overwhelming sense of the waste and wear we are so powerless to combat. I saw again the tall, naked house on the prairie, black and grim as a wooden fortress; the black pond where I had learned to swim, the rain-gullied clay about the naked house; the four dwarf ash-seedlings on which the dishcloths were always hung to dry before the kitchen door. The world there is the flat world of the ancients; to the east, a cornfield that stretched to daybreak; to the west, a corral that stretched to sunset; between, the sordid conquests of peace, more merciless than those of war.

The overture closed. My aunt released my coat-sleeve, but she said nothing. She sat staring at the orchestra through a dullness of thirty years, through the films made little by little, by each of the three hundred and sixty-five days in every one of them. What, I wondered, did she get from it? She had been a good pianist in her day, I knew, and her musical education had been broader than that of most music-teachers of a quarter of a century ago. She had often told me of Mozart's operas and Meyerbeer's, and I could remember hearing her sing, years ago, certain melodies of Verdi's. When I had fallen ill with a fever she used to sit by my cot in the evening, while the cool night wind blew in through the faded mosquito-netting tacked over the window, and I lay watching a bright star that burned red above the cornfield, and sing 'Home to our mountains, oh, let us return!' in a way fit to break the heart of a Vermont boy near dead of homesickness already.

I watched her closely through the prelude to Tristan and Isolde, trying vainly to conjecture what that warfare of motifs, that seething turmoil of strings and winds, might mean to her. Had this music any message for her? Did or did not a new planet swim into her ken? Wagner had been a sealed book to Americans before the sixties. Had she anything left with which to comprehend this glory that had flashed around the world since she had gone from it? I was in a fever of curiosity, but Aunt Georgiana sat silent upon her peak in Darien. She preserved this utter immobility throughout the numbers from the 'Flying Dutchman,' though her fingers worked mechanically upon her black dress, as though of themselves they were recalling the piano score they had once played. Poor old hands! They were stretched and pulled and twisted into mere tentacles to hold, and lift, and knead with; the palms unduly swollen, the fingers bent and knotted, on one of them a thin worn band that had once been a wedding-ring. As I pressed and gently quieted one of those groping hands, I remembered, with quivering eyelids, their services for me in other days.

Soon after the tenor began the Prize Song, I heard a quick-drawn breath, and turned to my aunt. Her eyes were closed, but the tears were glistening on her cheeks, and I think in a moment more they were in my eyes as well. It never really dies, then, the soul? It withers to the outward eye only, like that strange moss which can lie on a dusty shelf half a century and yet, if placed in water, grows green again. My aunt wept gently throughout the development and elaboration of the melody.

During the intermission before the second half of the concert, I questioned my aunt and found that the Prize Song was not new to her. Some years before there had drifted to the farm in Red Willow County a young German, a tramp cow-puncher, who had sung in the chorus at Baireuth, when he was a boy, along with the other peasant boys and girls. Of a Sunday morning he used to sit on his gingham-sheeted bed in the hands' bedroom, which opened off the kitchen, cleaning the leather of his boots and saddle, and singing the Prize Song, while my aunt went about her work in the kitchen. She had hovered about him until she had prevailed upon him to join the country church, though his sole fitness for this step, so far as I could gather, lay in his boyish face and his possession of this divine melody. Shortly afterward he had gone to town on the Fourth of July, been drunk for several days, lost his money at a faro-table, ridden a saddled Texan steer on a bet, and disappeared with a fractured collar-bone.

'Well, we have come to better things than the old Trovatore at any rate, Aunt Georgie?' I queried, with well-meant jocularity.

Her lip quivered and she hastily put her handkerchief up to her mouth. From behind it she murmured, 'And you have been hearing this ever since you left me, Clark?' Her question was the gentlest and saddest of reproaches.

'But do you get it, Aunt Georgiana, the astonishing structure of it all?' I persisted.

'Who could?' she said, absently; 'why should one?'

The second half of the programme consisted of four numbers from the Ring. This was followed by the forest music from Siegfried, and the programme closed with Siegfried's funeral march. My aunt wept quietly, but almost continuously. I was perplexed as to what measure of musical comprehension was left to her, to her who had heard nothing but the singing of gospel hymns in Methodist services at the square frame school-house on Section Thirteen. I was unable to gauge how much of it had been dissolved in soapsuds, or worked into bread, or milked into the bottom of a pail.

The deluge of sound poured on and on; I never knew what she found in the shining current of it; I never knew how far it bore her, or past what happy islands, or under what skies. From the trembling of her face I could well believe that the Siegfried march, at least, carried her out where the myriad graves are, out into the gray, burying-grounds of the sea; or into some world of death vaster yet, where, from the beginning of the world, hope has lain down with hope, and dream with dream and, renouncing, slept.

The concert was over; the people filed out of the hall chattering and laughing, glad to relax and find the living level again, but my kinswoman made no effort to rise. I spoke gently to her. She burst into tears and sobbed pleadingly, 'I don't want to go, Clark, I don't want to go!'

I understood. For her, just outside the door of the concert-hall, lay the black pond with the cattle-tracked bluffs, the tall, unpainted house, naked as a tower, with weather-curled boards; the crook-backed ash-seedlings where the dishcloths hung to dry, the gaunt, moulting turkeys picking up refuse about the kitchen door.

11

The Mission of Mr Scatters

(1904)

Paul Laurence Dunbar

It took something just short of a revolution to wake up the sleepy little town of Miltonville. Through the slow, hot days it drowsed along like a lazy dog, only half rousing now and then to snap at some flying rumour, and relapsing at once into its pristine somnolence.

It was not a dreamless sleep, however, that held the town in chains. It had its dreams – dreams of greatness, of wealth, of consequence and of growth. Granted that there was no effort to realise these visions, they were yet there, and, combined with the memory of a past that was not without credit, went far to give tone to its dormant spirit.

It was a real spirit, too; the gallant Bourbon spirit of the old South; of Kentucky when she is most the daughter of Virginia, as was evidenced in the awed respect which all Miltonvillians, white and black alike, showed to Major Richardson in his house on the hill. He was part of the traditions of the place. It was shown in the conservatism of the old white families, and a certain stalwart if reflected self-respect in the older coloured inhabitants.

In all the days since the school had been founded and Mr Dunkin's marriage to the teacher had raised a brief ripple of excitement, these coloured people had slumbered. They were still slumbering that hot August day, unmindful of the sensation that lay at their very doors, heedless of the portents that said as plain as preaching, 'Miltonville, the time is at hand, awake!'

So it was that that afternoon there were only a few loungers, and these not very alert, about the station when the little train wheezed and puffed its way into it. It had been so long since anyone save those whom they knew had alighted at Miltonville that the loungers had lost faith, and with it curiosity, and now they scarcely changed their positions as the little engine stopped with a snort of disgust. But in an instant indifference had fled as the mist before the sun, and every eye on the platform was staring and white. It is the unexpected that always happens, and yet humanity never gets accustomed to it. The loafers, white and black, had assumed a sitting posture, and then they had stood up. For from the cars there had alighted the wonder of a stranger – a Negro stranger, gorgeous

11　The Mission of Mr Scatters

of person and attire. He was dressed in a suit of black cloth. A long coat was buttoned close around his tall and robust form. He was dead black, from his shiny top hat to his not less shiny boots, and about him there was the indefinable air of distinction. He stood looking about the platform for a moment, and then stepped briskly and decisively toward the group that was staring at him with wide eyes. There was no hesitation in that step. He walked as a man walks who is not in the habit of being stopped, who has not known what it is to be told, 'Thus far shalt thou go and no further.'

'Can you tell me where I can find the residence of Mr Isaac Jackson?' he asked sonorously as he reached the stupefied loungers. His voice was deep and clear.

Someone woke from his astonishment and offered to lead him thither, and together the two started for their destination, the stranger keeping up a running fire of comment on the way. Had his companion been a close observer and known anything about the matter, he would have found the newcomer's English painfully, unforgivably correct. A language should be like an easy shoe on a flexible foot, but to one unused to it, it proves rather a splint on a broken limb. The stranger stalked about in conversational splints until they arrived at Isaac Jackson's door. Then giving his guide a dime, he dismissed him with a courtly bow, and knocked.

It was a good thing that Martha Ann Jackson had the innate politeness of her race well to the fore when she opened the door upon the radiant creature, or she would have given voice to the words that were in her heart: 'Good Lawd, what is dis?'

'Is this the residence of Mr Isaac Jackson?' in the stranger's suavest voice.

'Yes, suh, he live hyeah.'

'May I see him? I desire to see him upon some business.' He handed her his card, which she carefully turned upside down, glanced at without understanding, and put in her apron pocket as she replied:

'He ain't in jes' now, but ef you'll step in an' wait, I'll sen' one o' de chillen aftah him.'

'I thank you, madam, I thank you. I will come in and rest from the fatigue of my journey. I have travelled a long way, and rest in such a pleasant and commodious abode as your own appears to be will prove very grateful to me.'

She had been half afraid to invite this resplendent figure into her humble house, but she felt distinctly flattered at his allusion to the home which she had helped Isaac to buy, and by the alacrity with which the stranger accepted her invitation.

She ushered him into the front room, mentally thanking her stars that she had forced the reluctant Isaac to buy a bright new carpet a couple of months before.

A child was despatched to find and bring home the father, while Martha Ann, hastily slipping out of her work-dress and into a starched calico, came in to keep her visitor company.

His name proved to be Scatters, and he was a most entertaining and ingratiating man. It was evident that he had some important business with Isaac Jackson, but that it was mysterious was shown by the guarded way in which he occasionally hinted at it as he tapped the valise he carried and nodded knowingly.

Time had never been when Martha Ann Jackson was so flustered. She was charmed and frightened and flattered. She could only leave Mr Scatters long enough to give orders to her daughter, Lucy, to prepare such a supper as that household had never seen before; then she returned to sit again at his feet and listen to his words of wisdom.

The supper progressed apace, and the savour of it was already in the stranger's nostrils. Upon this he grew eloquent and was about to divulge his secret to the hungry-eyed woman when the trampling of Isaac's boots upon the walk told him that he had only a little while longer to contain himself, and at the same time to wait for the fragrant supper.

Now, it is seldom that a man is so well impressed with a smooth-tongued stranger as is his wife. Usually his hard-headedness puts him on the defensive against the blandishments of the man who has won his better half's favour, and, however honest the semi-fortunate individual may be, he despises him for his attainments. But it was not so in this case. Isaac had hardly entered the house and received his visitor's warm handclasp before he had become captive to his charm. Business, business – no, his guest had been travelling and he must be both tired and hungry. Isaac would hear of no business until they had eaten. Then, over a pipe, if the gentleman smoked, they might talk at their ease.

Mr Scatters demurred, but in fact nothing could have pleased him better, and the open smile with which he dropped into his place at the table was very genuine and heartfelt. Genuine, too, were his praises of Lucy's cooking; of her flaky buscuits and mealy potatoes. He was pleased all through and he did not hesitate to say so.

It was a beaming group that finally rose heavily laden from the supper table.

Over a social pipe a little later, Isaac Jackson heard the story that made his eyes bulge with interest and his heart throb with eagerness.

Mr Scatters began, tapping his host's breast and looking at him fixedly, 'You had a brother some years ago named John.' It was more like an accusation than a question.

'Yes, suh, I had a brothah John.'

'Uh, huh, and that brother migrated to the West Indies.'

'Yes, suh, he went out to some o' dem outlandish places.'

'Hold on, sir, hold on, I am a West Indian myself.'

'I do' mean no erfence, 'ceptin' dat John allus was of a rovin' dispersition.'

'Very well, you know no more about your brother after his departure for the West Indies?'

'No, suh.'

'Well, it is my mission to tell you the rest of the story. Your brother John landed at Cuba, and after working about some years and living frugally, he went into the coffee business, in which he became rich.'

'Rich?'

'Rich, sir.'

'Why, bless my soul, who'd 'a evah thought that of John? Why, suh, I'm sho'ly proud to hyeah it. Why don't he come home an' visit a body?'

'Ah, why?' said Mr Scatters dramatically. 'Now comes the most painful part of my mission. "In the midst of life we are in death."' Mr Scatters sighed, Isaac sighed and wiped his eyes. 'Two years ago your brother departed this life.'

'Was he saved?' Isaac asked in a choked voice. Scatters gave him one startled glance, and then answered hastily, 'I am happy to say that he was.'

'Poor John! He gone an' me lef'.'

'Even in the midst of our sorrows, however, there is always a ray of light. Your brother remembered you in his will.'

'Remembered me?'

'Remembered you, and as one of the executors of his estate,' – Mr Scatters rose and went softly over to his valise, from which he took a large square package. He came back with it, holding it as if it were something sacred, – 'as one of the executors of his estate, which is now settled, I was commissioned to bring you this.' He tapped the package. 'This package, sealed as you see with the seal of Cuba, contains five thousand dollars in notes and bonds.'

Isaac gasped and reached for the bundle, but it was withdrawn. 'I am, however, not to deliver it to you yet. There are certain formalities which my country demands to be gone through with, after which I deliver my message and return to the fairest of lands, to the Gem of the Antilles. Let me congratulate you, Mr Jackson, upon your good fortune.'

Isaac yielded up his hand mechanically. He was dazed by the vision of this sudden wealth.

'Fi' thousan' dollahs,' he repeated.

'Yes, sir, five thousand dollars. It is a goodly sum, and in the meantime, until court convenes, I wish you to recommend some safe place in which to put this money, as I do not feel secure with it about my person, nor would it be secure if it were known to be in your house.'

'I reckon Albert Matthews' grocery would be the safes' place fu' it. He's got one o' dem i'on saftes.'

'The very place. Let us go there at once, and after that I will not encroach upon your hospitality longer, but attempt to find a hotel.'

'Hotel nothin',' said Isaac emphatically. 'Ef my house ain't too common, you'll stay right thaih ontwell co't sets.'

'This is very kind of you, Mr Jackson, but really I couldn't think of being such a charge upon you and your good wife.'

''Tain't no charge on us; we'll be glad to have you. Folks hyeah in Miltonville has little enough comp'ny, de Lawd knows.'

Isaac spoke the truth, and it was as much the knowledge that he would be the envy of all the town as his gratitude to Scatters that prompted him to prevail upon his visitor to stay.

Scatters was finally persuaded, and the men only paused long enough in the house to tell the curiosity-eaten Martha Ann the news, and then started for Albert Matthews' store. Scatters carried the precious package, and Isaac was armed with an old shotgun lest anyone should suspect their treasure and attack them. Five thousand dollars was not to be carelessly handled!

As soon as the men were gone, Martha Ann started out upon her rounds, and her proud tongue did for the women portion of Miltonville what the visit to Matthews' store did for the men. Did Mrs So-and-So remember brother John? Indeed she did. And when the story was told, it was a 'Well, well, well! he used to be an ol' beau o' mine.' Martha Ann found no less than twenty women of her acquaintance for whom her brother John seemed to have entertained tender feelings.

The corner grocery store kept by Albert Matthews was the general gathering-place for the coloured male population of the town. It was a small, one-roomed building, almost filled with barrels, boxes, and casks.

Pride as well as necessity had prompted Isaac to go to the grocery just at this time, when it would be quite the fullest of men. He had not calculated wrongly when he reckoned upon the sensation that would be made by his entrance with the distinguished-looking stranger. The excitement was all the most hungry could have wished for. The men stared at Jackson and his companion with wide-open eyes. They left off chewing tobacco and telling tales. A half-dozen of them forgot to avail themselves of the joy of spitting, and Albert Matthews, the proprietor, a weazened little brown-skinned man, forgot to lay his hand upon the scale in weighing out a pound of sugar.

With a humility that was false on the very face of it, Isaac introduced his guest to the grocer and the three went off together mysteriously into a corner. The matter was duly explained and the object of the visit told. Matthews burned with envy of his neighbour's good fortune.

'I do' reckon, Mistah Scatters, dat we bettah not let de othah folks in de sto' know anything 'bout dis hyeah bus'ness of ouahs. I got to be 'sponsible fu dat money, an' I doesn't want to tek no chances.'

'You are perfectly right, sir, perfectly right. You are responsible, not only for the money itself, but for the integrity of this seal which means the dignity of government.'

Matthews looked sufficiently impressed, and together they all went their way among the barrels and boxes to the corner where the little safe stood. With many turnings and twistings the door was opened, the package inclosed and the safe shut again. Then they all rose solemnly and went behind the counter to sample something that Matthews had. This was necessary as a climax, for they had performed, not a mere deed, but a ceremonial.

'Of course, you'll say nothing about this matter at all, Mr Matthews,' said Scatters, thereby insuring publicity to his affair.

There were a few introductions as the men passed out, but hardly had their backs turned when a perfect storm of comment and inquiry broke about the grocer's head. So it came to pass, that with many mysterious nods and head shakings, Matthews first hinted at and then told the story.

11   The Mission of Mr Scatters

For the first few minutes the men could scarcely believe what they had heard. It was so utterly unprecedented. Then it dawned upon them that it might be so, and discussion and argument ran rife for the next hour.

The story flew like wildfire, there being three things in this world which interest all sorts and conditions of men alike: great wealth, great beauty, and great love. Whenever Mr Scatters appeared he was greeted with deference and admiration. Any man who had come clear from Cuba on such an errand to their fellow-townsman deserved all honour and respect. His charming manners confirmed, too, all that preconceived notions had said of him. He became a social favourite. It began with Mr and Mrs Dunkin's calling upon him. Then followed Alonzo Taft, and when the former two gave a reception for the visitor, his position was assured. Miltonville had not yet arisen to the dignity of having a literary society. He now founded one and opened it himself with an address so beautiful, so eloquent and moving that Mr Dunkin bobbed his head dizzy in acquiescence, and Aunt Hannah Payne thought she was in church and shouted for joy.

The little town had awakened from its long post-bellum slumber and accepted with eagerness the upward impulse given it. It stood aside and looked on with something like adoration when Mr Scatters and Mrs Dunkin met and talked of ineffable things – things far above the ken of the average mortal.

When Mr Scatters found that his mission was known, he gave up further attempts at concealing it and talked freely about the matter. He expatiated at length upon the responsibility that devolved upon him and his desire to discharge it, and he spoke glowingly of the great government whose power was represented by the seal which held the package of bonds. Not for one day would he stay away from his beloved Cuba, if it were not that that seal had to be broken in the presence of the proper authorities. So, however reluctant he might be to stay, it was not for him to shirk his task: he must wait for the sitting of court.

Meanwhile the Jacksons lived in an atmosphere of glory. The womenfolk purchased new dresses, and Isaac got a new wagon on the strength of their good fortune. It was nothing to what they dreamed of doing when they had the money positively in hand. Mr Scatters still remained their guest, and they were proud of it.

What pleased them most was that their distinguished visitor seemed not to look down upon, but rather to be pleased with, their homely fare. Isaac had further cause for pleasure when his guest came to him later with a great show of frank confidence to request the loan of fifty dollars.

'I should not think of asking even this small favour of you but that I have only Cuban money with me and I knew you would feel distressed if you knew that I went to the trouble of sending this money away for exchange on account of so small a sum.'

This was undoubtedly a mark of special confidence. It suddenly made Isaac feel as if the grand creature had accepted and labelled him as a brother and an equal. He hastened to Matthews' safe, where he kept his own earnings; for the grocer was banker as well.

With reverent hands they put aside the package of bonds and together counted out the required half a hundred dollars. In a little while Mr Scatters' long, graceful fingers had closed over it.

Mr Jackson's cup of joy was now full. It had but one bitter drop to mar its sweetness. That was the friendship that had sprung up between the Cuban and Mr Dunkin. They frequently exchanged visits, and sat long together engaged in conversation from which Isaac was excluded. This galled him. He felt that he had a sort of proprietary interest in his guest. And any infringement of this property right he looked upon with distinct disfavour. So that it was with no pleasant countenance that he greeted Mr Dunkin when he called on a certain night.

'Mr Scatters is gone out,' he said, as the old man entered and deposited his hat on the floor.

'Dat's all right, Isaac,' said Mr Dunkin slowly, 'I didn't come to see de gent'man. I come to see you.'

The cloud somewhat lifted from Isaac's brow. Mr Dunkin was a man of importance and it made a deal of difference whom he was visiting.

He seemed a little bit embarrassed, however, as to how to open conversation. He hummed and hawed and was visibly uneasy. He tried to descant upon the weather, but the subject failed him. Finally, with an effort, he hitched his chair nearer to his host's and said in a low voice, 'Ike, I reckon you has de confidence of Mistah Scatters?'

'I has,' was the proud reply, 'I has.'

'Hum! uh! huh! Well – well – has you evah loant him any money?'

Isaac was aghast. Such impertinence!

'Mistah Dunkin,' he began, 'I considah ...'

'Hol' on, Ike!' broke in Dunkin, laying a soothing hand on the other's knee, 'don' git on yo' high hoss. Dis hyeah's a impo'tant mattah.'

'I ain't got nothin' to say.'

'He ain't never tol' you 'bout havin' nothin' but Cubian money on him?'

Isaac started.

'I see he have. He tol' me de same thing.'

The two men sat staring suspiciously into each other's faces.

'He got a hun'ed an' fifty dollahs f'om me,' said Dunkin.

'I let him have fifty,' added Jackson weakly.

'He got a hun'ed an' fifty dollahs f'om thews. Dat's how I come to git 'spicious. He tol' him de same sto'y.'

Again that pregnant look flashed between them, and they both rose and went out of the house.

They hurried down to Matthews' grocery. The owner was waiting for them there. There was solemnity, but no hesitation, in the manner with which they now went to the safe. They took out the package hastily and with ruthless hands. This was no ceremonial now. The seal had no longer any fears for them. They tore it off. They tore the wrappers. Then paper. Neatly folded paper. More wrapping paper. Newspapers. Nothing more. Of bills or bonds – nothing. With the debris of the mysterious parcel scattered about their feet, they stood up and looked at each other.

'I nevah did believe in furriners nohow,' said Mr Dunkin sadly.

'But he knowed all about my brothah John.'

'An' he sho'ly did make mighty fine speeches. Maybe we's missed de money.' This from the grocer.

Together they went over the papers again, with the same result.

'Do you know where he went to-night, Ike?'

'No.'

'Den I reckon we's seed de las' o' him.'

'But he lef' his valise.'

'Yes, an' he lef' dis,' said Dunkin sternly, pointing to the paper on the floor. 'He sho'ly is mighty keerless of his valybles.'

'Let's go git de constable,' said the practical Matthews.

They did, though they felt that it would be unavailing.

The constable came and waited at Jackson's house. They had been there about half an hour, talking the matter over, when what was their surprise to hear Mr Scatters' step coming jauntily up the walk. A sudden panic of terror and shame seized them. It was as if they had wronged him. Suppose, after all, everything should come right and he should be able to explain? They sat and trembled until he entered. Then the constable told him his mission.

Mr Scatters was surprised. He was hurt. Indeed, he was distinctly grieved that his friends had had so little confidence in him. Had he been to them anything but a gentleman, a friend, and an honest man? Had he not come a long distance from his home to do one of them a favour? They hung their heads. Martha Ann, who was listening at the door, was sobbing audibly. What had he done thus to be humiliated? He saw the effect of his words and pursued it. Had he not left in the care of one of their own number security for his integrity in the shape of the bonds?

The effect of his words was magical. Every head went up and three pairs of flashing eyes were bent upon him. He saw and knew that they knew. He had not thought that they would dare to violate the seal around which he had woven such a halo. He saw that all was over, and, throwing up his hands with a despairing gesture, he bowed graciously and left the room with the constable.

All Miltonville had the story next day, and waited no less eagerly than before for the 'settin' of co't.'

To the anger and chagrin of Miltonvillians, Fox Run had the honour and distinction of being the county seat, and thither they must go to the sessions; but never did they so forget their animosities as on the day set for the trial of Scatters. They overlooked the pride of the Fox Runners, their cupidity and their vaunting arrogance. They ignored the indignity of showing interest in anything that took place in that village, and went in force, eager, anxious, and curious. Ahorse, afoot, by oxcart, by mule-wagon, white, black, high, low, old, and young of both sexes invaded Fox Run and swelled the crowd of onlookers until, with pity for the very anxiety of the people, the humane judge decided to discard the now inadequate court-room and hold the sessions on the village green. Here an impromptu bar was set up, and over against it were ranged the benches, chairs, and camp-stools of the spectators.

Every man of prominence in the county was present. Major Richardson, though now retired, occupied a distinguished position within the bar. Old Captain Howard shook hands familiarly with the judge and nodded to the assembly as though he himself had invited them all to be present. Former Judge Durbin sat with his successor on the bench.

Court opened and the first case was called. It gained but passing attention. There was bigger game to be stalked. A hog-stealing case fared a little better on account of the intimateness of the crime involved. But nothing was received with such awed silence as the case of the State against Joseph Scatters. The charge was obtaining money under false pretences, and the plea 'Not Guilty.'

The witnesses were called and their testimony taken. Mr Scatters was called to testify in his own defence, but refused to do so. The prosecution stated its case and proceeded to sum up the depositions of the witnesses. As there was no attorney for the defence, the State's attorney delivered a short speech, in which the guilt of the defendant was plainly set forth. It was as clear as day. Things looked very dark for Mr Scatters of Cuba.

As the lawyer sat down, and ere the case could be given to the jury, he rose and asked permission of the Court to say a few words.

This was granted him.

He stood up among them, a magnificent, strong, black figure. His eyes swept the assembly, judge, jury, and spectators with a look half amusement, half defiance.

'I have pleaded not guilty,' he began in a low, distinct voice that could be heard in every part of the inclosure, 'and I am not guilty of the spirit which is charged against me, however near the letter may touch me. I did use certain knowledge that I possessed, and the seal which I happened to have from an old government position, to defraud – that is the word, if you will – to defraud these men out of the price of their vanity and their cupidity. But it was not a long-premeditated thing. I was within a few miles of your town before the idea occurred to me. I was in straits. I stepped from the brink of great poverty into the midst of what you are pleased to deem a greater crime.'

The Court held its breath. No such audacity had ever been witnessed in the life of Fox Run.

Scatters went on, warming to his subject as he progressed. He was eloquent and he was pleasing. A smile flickered over the face of Major Richardson and was reflected in the features of many others as the speaker burst forth:

11   The Mission of Mr Scatters

'Gentlemen, I maintain that instead of imprisoning you should thank me for what I have done. Have I not taught your community a lesson? Have I not put a check upon their credulity and made them wary of unheralded strangers?'

He had. There was no disputing that. The judge himself was smiling, and the jurymen were nodding at each other.

Scatters had not yet played his trump card. He saw that the time was ripe. Straightening his form and raising his great voice, he cried: 'Gentlemen, I am guilty according to the letter of the law, but from that I appeal to the men who make and have made the law. From the hard detail of this new day, I appeal to the chivalry of the old South which has been told in story and sung in song. From men of vindictiveness I appeal to men of mercy. From plebeians to aristocrats. By the memory of the sacred names of the Richardsons' – the Major sat bolt upright and dropped his snuffbox – 'the Durbins' – the ex-judge couldn't for his life get his pince-nez on – 'the Howards' – the captain openly rubbed his hands – 'to the memory that those names call up I appeal, and to the living and honourable bearers of them present. And to you, gentlemen of the jury, the lives of whose fathers went to purchase this dark and bloody ground, I appeal from the accusation of these men, who are not my victims, not my dupes, but their own.'

There was a hush when he was done. The judge read the charge to the jury, and it was favourable – very. And – well, Scatters had taught the darkies a lesson; he had spoken of their families and their traditions, he knew their names, and – oh, well, he was a good fellow after all – what was the use?

The jury did not leave their seats, and the verdict was acquittal.

Scatters thanked the Court and started away; but he met three ominous-looking pairs of eyes, and a crowd composed of angry Negroes was flocking toward the edge of the green.

He came back.

'I think I had better wait until the excitement subsides,' he said to Major Richardson.

'No need of that, suh, no need of that. Here, Jim,' he called to his coachman, 'take Mr Scatters wherever he wants to go, and remember, I shall hold you responsible for his safety.'

'Yes, suh,' said Jim.

'A thousand thanks, Major,' said the man with the mission.

'Not at all, suh. By the way, that was a very fine effort of yours this afternoon. I was greatly moved by it. If you'll give me your address I'll send you a history of our family, suh, from the time they left Vuhginia and before.'

Mr Scatters gave him the address, and smiled at the three enemies, who still waited on the edge of the green.

'To the station,' he said to the driver.

12

Sultana's Dream

(1905)

Begum Rokeya Sakhawat Hossain

One evening I was lounging in an easy chair in my bedroom and thinking lazily of the condition of Indian womanhood. I am not sure whether I dozed off or not. But, as far as I remember, I was wide awake. I saw the moonlit sky sparkling with thousands of diamond-like stars, very distinctly.

All on a sudden a lady stood before me; how she came in, I do not know. I took her for my friend, Sister Sara.

'Good morning,' said Sister Sara. I smiled inwardly as I knew it was not morning, but starry night. However, I replied to her, saying, 'How do you do?'

'I am all right, thank you. Will you please come out and have a look at our garden?'

I looked again at the moon through the open window, and thought there was no harm in going out at that time. The men-servants outside were fast asleep just then, and I could have a pleasant walk with Sister Sara.

I used to have my walks with Sister Sara, when we were at Darjeeling. Many a time did we walk hand in hand and talk light-heartedly in the botanical gardens there. I fancied, Sister Sara had probably come to take me to some such garden and I readily accepted her offer and went out with her.

When walking I found to my surprise that it was a fine morning. The town was fully awake and the streets alive with bustling crowds. I was feeling very shy, thinking I was walking in the street in broad daylight, but there was not a single man visible.

Some of the passers-by made jokes at me. Though I could not understand their language, yet I felt sure they were joking. I asked my friend, 'What do they say?'

'The women say that you look very mannish.'

'Mannish?' said I, 'What do they mean by that?'

'They mean that you are shy and timid like men.'

'Shy and timid like men?' It was really a joke. I became very nervous, when I found that my companion was not Sister Sara, but a stranger. Oh, what a fool had I been to mistake this lady for my dear old friend, Sister Sara.

She felt my fingers tremble in her hand, as we were walking hand in hand.

'What is the matter, dear?' she said affectionately. 'I feel somewhat awkward,' I said in a rather apologizing tone, 'as being a purdahnishin woman I am not accustomed to walking abut unveiled.'

'You need not be afraid of coming across a man here. This is Ladyland, free from sin and harm. Virtue herself reigns here.'

By and by I was enjoying the scenery. Really it was very grand. I mistook a patch of green grass for a velvet cushion. Feeling as if I were walking on a soft carpet, I looked down and found the path covered with moss and flowers.

'How nice it is,' said I.

'Do you like it?' asked Sister Sara. (I continued calling her 'Sister Sara,' and she kept calling me by my name.)

'Yes, very much; but I do not like to tread on the tender and sweet flowers.'

'Never mind, dear Sultana; your treading will not harm them; they are street flowers.'

'The whole place looks like a garden,' said I admiringly. 'You have arranged every plant so skillfully.'

'Your Calcutta could become a nicer garden than this if only your countrymen wanted to make it so.'

'They would think it useless to give so much attention to horticulture, while they have so many other things to do.'

'They could not find a better excuse,' said she with smile.

I became very curious to know where the men were. I met more than a hundred women while walking there, but not a single man.

'Where are the men?' I asked her.

'In their proper places, where they ought to be.'

'Pray let me know what you mean by "their proper places".'

'O, I see my mistake, you cannot know our customs, as you were never here before. We shut our men indoors.'

'Just as we are kept in the zenana?'

'Exactly so.'

'How funny,' I burst into a laugh. Sister Sara laughed too.

'But dear Sultana, how unfair it is to shut in the harmless women and let loose the men.'

'Why? It is not safe for us to come out of the zenana, as we are naturally weak.'

'Yes, it is not safe so long as there are men about the streets, nor is it so when a wild animal enters a marketplace.'

'Of course not.'

'Suppose, some lunatics escape from the asylum and begin to do all sorts of mischief to men, horses and other creatures; in that case what will your countrymen do?'

'They will try to capture them and put them back into their asylum.'

'Thank you! And you do not think it wise to keep sane people inside an asylum and let loose the insane?'

'Of course not!' said I laughing lightly.

'As a matter of fact, in your country this very thing is done! Men, who do or at least are capable of doing no end of mischief, are let loose and the innocent women, shut up in the zenana! How can you trust those untrained men out of doors?'

'We have no hand or voice in the management of our social affairs. In India man is lord and master, he has taken to himself all powers and privileges and shut up the women in the zenana.'

'Why do you allow yourselves to be shut up?'

'Because it cannot be helped as they are stronger than women.'

'A lion is stronger than a man, but it does not enable him to dominate the human race. You have neglected the duty you owe to yourselves and you have lost your natural rights by shutting your eyes to your own interests.'

'But my dear Sister Sara, if we do everything by ourselves, what will the men do then?'

'They should not do anything, excuse me; they are fit for nothing. Only catch them and put them into the zenana.'

'But would it be very easy to catch and put them inside the four walls?' said I. 'And even if this were done, would all their business – political and commercial – also go with them into the zenana?'

Sister Sara made no reply. She only smiled sweetly. Perhaps she thought it useless to argue with one who was no better than a frog in a well.

By this time we reached Sister Sara's house. It was situated in a beautiful heart-shaped garden. It was a bungalow with a corrugated iron roof. It was cooler and nicer than any of our rich buildings. I cannot describe how neat and how nicely furnished and how tastefully decorated it was.

We sat side by side. She brought out of the parlour a piece of embroidery work and began putting on a fresh design.

'Do you know knitting and needle work?'

'Yes; we have nothing else to do in our zenana.'

'But we do not trust our zenana members with embroidery!' she said laughing, 'as a man has not patience enough to pass thread through a needle hole even!'

'Have you done all this work yourself?' I asked her pointing to the various pieces of embroidered teapoy cloths.

'Yes.'

'How can you find time to do all these? You have to do the office work as well? Have you not?'

'Yes. I do not stick to the laboratory all day long. I finish my work in two hours.'

'In two hours! How do you manage? In our land the officers – magistrates, for instance – work seven hours daily.'

'I have seen some of them doing their work. Do you think they work all the seven hours?'

'Certainly they do!'

'No, dear Sultana, they do not. They dawdle away their time in smoking. Some smoke two or three choroots during the office time. They talk much about their work, but do little. Suppose one choroot takes half an hour to burn off, and a man smokes twelve choroots daily; then you see, he wastes six hours every day in sheer smoking.'

We talked on various subjects, and I learned that they were not subject to any kind of epidemic disease, nor did they suffer from mosquito bites as we do. I was very much astonished to hear that in Ladyland no one died in youth except by rare accident.

'Will you care to see our kitchen?' she asked me.

'With pleasure,' said I, and we went to see it. Of course the men had been asked to clear off when I was going there. The kitchen was situated in a beautiful vegetable garden. Every creeper, every tomato plant was itself an ornament. I found no smoke, nor any chimney either in the kitchen – it was clean and bright; the windows were decorated with flower gardens. There was no sign of coal or fire.

'How do you cook?' I asked.

'With solar heat,' she said, at the same time showing me the pipe, through which passed the concentrated sunlight and heat. And she cooked something then and there to show me the process.

'How did you manage to gather and store up the sun heat?' I asked her in amazement.

'Let me tell you a little of our past history then. Thirty years ago, when our present Queen was thirteen years old, she inherited the throne. She was Queen in name only, the Prime Minister really ruling the country.

'Our good Queen liked science very much. She circulated an order that all the women in her country should be educated. Accordingly a number of girls' schools were founded and supported by the government. Education was spread far and wide among women. And early marriage also was stopped. No woman was to be allowed to marry before she was twenty-one. I must tell you that, before this change we had been kept in strict purdah.'

'How the tables are turned,' I interposed with a laugh.

'But the seclusion is the same,' she said. 'In a few years we had separate universities, where no men were admitted.'

'In the capital, where our Queen lives, there are two universities. One of these invented a wonderful balloon, to which they attached a number of pipes. By means of this captive balloon which they managed to keep afloat above the cloud-land, they could draw as much water from the atmosphere as they pleased. As the water was incessantly being drawn by the university people no cloud gathered and the ingenious Lady Principal stopped rain and storms thereby.'

'Really! Now I understand why there is no mud here!' said I. But I could not understand how it was possible to accumulate water in the pipes. She explained to me how it was done, but I was unable to understand her, as my scientific knowledge was very limited. However, she went on ...

'When the other university came to know of this, they became exceedingly jealous and tried to do something more extraordinary still. They invented an instrument by which they could collect as much sun-heat as they wanted. And they kept the heat stored up to be distributed among others as required.

'While the women were engaged in scientific research, the men of this country were busy increasing their military power. When they came to know that the female universities were able to draw water from the atmosphere and collect heat from the sun, they only laughed at the members of the universities and called the whole thing "a sentimental nightmare"!'

'Your achievements are very wonderful indeed! But tell me, how you managed to put the men of your country into the zenana. Did you entrap them first?'

'No.'

'It is not likely that they would surrender their free and open-air life of their own accord and confine themselves within the four walls of the zenana! They must have been overpowered.'

'Yes, they have been!'

'By whom? By some lady warriors, I suppose?'

'No, not by arms.'

'Yes, it cannot be so. Men's arms are stronger than women's. Then?'

'By brain.'

'Even their brains are bigger and heavier than women's. Are they not?'

'Yes, but what of that? An elephant also has got a bigger and heavier brain than a man has. Yet man can enchain elephants and employ them, according to their own wishes.'

'Well said, but tell me please, how it all actually happened. I am dying to know it!'

'Women's brains are somewhat quicker than men's. Ten years ago, when the military officers called our scientific discoveries "a sentimental nightmare," some of the young ladies wanted to say something in reply to those remarks. But both the Lady Principals restrained them and said, they should reply not by word, but by deed, if ever they got the opportunity. And they had not long to wait for that opportunity.'

'How marvellous!' I heartily clapped my hands. 'And now the proud gentlemen are dreaming sentimental dreams themselves.'

'Soon afterwards certain persons came from a neighbouring country and took shelter in ours. They were in trouble having committed some political offence. The king who cared more for power than for good government asked our kind-hearted Queen to hand them over to his officers. She refused, as it was against her principle to turn out refugees. For this refusal the king declared war against our country.

'Our military officers sprang to their feet at once and marched out to meet the enemy.

'The enemy however, was too strong for them. Our soldiers fought bravely, no doubt. But in spite of all their bravery the foreign army advanced step by step to invade our country.

'Nearly all the men had gone out to fight; even a boy of sixteen was not left home. Most of our warriors were killed, the rest driven back and the enemy came within twenty-five miles of the capital.

'A meeting of a number of wise ladies was held at the Queen's palace to advise as to what should be done to save the land.

'Some proposed to fight like soldiers; others objected and said that women were not trained to fight with swords and guns, nor were they accustomed to fighting with any weapons. A third party regretfully remarked that they were hopelessly weak of body.

'If you cannot save your country for lack of physical strength,' said the Queen, 'try to do so by brain power.'

'There was a dead silence for a few minutes. Her Royal Highness said again, 'I must commit suicide if the land and my honour are lost.'

'Then the Lady Principal of the second university (who had collected sun-heat), who had been silently thinking during the consultation, remarked that they were all but lost, and there was little hope left for them. There was, however, one plan which she would like to try, and this would be her first and last efforts; if she failed in this, there would be nothing left but to commit suicide. All present solemnly vowed that they would never allow themselves to be enslaved, no matter what happened.

'The Queen thanked them heartily, and asked the Lady Principal to try her plan.

'The Lady Principal rose again and said, "before we go out the men must enter the zenanas. I make this prayer for the sake of purdah." "Yes, of course," replied Her Royal Highness.

'On the following day the Queen called upon all men to retire into zenanas for the sake of honour and liberty.

'Wounded and tired as they were, they took that order rather for a boon! They bowed low and entered the zenanas without uttering a single word of protest. They were sure that there was no hope for this country at all.

'Then the Lady Principal with her two thousand students marched to the battle field, and arriving there directed all the rays of the concentrated sunlight and heat towards the enemy.

'The heat and light were too much for them to bear. They all ran away panic-stricken, not knowing in their bewilderment how to counteract that scorching heat. When they fled away leaving their guns and other ammunitions of war, they were burnt down by means of the same sun heat.

'Since then no one has tried to invade our country any more.'

'And since then your countrymen never tried to come out of the zenana?'

'Yes, they wanted to be free. Some of the police commissioners and district magistrates sent word to the Queen to the effect that the military officers certainly deserved to be imprisoned for their failure; but they never neglected their duty and therefore they should not be punished and they prayed to be restored to their respective offices.

'Her Royal Highness sent them a circular letter intimating to them that if their services should ever be needed they would be sent for, and that in the meanwhile they should remain where they were.

'Now that they are accustomed to the purdah system and have ceased to grumble at their seclusion, we call the system "Murdana" instead of "zenana".'

'But how do you manage,' I asked Sister Sara, 'to do without the police or magistrates in case of theft or murder?'

'Since the "Murdana" system has been established, there has been no more crime or sin; therefore we do not require a policeman to find out a culprit, nor do we want a magistrate to try a criminal case.'

'That is very good, indeed. I suppose if there was any dishonest person, you could very easily chastise her. As you gained a decisive victory without shedding a single drop of blood, you could drive off crime and criminals too without much difficulty!'

'Now, dear Sultana, will you sit here or come to my parlour?' she asked me.

'Your kitchen is not inferior to a queen's boudoir!' I replied with a pleasant smile, 'but we must leave it now; for the gentlemen may be cursing me for keeping them away from their duties in the kitchen so long.' We both laughed heartily.

'How my friends at home will be amused and amazed, when I go back and tell them that in the far-off Ladyland, ladies rule over the country and control all social matters, while gentlemen are kept in the Murdanas to mind babies, to cook and to do all sorts of domestic work; and that cooking is so easy a thing that it is simply a pleasure to cook!'

'Yes, tell them about all that you see here.'

'Please let me know, how you carry on land cultivation and how you plough the land and do other hard manual work.'

'Our fields are tilled by means of electricity, which supplies motive power for other hard work as well, and we employ it for our aerial conveyances too. We have no rail road nor any paved streets here.'

'Therefore neither street nor railway accidents occur here,' said I. 'Do not you ever suffer from want of rainwater?' I asked.

'Never since the "water balloon" has been set up. You see the big balloon and pipes attached thereto. By their aid we can draw as much rainwater as we require. Nor do we ever suffer from flood or thunderstorms. We are all very busy making Nature yield as much as she can. We do not find time to quarrel with one another as we never sit idle. Our noble Queen is exceedingly fond of botany; it is her ambition to convert the whole country into one grand garden.'

'The idea is excellent. What is your chief food?'

'Fruits.'

'How do you keep your country cool in hot weather? We regard the rainfall in summer as a blessing from heaven.'

'When the heat becomes unbearable, we sprinkle the ground with plentiful showers drawn from the artificial fountains. And in cold weather we keep our room warm with sun heat.'

She showed me her bathroom, the roof of which was removable. She could enjoy a shower bath whenever she liked, by simply removing the roof (which was like the lid of a box) and turning on the tap of the shower pipe.

'You are a lucky people!' ejaculated I. 'You know no want. What is your religion, may I ask?'

'Our religion is based on Love and Truth. It is our religious duty to love one another and to be absolutely truthful. If any person lies, she or he is ...'

'Punished with death?'

'No, not with death. We do not take pleasure in killing a creature of God, especially a human being. The liar is asked to leave this land for good and never to come to it again.'

'Is an offender never forgiven?'

'Yes, if that person repents sincerely.'

'Are you not allowed to see any man, except your own relations?'

'No one except sacred relations.'

'Our circle of sacred relations is very limited; even first cousins are not sacred.'

'But ours is very large; a distant cousin is as sacred as a brother.'

'That is very good. I see purity itself reigns over your land. I should like to see the good Queen, who is so sagacious and far-sighted and who has made all these rules.'

'All right,' said Sister Sara.

Then she screwed a couple of seats onto a square piece of plank. To this plank she attached two smooth and well-polished balls. When I asked her what the balls were for, she said they were hydrogen balls and they were used to overcome the force of gravity. The balls were of different capacities to be used according to the different weights desired to be overcome. She then fastened to the air-car two wing-like blades, which, she said, were worked by electricity. After we were comfortably seated she touched a knob and the blades began to whirl, moving faster and faster every moment. At first we were raised to the height of about six or seven feet and then off we flew. And before I could realize that we had commenced moving, we reached the garden of the Queen.

My friend lowered the air-car by reversing the action of the machine, and when the car touched the ground the machine was stopped and we got out.

I had seen from the air-car the Queen walking on a garden path with her little daughter (who was four years old) and her maids of honour.

'Halloo! You here!' cried the Queen addressing Sister Sara. I was introduced to Her Royal Highness and was received by her cordially without any ceremony.

I was very much delighted to make her acquaintance. In the course of the conversation I had with her, the Queen told me that she had no objection to permitting her subjects to trade with other countries. 'But,' she continued, 'no trade was possible with countries where the women were kept in the zenanas and so unable to come and trade with us. Men, we find, are rather of lower morals and so we do not like dealing with them. We do not covet other people's land, we do not fight for a piece of diamond though it may be a thousand-fold brighter than the Koh-i-Noor, nor do we grudge a ruler his peacock throne. We dive deep into the ocean of knowledge and try to find out the precious gems, which Nature has kept in store for us. We enjoy Nature's gifts as much as we can.'

After taking leave of the Queen, I visited the famous universities, and was shown some of their manufactories, laboratories and observatories.

After visiting the above places of interest we got again into the air-car, but as soon as it began moving, I somehow slipped down and the fall startled me out of my dream. And on opening my eyes, I found myself in my own bed lounging in the easy-chair!

13

The Preliminaries

(1910)

Cornelia A P Comer

I

Young Oliver Pickersgill was in love with Peter Lannithorne's daughter. Peter Lannithorne was serving a six-year term in the penitentiary for embezzlement.

It seemed to Ollie that there was only one right-minded way of looking at these basal facts of his situation. But this simple view of the matter was destined to receive several shocks in the course of his negotiations for Ruth Lannithorne's hand. I say negotiations advisedly. Most young men in love have only to secure the consent of the girl and find enough money to go to housekeeping. It is quite otherwise when you wish to marry into a royal family, or to ally yourself with a criminal's daughter. The preliminaries are more complicated.

Ollie thought a man ought to marry the girl he loves, and prejudices be hanged! In the deeps of his soul, he probably knew this to be the magnanimous, manly attitude, but certainly there was no condescension in his outward bearing when he asked Ruth Lannithorne to be his wife. Yet she turned on him fiercely, bristling with pride and tense with over-wrought nerves.

'I will never marry any one,' she declared, 'who doesn't respect my father as I do!'

If Oliver's jaw fell, it is hardly surprising. He had expected her to say she would never marry into a family where she was not welcome. He had planned to get around the natural objections of his parents somehow – the details of this were vague in his mind – and then he meant to reassure her warmly, and tell her that personal merit was the only thing that counted with him or his. He may have visualized himself as wiping away her tears and gently raising her to share the safe social pedestal whereon the Pickersgills were firmly planted. The young do have these visions not infrequently. But to be asked to respect Peter Lannithorne, about whom he knew practically nothing save his present address!

'I don't remember that I ever saw your father, Ruth,' he faltered.

'He was the best man,' said the girl excitedly, 'the kindest, the most indulgent. – That's another thing, Ollie. I will never marry an indulgent man, nor one who will let his wife manage him. If it hadn't been for mother – ' She broke off abruptly.

Ollie tried to look sympathetic and not too intelligent. He had heard that Mrs Lannithorne was considered difficult.

'I oughtn't to say it, but can't explain father unless I do. Mother nagged; she wanted more money than there was; she made him feel her illnesses, and our failings, and the overdone beefsteak, and the under-done bread, – everything that went wrong, always, was his fault. His fault – because he didn't make more money. We were on the edge of things, and she wanted to be in the middle, as she was used to being. Of course, she really hasn't been well, but I think it's mostly nerves,' said Ruth, with the terrible hardness of the young. 'Anyhow, she might just as well have stuck knives into him as to say the things she did. It hurt him – like knives, I could see him wince – and try harder – and get discouraged – and then, at last – ' The girl burst into a passion of tears.

Oliver tried to soothe her. Secretly he was appalled at these squalid revelations of discordant family life. The domestic affairs of the Pickersgills ran smoothly, in affluence and peace. Oliver had never listened to a nagging woman in his life. He had an idea that such phenomena were confined to the lower classes.

'Don't you care for me at all, Ruth?'

The girl crumpled her wet handkerchief. 'Ollie, you're the most beautiful thing that ever happened – except my father. He was beautiful, too; indeed, indeed, he was. I'll never think differently. I can't. He tried so hard.'

All the latent manliness in the boy came to the surface and showed itself.

'Ruth, darling, I don't want you to think differently. It's right for you to be loyal and feel as you do. You see, you know, and the world doesn't. I'll take what you say and do as you wish. You mustn't think I'm on the other side. I'm not. I'm on your side, wherever that is. When the time comes I'll show you. You may trust me, Ruth.'

He was eager, pleading, earnest. He looked at the moment so good, so loving and sincere, that the girl, out of her darker experience of life, wondered wistfully if it were really true that Providence ever let people just live their lives out like that – being good, and prosperous, and generous, advancing from happiness to happiness, instead of stubbing along painfully as she felt she had done, from one bitter experience to another, learning to live by failures.

It must be beautiful to learn from successes instead, as it seemed to her Oliver had done. How could any one refuse to share such a radiant life when it was offered? As for loving Oliver, that was a foregone conclusion. Still, she hesitated.

'You're awfully dear and good to me, Ollie,' she said. 'But I want you to see father. I want you to go and talk to him about this, and know him for yourself. I know I'm asking a hard thing of you, but, truly, I believe it's best. If *he* says it's all right for me to marry you, I will – if your family want me, of course,' she added as an afterthought.

'Oughtn't I to speak to your mother?' hesitated Oliver.

'Oh, – mother? Yes, I suppose she'd like it,' said Ruth, absent-mindedly. 'Mother has views about getting married, Ollie. I dare say she'll want to tell you what they are. You mustn't think they're my views, though.'

'I'd rather hear yours, Ruth.'

She flashed a look at him that opened for him the heavenly deeps that lie before the young and the loving, and he had a sudden vision of their life as a long sunlit road, winding uphill, winding down, but sunlit always – because looks like that illumine any dusk.

'I'll tell you my views – some day,' Ruth said softly. 'But first – '

'First I must talk to my father, your mother, your father.' Oliver checked them off on his fingers. 'Three of them. Seems to me that's a lot of folks to consult about a thing that doesn't really concern anybody but you and me!'

II

After the fashion of self-absorbed youth, Oliver had never noticed Mrs Lannithorne especially. She had been to him simply a sallow little figure in the background of Ruth's vivid young life; someone to be spoken to very politely, but otherwise of no particular moment.

If his marital negotiations did nothing else for him, they were at least opening his eyes to the significance of the personalities of older people.

The things Ruth said about her mother had prepared him to find that lady querulous and difficult, but essentially negligible. Face to face with Mrs Lannithorne, he had a very different impression. She received him in the upstairs sitting-room to which her semi-invalid habits usually confined her. Wrapped in a white wool shawl and lying in a long Canton lounging-chair by a sunshiny window, she put out a chilly hand in greeting, and asked the young man to be seated.

Oliver, scanning her countenance, received an unexpected impression of dignity. She was thin and nervous, with big dark eyes peering out of a pale, narrow face; she might be a woman with a grievance, but he apprehended something beyond mere fretfulness in the discontent of her expression. There was suffering and thought in her face, and even when the former is exaggerated and the latter erroneous, these are impressive things.

'Mrs Lannithorne, have you any objection to letting Ruth marry me?'

'Mr Pickersgill, what are your qualifications for the care of a wife and family?'

Oliver hesitated. 'Why, about what anybody's are, I think,' he said, and was immediately conscious of the feebleness of this response. 'I mean,' he added, flushing to the roots of his blond hair, 'that my prospects in life are fair. I am in my father's office, you know. I am to have a small share in the business next year. I needn't tell you that the firm is a good one. If you want to know about my qualifications as a lawyer – why, I can refer you to people who can tell you if they think I am promising.'

'Do your family approve of this marriage?'

'I haven't talked to them about it yet.'

'Have you ever saved any money of your own earning, or have you any property in your own name?'

Oliver thought guiltily of his bank account, which had a surprising way of proving, when balanced, to be less than he expected.

'Well, – not exactly.'

'In other words, then, Mr Pickersgill, you are a young and absolutely untried man; you are in your father's employ and practically at his mercy; you propose a great change in your life of which you do not know that he approves; you have no resources of your own, and you are not even sure of your earning capacity if your father's backing were withdrawn. In these circumstances you plan to double your expenses and assume the whole responsibility of another person's life, comfort, and happiness. Do you think that you have shown me that your qualifications are adequate?'

All this was more than a little disconcerting. Oliver was used to being accepted as old Pickersgill's only son – which meant a cheerfully accorded background of eminence, ability, and comfortable wealth. It had not occurred to him to detach himself from that background and see how he looked when separated from it. He felt a little angry, and also a little ashamed of the fact that he did not bulk larger as a personage, apart from his environment. Nevertheless, he answered her question honestly.

'No, Mrs Lannithorne, I don't think that I have.'

She did not appear to rejoice in his discomfiture. She even seemed a little sorry for it, but she went on quietly: –

'Don't think I am trying to prove that you are the most ineligible young man in the city. But it is absolutely necessary that a man should stand on his own feet, and firmly, before he undertakes to look after other lives than his own. Otherwise there is nothing but misery for the woman and children who depend upon him. It is a serious business, getting married.'

'I begin to think it is,' muttered Oliver blankly.

'I don't *want* my daughters to marry,' said Mrs Lannithorne. 'The life is a thousand times harder than that of the self-supporting woman – harder work, fewer rewards, less enjoyment, less security. That is true even of an ordinarily happy marriage. And if they are not happy – Oh, the bitterness of them!'

She was speaking rapidly now, with energy, almost with anguish. Oliver, red in the face, subdued, but eager to refute her out of the depths and heights of his inexperience, held himself rigidly still and listened.

'Did you ever hear that epigram of Disraeli – that all men should marry, but no women? That is what I believe! At least, if women must marry, let others do it, not my children, not my little girls! – It is curious, but that is how we always think of them. When they are grown they are often uncongenial. My daughter Ruth does not love me deeply, nor am I greatly drawn to her now, as an individual, a personality, – but Ruth was such a dear baby! I can't bear to have her suffer.'

13 The Preliminaries

Oliver started to protest, hesitated, bit his lip, and subsided. After all, did he dare say that his wife would never suffer? The woman opposite looked at him with hostile, accusing eyes, as if he incarnated in his youthful person all the futile masculinity in the world.

'Do you think a woman who has suffered willingly gives her children over to the same fate?' she demanded passionately. 'I wish I could make you see it for five minutes as I see it, you, young, careless, foolish! Why, you know nothing – nothing! Listen to me. The woman who marries gives up everything, or at least jeopardizes everything: her youth, her health, her life perhaps, certainly her individuality. She acquires the permanent possibility of self-sacrifice. She does it gladly, but she does not know what she is doing. In return, is it too much to ask that she be assured a roof over her head, food to her mouth, clothes to her body? How many men marry without being sure that they have even so much to offer? You yourself, of what are you sure? Is your arm strong? Is your heart loyal? Can you shelter her soul as well as her body? I know your father has money. Perhaps you can care for her creature needs, but that isn't all. For some women life is one long affront, one slow humiliation. How do I know you are not like that?'

'Because I'm not, that's all!' said Oliver Pickersgill abruptly, getting to his feet.

He felt badgered, baited, indignant, yet he could not tell this frail, excited woman what he thought. There were things one didn't say, although Mrs Lannithorne seemed to ignore the fact. She went on ignoring it.

'I know what you are thinking,' she said, 'that I would regard these matters differently if I had married another man. That is not wholly true. It is because Peter Lannithorne was a good man at heart, and tried to play the man's part as well as he knew how, and because it was partly my own fault that he failed so miserably, that I have thought of it all so much. And the end of all my thinking is that I don't want my daughters to marry.'

Oliver was white now, and a little unsteady. He was also confused. There was the note of truth in what she said, but he felt that she said it with too much excitement, with too great facility. He had the justified masculine distrust of feminine fluency as hysterical. Nothing so presented could carry full conviction. And he felt physically bruised and battered, as if he had been beaten with actual rods instead of stinging words; but he was not yet defeated.

'Mrs Lannithorne, what do you wish me to understand from all this. Do you forbid Ruth and me to marry – is that it?'

She looked at him dubiously. She felt so fiercely the things she had been saying that she could not feel them continuously. She, too, was exhausted.

Oliver Pickersgill had a fine head, candid eyes, a firm chin, strong capable hands. He was young, and the young know nothing, but it might be that there was the making of a man in him. If Ruth must marry, perhaps him as well as another. But she did not trust her own judgment, even of such hands, such eyes, and such a chin. Oh, if the girls would only believe her, if they would only be content to trust the wisdom she had distilled from the bitterness of life! But the young know nothing, and believe only the lying voices in their own hearts!

'I wish you would see Ruth's father,' she said suddenly. 'I am prejudiced. I ought not to have to deal with these questions. I tell you, I pray Heaven none of them may marry – ever; but, just the same, they will! Go ask Peter Lannithorne if he thinks his daughter Ruth has a fighting chance for happiness as your wife. Let him settle it. I have told you what I think. I am done.'

'I shall be very glad to talk with Ruth's father about the matter,' said Oliver with a certain emphasis on *father*. 'Perhaps he and I shall be able to understand each other better. Good-morning, Mrs Lannithorne!'

III

Oliver Pickersgill Senior turned his swivel-chair about, bit hard on the end of his cigar, and stared at his only son.

'What's that?' he said abruptly. 'Say that again.'

Oliver Junior winced, not so much at the words as at his father's face.

'I want to marry Ruth Lannithorne,' he repeated steadily.

There was a silence. The elder Pickersgill looked at his son long and hard from under lowered brows. Oliver had never seen his father look at him like that before: as if he were a rank outsider, some detached person whose doings were to be scrutinized coldly and critically, and judged on their merits. It is a hard hour for a beloved child when he first sees that look in heretofore indulgent parental eyes. Young Oliver felt a weight at his heart, but he sat the straighter, and did not flinch before the appraising glance.

'So you want to marry Peter Lannithorne's daughter, do you? Well, now what is there in the idea of marrying a jail-bird's child that you find especially attractive?'

'Of course I might say that I've seen something of business men in this town, Ross, say, and Worcester, and Jim Stone, and that if it came to a choice between their methods and Lannithorne's, his were the squarer, for he settled up, and is paying the price besides. But I don't know that there's any use saying that. I don't want to marry any of their daughters – and you wouldn't want me to. You know what Ruth Lannithorne is as well as I do. If there's a girl in town that's finer-grained, or smarter, or prettier, I'd like to have you point her out! And she has a sense of honor like a man's. I don't know another girl like her in that. She knows what's fair,' said the young man.

Mr Pickersgill's face relaxed a little. Oliver was making a good argument with no mushiness about it, and he had a long-settled habit of appreciating Ollie's arguments.

'She knows what's fair, does she? Then what does she say about marrying you?'

'She says she won't marry anybody who doesn't respect her father as she does!'

At this the parent grinned a little, grimly it is true, but appreciatively. He looked past Oliver's handsome, boyish head, out of the window, and was silent for a time. When he spoke, it was gravely, not angrily.

'Oliver, you're young. The things I'm as sure of as two and two, you don't yet believe at all. Probably you won't believe 'em if I put them to you, but it's up to me to do it.

13   The Preliminaries

Understand, I'm not getting angry and doing the heavy father over this. I'm just telling you how some things are in this world, – facts, like gravitation and atmospheric pressure. Ruth Lannithorne is a good girl, I don't doubt. This world is chuck full of good girls. It makes *some* difference which one of 'em you marry, but not nearly so much difference as you think it does. What matters, from forty on, for the rest of your life, is the kind of inheritance you've given your children. You don't know it yet, but the thing that's laid on men and women to do is to give their children as good an inheritance as they can. Take it from me that this is Gospel truth, can't you? Your mother and I have done the best we can for you and your sisters. You come from good stock, and by that I mean honest blood. You've got to pass it on untainted. Now – hold on!' he held up a warning hand as Oliver was about to interrupt hotly. 'Wait till I'm through – and then think it over. I'm not saying that Peter Lannithorne's blood isn't as good as much that passes for untainted, or that Ruth isn't a fine girl. I'm only telling you this: when first you look into your son's face, every failing of your own will rise up to haunt you because you will wish for nothing on God's earth so much as that that boy shall have a fair show in life and be a better man than you. You will thank Heaven for every good thing you know of in your blood and in your wife's, and you will regret every meanness, every weakness, that he may inherit, more than you knew it was in you to regret anything. Do you suppose when that hour comes to you that you'll want to remember his grandfather was a convict? How will you face that down?'

Young Oliver's face was pale. He had never thought of things like this. He made no response for a while. At last he asked, –

'What kind of a man is Peter Lannithorne?'

'Eh? What kind of – ? Oh, well, as men go, there have been worse ones. You know how he came to get sent up. He speculated, and he borrowed some of another man's money without asking, for twenty-four hours, to protect his speculation. He didn't lose it, either! There's a point where his case differs from most. He pulled the thing off and made enough to keep his family going in decent comfort, and he paid the other money back; but they concluded to make an example of him, so they sent him up. It was just, yes, and he said so himself. At the same time there are a great many more dishonest men out of prison than Peter Lannithorne, though he is in it. I meet 'em every day, and I ought to know. But that's not the point. As you said yourself, you don't want to marry their daughters. Heaven forbid that you should! You want to marry his daughter. And he was weak. He was tempted and fell – and got found out. He is a convict, and the taint sticks. The Lord knows why the stain of unsuccessful dishonesty should stick longer than the stain of successful dishonesty. I don't. But we know it does. That is the way things are. Why not marry where there is no taint?'

'Father – ?'

'Yes, Ollie.'

'Father, see here. He was weak and gave way – *once*! Are there any men in the world who haven't given way at least *once* about something or other? – are there, father?'

There was a note of anguish in the boy's voice. Perhaps he was being pushed too far. Oliver Pickersgill Senior cleared his throat, paused, and at last answered sombrely, –

'God knows, Ollie. I don't. I won't say there are.'

'Well, then – '

'See here!' his father interrupted sharply. 'Of course I see your argument. I won't meet it. I shan't try. It doesn't change my mind even if it is a good argument. We'll never get anywhere, arguing along those lines. I'll propose something else. Suppose you go ask Peter Lannithorne whether you shall marry his daughter or not. Yes, ask him. He knows what's what as well as the next man. Ask Peter Lannithorne what a man wants in the family of the woman he marries.'

There was a note of finality in the older man's voice. Ollie recognized it drearily. All roads led to Lannithorne, it seemed. He rose, oppressed with the sense that henceforward life was going to be full of unforeseen problems; that things which, from afar, looked simple, and easy, and happy, were going to prove quite otherwise. Mrs Lannithorne had angered rather than frightened him, and he had held his own with her; but this was his very own father who was piling the load on his shoulders and filling his heart with terror of the future. What was it, after all, this adventure of the married life whereof these seasoned travelers spoke so dubiously? Could it really be that it was not the divine thing it seemed when he and Ruth looked into each other's eyes?

He crossed the floor dejectedly, with the step of an older man, but at the door he shook himself and looked back.

'Say, dad!'

'Yes, Ollie.'

'Everybody is so terribly depressing about this thing, it almost scares me. Aren't there really any happy times for married people, ever? You and Mrs Lannithorne make me feel there aren't; but somehow I have a hunch that Ruth and I know best! Own up now! Are you and mother miserable? You never looked it!'

His father surveyed him with an expression too wistful to be complacent. Ah, those broad young shoulders that must be fitted to the yoke! Yet for what other end was their strength given them? Each man must take his turn.

'It's not a soft snap. I don't know anything worth while that is. But there are compensations. You'll see what some of them are when your boys begin to grow up.'

IV

Across Oliver's young joy fell the shadow of fear. If, as his heart told him, there was nothing to be afraid of, why were his elders thus cautious and terrified? He felt himself affected by their alarms all the more potently because his understanding of them was vague. He groped his way in fog. How much ought he to be influenced by Mrs Lannithorne's passionate protests and his father's stern warnings? He realized all at once that the admonitory attitude of age to youth is rooted deep in immortal necessity. Like most lads, he had never thought of it before save as an unpleasant parental habit. But fear changes the point of view, and Oliver had begun to be afraid.

13 The Preliminaries

Then again, before him loomed the prospect of his interview with Peter Lannithorne. This was a very concrete unpleasantness. Hang it all! Ruth was worth any amount of trouble, but still it was a tough thing to have to go down to the state capital and seek one's future father-in-law in his present boarding-place! One oughtn't to have to plough through that particular kind of difficulty on such an errand. Dimly he felt that the path to the Most Beautiful should be rose-lined and soft to the feet of the approaching bridegroom. But, apparently, that wasn't the way such paths were laid out. He resented this bitterly, but he set his jaws and proceeded to make his arrangements.

It was not difficult to compass the necessary interview. He knew a man who knew the warden intimately. It was quickly arranged that he was to see Peter Lannithorne in the prison library, quite by himself.

Oliver dragged himself to that conference by the sheer strength of his developing will. Every fibre of his being seemed to protest and hold back. Consequently he was not in the happiest imaginable temper for important conversation.

The prison library was a long, narrow room, with bookcases to the ceiling on one side and windows to the ceiling on the other. There were red geraniums on brackets up the sides of the windows, and a canary's cage on a hook gave the place a false air of domesticity, contradicted by the barred sash. Beneath, there was a window-seat, and here Oliver Pickersgill awaited Lannithorne's coming.

Ollie did not know what he expected the man to be like, but his irritated nerves were prepared to resent and dislike him, whatever he might prove. He held himself rigidly as he waited, and he could feel the muscles of his face setting themselves into hard lines.

When the door opened and some one approached him, he rose stiffly and held out his hand like an automaton.

'How do you do, Mr Lannithorne? I am Oliver Pickersgill, and I have come – I have come – '

His voice trailed off into silence, for he had raised his eyes perfunctorily to Peter Lannithorne's face, and the things printed there made him forget himself and the speech he had prepared.

He saw a massive head topping an insignificant figure. A fair man was Peter Lannithorne, with heavy reddish hair, a bulging forehead, and deep-set gray eyes with a light behind them. His features were irregular and unnoticeable, but the sum-total of them gave the impression of force. It was a strong face, yet you could see that it had once been a weak one. It was a tremendously human face, a face like a battle-ground, scarred and seamed and lined with the stress of invisible conflicts. There was so much of struggle and thought set forth in it that one involuntarily averted one's gaze. It did not seem decent to inspect so much of the soul of a man as was shown in Peter Lannithorne's countenance. Not a triumphant face at all, and yet there was peace in it. Somehow, the man had achieved something, arrived somewhere, and the record of the journey was piteous and terrible. Yet it drew the eyes in awe as much as in wonder, and in pity not at all!

These things were startlingly clear to Oliver. He saw them with a vividness not to be overestimated. This was a prison. This might be a convict, but he was a man. He was a man who knew things and would share his knowledge. His wisdom was as patent as his suffering, and both stirred young Oliver's heart to its depths. His pride, his irritation, his rigidity vanished in a flash. His fears were in abeyance. Only his wonder and his will to learn were left.

Lannithorne did not take the offered hand, yet did not seem to ignore it. He came forward quietly and sat down on the window-seat, half turning so that he and Oliver faced each other.

'Oliver Pickersgill?' he said. 'Then you are Oliver Pickersgill's son.'

'Yes, Mr Lannithorne. My father sent me here – my father, and Mrs Lannithorne, and Ruth.'

At his daughter's name a light leaped into Peter Lannithorne's eyes that made him look even more acutely and painfully alive than before.

'And what have you to do with Ruth, or her mother?' the man asked.

Here it was! The great moment was facing him. Oliver caught his breath, then went straight to the point.

'I want to marry your daughter, Mr Lannithorne. We love each other very much. But – I haven't quite persuaded her, and I haven't persuaded Mrs Lannithorne and my father at all. They don't see it. They say things – all sorts of dreadful things,' said the boy. 'You would think they had never been young and – cared for anybody. They seem to have forgotten what it means. They try to make us afraid – just plain afraid. How am I to suppose that they know best about Ruth and me?'

Lannithorne looked across at the young man long and fixedly. Then a great kindliness came into his beaten face, and a great comprehension. Oliver, meeting his eyes, had a sudden sense of shelter, and felt his haunting fears allayed. It was absurd and incredible, but this man made him feel comfortable, yes, and eager to talk things over.

'They all said you would know. They sent me to you.'

Peter Lannithorne smiled faintly to himself. He had not left his sense of humor behind him in the outside world.

'They sent you to me, did they, boy? And what did they tell you to ask me? They had different motives, I take it.'

'Rather! Ruth said you were the best man she had ever known, and if you said it was right for her to marry me, she would. Mrs Lannithorne said I should ask you if you thought Ruth had a fighting chance for happiness with me. She doesn't want Ruth to marry anybody, you see. My father – my father' – Oliver's voice shook with his consciousness of the cruelty of what was to follow, but he forced himself to steadiness and got the words out – 'said I was to ask you what a man wants in the family of the woman he marries. He said you knew what was what, and I should ask you what to do.'

13 The Preliminaries

Lannithorne's face was very grave, and his troubled gaze sought the floor. Oliver, convicted of brutality and conscience-smitten, hurried on, 'And now that I've seen you, I want to ask you a few things for myself, Mr Lannithorne. I – I believe you know.'

The man looked up and held up an arresting hand. 'Let me clear the way for you a little,' he said. 'It was a hard thing for you to come and seek me out in this place. I like your coming. Most young men would have refused, or come in a different spirit. I want you to understand that if in Ruth's eyes, and my wife's, and your father's, my counsel has value, it is because they think I see things as they are. And that means, first of all, that I know myself for a man who committed a crime, and is paying the penalty. I am satisfied to be paying it. As I see justice, it is just. So, if I seem to wince at your necessary allusions to it, that is part of the price. I don't want you to feel that you are blundering or hurting me more than is necessary. You have got to lay the thing before me as it is.'

Something in the words, in the dry, patient manner, in the endurance of the man's face, touched Oliver to the quick and made him feel all manner of new things: such as a sense of the moral poise of the universe, acquiescence in its retributions, and a curious pride, akin to Ruth's own, in a man who could meet him after this fashion, in this place.

'Thank you, Mr Lannithorne,' he said. 'You see, it's this way, sir. Mrs Lannithorne says – '

And he went on eagerly to set forth his new problems as they had been stated to him.

'Well, there you have it,' he concluded at last. 'For myself, the things they said opened chasms and abysses. Mrs Lannithorne seemed to think I would hurt Ruth. My father seemed to think Ruth would hurt me. *Is* married life something to be afraid of? When I look at Ruth, I am sure everything is all right. It may be miserable for other people, but how could it be miserable for Ruth and me?'

Peter Lannithorne looked at the young man long and thoughtfully again before he answered. Oliver felt himself measured and estimated, but not found wanting. When the man spoke, it was slowly and with difficulty, as if the habit of intimate, convincing speech had been so long disused that the effort was painful. The sentences seemed wrung out of him, one by one.

'They haven't the point of view,' he said. 'It is life that is the great adventure. Not love, not marriage, not business. They are just chapters in the book. The main thing is to take the road fearlessly, – to have courage to live one's life.'

'Courage?'

Lannithorne nodded.

'That is the great word. Don't you see what ails your father's point of view, and my wife's? One wants absolute security in one way for Ruth; the other wants absolute security in another way for you. And security – why, it's just the one thing a human being can't have, the thing that's the damnation of him if he gets it! The reason it is so hard for a rich man to enter the kingdom of Heaven is that he has that false sense of security. To demand it just disintegrates a man. I don't know why. It does.'

Oliver shook his head uncertainly.

'I don't quite follow you, sir. Oughtn't one to try to be safe?'

'One ought to try, yes. That is common prudence. But the point is that, whatever you do or get, you aren't after all secure. There is no such condition, and the harder you demand it, the more risk you run. So it is up to a man to take all reasonable precautions about his money, or his happiness, or his life, and trust the rest. What every man in the world is looking for is the sense of having the mastery over life. But I tell you, boy, there is only one thing that really gives it!'

'And that is – ?'

Lannithorne hesitated perceptibly. For the thing he was about to tell this undisciplined lad was his most precious possession; it was the piece of wisdom for which he had paid with the years of his life. No man parts lightly with such knowledge.

'It comes,' he said, with an effort, 'with the knowledge of our power to endure. That's it. *You are safe only when you can stand everything that can happen to you.* Then and then only! Endurance is the measure of a man.'

Oliver's heart swelled within him as he listened, and his face shone, for these words found his young soul where it lived. The chasms and abysses in his path suddenly vanished, and the road lay clear again, winding uphill, winding down, but always lit for Ruth and him by the light in each other's eyes. For surely neither Ruth nor he could ever fail in courage!

'Sometimes I think it is harder to endure what we deserve, like me,' said Lannithorne, 'than what we don't. I was afraid, you see, afraid for my wife and all of them. Anyhow, take my word for it. Courage is security. There is no other kind.'

'Then – Ruth and I – '

'Ruth is the core of my heart!' said Lannithorne thickly. 'I would rather die than have her suffer more than she must. But she must take her chances like the rest. It is the law of things. If you know yourself fit for her, and feel reasonably sure you can take care of her, you have a right to trust the future. Myself, I believe there is Some One to trust it to. As for the next generation, God and the mothers look after that! You may tell your father so from me. And you may tell my wife I think there is the stuff of a man in you. And Ruth – tell Ruth – '

He could not finish. Oliver reached out and found his hand and wrung it hard.

'I'll tell her, sir, that I feel about her father as she does! And that he approves of our venture. And I'll tell myself, always, what you've just told me. Why, it *must* be true! You needn't be afraid I'll forget – when the time comes for remembering.'

Finding his way out of the prison yard a few minutes later, Oliver looked, unseeing, at the high walls that soared against the blue spring sky. He could not realize them, there was such a sense of light, air, space, in his spirit.

Apparently, he was just where he had been an hour before, with all his battles still to fight, but really he knew they were already won, for his weapon had been forged and put in his hand. He left his boyhood behind him as he passed that stern threshold, for the last hour had made a man of him, and a prisoner had given him the master-key that opens every door.

14

Araby

(1914)

James Joyce

North Richmond Street, being blind, was a quiet street except at the hour when the Christian Brothers' School set the boys free. An uninhabited house of two storeys stood at the blind end, detached from its neighbours in a square ground. The other houses of the street, conscious of decent lives within them, gazed at one another with brown imperturbable faces.

The former tenant of our house, a priest, had died in the back drawing-room. Air, musty from having been long enclosed, hung in all the rooms, and the waste room behind the kitchen was littered with old useless papers. Among these I found a few paper-covered books, the pages of which were curled and damp: *The Abbot*, by Walter Scott, *The Devout Communicant* and *The Memoirs of Vidocq*. I liked the last best because its leaves were yellow. The wild garden behind the house contained a central apple-tree and a few straggling bushes under one of which I found the late tenant's rusty bicycle-pump. He had been a very charitable priest; in his will he had left all his money to institutions and the furniture of his house to his sister.

When the short days of winter came dusk fell before we had well eaten our dinners. When we met in the street the houses had grown sombre. The space of sky above us was the colour of ever-changing violet and towards it the lamps of the street lifted their feeble lanterns. The cold air stung us and we played till our bodies glowed. Our shouts echoed in the silent street. The career of our play brought us through the dark muddy lanes behind the houses where we ran the gauntlet of the rough tribes from the cottages, to the back doors of the dark dripping gardens where odours arose from the ashpits, to the dark odorous stables where a coachman smoothed and combed the horse or shook music from the buckled harness. When we returned to the street light from the kitchen windows had filled the areas. If my uncle was seen turning the corner we hid in the shadow until we had seen him safely housed. Or if Mangan's sister came out on the doorstep to call her brother in to his tea we watched her from our shadow peer up and down the street. We waited to see whether she would remain or go in and, if she remained, we left our shadow and walked up to Mangan's steps resignedly. She was waiting for us, her figure defined by the light from the half-opened door. Her brother always teased her before he obeyed and I stood by the railings looking at her. Her dress swung as she moved her body and the soft rope of her hair tossed from side to side.

Every morning I lay on the floor in the front parlour watching her door. The blind was pulled down to within an inch of the sash so that I could not be seen. When she came out on the doorstep my heart leaped. I ran to the hall, seized my books and followed her. I kept her brown figure always in my eye and, when we came near the point at which our ways diverged, I quickened my pace and passed her. This happened morning after morning. I had never spoken to her, except for a few casual words, and yet her name was like a summons to all my foolish blood.

Her image accompanied me even in places the most hostile to romance. On Saturday evenings when my aunt went marketing I had to go to carry some of the parcels. We walked through the flaring streets, jostled by drunken men and bargaining women, amid the curses of labourers, the shrill litanies of shop-boys who stood on guard by the barrels of pigs' cheeks, the nasal chanting of street-singers, who sang a *come-all-you* about O'Donovan Rossa, or a ballad about the troubles in our native land. These noises converged in a single sensation of life for me: I imagined that I bore my chalice safely through a throng of foes. Her name sprang to my lips at moments in strange prayers and praises which I myself did not understand. My eyes were often full of tears (I could not tell why) and at times a flood from my heart seemed to pour itself out into my bosom. I thought little of the future. I did not know whether I would ever speak to her or not or, if I spoke to her, how I could tell her of my confused adoration. But my body was like a harp and her words and gestures were like fingers running upon the wires.

One evening I went into the back drawing-room in which the priest had died. It was a dark rainy evening and there was no sound in the house. Through one of the broken panes I heard the rain impinge upon the earth, the fine incessant needles of water playing in the sodden beds. Some distant lamp or lighted window gleamed below me. I was thankful that I could see so little. All my senses seemed to desire to veil themselves and, feeling that I was about to slip from them, I pressed the palms of my hands together until they trembled, murmuring: *O love! O love!* many times.

At last she spoke to me. When she addressed the first words to me I was so confused that I did not know what to answer. She asked me was I going to *Araby*. I forget whether I answered yes or no. It would be a splendid bazaar, she said; she would love to go.

– And why can't you? I asked.

While she spoke she turned a silver bracelet round and round her wrist. She could not go, she said, because there would be a retreat that week in her convent. Her brother and two other boys were fighting for their caps and I was alone at the railings. She held one of the spikes, bowing her head towards me. The light from the lamp opposite our door caught the white curve of her neck, lit up her hair that rested there and, falling, lit up the hand upon the railing. It fell over one side of her dress and caught the white border of a petticoat, just visible as she stood at ease.

– It's well for you, she said.

– If I go, I said, I will bring you something.

What innumerable follies laid waste my waking and sleeping thoughts after that evening! I wished to annihilate the tedious intervening days. I chafed against the work of school. At night in my bedroom and by day in the classroom her image came between me and the page I strove to read. The syllables of the word *Araby* were called to me through the silence in which my soul luxuriated and cast an Eastern enchantment over me. I asked for leave to go to the bazaar on Saturday night. My aunt was surprised and hoped it was not some Freemason affair. I answered few questions in class. I watched my master's face pass from amiability to sternness; he hoped I was not beginning to idle. I could not call my wandering thoughts together. I had hardly any patience with the serious work of life which, now that it stood between me and my desire, seemed to me child's play, ugly monotonous child's play.

On Saturday morning I reminded my uncle that I wished to go to the bazaar in the evening. He was fussing at the hallstand, looking for the hat-brush, and answered me curtly:

– Yes, boy, I know.

As he was in the hall I could not go into the front parlour and lie at the window. I left the house in bad humour and walked slowly towards the school. The air was pitilessly raw and already my heart misgave me.

When I came home to dinner my uncle had not yet been home. Still it was early. I sat staring at the clock for some time and, when its ticking began to irritate me, I left the room. I mounted the staircase and gained the upper part of the house. The high cold empty gloomy rooms liberated me and I went from room to room singing. From the front window I saw my companions playing below in the street. Their cries reached me weakened and indistinct and, leaning my forehead against the cool glass, I looked over at the dark house where she lived. I may have stood there for an hour, seeing nothing but the brown-clad figure cast by my imagination, touched discreetly by the lamplight at the curved neck, at the hand upon the railings and at the border below the dress.

When I came downstairs again I found Mrs Mercer sitting at the fire. She was an old garrulous woman, a pawnbroker's widow, who collected used stamps for some pious purpose. I had to endure the gossip of the tea-table. The meal was prolonged beyond an hour and still my uncle did not come. Mrs Mercer stood up to go: she was sorry she couldn't wait any longer, but it was after eight o'clock and she did not like to be out late, as the night air was bad for her. When she had gone I began to walk up and down the room, clenching my fists. My aunt said:

– I'm afraid you may put off your bazaar for this night of Our Lord.

At nine o'clock I heard my uncle's latchkey in the halldoor. I heard him talking to himself and heard the hallstand rocking when it had received the weight of his overcoat. I could interpret these signs. When he was midway through his dinner I asked him to give me the money to go to the bazaar. He had forgotten.

– The people are in bed and after their first sleep now, he said.

I did not smile. My aunt said to him energetically:

– Can't you give him the money and let him go? You've kept him late enough as it is.

My uncle said he was very sorry he had forgotten. He said he believed in the old saying: *All work and no play makes Jack a dull boy*. He asked me where I was going and, when I had told him a second time he asked me did I know *The Arab's Farewell to his Steed*. When I left the kitchen he was about to recite the opening lines of the piece to my aunt.

I held a florin tightly in my hand as I strode down Buckingham Street towards the station. The sight of the streets thronged with buyers and glaring with gas recalled to me the purpose of my journey. I took my seat in a third-class carriage of a deserted train. After an intolerable delay the train moved out of the station slowly. It crept onward among ruinous houses and over the twinkling river. At Westland Row Station a crowd of people pressed to the carriage doors; but the porters moved them back, saying that it was a special train for the bazaar. I remained alone in the bare carriage. In a few minutes the train drew up beside an improvised wooden platform. I passed out on to the road and saw by the lighted dial of a clock that it was ten minutes to ten. In front of me was a large building which displayed the magical name.

I could not find any sixpenny entrance and, fearing that the bazaar would be closed, I passed in quickly through a turnstile, handing a shilling to a weary-looking man. I found myself in a big hall girdled at half its height by a gallery. Nearly all the stalls were closed and the greater part of the hall was in darkness. I recognised a silence like that which pervades a church after a service. I walked into the centre of the bazaar timidly. A few people were gathered about the stalls which were still open. Before a curtain, over which the words *Café Chantant* were written in coloured lamps, two men were counting money on a salver. I listened to the fall of the coins.

Remembering with difficulty why I had come I went over to one of the stalls and examined porcelain vases and flowered tea-sets. At the door of the stall a young lady was talking and laughing with two young gentlemen. I remarked their English accents and listened vaguely to their conversation.

– O, I never said such a thing!

– O, but you did!

– O, but I didn't!

– Didn't she say that?

– Yes. I heard her.

– O, there's a ... fib!

Observing me the young lady came over and asked me did I wish to buy anything. The tone of her voice was not encouraging; she seemed to have spoken to me out of a sense of duty. I looked humbly at the great jars that stood like eastern guards at either side of the dark entrance to the stall and murmured:

– No, thank you.

The young lady changed the position of one of the vases and went back to the two young men. They began to talk of the same subject. Once or twice the young lady glanced at me over her shoulder.

14   Araby

    I lingered before her stall, though I knew my stay was useless, to make my interest in her wares seem the more real. Then I turned away slowly and walked down the middle of the bazaar. I allowed the two pennies to fall against the sixpence in my pocket. I heard a voice call from one end of the gallery that the light was out. The upper part of the hall was now completely dark.

    Gazing up into the darkness I saw myself as a creature driven and derided by vanity; and my eyes burned with anguish and anger.

15

The Mark on the Wall

(1917)

Virginia Woolf

Perhaps it was the middle of January in the present year that I first looked up and saw the mark on the wall. In order to fix a date it is necessary to remember what one saw. So now I think of the fire; the steady film of yellow light upon the page of my book; the three chrysanthemums in the round glass bowl on the mantelpiece. Yes, it must have been the winter time, and we had just finished our tea, for I remember that I was smoking a cigarette when I looked up and saw the mark on the wall for the first time. I looked up through the smoke of my cigarette and my eye lodged for a moment upon the burning coals, and that old fancy of the crimson flag flapping from the castle tower came into my mind, and I thought of the cavalcade of red knights riding up the side of the black rock. Rather to my relief the sight of the mark interrupted the fancy, for it is an old fancy, an automatic fancy, made as a child perhaps. The mark was a small round mark, black upon the white wall, about six or seven inches above the mantelpiece.

How readily our thoughts swarm upon a new object, lifting it a little way, as ants carry a blade of straw so feverishly, and then leave it ... If that mark was made by a nail, it can't have been for a picture, it must have been for a miniature – the miniature of a lady with white powdered curls, powder-dusted cheeks, and lips like red carnations. A fraud of course, for the people who had this house before us would have chosen pictures in that way – an old picture for an old room. That is the sort of people they were – very interesting people, and I think of them so often, in such queer places, because one will never see them again, never know what happened next. They wanted to leave this house because they wanted to change their style of furniture, so he said, and he was in process of saying that in his opinion art should have ideas behind it when we were torn asunder, as one is torn from the old lady about to pour out tea and the young man about to hit the tennis ball in the back garden of the suburban villa as one rushes past in the train.

But as for that mark, I'm not sure about it; I don't believe it was made by a nail after all; it's too big, too round, for that. I might get up, but if I got up and looked at it, ten to one I shouldn't be able to say for certain; because once a thing's done, no one ever knows how it happened. Oh! dear me, the mystery of life! The inaccuracy of thought! The ignorance of humanity! To show how very little control of our possessions we have – what an accidental affair this living is after all our civilization – let me just count over a few of the things lost in one lifetime, beginning, for that seems always the most mysterious of losses – what cat would gnaw, what rat would nibble – three pale blue canisters of book-binding tools? Then there were the bird cages, the iron hoops, the steel skates, the Queen Anne coal-scuttle, the bagatelle board, the hand organ – all gone, and jewels, too. Opals and emeralds, they lie about the roots of turnips. What a scraping paring affair it is to be sure! The wonder is that I've any clothes on my back, that I sit surrounded by solid furniture at this moment. Why, if one wants to compare life to anything, one must liken it to being blown through the Tube at fifty miles an hour – landing at the other end without a single hairpin in one's hair! Shot out at the feet of God entirely naked! Tumbling head over heels in the asphodel meadows like brown paper parcels pitched down a shoot in the post office! With one's hair flying back like the tail of a race-horse. Yes, that seems to express the rapidity of life, the perpetual waste and repair; all so casual, all so haphazard ...

But after life. The slow pulling down of thick green stalks so that the cup of the flower, as it turns over, deluges one with purple and red light. Why, after all, should one not be born there as one is born here, helpless, speechless, unable to focus one's eyesight, groping at the roots of the grass, at the toes of the Giants? As for saying which are trees, and which are men and women, or whether there are such things, that one won't be in a condition to do for fifty years or so. There will be nothing but spaces of light and dark, intersected by thick stalks, and rather higher up perhaps, rose-shaped blots of an indistinct colour – dim pinks and blues – which will, as time goes on, become more definite, become – I don't know what ...

And yet that mark on the wall is not a hole at all. It may even be caused by some round black substance, such as a small rose leaf, left over from the summer, and I, not being a very vigilant housekeeper – look at the dust on the mantelpiece, for example, the dust which, so they say, buried Troy three times over, only fragments of pots utterly refusing annihilation, as one can believe.

The tree outside the window taps very gently on the pane ... I want to think quietly, calmly, spaciously, never to be interrupted, never to have to rise from my chair, to slip easily from one thing to another, without any sense of hostility, or obstacle. I want to sink deeper and deeper, away from the surface, with its hard separate facts. To steady myself, let me catch hold of the first idea that passes ... Shakespeare ... Well, he will do as well as another. A man who sat himself solidly in an arm-chair, and looked into the fire, so – A shower of ideas fell perpetually from some very high Heaven down through his mind. He leant his forehead on his hand, and people, looking in through the open door, – for this scene is supposed to take place on a summer's evening – But how dull this is, this historical fiction! It doesn't interest me at all. I wish I could hit upon a pleasant track of thought, a track indirectly reflecting credit upon myself, for those are the pleasantest thoughts, and very frequent even in the minds of modest mouse-coloured people, who believe genuinely that they dislike to hear their own praises. They are not thoughts directly praising oneself; that is the beauty of them; they are thoughts like this:

'And then I came into the room. They were discussing botany. I said how I'd seen a flower growing on a dust heap on the site of an old house in Kingsway. The seed, I said, must have been sown in the reign of Charles the First. What flowers grew in the reign of Charles the First?' I asked – (but I don't remember the answer). Tall flowers with purple tassels to them perhaps. And so it goes on. All the time I'm dressing up the figure of myself in my own mind, lovingly, stealthily, not openly adoring it, for if I did that, I should catch myself out, and stretch my hand at once for a book in self-protection. Indeed, it is curious how instinctively one protects the image of oneself from idolatry or any other handling that could make it ridiculous, or too unlike the original to be believed in any longer. Or is it not so very curious after all? It is a matter of great importance. Suppose the looking glass smashes, the image disappears, and the romantic figure with the green of forest depths all about it is there no longer, but only that shell of a person which is seen by other people – what an airless, shallow, bald, prominent world it becomes! A world not to be lived in. As we face each other in omnibuses and underground railways we are looking into the mirror; that accounts for the vagueness, the gleam of glassiness, in our eyes. And the novelists in future will realize more and more the importance of these reflections, for of course there is not one reflection but an almost infinite number; those are the depths they will explore, those the phantoms they will pursue, leaving the description of reality more and more out of their stories, taking a knowledge of it for granted, as the Greeks did and Shakespeare perhaps – but these generalizations are very worthless. The military sound of the word is enough. It recalls leading articles, cabinet ministers – a whole class of things indeed which as a child one thought the thing itself, the standard thing, the real thing, from which one could not depart save at the risk of nameless damnation. Generalizations bring back somehow Sunday in London, Sunday afternoon walks, Sunday luncheons, and also ways of speaking of the dead, clothes, and habits – like the habit of sitting all together in one room until a certain hour, although nobody liked it. There was a rule for everything. The rule for tablecloths at that particular period was that they should be made of tapestry with little yellow compartments marked upon them, such as you may see in photographs of the carpets in the corridors of the royal palaces. Tablecloths of a different kind were not real tablecloths. How shocking, and yet how wonderful it was to discover that these real things, Sunday luncheons, Sunday walks, country houses, and tablecloths were not entirely real, were indeed half phantoms, and the damnation which visited the disbeliever in them was only a sense of illegitimate freedom. What now takes the place of those things I wonder, those real standard things? Men perhaps, should you be a woman; the masculine point of view which governs our lives, which sets the standard, which establishes Whitaker's Table of Precedency, which has become, I suppose, since the war half a phantom to many men and women, which soon, one may hope, will be laughed into the dustbin where the phantoms go, the mahogany sideboards and the Landseer prints, Gods and Devils, Hell and so forth, leaving us all with an intoxicating sense of illegitimate freedom – if freedom exists ...

In certain lights that mark on the wall seems actually to project from the wall. Nor is it entirely circular. I cannot be sure, but it seems to cast a perceptible shadow, suggesting that if I ran my finger down that strip of the wall it would, at a certain point, mount and descend a small tumulus, a smooth tumulus like those barrows on the South Downs which are, they say, either tombs or camps. Of the two I should prefer them to be tombs, desiring melancholy like most English people, and finding it natural at the end of a walk to think of the bones stretched beneath the turf ... There must be some book about it. Some antiquary must have dug up those bones and given them a name ... What sort of a man is an antiquary, I wonder? Retired colonels for the most part, I daresay, leading parties of aged labourers to the top here, examining clods of earth and stone, and getting into correspondence with the neighbouring clergy, which, being opened at breakfast time, gives them a feeling of importance, and the comparison of arrow-heads necessitates cross-country journeys to the county towns, an agreeable necessity both to them and to their elderly wives, who wish to make plum jam or to clean out the study, and have every reason for keeping that great question of the camp or the tomb in perpetual suspension, while the Colonel himself feels agreeably philosophic in accumulating evidence on both sides of the question. It is true that he does finally incline to believe in the camp; and, being opposed, indites a pamphlet which he is about to read at the quarterly meeting of the local society when a stroke lays him low, and his last conscious thoughts are not of wife or child, but of the camp and that arrowhead there, which is now in the case at the local museum, together with the foot of a Chinese murderess, a handful of Elizabethan nails, a great many Tudor clay pipes, a piece of Roman pottery, and the wine-glass that Nelson drank out of – proving I really don't know what.

No, no, nothing is proved, nothing is known. And if I were to get up at this very moment and ascertain that the mark on the wall is really – what shall we say? – the head of a gigantic old nail, driven in two hundred years ago, which has now, owing to the patient attrition of many generations of housemaids, revealed its head above the coat of paint, and is taking its first view of modern life in the sight of a white-walled fire-lit room, what should I gain? – Knowledge? Matter for further speculation? I can think sitting still as well as standing up. And what is knowledge? What are our learned men save the descendants of witches and hermits who crouched in caves and in woods brewing herbs, interrogating shrew-mice and writing down the language of the stars? And the less we honour them as our superstitions dwindle and our respect for beauty and health of mind increases ... Yes, one could imagine a very pleasant world. A quiet, spacious world, with the flowers so red and blue in the open fields. A world without professors or specialists or house-keepers with the profiles of policemen, a world which one could slice with one's thought as a fish slices the water with his fin, grazing the stems of the water-lilies, hanging suspended over nests of white sea eggs ... How peaceful it is down here, rooted in the centre of the world and gazing up through the grey waters, with their sudden gleams of light, and their reflections – if it were not for Whitaker's Almanack – if it were not for the Table of Precedency!

I must jump up and see for myself what that mark on the wall really is – a nail, a rose-leaf, a crack in the wood?

Here is nature once more at her old game of self-preservation. This train of thought, she perceives, is threatening mere waste of energy, even some collision with reality, for who will ever be able to lift a finger against Whitaker's Table of Precedency? The Archbishop of Canterbury is followed by the Lord High Chancellor; the Lord High

Chancellor is followed by the Archbishop of York. Everybody follows somebody, such is the philosophy of Whitaker; and the great thing is to know who follows whom. Whitaker knows, and let that, so Nature counsels, comfort you, instead of enraging you; and if you can't be comforted, if you must shatter this hour of peace, think of the mark on the wall.

I understand Nature's game – her prompting to take action as a way of ending any thought that threatens to excite or to pain. Hence, I suppose, comes our slight contempt for men of action – men, we assume, who don't think. Still, there's no harm in putting a full stop to one's disagreeable thoughts by looking at a mark on the wall.

Indeed, now that I have fixed my eyes upon it, I feel that I have grasped a plank in the sea; I feel a satisfying sense of reality which at once turns the two Archbishops and the Lord High Chancellor to the shadows of shades. Here is something definite, something real. Thus, waking from a midnight dream of horror, one hastily turns on the light and lies quiescent, worshipping the chest of drawers, worshipping solidity, worshipping reality, worshipping the impersonal world which is a proof of some existence other than ours. That is what one wants to be sure of ... Wood is a pleasant thing to think about. It comes from a tree; and trees grow, and we don't know how they grow. For years and years they grow, without paying any attention to us, in meadows, in forests, and by the side of rivers – all things one likes to think about. The cows swish their tails beneath them on hot afternoons; they paint rivers so green that when a moorhen dives one expects to see its feathers all green when it comes up again. I like to think of the fish balanced against the stream like flags blown out; and of water-beetles slowly raising domes of mud upon the bed of the river. I like to think of the tree itself: first the close dry sensation of being wood; then the grinding of the storm; then the slow, delicious ooze of sap. I like to think of it, too, on winter's nights standing in the empty field with all leaves close-furled, nothing tender exposed to the iron bullets of the moon, a naked mast upon an earth that goes tumbling, tumbling, all night long. The song of birds must sound very loud and strange in June; and how cold the feet of insects must feel upon it, as they make laborious progresses up the creases of the bark, or sun themselves upon the thin green awning of the leaves, and look straight in front of them with diamond-cut red eyes ... One by one the fibres snap beneath the immense cold pressure of the earth, then the last storm comes and, falling, the highest branches drive deep into the ground again. Even so, life isn't done with; there are a million patient, watchful lives still for a tree, all over the world, in bedrooms, in ships, on the pavement, lining rooms, where men and women sit after tea, smoking cigarettes. It is full of peaceful thoughts, happy thoughts, this tree. I should like to take each one separately – but something is getting in the way ... Where was I? What has it all been about? A tree? A river? The Downs? Whitaker's Almanack? The fields of asphodel? I can't remember a thing. Everything's moving, falling, slipping, vanishing ... There is a vast upheaval of matter. Someone is standing over me and saying –

'I'm going out to buy a newspaper.'

'Yes?'

'Though it's no good buying newspapers ... Nothing ever happens. Curse this war; God damn this war! ... All the same, I don't see why we should have a snail on our wall.'

Ah, the mark on the wall! It was a snail.

16

The Interlopers

(1919)

Saki (Hector Hugh Munro)

In a forest of mixed growth somewhere on the eastern spurs of the Karpathians, a man stood one winter night watching and listening, as though he waited for some beast of the woods to come within the range of his vision, and, later, of his rifle. But the game for whose presence he kept so keen an outlook was none that figured in the sportsman's calendar as lawful and proper for the chase; Ulrich von Gradwitz patrolled the dark forest in quest of a human enemy.

    The forest lands of Gradwitz were of wide extent and well stocked with game; the narrow strip of precipitous woodland that lay on its outskirt was not remarkable for the game it harboured or the shooting it afforded, but it was the most jealously guarded of all its owner's territorial possessions. A famous law suit, in the days of his grandfather, had wrested it from the illegal possession of a neighbouring family of petty landowners; the dispossessed party had never acquiesced in the judgment of the Courts, and a long series of poaching affrays and similar scandals had embittered the relationships between the families for three generations. The neighbour feud had grown into a personal one since Ulrich had come to be head of his family; if there was a man in the world whom he detested and wished ill to it was Georg Znaeym, the inheritor of the quarrel and the tireless game-snatcher and raider of the disputed border-forest. The feud might, perhaps, have died down or been compromised if the personal ill-will of the two men had not stood in the way; as boys they had thirsted for one another's blood, as men each prayed that misfortune might fall on the other, and this wind-scourged winter night Ulrich had banded together his foresters to watch the dark forest, not in quest of four-footed quarry, but to keep a look-out for the prowling thieves whom he suspected of being afoot from across the land boundary. The roebuck, which usually kept in the sheltered hollows during a storm-wind, were running like driven things to-night, and there was movement and unrest among the creatures that were wont to sleep through the dark hours. Assuredly there was a disturbing element in the forest, and Ulrich could guess the quarter from whence it came.

He strayed away by himself from the watchers whom he had placed in ambush on the crest of the hill, and wandered far down the steep slopes amid the wild tangle of undergrowth, peering through the tree trunks and listening through the whistling and skirling of the wind and the restless beating of the branches for sight and sound of the marauders. If only on this wild night, in this dark, lone spot, he might come across Georg Znaeym, man to man, with none to witness – that was the wish that was uppermost in his thoughts. And as he stepped round the trunk of a huge beech he came face to face with the man he sought.

The two enemies stood glaring at one another for a long silent moment. Each had a rifle in his hand, each had hate in his heart and murder uppermost in his mind. The chance had come to give full play to the passions of a lifetime. But a man who has been brought up under the code of a restraining civilisation cannot easily nerve himself to shoot down his neighbour in cold blood and without word spoken, except for an offence against his hearth and honour. And before the moment of hesitation had given way to action a deed of Nature's own violence overwhelmed them both. A fierce shriek of the storm had been answered by a splitting crash over their heads, and ere they could leap aside a mass of falling beech tree had thundered down on them. Ulrich von Gradwitz found himself stretched on the ground, one arm numb beneath him and the other held almost as helplessly in a tight tangle of forked branches, while both legs were pinned beneath the fallen mass. His heavy shooting-boots had saved his feet from being crushed to pieces, but if his fractures were not as serious as they might have been, at least it was evident that he could not move from his present position till some one came to release him. The descending twig had slashed the skin of his face, and he had to wink away some drops of blood from his eyelashes before he could take in a general view of the disaster. At his side, so near that under ordinary circumstances he could almost have touched him, lay Georg Znaeym, alive and struggling, but obviously as helplessly pinioned down as himself. All round them lay a thick-strewn wreckage of splintered branches and broken twigs.

Relief at being alive and exasperation at his captive plight brought a strange medley of pious thank-offerings and sharp curses to Ulrich's lips. Georg, who was nearly blinded with the blood which trickled across his eyes, stopped his struggling for a moment to listen, and then gave a short, snarling laugh.

'So you're not killed, as you ought to be, but you're caught, anyway,' he cried; 'caught fast. Ho, what a jest, Ulrich von Gradwitz snared in his stolen forest. There's real justice for you!'

And he laughed again, mockingly and savagely.

'I'm caught in my own forest-land,' retorted Ulrich. 'When my men come to release us you will wish, perhaps, that you were in a better plight than caught poaching on a neighbour's land, shame on you.'

Georg was silent for a moment; then he answered quietly:

'Are you sure that your men will find much to release? I have men, too, in the forest to-night, close behind me, and *they* will be here first and do the releasing. When they drag me out from under these damned branches it won't need much clumsiness on their part to roll this mass of trunk right over on the top of you. Your men will find you dead under a fallen beech tree. For form's sake I shall send my condolences to your family.'

'It is a useful hint,' said Ulrich fiercely. 'My men had orders to follow in ten minutes time, seven of which must have gone by already, and when they get me out – I will remember the hint. Only as you will have met your death poaching on my lands I don't think I can decently send any message of condolence to your family.'

'Good,' snarled Georg, 'good. We fight this quarrel out to the death, you and I and our foresters, with no cursed interlopers to come between us. Death and damnation to you, Ulrich von Gradwitz.'

'The same to you, Georg Znaeym, forest-thief, game-snatcher.'

Both men spoke with the bitterness of possible defeat before them, for each knew that it might be long before his men would seek him out or find him; it was a bare matter of chance which party would arrive first on the scene.

Both had now given up the useless struggle to free themselves from the mass of wood that held them down; Ulrich limited his endeavours to an effort to bring his one partially free arm near enough to his outer coat-pocket to draw out his wine-flask. Even when he had accomplished that operation it was long before he could manage the unscrewing of the stopper or get any of the liquid down his throat. But what a Heaven-sent draught it seemed! It was an open winter, and little snow had fallen as yet, hence the captives suffered less from the cold than might have been the case at that season of the year; nevertheless, the wine was warming and reviving to the wounded man, and he looked across with something like a throb of pity to where his enemy lay, just keeping the groans of pain and weariness from crossing his lips.

'Could you reach this flask if I threw it over to you?' asked Ulrich suddenly; 'there is good wine in it, and one may as well be as comfortable as one can. Let us drink, even if to-night one of us dies.'

'No, I can scarcely see anything; there is so much blood caked round my eyes,' said Georg, 'and in any case I don't drink wine with an enemy.'

Ulrich was silent for a few minutes, and lay listening to the weary screeching of the wind. An idea was slowly forming and growing in his brain, an idea that gained strength every time that he looked across at the man who was fighting so grimly against pain and exhaustion. In the pain and languor that Ulrich himself was feeling the old fierce hatred seemed to be dying down.

'Neighbour,' he said presently, 'do as you please if your men come first. It was a fair compact. But as for me, I've changed my mind. If my men are the first to come you shall be the first to be helped, as though you were my guest. We have quarrelled like devils all our lives over this stupid strip of forest, where the trees can't even stand upright in a breath of wind. Lying here to-night thinking I've come to think we've been rather fools; there are better things in life than getting the better of a boundary dispute. Neighbour, if you will help me to bury the old quarrel I – I will ask you to be my friend.'

Georg Znaeym was silent for so long that Ulrich thought, perhaps, he had fainted with the pain of his injuries. Then he spoke slowly and in jerks.

'How the whole region would stare and gabble if we rode into the market-square together. No one living can remember seeing a Znaeym and a von Gradwitz talking to one another in friendship. And what peace there would be among the forester folk if we ended our feud to-night. And if we choose to make peace among our people there is none other to interfere, no interlopers from outside ... You would come and keep the Sylvester night beneath my roof, and I would come and feast on some high day at your castle ... I would never fire a shot on your land, save when you invited me as a guest; and you should come and shoot with me down in the marshes where the wildfowl are. In all the countryside there are none that could hinder if we willed to make peace. I never thought to have wanted to do other than hate you all my life, but I think I have changed my mind about things too, this last half-hour. And you offered me your wine-flask ... Ulrich von Gradwitz, I will be your friend.'

For a space both men were silent, turning over in their minds the wonderful changes that this dramatic reconciliation would bring about. In the cold, gloomy forest, with the wind tearing in fitful gusts through the naked branches and whistling round the tree-trunks, they lay and waited for the help that would now bring release and succour to both parties. And each prayed a private prayer that his men might be the first to arrive, so that he might be the first to show honourable attention to the enemy that had become a friend.

Presently, as the wind dropped for a moment, Ulrich broke silence.

'Let's shout for help,' he said, 'in this lull our voices may carry a little way.'

'They won't carry far through the trees and undergrowth,' said Georg, 'but we can try. Together, then.'

The two raised their voices in a prolonged hunting call.

'Together again,' said Ulrich a few minutes later, after listening in vain for an answering halloo.

'I heard nothing but the pestilential wind,' said Georg hoarsely.

There was silence again for some minutes, and then Ulrich gave a joyful cry.

'I can see figures coming through the wood. They are following in the way I came down the hillside.'

Both men raised their voices in as loud a shout as they could muster.

'They hear us! They've stopped. Now they see us. They're running down the hill towards us,' cried Ulrich.

'How many of them are there?' asked Georg.

'I can't see distinctly,' said Ulrich; 'nine or ten.'

'Then they are yours,' said Georg; 'I had only seven out with me.'

'They are making all the speed they can, brave lads,' said Ulrich gladly.

16 The Interlopers

'Are they your men?' asked Georg. 'Are they your men?' he repeated impatiently as Ulrich did not answer.

'No,' said Ulrich with a laugh, the idiotic chattering laugh of a man unstrung with hideous fear.

'Who are they?' asked Georg quickly, straining his eyes to see what the other would gladly not have seen.

'*Wolves.*'

17

The Nightmare Room

(1921)

Arthur Conan Doyle

The sitting-room of the Masons was a very singular apartment. At one end it was furnished with considerable luxury. The deep sofas, the low, luxurious chairs, the voluptuous statuettes, and the rich curtains hanging from deep and ornamental screens of metal-work made a fitting frame for the lovely woman who was the mistress of the establishment. Mason, a young but wealthy man of affairs, had clearly spared no pains and no expense to meet every want and every whim of his beautiful wife. It was natural that he should do so, for she had given up much for his sake. The most famous dancer in France, the heroine of a dozen extraordinary romances, she had resigned her life of glittering pleasure in order to share the fate of the young American, whose austere ways differed so widely from her own. In all that wealth could buy he tried to make amends for what she had lost. Some might perhaps have thought it in better taste had he not proclaimed this fact – had he not even allowed it to be printed – but save for some personal peculiarities of the sort, his conduct was that of a husband who has never for an instant ceased to be a lover. Even the presence of spectators would not prevent the public exhibition of his overpowering affection.

But the room was singular. At first it seemed familiar, and yet a longer acquaintance made one realize its sinister peculiarities. It was silent – very silent. No footfall could be heard upon those rich carpets and heavy rugs. A struggle – even the fall of a body – would make no sound. It was strangely colourless also, in a light which seemed always subdued. Nor was it all furnished in equal taste. One would have said that when the young banker had lavished thousands upon this boudoir, this inner jewel-case for his precious possession, he had failed to count the cost and had suddenly been arrested by a threat to his own solvency. It was luxurious where it looked out upon the busy street below. At the farther side it was bare, spartan, and reflected rather the taste of a most ascetic man than of a pleasure-loving woman. Perhaps that was why she only came there for a few hours, sometimes two, sometimes four, in the day, but while she was there she lived intensely, and within this nightmare room Lucille Mason was a very different and a more dangerous woman than elsewhere.

17 The Nightmare Room

Dangerous – that was the word. Who could doubt it who saw her delicate figure stretched upon the great bearskin which draped the sofa. She was leaning upon her right elbow, her delicate but determined chin resting upon her hand, while her eyes, large and languishing, adorable but inexorable, stared out in front of her with a fixed intensity which had in it something vaguely terrible. It was a lovely face – a child's face, and yet Nature had placed there some subtle mark, some indefinable expression, which told that a devil lurked within. It had been noticed that dogs shrank from her, and that children screamed and ran from her caresses. There are instincts which are deeper than reason.

Upon this particular afternoon something had greatly moved her. A letter was in her hand, which she read and re-read with a tightening of those delicate little eyebrows and a grim setting of those delicious lips. Suddenly she started, and a shadow of fear softened the feline menace of her features. She raised herself upon her arm, and her eyes were fixed eagerly upon the door. She was listening intently – listening for something which she dreaded. For a moment a smile of relief played over her expressive face. Then with a look of horror she stuffed her letter into her dress. She had hardly done so before the door opened, and a young man came briskly into the room. It was Archie Mason, her husband – the man whom she had loved, the man for whom she had sacrificed her European fame, the man whom now she regarded as the one obstacle to a new and wonderful experience.

The American was a man about thirty, clean-shaven, athletic, dressed to perfection in a closely-cut suit, which outlined his perfect figure. He stood at the door with his arms folded, looking intently at his wife, with a face which might have been a handsome, sun-tinted mask save for those vivid eyes. She still leaned upon her elbow, but her eyes were fixed on his. There was something terrible in the silent exchange. Each interrogated the other, and each conveyed the thought that the answer to their question was vital. He might have been asking, 'What have you done?' She in her turn seemed to be saying, 'What do you know?' Finally, he walked forward, sat down upon the bearskin beside her, and taking her delicate ear gently between his fingers, turned her face towards his.

'Lucille,' he said, 'are you poisoning me?'

She sprang back from his touch with horror in her face and protests upon her lips. Too moved to speak, her surprise and her anger showed themselves rather in her darting hands and her convulsed features. She tried to rise, but his grasp tightened upon her wrist. Again he asked a question, but this time it had deepened in its terrible significance.

'Lucille, why are you poisoning me?'

'You are mad, Archie! Mad!' she gasped.

His answer froze her blood. With pale parted lips and blanched cheeks she could only stare at him in helpless silence, whilst he drew a small bottle from his pocket and held it before her eyes.

'It is from your jewel-case!' he cried.

Twice she tried to speak and failed. At last the words came slowly one by one from her contorted lips: 'At least I never used it.'

Again his hand sought his pocket. From it he drew a sheet of paper, which he unfolded and held before her.

'It is the certificate of Dr Angus. It shows the presence of twelve grains of antimony. I have also the evidence of Du Val, the chemist who sold it.'

Her face was terrible to look at. There was nothing to say. She could only lie with that fixed hopeless stare like some fierce creature in a fatal trap.

'Well?' he asked.

There was no answer save a movement of desperation and appeal.

'Why?' he said. 'I want to know why.' As he spoke his eye caught the edge of the letter which she had thrust into her bosom. In an instant he had snatched it. With a cry of despair she tried to regain it, but he held her off with one hand while his eyes raced over it.

'Campbell!' he gasped. 'It was Campbell!'

She had found her courage again. There was nothing more to conceal. Her face set hard and firm. Her eyes were deadly as daggers.

'Yes,' she said, 'it is Campbell.'

'My God! Campbell of all men!'

He rose and walked swiftly about the room. Campbell, the grandest man that he had ever known, a man whose whole life had been one long record of self-denial, of courage, of every quality which marks the chosen man. And yet, he, too, had fallen a victim to this siren, and had been dragged down to such a level that he had betrayed, in intention if not in actual deed, the man whose hand he shook in friendship. It was incredible – and yet here was the passionate, pleading letter imploring his wife to fly and share the fate of a penniless man. Every word of the letter showed that Campbell had at least no thought of Mason's death, which would have removed all difficulties. That devilish solution was the outcome of the deep and wicked brain which brooded within that perfect habitation.

Mason was a man in a million, a philosopher, a thinker, with a broad and tender sympathy for others. For an instant his soul had been submerged in his bitterness. He could for that brief period have slain both his wife and Campbell, and gone to his own death with the serene mind of a man who has done his plain duty. But already, as he paced the room, milder thoughts had begun to prevail. How could he blame Campbell? He knew the absolute witchery of this woman. It was not only her wonderful physical beauty. She had a unique power of seeming to take an interest in a man, in writhing into his inmost conscience, in penetrating those parts of his nature which were too sacred for the world, and in seeming to stimulate him towards ambition and even towards virtue. It was just there that the deadly cleverness of her net was shown. He remembered how it had been in his own case. She was free then – or so he thought – and he had been able to marry her. But suppose she had not been free. Suppose she had been married. And suppose she had taken possession of his soul in the same way. Would he have stopped there? Would he have been able to draw off with his unfulfilled longings? He was bound to admit that with all his New England strength he could not have done so. Why, then, should he feel so bitter with his unfortunate friend who was in the same position? It was pity and sympathy which filled his mind as he thought of Campbell.

And she? There she lay upon the sofa, a poor broken butterfly, her dreams dispersed, her plot detected, her future dark and perilous. Even for her, poisoner as she was, his heart relented. He knew something of her history. He knew her as a spoiled child from birth, untamed, unchecked, sweeping everything easily before her from her cleverness, her beauty, and her charm. She had never known an obstacle. And now one had risen across her path, and she had madly and wickedly tried to remove it. But if she had wished to remove it, was not that in itself a sign that he had been found wanting – that he was not the man who could bring her peace of mind and contentment of heart? He was too stern and self-contained for that sunny volatile nature. He was of the North, and she of the South, drawn strongly together for a time by the law of opposites, but impossible for permanent union. He should have seen to this – he should have understood it. It was on him, with his superior brain, that the responsibility for the situation lay. His heart softened towards her as it would to a little child which was in helpless trouble. For a time he had paced the room in silence, his lips compressed, his hands clenched till his nails had marked his palms. Now with a sudden movement he sat beside her and took her cold and inert hand in his. One thought beat in his brain. 'Is it chivalry, or is it weakness?' The question sounded in his ears, it framed itself before his eyes, he could almost fancy that it materialized itself and that he saw it in letters which all the world could read.

It had been a hard struggle, but he had conquered.

'You shall choose between us, dear,' he said. 'If really you are sure – *sure*, you understand – that Campbell could make you happy as a husband, I will not be the obstacle.'

'A divorce!' she gasped.

His hand closed upon the bottle of poison. 'You can call it that,' said he.

A new strange light shone in her eyes as she looked at him. This was a man who had been unknown to her. The hard, practical American had vanished. In his place she seemed to have a glimpse of a hero, and a saint, a man who could rise to an inhuman height of unselfish virtue. Both her hands were round that which held the fatal phial.

'Archie,' she cried, 'you could forgive me even that!'

He smiled at her. 'You are only a little wayward kiddie after all.'

Her arms were outstretched to him when there was a tap at the door, and the maid entered in the strange silent fashion in which all things moved in that nightmare room. There was a card on the tray. She glanced at it.

'Captain Campbell! I will not see him.'

Mason sprang to his feet.

'On the contrary, he is most welcome. Show him up this instant.'

A few minutes later a tall, sun-burned young soldier had been ushered into the room. He came forward with a smile upon his pleasant features, but as the door closed behind him, and the faces before him resumed their natural expressions, he paused irresolutely and glanced from one to the other.

'Well?' he asked.

Mason stepped forward and laid his hand upon his shoulder.

'I bear no ill-will,' he said.

'Ill-will?'

'Yes, I know all. But I might have done the same myself had the position been reversed.'

Campbell stepped back and looked a question at the lady. She nodded and shrugged her graceful shoulders. Mason smiled.

'You need not fear that it is a trap for a confession. We have had a frank talk upon the matter. See, Jack, you were always a sportsman. Here's a bottle. Never mind how it came here. If one or other of us drink it, it would clear the situation.' His manner was wild, almost delirious. 'Lucille, which shall it be?'

There had been a strange force at work in the nightmare room. A third man was there, though not one of the three who had stood in the crisis of their life's drama had time or thought for him. How long he had been there – how much he had heard – none could say. In the corner farthest from the little group he lay crouched against the wall, a sinister snake-like figure, silent and scarcely moving save for a nervous twitching of his clenched right hand. He was concealed from view by a square case and by a dark cloth drawn cunningly above it, so as to screen his features. Intent, watching eagerly every new phase of the drama, the moment had almost come for his intervention. But the three thought little of that. Absorbed in the interplay of their own emotions they had lost sight of a force stronger than themselves – a force which might at any moment dominate the scene.

'Are you game, Jack?' asked Mason.

The soldier nodded.

'No! – for God's sake, no!' cried the woman.

Mason had uncorked the bottle, and turning to the side table he drew out a pack of cards. Cards and bottle stood together.

'We can't put the responsibility on her,' he said. 'Come, Jack, the best of three.'

The soldier approached the table. He fingered the fatal cards. The woman, leaning upon her hand, bent her face forward and stared with fascinated eyes.

Then and only then the bolt fell.

The stranger had risen, pale and grave.

All three were suddenly aware of his presence. They faced him with eager inquiry in their eyes. He looked at them coldly, sadly, with something of the master in his bearing.

'How is it?' they asked, all together.

'Rotten!' he answered. 'Rotten! We'll take the whole reel once more tomorrow.'

18

The Return

(1923)

Elizabeth Bowen

Mr and Mrs Tottenham had come home.

The moist brown gravel of the drive and sweep bore impress of their fly wheels. Lydia Broadbent listened from the doorstep to the receding gritty rumble of the empty fly, and the click and rattle as the gate swung to. Behind her, in the dusky hall, Mr Tottenham shouted directions for the disposal of the luggage, flustered servants bumped against each other and recoiled, and Porloch the gardener shouldered the heavy trunks with gasps and lurches, clutching at the banisters until they creaked.

Lydia heard Mrs Tottenham burst open the drawing-room door and cross the threshold with her little customary pounce, as though she hoped to catch somebody unawares. She pictured her looking resentfully round her, and knew that presently she would hear her tweaking at the curtains. During her six weeks of solitude the house had grown very human to Lydia. She felt now as if it were drawing itself together into a nervous rigour, as a man draws himself together in suffering irritation at the entrance of a fussy wife.

'Were these all the letters, Lydia? I hope none were forwarded to Wickly? Porloch, do be careful of the paint! The fly was very stuffy, Lydia. I wish you'd ordered one of Bicklesfield's. His are always clean.'

Mrs Tottenham had darted out of the drawing-room, swept up her letters from the table, and stood hesitating at the bottom of the stairs.

'You might order tea immediately. Yes, the drawing-room for to-day.' A red shimmer of firelight invited them through the open door. 'Herbert, *Her*-bert!'

Mr Tottenham was clattering in the smoking-room. His face peered crossly at them round the door.

'I wondered if you had gone upstairs. Porloch has been very careless of the paint. You might have watched him, Lydia!' She vanished slowly into the gloom above.

Lydia went into the drawing-room and stood warming her hands before the fire. A servant with a lighted taper passed from gas-bracket to gas-bracket and the greenish lights sprang upwards in her wake. Outside the brown gloom deepened over the November garden. The young distorted trees loomed dark and sullen, the air was thick with moisture, heavy with decay.

To-day there had been no time to think. Lydia was aware but dimly of a sense of desolation and of loss. Something was shattered that had built itself around her during these coherent weeks, something violated which had been sacred unawares. Every fibre of her quivered with hostility to these invaders who were the owners of the house. She was at odds with herself again, at odds with her surroundings. She stared at her gaunt reflection in the fireplace and knew that her best companion had drawn back again, forbidding her. She would be baffled once again by the hostility of Lydia Broadbent, her derision, her unsparing scorn. 'I was such friends with myself when they left us together; we were so harmonious and at ease with each other, me and myself and the house. Now we are afraid and angry with each other again.'

Mr and Mrs Tottenham were impossible. They were childless, humourless and dyspeptic. They were not even funny. There was nothing bizarre about them, or tragic or violent or farcical. They neither loved nor hated each other, there was nothing they did not know about each other; no mystery or fear between them. In the early days of their marriage they had been actively and articulately unhappy. She had had a lover; he had left her for months together and lived in some drab wickedness elsewhere. Then her lover had deserted her, he had been left more money; they had drifted together again, bought 'The Laurels,' spun their shams and miseries around them like a web and lurked within them. They visited, were reputable and entertained; and kept a home for Mr Tottenham's nephew, their expectant heir.

'Lydia?'

The thin voice fluted over the banisters. Lydia hurried upstairs, flicked at a panel of Mrs Tottenham's door and entered, her footsteps muffled among the woolliness of many rugs. There was a blot of yellow light from a candle on the writing-table. Mrs Tottenham stood beside the bed, staring at two sheets of close-written paper and an envelope, which she held out fan-wise between rigid fingers, as one holding a hand at cards.

'Did – has my husband taken his mail yet? Did he overlook the letters?'

'I think Mr Tottenham's post is still lying on the hall table. Is there anything you want to show him?' They had all their correspondence in common; it was quite impersonal.

'No, no, Lydia, shut the door, please. Is tea up? It is draughty: I should have liked a fire. You might get the things out of my dressing-bag – there, it's over on the sofa.'

This constant attendance was to begin again. Lydia was well schooled to it; why had she forgotten?

She unpacked the combs and brushes, and Mrs Tottenham fidgeted before the glass.

'Light the gas, please. I hate this half-light!' There was resentment in her glance towards the window, where the last day-light leaked in faintly through draperies of parchment-coloured lace. Why was Mrs Tottenham so agitated, tugging her hat off and patting at her crimped and faded hair?

She bent to a level with the mirror; haggard-eyed and grinning with anxiety, she searched her bleached and baggy face to find what prettiness was there. Lydia watched her with apathetic curiosity from where, on her knees beside the sofa, she unwrapped the shoes and bottles from their little holland bags.

'Have you seen the photo,' asked Mrs Tottenham suddenly, 'of me when I was twenty-five? On the chiffonier – the plush-framed one – you *must* know it!'

Lydia assented.

'It's a good one, isn't it? D'you think it's like me – now, I mean?'

'Quite a likeness, really, considering.'

'*Considering?*' (How sharp her voice was!)

'Oh, change of fashions makes a difference, doesn't it, and, well … time, of course.'

'Of course I know it wasn't taken yesterday, Lydia. *I* don't need telling. But I'm a lot younger than Mr Tottenham to look at. There was a gentleman at the Hydro took us for father and daughter, really he did!'

Her voice was by turns peremptory, confidential, almost appealing. It died out into silence.

The room was restive and disturbed. 'Oh, you unhappy house,' thought Lydia. 'They have broken into your silence and given you nothing in return.'

'Tea will be ready, I think,' she reminded. Mrs Tottenham turned sharply from the glass, and Lydia saw with amazement that she had reddened her lips. They shone with sticky brightness in her sallow face.

Mrs Tottenham was conscious of her glance. 'Shows rather, doesn't it?' she queried diffidently, and rubbed her mouth with the back of her hand till the red was smeared out over her cheeks.

'One looks so washy after a journey. Just a touch of colour – one wouldn't notice it, hardly, if it wasn't for the glare.' Her muttered extenuations were not addressed to Lydia.

They heard the tea-tray rattling through the hall. Lydia turned the light out, and they prepared to descend. Mrs Tottenham pawed her in the twilight. 'You needn't mention to Mr Tottenham I've opened any of my letters. I'll be showing him the rest. This one was rather particular – from a friend of mine, it was.' An appeal still quavered in her husky tones which her paid companion had never heard before.

From the drawing-room they saw Mr Tottenham scurrying across the grass, drawn tea-wards by the lighted window. There was something quick and furtive about him; Lydia had never been able to determine whether he dodged and darted as pursuer or pursued.

'Wretched evening, wretched.' He chattered his way across the crowded room. 'Been talking to Porloch – garden's in an awful way; shrubberies like a jungle. Did 'e sell the apples?'

He darted the inquiry at Lydia, turning his head sharply towards her, with his eyes averted as though he could not bear to look at her. At first she had imagined that her appearance repulsed him. She knew herself for a plain woman, but now she had learnt that he never looked at anybody if he could avoid it.

'Oh, he sold them well, I believe. I thought he wrote about them?'

'Oh yes, yes, sharp man, Porloch. Dickie been running round for his things?'

'Not often. He says he wants his letters forwarded to Elham till further notice.'

The reference to Elham tickled Dickie's uncle. He put his cup down, giggled, mopped at his mouth and darted a side glance at his wife.

Mrs Tottenham was not listening. She sat very stiff and upright, staring straight before her, crumbling at her cake.

'Hey, Mollie! Dickie's gone to Elham. Didgehear that? Pore old Dickie's gone to Elham again! Never wrote and told me, never told me anything. The young dog!'

The silence was once more outraged by his falsetto giggles.

He held his cup out for Lydia to refill, and she watched with fascination the convulsive movements his throat made while he drank.

'Hey, Mollie! Don't forget we're going to the Gunnings to-morrow. Write it down, my dear girl, write it down, and tell them about orderin' the cab.' He always referred to Lydia obliquely as 'they' or 'them.'

'Gunnin's a good fellow,' he informed the fireplace.

'This cake is uneatable, Lydia. Wherever did you buy it?' Her grumble lacked conviction; it was a perfunctory concession to her distrust of her companion's housekeeping.

'Birch's. I'm sorry, Mrs Tottenham. Aren't you ready for more tea? It's nice and hot for you, isn't it, after the journey?'

Lydia felt as though she had caught her own eye, and was embarrassed and discomfited. She listened with derision to her glib and sugary banalities of speech. 'The perfect companion!' taunted the hostile self. 'What about all those fine big truths and principles we reasoned out together? Yesterday we believed you were sincere. "*Nice and hot after the journey*." Bah!'

The mirror in the overmantel now fascinated Mrs Tottenham. She finished her tea mechanically, laid her cup down and stood before the fireplace, patting and tweaking at her hair. Her husband looked at her contemptuously. 'Pretty little daughter I've got!' he mumbled, with his mouth full of cake. It was a bitter comment on the mistake made by the gentleman at the Hydro.

Mrs Tottenham put her hands before her face and hurried from the room.

Lydia began to gather up the tea things, and a servant darkened the windows with a musty clatter of Venetian blinds. Mr Tottenham's chair creaked as he stretched his legs out to the fire. The room was hot with the smell of tea and tea-cakes, and the smell of upholstery and wilting ferns was drawn out by the heat.

The hall outside was cold and quiet. The sense of the afternoon's invasion had subsided from it like a storm. Through a strip of door the morning-room beckoned her with its associations of the last six weeks. She saw the tall uncurtained windows grey-white in the gloom.

Her book lay open on a table: she shut it with a sense of desolation. It would never be finished now, it was too good a thing to read while *they* were in the house; to be punctuated by *her* petulant insistent chatter, *his* little shuffling, furtive steps. If only this room were all her own: inviolable. She could leave the rest of the house to them, to mar and bully, if she had only a few feet of silence of her own, to exclude the world from, to build up in something of herself.

If she did not go upstairs now Mrs Tottenham would call her, and that, in this room, would be more than she could bear. Vaguely she pictured headlines: '"Laurels" Murder Mystery. Bodies in a Cistern. Disappearance of Companion.' The darkness was all lurid with her visionary crime.

Mrs Tottenham had not been round the house. She did not say the rooms smelt mouldy, and she left the curtain-draperies alone.

Lydia wondered deeply.

'Did you know Sevenoaks?'

The question abashed her. What had Mrs Tottenham to do with Sevenoaks?

'N – no. Scarcely. I've been over there sometimes for the day, from Orpington.'

'A friend of mine lives there – a Mr Merton. He wrote to me to-day. He's come back from the Colonies and bought a place there. It's funny to hear from an old friend, suddenly. It makes me feel quite funny, really.'

She did not sound funny. Her voice was high-pitched with agitation. Lydia had been told all about Mrs Tottenham's friends, and seldom listened. But she did not remember Mr Merton.

'He wants to come and see us. I really hardly like, you know, to suggest the idea to Mr Tottenham.'

'I thought you'd all your friends in common. How well these night-dresses have washed! They must have laundered nicely at the Hydro.'

'Ah, but this is different, you see.' She laughed a little conscious laugh. 'Mr Merton was a particular *friend* of mine. I – Mr Tottenham didn't used to know him.'

'I see,' said Lydia vaguely. 'A friend of yours before your marriage.'

'Well, no. You see, I was very young when I was married. Quite an inexperienced young girl – a child, you might almost say.'

Lydia supposed that Mrs Tottenham *had* been young. She strained her imagination to the effort.

'I did very well for myself when I married Mr Tottenham,' the wife said sharply. 'I must say I never was a fool. My mother'd never brought me up to go about, but we did a good deal of entertaining at one time, Mr Tottenham's friends and my own, and we always had things very nice and showy. But it was a lonely life.'

Mrs Tottenham's confidences were intolerable. Better a hundred times that she should nag.

'So you liked the Hydro – found it really comfortable?'

'Oh yes. But it's the coming back – to this … Lydia, you're a good sort of girl. I wonder if I ought to tell you.'

'Don't tell me anything you would regret,' said Lydia defensively, jerking at the drawer-handles.

'You see, Mr Merton was a good deal to me at one time; then we tore it, and he went off to Canada and married there. I heard he'd been unhappy, and that there was the rumour of a split. Of course he didn't write or anything; we had ab-so-lutely *torn* it; but I couldn't help hearing things, and she seems to have been a really bad sort of woman – there were children, too. He's bringing the children back with him to Sevenoaks.

'He wants to come and see me. He's been thinking about me a great deal, he says, and wondering if I've changed, and wishing – He always was a straight sort of man; it was only circumstances drove him crooked. I daresay I was a good bit to blame. I've kept his photograph, though I know I didn't ought, but I liked having it by me to look at.'

She had unlocked a drawer and held a stiff-backed photograph up beneath the light, scrutinising it. Lydia listened to a distant surge of movement in the house beneath her; steps across the oil-cloth, windows shutting, voices cut off by the swinging of a door. She felt, revoltedly, as though Mrs Tottenham were stepping out of her clothes.

'He says he's hardly changed at all. Seventeen years – they go past you like a flash, he says, when you're working.'

'Seventeen years,' said Lydia deliberately, 'are bound to make a difference to a woman. Did you care for him?'

Mrs Tottenham made no answer; she was staring at the photograph. Her eyes dilated, and she licked her lips.

'I suppose you'll be glad to see him again?' suggested Lydia. She felt suddenly alert and interested, as though she were watching through the lens of a microscope some tortured insect twirling on a pin.

Mrs Tottenham sat down stiffly on the sofa, and laid the photo on her lap. Suddenly she clasped her hands and put them up before her eyes.

'I couldn't,' she gasped. 'Not after all these years I couldn't. Not like this. O Lord, I've got so ugly! I can't pretend – I haven't got the heart to risk it. It's been so real to me, I couldn't bear to lose him.

'It's all gone, it's all gone. I've been pretending. I used to be a fine figure of a woman. How can I have the heart to care when I couldn't keep him caring?'

'You broke it off. It was all over and done with, you told me so. It was wrong, besides. Why should either of you want to rake it up when it was all past and done with seventeen years ago?'

'Because it *was* wrong. It's this awful *rightness* that's killing me. My husband's been a bad man, too, but here we both are, smirking and grinning at each other, just to keep hold of something we neither of us want.'

Lydia was terrified by the dry, swift sobbing. She felt suddenly hard and priggish and immature. All her stresses, her fears and passions, were such twilight things.

18 The Return

Mrs Tottenham stood upright and held the photograph in the flame of the gas jet, watching the ends curl upwards. For all her frizzled hair and jingling ornaments and smudgy tentative cosmetics she was suddenly elemental and heroic.

It was over.

Lydia went quietly out of the room and shut the door behind her.

The place was vibrant with the humanity of Mrs Tottenham. It was as though a child had been born in the house.

19

The Woman at the Store

(1924)

Katherine Mansfield

All that day the heat was terrible. The wind blew close to the ground; it rooted among the tussock grass, slithered along the road, so that the white pumice dust swirled in our faces, settled and sifted over us and was like a dry-skin itching for growth on our bodies. The horses stumbled along, coughing and chuffing. The pack-horse was sick – with a big open sore rubbed under the belly. Now and again she stopped short, threw back her head, looked at us as though she were going to cry, and whinnied. Hundreds of larks shrilled; the sky was slate colour, and the sound of the larks reminded me of slate pencils scraping over its surface. There was nothing to be seen but wave after wave of tussock grass, patched with purple orchids and manuka bushes covered with thick spider webs.

Jo rode ahead. He wore a blue galatea shirt, corduroy trousers and riding boots. A white handkerchief, spotted with red – it looked as though his nose had been bleeding on it – was knotted round his throat. Wisps of white hair straggled from under his wideawake – his moustache and eyebrows were called white – he slouched in the saddle, grunting. Not once that day had he sung

>'I don't care, for don't you see,
>
>My wife's mother was in front of me!'

It was the first day we had been without it for a month, and now there seemed something uncanny in his silence. Jim rode beside me, white as a clown; his black eyes glittered and he kept shooting out his tongue and moistening his lips. He was dressed in a Jaeger vest and a pair of blue duck trousers, fastened round the waist with a plaited leather belt. We had hardly spoken since dawn. At noon we had lunched off fly biscuits and apricots by the side of a swampy creek.

'My stomach feels like the crop of a hen,' said Jo. 'Now then, Jim, you're the bright boy of the party – where's this 'ere store you kep' on talking about. "Oh yes," you says,

The Woman at the Store

"I know a fine store, with a paddock for the horses and a creek runnin' through, owned by a friend of mine who'll give yer a bottle of whisky before 'e shakes hands with yer." I'd like ter see that place – merely as a matter of curiosity – not that I'd ever doubt yer word – as yer know very well – *but …*'

Jim laughed. 'Don't forget there's a woman too, Jo, with blue eyes and yellow hair, who'll promise you something else before she shakes hands with you. Put that in your pipe and smoke it.'

'The heat's making you balmy,' said Jo. But he dug his knees into the horse. We shambled on. I half fell asleep and had a sort of uneasy dream that the horses were not moving forward at all – then that I was on a rocking-horse, and my old mother was scolding me for raising such a fearful dust from the drawing-room carpet. 'You've entirely worn off the pattern of the carpet,' I heard her saying, and she gave the reins a tug. I snivelled and woke to find Jim leaning over me, maliciously smiling.

'That was a case of all but,' said he. 'I just caught you. What's up? Been bye-bye?'

'No!' I raised my head. 'Thank the Lord we're arriving somewhere.'

We were on the brow of the hill, and below us there was a whare roofed with corrugated iron. It stood in a garden, rather far back from the road – a big paddock opposite, and a creek and a clump of young willow trees. A thin line of blue smoke stood up straight from the chimney of the whare; and as I looked a woman came out, followed by a child and a sheep dog – the woman carrying what appeared to me a black stick. She made gestures at us. The horses put on a final spurt, Jo took off his wideawake, shouted, threw out his chest, and began singing 'I don't care, for don't you see …' The sun pushed through the pale clouds and shed a vivid light over the scene. It gleamed on the woman's yellow hair, over her flapping pinafore and the rifle she was carrying. The child hid behind her, and the yellow dog, a mangy beast, scuttled back into the whare, his tail between his legs. We drew rein and dismounted.

'Hallo,' screamed the woman. 'I thought you was three 'awks. My kid comes runnin' in ter me. "Mumma," says she, "there's three brown things comin' over the 'ill," says she. An' I comes out smart, I can tell yer. "They'll be 'awks," I says to her. Oh, the 'awks about 'ere, yer wouldn't believe.'"

The 'kid' gave us the benefit of one eye from behind the woman's pinafore – then retired again.

'Where's your old man?' asked Jim.

The woman blinked rapidly, screwing up her face.

'Away shearin'. Bin away a month. I suppose ye're not goin' to stop, are yer? There's a storm comin' up.'

'You bet we are,' said Jo. 'So you're on your lonely, missus?'

She stood, pleating the frills of her pinafore, and glancing from one to the other of us, like a hungry bird. I smiled at the thought of how Jim had pulled Jo's leg about her. Certainly her eyes were blue, and what hair she had was yellow, but ugly. She was a figure of fun. Looking at her, you felt there was nothing but sticks and wires under that pinafore – her front teeth were knocked out, she had red, pulpy hands and she wore on her feet a pair of dirty Bluchers.

'I'll go and turn out the horses,' said Jim. 'Got any embrocation? Poi's rubbed herself to hell!'

''Arf a mo!' The woman stood silent a moment, her nostrils expanding as she breathed. Then she shouted violently, 'I'd rather you didn't stop … You *can't*, and there's the end of it. I don't let out that paddock any more. You'll have to go on; I ain't got nothing!'

'Well, I'm blest!' said Jo heavily. He pulled me aside. 'Gone a bit off 'er dot,' he whispered. 'Too much alone, *you know*,' very significantly. 'Turn the sympathetic tap on 'er, she'll come round all right.'

But there was no need – she had come round by herself.

'Stop if yer like!' she muttered, shrugging her shoulders. To me – 'I'll give yer the embrocation if yer come along.'

'Right-o, I'll take it down to them.' We walked together up the garden path. It was planted on both sides with cabbages. They smelled like stale dish-water. Of flowers there were double poppies and sweet-williams. One little patch was divided off by pawa shells – presumably it belonged to the child – for she ran from her mother and began to grub in it with a broken clothes-peg. The yellow dog lay across the doorstep, biting fleas; the woman kicked him away.

'Gar-r, get away, you beast … the place ain't tidy. I 'aven't 'ad time ter fix things to-day – been ironing. Come right in.'

It was a large room, the walls plastered with old pages of English periodicals. Queen Victoria's Jubilee appeared to be the most recent number. A table with an ironing board and wash-tub on it, some wooden forms, a black horsehair sofa and some broken cane chairs pushed against the walls. The mantelpiece above the stove was draped in pink paper, further ornamented with dried grasses and ferns and a coloured print of Richard Seddon. There were four doors – one, judging from the smell, led into the 'Store," one on to the 'backyard,' through a third I saw the bedroom. Flies buzzed in circles round the ceiling, and treacle papers and bundles of dried clover were pinned to the window curtains.

I was alone in the room; she had gone into the store for the embrocation. I heard her stamping about and muttering to herself: 'I got some, now where did I put that bottle? … It's behind the pickles … no, it ain't.' I cleared a place on the table and sat there, swinging my legs. Down in the paddock I could hear Jo singing and the sound of hammer strokes as Jim drove in the tent pegs. It was sunset. There is no twilight in our New Zealand days, but a curious half-hour when everything appears grotesque – it frightens – as though the savage spirit of the country walked abroad and sneered at what it saw. Sitting alone in the hideous room I grew afraid. The woman next door was a long time finding that stuff. What was she doing in there? Once I thought I heard her bang her hands down on the counter, and once she half moaned, turning it into a cough and clearing her throat. I wanted to shout 'Buck up!' but I kept silent.

'Good Lord, what a life!' I thought. 'Imagine being here day in, day out, with that rat of a child and a mangy dog. Imagine bothering about ironing. *Mad*, of course she's mad! Wonder how long she's been here – wonder if I could get her to talk.'

At that moment she poked her head round the door.

'Wot was it yer wanted?' she asked.

'Embrocation.'

'Oh, I forgot. I got it, it was in front of the pickle jars.'

She handed me the bottle.

'My, you do look tired, you do! Shall I knock yer up a few scones for supper! There's some tongue in the store, too, and I'll cook yer a cabbage if you fancy it.'

'Right-o.' I smiled at her. 'Come down to the paddock and bring the kid for tea.'

She shook her head, pursing up her mouth.

'Oh no. I don't fancy it. I'll send the kid down with the things and a billy of milk. Shall I knock up a few extry scones to take with yer ter-morrow?'

'Thanks.'

She came and stood by the door.

'How old is the kid?'

'Six – come next Christmas. I 'ad a bit of trouble with 'er one way an' another. I 'adn't any milk till a month after she was born and she sickened like a cow.'

'She's not like you – takes after her father?' Just as the woman had shouted her refusal at us before, she shouted at me then.

'No, she don't! She's the dead spit of me. Any fool could see that. Come on in now, Else, you stop messing in the dirt.'

I met Jo climbing over the paddock fence.

'What's the old bitch got in the store?' he asked.

'Don't know – didn't look.'

'Well, of all the fools. Jim's slanging you. What have you been doing all the time?'

'She couldn't find this stuff. Oh, my shakes, you are smart!'

Jo had washed, combed his wet hair in a line across his forehead, and buttoned a coat over his shirt. He grinned.

Jim snatched the embrocation from me. I went to the end of the paddock where the willows grew and bathed in the creek. The water was clear and soft as oil. Along the edges held by the grass and rushes white foam tumbled and bubbled. I lay in the water and looked up at the trees that were still a moment, then quivered lightly and again were still. The air smelt of rain. I forgot about the woman and the kid until I came back to the tent. Jim lay by the fire watching the billy boil.

I asked where Jo was, and if the kid had brought our supper.

'Pooh,' said Jim, rolling over and looking up at the sky. 'Didn't you see how Jo had been titivating? He said to me before he went up to the whare, "Dang it! she'll look better by night light – at any rate, my buck, she's female flesh!"'

'You had Jo about her looks – you had me too.'

'No – look here. I can't make it out. It's four years since I came past this way and I stopped here two days. The husband was a pal of mine once, down the West Coast – a fine, big chap, with a voice on him like a trombone. She's been barmaid down the Coast – as pretty as a wax doll. The coach used to come this way then once a fortnight, that was before they opened the railway up Napier way, and she had no end of a time! Told me once in a confidential moment that she knew one hundred and twenty-five different ways of kissing!'

'Oh, go on, Jim! She isn't the same woman!'

"Course she is … I can't make it out. What I think is the old man's cleared out and left her: that's all my eye about shearing. Sweet life! The only people who come through now are Maoris and sundowners!'

Through the dark we saw the gleam of the kid's pinafore. She trailed over to us with a basket in her hand, the milk billy in the other. I unpacked the basket, the child standing by.

'Come over here,' said Jim, snapping his fingers at her.

She went, the lamp from the inside of the tent cast a bright light over her. A mean, undersized brat, with whitish hair and weak eyes. She stood, legs wide apart and her stomach protruding.

'What do you do all day?' asked Jim.

She scraped out one ear with her little finger, looked at the result and said, 'Draw.'

'Huh! What do you draw? Leave your ears alone!'

'Pictures.'

'What on?'

'Bits of butter paper an' a pencil of my Mumma's.'

'Boh! What a lot of words at one time!' Jim rolled his eyes at her. 'Baa-lambs and moo-cows?'

'No, everything. I'll draw all of you when you're gone, and your horses and the tent, and that one' – she pointed to me – 'with no clothes on in the creek. I looked at her where she couldn't see me from.'

'Thanks very much. How ripping of you,' said Jim. 'Where's Dad?'

The kid pouted. 'I won't tell you because I don't like yer face!' She started operations on the other ear.

'Here,' I said. 'Take the basket, get along home and tell the other man supper's ready.'

'I don't want to.'

19 The Woman at the Store

'I'll give you a box on the ear if you don't,' said Jim savagely.

'Hie! I'll tell Mumma. I'll tell Mumma.' The kid fled.

We ate until we were full, and had arrived at the smoke stage before Jo came back, very flushed and jaunty, a whisky bottle in his hand.

'"Ave a drink – you two!' he shouted, carrying off matters with a high hand. ''Ere, shove along the cups.'

'One hundred and twenty-five different ways,' I murmured to Jim.

'What's that? Oh! stow it!' said Jo. 'Why 'ave you always got your knife into me. You gas like a kid at a Sunday School beano. She wants us to go there to-night and have a comfortable chat. I' – he waved his hand airily – 'I got 'er round.'

'Trust you for that,' laughed Jim. 'But did she tell you where the old man's got to?'

Jo looked up. 'Shearing! You 'eard 'er, you fool!'

The woman had fixed up the room, even to a light bouquet of sweet-williams on the table. She and I sat one side of the table, Jo and Jim the other. An oil lamp was set between us, the whisky bottle and glasses, and a jug of water. The kid knelt against one of the forms, drawing on butter paper; I wondered, grimly, if she was attempting the creek episode. But Jo had been right about night time. The woman's hair was tumbled – two red spots burned in her cheeks – her eyes shone – and we knew that they were kissing feet under the table. She had changed the blue pinafore for a white calico dressing-jacket and a black skirt – the kid was decorated to the extent of a blue sateen hair ribbon. In the stifling room, with the flies buzzing against the ceiling and dropping on to the table, we got slowly drunk.

'Now listen to me,' shouted the woman, banging her fist on the table. 'It's six years since I was married, and four miscarriages. I says to 'im, I says, what do you think I'm doin' up 'ere? If you was back at the Coast I'd 'ave you lynched for child murder. Over and over I tells 'im – you've broken my spirit and spoiled my looks, and wot for – that's wot I'm driving at.' She clutched her head with her hands and stared round at us. Speaking rapidly, 'Oh, some days – an' months of them – I 'ear them two words knockin' inside me all the time – "Wot for!" but sometimes I'll be cooking the spuds an' I lifts the lid off to give 'em a prong and I 'ears, quite suddin again, "Wot for!" Oh! I don't mean only the spuds and the kid – I mean – I mean,' she hiccoughed – 'you know what I mean, Mr Jo.'

'I know,' said Jo, scratching his head.

'Trouble with me is,' she leaned across the table, 'he left me too much alone. When the coach stopped coming, sometimes he'd go away days, sometimes he'd go away weeks, and leave me ter look after the store. Back 'e'd come – pleased as Punch. "Oh, 'allo," 'e'd say. "'Ow are you gettin' on? Come and give us a kiss." Sometimes I'd turn a bit nasty, and then 'e'd go off again, and if I took it all right, 'e'd wait till 'e could twist me round 'is finger, then 'e'd say, "Well, so long, I'm off," and do you think I could keep 'im? – not me!'

'Mumma,' bleated the kid, 'I made a picture of them on the 'ill, an' you an' me an' the dog down below.'

'Shut your mouth!' said the woman.

A vivid flash of lightning played over the room – we heard the mutter of thunder.

'Good thing that's broke loose,' said Jo. 'I've 'ad it in me 'ead for three days.'

'Where's your old man now?' asked Jim slowly.

The woman blubbered and dropped her head on to the table. 'Jim, 'e's gone shearin' and left me alone again,' she wailed.

''Ere, look out for the glasses,' said Jo. 'Cheer-o, 'ave another drop. No good cryin' over spilt 'usbands! You, Jim, you blasted cuckoo!'

'Mr Jo,' said the woman, drying her eyes on her jacket frill, 'you're a gent, an' if I was a secret woman I'd place any confidence in your 'ands. I don't mind if I do 'ave a glass on that.'

Every moment the lightning grew more vivid and the thunder sounded nearer. Jim and I were silent – the kid never moved from her bench. She poked her tongue out and blew on her paper as she drew.

'It's the loneliness,' said the woman, addressing Jo – he made sheep's eyes at her – 'and bein' shut up 'ere like a broody 'en.' He reached his hand across the table and held hers, and though the position looked most uncomfortable when they wanted to pass the water and whisky, their hands stuck together as though glued. I pushed back my chair and went over to the kid, who immediately sat flat down on her artistic achievements and made a face at me.

'You're not to look,' said she.

'Oh, come on, don't be nasty!' Jim came over to us, and we were just drunk enough to wheedle the kid into showing us. And those drawings of hers were extraordinary and repulsively vulgar. The creations of a lunatic with a lunatic's cleverness. There was no doubt about it, the kid's mind was diseased. While she showed them to us, she worked herself up into a mad excitement, laughing and trembling, and shooting out her arms.

'Mumma,' she yelled. 'Now I'm going to draw them what you told me I never was to – now I am.'

The woman rushed from the table and beat the child's head with the flat of her hand.

'I'll smack you with yer clothes turned up if yer dare say that again,' she bawled.

Jo was too drunk to notice, but Jim caught her by the arm. The kid did not utter a cry. She drifted over to the window and began picking flies from the treacle paper.

We returned to the table – Jim and I sitting one side, the woman and Jo, touching shoulders, the other. We listened to the thunder, saying stupidly, 'That was a near one,' 'There it goes again,' and Jo, at a heavy hit, 'Now we're off,' 'Steady on the brake,' until rain began to fall, sharp as cannon shot on the iron roof.

'You'd better doss here for the night,' said the woman.

19 The Woman at the Store

'That's right,' assented Jo, evidently in the know about this move.

'Bring up yer things from the tent. You two can doss in the store along with the kid – she's used to sleep in there and won't mind you.'

'Oh, Mumma, I never did,' interrupted the kid.

'Shut yer lies! An' Mr Jo can 'ave this room.'

It sounded a ridiculous arrangement, but it was useless to attempt to cross them, they were too far gone. While the woman sketched the plan of action, Jo sat, abnormally solemn and red, his eyes bulging, and pulling at his moustache.

'Give us a lantern,' said Jim, 'I'll go down to the paddock.' We two went together. Rain whipped in our faces, the land was light as though a bush fire was raging. We behaved like two children let loose in the thick of an adventure, laughed and shouted to each other, and came back to the whare to find the kid already bedded in the counter of the store. The woman brought us a lamp. Jo took his bundle from Jim, the door was shut.

'Good night all,' shouted Jo.

Jim and I sat on two sacks of potatoes. For the life of us we could not stop laughing. Strings of onions and half-hams dangled from the ceiling – wherever we looked there were advertisements for 'Camp Coffee' and tinned meats. We pointed at them, tried to read them aloud – overcome with laughter and hiccoughs. The kid in the counter stared at us. She threw off her blanket and scrambled to the floor, where she stood in her grey flannel night-gown rubbing one leg against the other. We paid no attention to her.

'Wot are you laughing at?' she said uneasily.

'You!' shouted Jim. 'The red tribe of you, my child.'

She flew into a rage and beat herself with her hands. 'I won't be laughed at, you curs – you.' He swooped down upon the child and swung her on to the counter.

'Go to sleep, Miss Smarty – or make a drawing – here's a pencil – you can use Mumma's account book.'

Through the rain we heard Jo creak over the boarding of the next room – the sound of a door being opened – then shut to.

'It's the loneliness,' whispered Jim.

'One hundred and twenty-five different ways – alas! my poor brother!'

The kid tore out a page and flung it at me.

'There you are,' she said. 'Now I done it ter spite Mumma for shutting me up 'ere with you two. I done the one she told me I never ought to. I done the one she told me she'd shoot me if I did. Don't care! Don't care!'

The kid had drawn the picture of the woman shooting at a man with a rook rifle and then digging a hole to bury him in.

She jumped off the counter and squirmed about on the floor biting her nails.

Jim and I sat till dawn with the drawing beside us. The rain ceased, the little kid fell asleep, breathing loudly. We got up, stole out of the whare, down into the paddock.

White clouds floated over a pink sky – a chill wind blew; the air smelled of wet grass. Just as we swung into the saddle Jo came out of the whare – he motioned to us to ride on.

'I'll pick you up later,' he shouted.

A bend in the road, and the whole place disappeared.

Note

'The Woman at the Store' was first published in 1912, and republished with minor amendments in 1924. The version of the story included in the present volume is the 1924 version.

20

Never

(1926)

H E Bates

It was afternoon: great clouds stumbled across the sky. In the drowsy, half-dark room the young girl sat in a heap near the window, scarcely moving herself, as if she expected a certain timed happening, such as a visit, sunset, a command. Slowly she would draw the fingers of one hand across the back of the other, in the little hollows between the guides, and move her lips in the same sad, vexed way in which her brows came together. And like this too, her eyes would shift about, from the near, shadowed fields, to the west hills, where the sun had dropped a strip of light, and to the woods between, looking like black scars one minute, and like friendly sanctuaries the next. It was all confused. There was the room, too. The white keys of the piano would now and then exercise a fascination over her which would keep her whole body perfectly still for perhaps a minute. But when this passed, full of hesitation, her fingers would recommence the slow exploration of her hands, and the restlessness took her again.

It was all confused. She was going away: already she had said a hundred times during the afternoon – 'I am going away, I am going away. I can't stand it any longer.' But she had made no attempt to go. In this same position, hour after hour had passed her and all she could think was: 'Today I'm going away. I'm tired here. I never do anything. It's dead, rotten.'

She said, or thought it all without the slightest trace of exultation and was sometimes even methodical when she began to consider: 'What shall I take? The blue dress with the rosette? Yes. What else? what else?' And then it would all begin again: 'Today I'm going away. I never do anything.'

It was true: she never did anything. In the mornings she got up late, was slow over her breakfast, over everything – her reading, her mending, her eating, her playing the piano, cards in the evening, going to bed. It was all slow – purposely done, to fill up the day. And it was true, day succeeded day and she never did anything different.

But today something was about to happen: no more cards in the evening, every evening the same, with her father declaring: 'I never have a decent hand, I thought the ace of trumps had gone! It's too bad!!' and no more: 'Nellie, it's ten o'clock – Bed!' and the slow unimaginative climb of the stairs. Today she was going away: no one knew, but it was so. She was catching the evening train to London.

'I'm going away. What shall I take? The blue dress with the rosette? What else?'

She crept upstairs with difficulty, her body stiff after sitting. The years she must have sat, figuratively speaking, and grown stiff! And as if in order to secure some violent reaction against it all she threw herself into the packing of her things with a nervous vigour, throwing in the blue dress first and after it a score of things she had just remembered. She fastened her bag: it was not heavy. She counted her money a dozen times. It was all right! It was all right. She was going away!

She descended into the now dark room for the last time. In the dining-room someone was rattling tea-cups, an unbearable, horribly domestic sound! She wasn't hungry: she would be in London by eight – eating now meant making her sick. It was easy to wait. The train went at 6.18. She looked it up again: 'Elden 6.13, Olde 6.18, London 7.53.'

She began to play a waltz. It was a slow, dreamy tune, ta-tum, tum, ta-tum, tum, ta-tum, tum, of which the notes slipped out in mournful, sentimental succession. The room was quite dark, she could scarcely see the keys, and into the tune itself kept insinuating: 'Elden 6.13, Olde 6.18,' impossible to mistake or forget.

As she played on she thought: 'I'll never play this waltz again. It has the atmosphere of this room. It's the last time!' The waltz slid dreamily to an end: for a minute she sat in utter silence, the room dark and mysterious, the air of the waltz quite dead, then the tea-cups rattled again and the thought came back to her: 'I'm going away!'

She rose and went out quietly. The grass on the roadside moved under the evening wind, sounding like many pairs of hands rubbed softly together. But there was no other sound, her feet were light, no one heard her, and as she went down the road she told herself: 'It's going to happen! It's come at last!'

'Elden 6.13. Olde 6.18.'

Should she go to Elden or Olde? At the crossroads she stood to consider, thinking that if she went to Elden no one would know her. But at Olde someone would doubtless notice her and prattle about it. To Elden, then, not that it mattered. Nothing mattered now. She was going, was as good as gone!

Her breast, tremulously warm, began to rise and fall as her excitement increased. She tried to run over the things in her bag and could remember only 'the blue dress with the rosette', which she had thrown in first and had since covered over. But it didn't matter. Her money was safe, everything was safe, and with that thought she dropped into a strange quietness, deepening as she went on, in which she had a hundred emotions and convictions. She was never going to strum that waltz again, she had played cards for the last, horrible time, the loneliness, the slowness, the oppression were ended, all ended.

'I'm going away!'

She felt warm, her body tingled with a light delicious thrill that was like the caress of a soft night-wind. There were no fears now. A certain indignation, approaching fury even, sprang up instead, as she thought: 'No one will believe I've gone. But it's true – I'm going at last.'

Her bag grew heavy. Setting it down in the grass she sat on it for a brief while, in something like her attitude in the dark room during the afternoon, and indeed actually began to rub her gloved fingers over the backs of her hands. A phrase or two of the waltz came back to her … That silly piano! Its bottom G was flat, had always been flat! How ridiculous! She tried to conjure up some sort of vision of London, but it was difficult and in the end she gave way again to the old cry: 'I'm going away.' And she was pleased more than ever deeply.

On the station a single lamp burned, radiating a fitful yellowness that only increased the gloom. And worse, she saw no one and in the cold emptiness traced and retraced her footsteps without the friendly assurance of another sound. In the black distance all the signals showed hard circles of red, looking as if they could never change. But she nevertheless told herself over and over again: 'I'm going away – I'm going away.' And later: 'I hate everyone. I've changed until I hardly know myself.'

Impatiently she looked for the train. It was strange. For the first time it occurred to her to know the time and she pulled back the sleeve of her coat. Nearly six-thirty! She felt cold. Up the line every signal displayed its red ring, mocking her. 'Six-thirty, of course, of course.' She tried to be careless. 'Of course, it's late, the train is late,' but the coldness, in reality her fear, increased rapidly, until she could no longer believe those words …

Great clouds, lower and more than ever depressing, floated above her head as she walked back. The wind had a deep note that was sad too. These things had not troubled her before, now they, also, spoke failure and foretold misery and dejection. She had no spirit, it was cold, and she was too tired even to shudder.

In the absolutely dark, drowsy room she sat down, telling herself: 'This isn't the only day. Some day I shall go. Some day.'

She was silent. In the next room they were playing cards and her father suddenly moaned: 'I thought the ace had gone.' Somebody laughed. Her father's voice came again: 'I never have a decent hand! I never have a decent hand! Never!'

It was too horrible! She couldn't stand it! She must do something to stop it! It was too much. She began to play the waltz again and the dreamy, sentimental arrangement made her cry.

'This isn't the only day,' she reassured herself. 'I shall go. Some day!'

And again and again as she played the waltz, bent her head and cried, she would tell herself that same thing:

'Some day! Some day!'

21

Atrophy

(1927)

Edith Wharton

I

Nora Frenway settled down furtively in her corner of the Pullman and, as the express plunged out of the Grand Central Station, wondered at herself for being where she was. The porter came along. 'Ticket?' 'Westover.' She had instinctively lowered her voice and glanced about her. But neither the porter nor her nearest neighbors – fortunately none of them known to her – seemed in the least surprised or interested by the statement that she was traveling to Westover.

Yet what an earth-shaking announcement it was! Not that she cared, now; not that anything mattered except the one overwhelming fact which had convulsed her life, hurled her out of her easy velvet-lined rut, and flung her thus naked to the public scrutiny ... Cautiously, again, she glanced about her to make doubly sure that there was no one, absolutely no one, in that Pullman whom she knew by sight.

Her life had been so carefully guarded, so inwardly conventional in a world where all the outer conventions were tottering, that no one had ever known she had a lover. No one – of that she was absolutely sure. All the circumstances of the case had made it necessary that she should conceal her real life – her only real life – from everyone about her; from her half-invalid irascible husband, his prying envious sisters, and the terrible monumental old chieftainess, her mother-in-law, before whom all the family quailed and humbugged and fibbed and fawned.

What nonsense to pretend that nowadays, even in big cities, in the world's greatest social centers, the severe old-fashioned standards had given place to tolerance, laxity and ease! You took up the morning paper, and you read of girl bandits, movie star divorces, 'hold-ups' at balls, murder and suicide and elopement, and a general welter of disjointed disconnected impulses and appetites; then you turned your eyes onto your own daily life, and found yourself as cribbed and cabined, as beset by vigilant family eyes, observant friends, all sorts of embodied standards, as any white muslin novel heroine of the sixties!

In a different way, of course. To the casual eye Mrs Frenway herself might have seemed as free as any of the young married women of her group. Poker playing, smoking, cocktail drinking, dancing, painting, short skirts, bobbed hair and the rest – when had these been denied to her? If by any outward sign she had differed too markedly from her kind – lengthened her skirts, refused to play for money, let her hair grow, or ceased to make up – her husband would have been the first to notice it, and to say: 'Are you ill? What's the matter? How queer you look! What's the sense of making yourself conspicuous?' For he and his kind had adopted all the old inhibitions and sanctions, blindly transferring them to a new ritual, as the receptive Romans did when strange gods were brought into their temples ...

The train had escaped from the ugly fringes of the city, and the soft spring landscape was gliding past her: glimpses of green lawns, budding hedges, pretty irregular roofs, and miles and miles of alluring tarred roads slipping away into mystery. How often she had dreamed of dashing off down an unknown road with Christopher!

Not that she was a woman to be awed by the conventions. She knew she wasn't. She had always taken their measure, smiled at them – and conformed. On account of poor George Frenway, to begin with. Her husband, in a sense, was a man to be pitied; his weak health, his bad temper, his unsatisfied vanity, all made him a rather forlornly comic figure. But it was chiefly on account of the two children that she had always resisted the temptation to do anything reckless. The least self-betrayal would have been the end of everything. Too many eyes were watching her, and her husband's family was so strong, so united – when there was anybody for them to hate – and at all times so influential, that she would have been defeated at every point, and her husband would have kept the children.

At the mere thought she felt herself on the brink of an abyss. 'The children are my religion,' she had once said to herself; and she had no other.

Yet here she was on her way to Westover ... Oh, what did it matter now? That was the worst of it – it was too late for anything between her and Christopher to matter! She was sure he was dying. The way in which his cousin, Gladys Brincker, had blurted it out the day before at Kate Salmer's dance: 'You didn't know – poor Kit? Thought you and he were such pals! Yes; awfully bad, I'm afraid. Return of the old trouble! I know there've been two consultations – they had Knowlton down. They say there's not much hope; and nobody but that forlorn frightened Jane mounting guard ...'

Poor Christopher! His sister Jane Aldis, Nora suspected, forlorn and frightened as she was, had played in his life a part nearly as dominant as Frenway and the children in Nora's. Loyally, Christopher always pretended that she didn't; talked of her indulgently as 'poor Jenny.' But didn't she, Nora, always think of her husband as 'poor George'? Jane Aldis, of course, was much less self-assertive, less demanding, than George Frenway; but perhaps for that very reason she would appeal all the more to a man's compassion. And somehow, under her unobtrusive air, Nora had – on the rare occasions when they met – imagined that Miss Aldis was watching and drawing her inferences. But then Nora always felt, where Christopher was concerned, as if her breast were a pane of glass through which her trembling palpitating heart could be seen as plainly as holy viscera in a reliquary. Her sober after-thought was that Jane Aldis was just a dowdy self-effacing old maid whose life was filled to the brim by looking after the Westover place for her brother, and seeing that the fires were lit and the rooms full of flowers when he brought down his friends for a weekend.

Ah, how often he had said to Nora: 'If I could have you to myself for a weekend at Westover' – quite as if it were the easiest thing imaginable, as far as his arrangements were concerned! And they had even pretended to discuss how it could be done. But somehow she fancied he said it because he knew that the plan, for her, was about as feasible as a weekend in the moon. And in reality her only visits to Westover had been made in the company of her husband, and that of other friends, two or three times, at the beginning ... For after that she wouldn't. It was three years now since she had been there.

Gladys Brincker, in speaking of Christopher's illness, had looked at Nora queerly, as though suspecting something. But no – what nonsense! No one had ever suspected Nora Frenway. Didn't she know what her friends said of her? 'Nora? No more temperament than a lamp post. Always buried in her books ... Never very attractive to men, in spite of her looks.' Hadn't she said that of other women, who perhaps, in secret, like herself ...?

The train was slowing down as it approached a station. She sat up with a jerk and looked at her wrist watch. It was half-past two, the station was Ockham; the next would be Westover. In less than an hour she would be under his roof, Jane Aldis would be receiving her in that low paneled room full of books, and she would be saying – what would she be saying?

She had gone over their conversation so often that she knew not only her own part in it but Miss Aldis's by heart. The first moments would of course be painful, difficult; but then a great wave of emotion, breaking down the barriers between the two anxious women, would fling them together. She wouldn't have to say much, to explain; Miss Aldis would just take her by the hand and lead her upstairs to the room.

That room! She shut her eyes, and remembered other rooms where she and he had been together in their joy and their strength ... No, not that; she must not think of that now. For the man she had met in those other rooms was dying; the man she was going to was some one so different from that other man that it was like a profanation to associate their images ... And yet the man she was going to was her own Christopher, the one who had lived in her soul: and how his soul must be needing hers, now that it hung alone on the dark brink! As if anything else mattered at such a moment! She neither thought nor cared what Jane Aldis might say or suspect; she wouldn't have cared if the Pullman had been full of prying acquaintances, or if George and all George's family had got in at that last station.

She wouldn't have cared a fig for any of them. Yet at the same moment she remembered having felt glad that her old governess, whom she used to go and see twice a year, lived at Ockham – so that if George did begin to ask questions, she could always say: 'Yes, I went to see poor old Fräulein; she's absolutely crippled now. I shall have to give her a Bath chair. Could you get me a catalogue of prices?' There wasn't a precaution she hadn't thought of – and now she was ready to scatter them all to the winds ...

Westover – *Junction!*

She started up and pushed her way out of the train. All the people seemed to be obstructing her, putting bags and suitcases in her way. And the express stopped for only two minutes. Suppose she should be carried on to Albany?

Westover Junction was a growing place, and she was fairly sure there would be a taxi at the station. There was one – she just managed to get to it ahead of a traveling man with a sample case and a new straw hat. As she opened the door a smell of damp hay and bad tobacco greeted her. She sprang in and gasped: 'To Oakfield. You know? Mr Aldis's place near Westover.'

II

It began exactly as she had expected. A surprised parlormaid – why surprised? – showed her into the low paneled room that was so full of his presence, his books, his pipes, his terrier dozing on the shabby rug. The parlormaid said she would go and see if Miss Aldis could come down. Nora wanted to ask if she were with her brother – and how he was. But she found herself unable to speak the words. She was afraid her voice might tremble. And why should she question the parlormaid, when in a moment, she hoped, she was to see Miss Aldis?

The woman moved away with a hushed step – the step which denotes illness in the house. She did not immediately return, and the interval of waiting in that room, so strange yet so intimately known, was a new torture to Nora. It was unlike anything she had imagined. The writing table with his scattered pens and letters was more than she could bear. His dog looked at her amicably from the hearth, but made no advances; and though she longed to stroke him, to let her hand rest where Christopher's had rested, she dared not for fear he should bark and disturb the peculiar hush of that dumb watchful house. She stood in the window and looked out at the budding shrubs and the bulbs pushing up through the swollen earth.

'This way, please.'

Her heart gave a plunge. Was the woman actually taking her upstairs to his room? Her eyes filled, she felt herself swept forward on a great wave of passion and anguish … But she was only being led across the hall into a stiff lifeless drawing room – the kind that bachelors get an upholsterer to do for them, and then turn their backs on forever. The chairs and sofas looked at her with an undisguised hostility, and then resumed the moping expression common to furniture in unfrequented rooms. Even the spring sun slanting in through the windows on the pale marquetry of a useless table seemed to bring no heat or light with it.

The rush of emotion subsided, leaving in Nora a sense of emptiness and apprehension. Supposing Jane Aldis should look at her with the cold eyes of this resentful room? She began to wish she had been friendlier and more cordial to Jane Aldis in the past. In her intense desire to conceal from everyone the tie between herself and Christopher she had avoided all show of interest in his family; and perhaps, as she now saw, excited curiosity by her very affectation of indifference.

No doubt it would have been more politic to establish an intimacy with Jane Aldis; and today, how much easier and more natural her position would have been! Instead of groping about – as she was again doing – for an explanation of her visit, she could have said: 'My dear, I came to see if there was anything in the world I could do to help you.'

She heard a hesitating step in the hall – a hushed step like the parlormaid's – and saw Miss Aldis pause near the half-open door. How old she had grown since their last meeting! Her hair, untidily pinned up, was gray and lanky. Her eyelids, always reddish, were swollen and heavy, her face sallow with anxiety and fatigue. It was odd to have feared so defenseless an adversary. Nora, for an instant, had the impression that Miss Aldis had wavered in the hall to catch a glimpse of her, take the measure of the situation. But perhaps she had only stopped to push back a strand of hair as she passed in front of a mirror.

'Mrs Frenway – how good of you!' She spoke in a cool detached voice, as if her real self were elsewhere and she were simply an automaton wound up to repeat the familiar forms of hospitality. 'Do sit down,' she said.

She pushed forward one of the sulky armchairs, and Nora seated herself stiffly, her handbag clutched on her knee, in the self-conscious attitude of a country caller.

'I came – '

'So good of you,' Miss Aldis repeated. 'I had no idea you were in this part of the world. Not the slightest.'

Was it a lead she was giving? Or did she know everything, and wish to extend to her visitor the decent shelter of a pretext? Or was she really so stupid –

'You're staying with the Brinckers, I suppose. Or the Northrups? I remember the last time you came to lunch here you motored over with Mr Frenway from Northrups'. That must have been two years ago, wasn't it?' She put the question with an almost sprightly show of interest.

'No – three years,' said Nora, mechanically.

'Was it? As long ago as that? Yes – you're right. That was the year we moved the big fern-leaved beech. I remember Mr Frenway was interested in tree moving, and I took him out to show him where the tree had come from. He *is* interested in tree moving, isn't he?'

'Oh, yes; very much.'

'We had those wonderful experts down to do it. "Tree doctors," they call themselves. They have special appliances, you know. The tree is growing better than it did before they moved it. But I suppose you've done a great deal of transplanting on Long Island.'

'Yes. My husband does a good deal of transplanting.'

'So you've come over from the Northrups'? I didn't even know they were down at Maybrook yet. I see so few people.'

'No; not from the Northrups'.'

'Oh – the Brinckers'? Hal Brincker was here yesterday, but he didn't tell me you were staying there.'

21 Atrophy

Nora hesitated. 'No. The fact is, I have an old governess who lives at Ockham. I go to see her sometimes. And so I came on to Westover –' She paused, and Miss Aldis interrogated brightly: 'Yes?' as if prompting her in a lesson she was repeating.

'Because I saw Gladys Brincker the other day, and she told me that your brother was ill.'

'Oh.' Miss Aldis gave the syllable its full weight, and set a full stop after it. Her eyebrows went up, as if in a faint surprise. The silent room seemed to close in on the two speakers, listening. A resuscitated fly buzzed against the sunny windowpane. 'Yes; he's ill,' she conceded at length.

'I'm so sorry; I ... he has been ... such a friend of ours ... so long ...'

'Yes; I've often heard him speak of you and Mr Frenway.' Another full stop sealed this announcement. ('No, she knows nothing,' Nora thought.) 'I remember his telling me that he thought a great deal of Mr Frenway's advice about moving trees. But then you see our soil is so different from yours. I suppose Mr Frenway has had your soil analyzed?'

'Yes; I think he has.'

'Christopher's always been a great gardener.'

'I hope he's not – not very ill? Gladys seemed to be afraid – '

'Illness is always something to be afraid of, isn't it?'

'But you're not – I mean, not anxious ... not seriously?'

'It's so kind of you to ask. The doctors seem to think there's no particular change since yesterday.'

'And yesterday?'

'Well, yesterday they seemed to think there might be.'

'A change, you mean?'

'Well, yes.'

'A change – I hope for the better?'

'They said they weren't sure; they couldn't say.'

The fly's buzzing had become so insistent in the still room that it seemed to be going on inside of Nora's head, and in the confusion of sound she found it more and more difficult to regain a lead in the conversation. And the minutes were slipping by, and upstairs the man she loved was lying. It was absurd and lamentable to make a pretense of keeping up this twaddle. She would cut through it, no matter how.

'I suppose you've had – a consultation?'

'Oh, yes; Dr Knowlton's been down twice.'

'And what does he – '

'Well; he seems to agree with the others.'

There was another pause, and then Miss Aldis glanced out of the window. 'Why, who's that driving up?' she inquired. 'Oh, it's your taxi, I suppose, coming up the drive.'

'Yes. I got out at the gate.' She dared not add: 'For fear the noise might disturb him.'

'I hope you had no difficulty in finding a taxi at the Junction?'

'Oh, no; I had no difficulty.'

'I think it was so kind of you to come – not even knowing whether you'd find a carriage to bring you out all this way. And I know how busy you are. There's always so much going on in town, isn't there, even at this time of year?'

'Yes; I suppose so. But your brother – '

'Oh, of course my brother won't be up to any sort of gaiety; not for a long time.'

'A long time; no. But you do hope – '

'I think everybody about a sick bed ought to hope, don't you?'

'Yes; but I mean – '

Nora stood up suddenly, her brain whirling. Was it possible that she and that woman had sat thus facing each other for half an hour, piling up this conversational rubbish, while upstairs, out of sight, the truth, the meaning of their two lives hung on the frail thread of one man's intermittent pulse? She could not imagine why she felt so powerless and baffled. What had a woman who was young and handsome and beloved to fear from a dowdy and insignificant old maid? Why, the antagonism that these very graces and superiorities would create in the other's breast, especially if she knew they were all spent in charming the being on whom her life depended. Weak in herself, but powerful from her circumstances, she stood at bay on the ruins of all that Nora had ever loved. 'How she must hate me – and I never thought of it,' mused Nora, who had imagined that she had thought of everything where her relation to her lover was concerned. Well, it was too late now to remedy her omission; but at least she must assert herself, must say something to save the precious minutes that remained and break through the stifling web of platitudes which her enemy's tremulous hand was weaving around her.

'Miss Aldis – I must tell you – I came to see – '

'How he was? So very friendly of you. He would appreciate it, I know. Christopher is so devoted to his friends.'

'But you'll – you'll tell him that I – '

'Of course. That you came on purpose to ask about him. As soon as he's a little bit stronger.'

'But I mean – now?'

'Tell him now that you called to inquire? How good of you to think of that too! Perhaps tomorrow morning, if he's feeling a little bit brighter – '

Nora felt her lips drying as if a hot wind had parched them. They would hardly move. 'But now – now – today.' Her voice sank to a whisper as she added: 'Isn't he conscious?'

'Oh, yes; he's conscious; he's perfectly conscious.' Miss Aldis emphasized this with another of her long pauses. 'He shall certainly be told that you called.' Suddenly she too got up from her seat and moved toward the window. 'I must seem dreadfully inhospitable, not even offering you a cup of tea. But the fact is, perhaps I ought to tell you – if you're thinking of getting back to Ockham this afternoon there's only one train that stops at the Junction after three o'clock.' She pulled out an old-fashioned enameled watch with a wreath of roses about the dial, and turned almost apologetically to Mrs Frenway. 'You ought to be at the station by four o'clock at the latest; and with one of those old Junction taxis ... I'm so sorry; I know I must appear to be driving you away.' A wan smile drew up her pale lips.

Nora knew just how long the drive from Westover Junction had taken, and understood that she was being delicately dismissed. Dismissed from life – from hope – even from the dear anguish of filling her eyes for the last time with the face which was the one face in the world to her! ('But then she does know everything,' she thought.)

'I mustn't make you miss your train, you know.'

'Miss Aldis, is he – has he seen anyone?' Nora hazarded in a painful whisper.

'Seen anyone? Well, there've been all the doctors – five of them! And then the nurses. Oh, but you mean friends, of course. Naturally.' She seemed to reflect. 'Hal Brincker, yes; he saw our cousin Hal yesterday – but not for very long.'

Hal Brincker! Nora knew what Christopher thought of his Brincker cousins – blighting bores, one and all of them, he always said. And in the extremity of his illness the one person privileged to see him had been – Hal Brincker! Nora's eyes filled; she had to turn them away for a moment from Miss Aldis's timid inexorable face.

'But today?' she finally brought out.

'No. Today he hasn't seen anyone; not yet.' The two women stood and looked at each other; then Miss Aldis glanced uncertainly about the room. 'But couldn't I – Yes, I ought at least to have asked you if you won't have a cup of tea. So stupid of me! There might still be time. I never take tea myself.' Once more she referred anxiously to her watch. 'The water is sure to be boiling, because the nurse's tea is just being taken up. If you'll excuse me a moment I'll go and see.'

'Oh, no; no!' Nora drew in a quick sob. 'How can you? ... I mean, I don't want any ...'

Miss Aldis looked relieved. 'Then I shall be quite sure that you won't reach the station too late.' She waited again, and then held out a long stony hand. 'So kind – I shall never forget your kindness. Coming all this way, when you might so easily have telephoned from town. Do please tell Mr Frenway how I appreciated it. You will remember to tell him, won't you? He sent me such an interesting collection of pamphlets about tree moving. I should like him to know how much I feel his kindness in letting you come.' She paused again, and pulled in her lips so that they became a narrow thread, a mere line drawn across her face by a ruler. 'But, no; I won't trouble you; I'll write to thank him myself.' Her hand ran out to an electric bell on the nearest table. It shrilled through the silence, and the parlormaid appeared with a stagelike promptness.

'The taxi, please? Mrs Frenway's taxi.'

The room became silent again. Nora thought: 'Yes; she knows everything.' Miss Aldis peeped for the third time at her watch, and then uttered a slight unmeaning laugh. The bluebottle banged against the window, and once more it seemed to Nora that its sonorities were reverberating inside her head. They were deafeningly mingled there with the explosion of the taxi's reluctant starting-up and its convulsed halt at the front door. The driver sounded his horn as if to summon her. 'He's afraid too that you'll be late!' Miss Aldis smiled.

The smooth slippery floor of the hall seemed to Nora to extend away in front of her for miles. At its far end she saw a little tunnel of light, a miniature maid, a toy taxi. Somehow she managed to travel the distance that separated her from them, though her bones ached with weariness, and at every step she seemed to be lifting a leaden weight. The taxi was close to her now, its door was open, she was getting in. The same smell of damp hay and bad tobacco greeted her. She saw her hostess standing on the threshold. 'To the Junction, driver – back to the Junction,' she heard Miss Aldis say. The taxi began to roll toward the gate. As it moved away Nora heard Miss Aldis calling: 'I'll be sure to write and thank Mr Frenway.'

22

A Lady's Beaded Bag

(1930)

Tennessee Williams

Through the chill of a November evening a small man trudged down an alley, bearing upon his shoulders a huge, bulging sack. He moved with that uneasy, half-unconscious stealth characteristic of an old and weary mongrel who realizes that his life can be preserved from its enemies through wariness alone. The profession which he followed was not illegitimate; he had no need of fearing molestation from the enforcers of the law. And yet his manner seemed to indicate a sense of guilt and fear of detection. He kept close to the walls of the garages as though seeking concealment in their shadows. He skirted widely the circles of radiance cast by the occasional alley lights. Whenever he encountered another alley-walker he lowered his head without glancing at the other's face. He had none of the defiant hardness and boldness common among most of his kind. He was oppressed with an almost maniacal sense of lowliness and shame.

He had been a trash-picker for fifteen years. He had spent each day following an unvarying route through the alleys of the city's exclusive residential section, delving among the contents of ash-pits for old shoes, broken and rusted metal objects, and bundles of soiled and ragged cloth. The fruits of his scavengery he sold for a pittance to dealers who could make use of such rubbish. It would have been an intolerably drear and colorless occupation had he not been sustained through all of those fifteen years by the hope of some day discovering among the trash something of great worth accidentally thrown there. A diamond ring or pin, a watch, earrings – something for which he might receive hundreds of dollars, bringing the fulfillment of his beggar-dreams.

There had been times when his heart had been made to leap simply by the sharp glitter of a bit of broken glass or golden tinfoil, glimpsed over the edge of an ash-pit. And though he had found nothing as yet of greater worth than the scraps of metal, leather, and cloth, hope had not died in him.

He had made it an inviolable rule always to complete his route. Therefore, though his sack was already packed to its capacity, he would not turn back this evening until he had traversed the last block of alley. With aching feet and back he trudged from pit to pit, stopping sometimes to exchange one piece of rubbish in his bag for another of slightly more value. He came at length to a pit whose contents were surmounted by a mauve-colored milliner's box, filled with a bundle of wrapping paper. He was prompted by some impulse to pull the box to the edge of the pit to look at it more closely. The sound of something heavy sliding beneath the bundled paper caught his attention. Removing the paper, he peered sharply into the interior of the box. He saw there one of those things for which he had been searching fifteen years. It was a lady's beaded bag.

For a moment greed was stronger than caution. With trembling fingers he seized the bag and started to lift it from its covert. But at that moment a door slammed and he quickly lifted the heel of an old shoe and pretended to examine it, while his heart hammered at his breast and his head swam with excitement. A lady's beaded bag!

The door slammed once more. He dropped the old heel, crouched closer against the pit. He reached once more into the interior of the box and found the beaded bag. He drew his fingers over its soft, cool surface with the lightness of a cautious Don Juan caressing a woman of whom he is not sure. Once more he scanned the vista of backyards before him to assure himself that he was unobserved; then with lightning speed removed the bag from the box and stuffed it into the pocket of his coat. It was done. The treasure was his.

With elaborately affected nonchalance he swung the sack over his shoulder and started slowly down the alley, betraying outwardly no sign that he had found in the pit anything of more importance than the milliner's box and the old heel that he had fingered. But in his pocket his hand was clasping the beaded bag – clasping it tightly, as though only through the cutting of the tiny cool beads into the hot flesh of his palm could he be made really to believe in its reality. With his fingers he found the opening of the bag. He squeezed them into its plushy interior. He could feel the coins and bills which it contained. It was fairly stuffed with them. Enchanting visions of the pleasures which this money could bring him passed kaleidoscopically before his eyes. He pictured himself clad in handsome clothes, dining upon delectable foods, enjoying for a while those luxuries and splendors of life of which he had yearningly dreamt for many years.

Before reaching the end of the alley he glanced once more behind him. And in the instant of that glance all of his rapturous dreams were shattered. Standing beside the ash-pit in which the bag had lain was a tall young man in the garb of a chauffeur. Their eyes met. And though the regard of the young chauffeur was perfectly casual, it brought panic to the trash-picker. He fancied that he could read in that regard a cold and stern accusation. The loss of the bag, he decided, must have been discovered; it had been traced to the ash-pit. The chauffeur had been sent by his mistress to retrieve it. In all probability, he knew that it had been taken by the trash-picker. He would notify the police. And the world of which the trash-picker had always been so insanely fearful would lay its cold, cruel hands upon him for having become a violater of its laws. The thought of that made him sick with terror; frantic as a small animal caught in a trap.

Of a sudden it occurred to his distracted mind that he might still save himself by surrendering the bag to its owner. Without another thought he hastened out of the alley and around the corner. He followed the walk until he came before a handsome residence of gray stone which he identified as the one in whose ash-pit he had found the bag.

Almost breathless with fear and awe, he scurried up its walk and steps to the grilled outer doors. He found the bell and gave it a brief ring. In a few moments the doors were opened up on a brightly lighted vestibule and he beheld hazily a young woman clad in an austerely cut uniform of black and white.

Barely raising his eyes to her face he lifted the bag, humbly as a priest would lift an offering to the altar of some wrathful god, and mumbled,

'I found this in the trash.'

Looking at the bag, the maid recognized it as one belonging to her employer. She realized that it must have been thrown in the trash-pit with the milliner's box which she had removed from her employer's room that morning. She feared, however, that she might be dismissed for carelessness should she tell the true circumstances of its loss and recovery. Therefore, upon bringing the bag to her employer's bedroom, where she was dressing for a dinner engagement, she said,

'Mrs Ferrabye, I found this lying on the piano.'

Without turning from her dressing table at which she was arranging her hair, the woman replied,

'Put it in my drawer, Hilda.'

A few minutes later a delivery man arrived with a belated package from a modiste's shop. The maid carried it up to her employer's room, laid it on the bed and gave her employer the bill. It amounted to several hundred dollars. The woman opened her beaded bag. She drew out that sum – practically all that the bag contained – and handed it to the maid. Then she lifted the lid of the box and raised from its tissue wrappings an evening wrap of diaphanous white material, sprinkled with glistening bits of metal. She held it beneath the light to survey it critically a moment; then dropped it upon the bed, marring the refined beauty of her face with a grimace of disgust.

'Honestly, I must have been out of my mind when I bought this thing. Why I could never dream of wearing anything so perfectly ridiculous.'

Turning back to the mirror and beginning once more to smooth the golden coils of her hair, her momentary annoyance passed, and her face quickly resumed its former expression of smiling self-satisfaction.

23

Excursion

(1949)

Herman Bosman

During the fourth year of my imprisonment, a very beautiful thing happened to me. I was working in the carpenters' shop still. A bracket had to be fitted into a guard-post on the pavement in front of the prison. The head-warder sent me out to do this job. I went there, escorted by a discipline-warder and accompanied by another convict. It was a wonderful adventure. Even now, when I think of it, twenty years later, that old thrill comes back to me once more.

'Get your tools,' the head-warder said to me, 'And the timber for a bracket.' To the discipline-warder he said, 'Get your gun.'

So we went out through the back-gate of the prison, the warder, the other convict and I. At the gate the warder got his revolver which he slung over his shoulder on a strap. The other convict and I were searched. The outside-warder opened the gate. Slowly, much too slowly, the gate creaked outward on its heavy iron hinges – and we saw the outside world.

Stout Cortez seeing the Pacific for the first time, from a peak on Darien ... All that sentimental rubbish. As though one piece of ocean could be different from any other piece of ocean ...

But in that moment of the gate swinging open very slowly, I saw the outside world again, after a period of four years.

'Forward,' the discipline-warder said.

It sounded like the voice of Divinity talking. It meant we were going down that road which I had seen only once before, four years ago, and the sight of which had made my throat contract, because I had been under the sentence of death, then, and as we had approached the gloomy exterior of the prison, and those forbidding-looking portals had reared up before me, it was with an unutterable despair that I had looked on that same road, for the last time.

We continued down that road, towards the front of the prison, where the guard-post was. Several times the discipline-warder had to shout at me to pick up my step. For every moment was ecstasy to me. I walked with an awful deliberation. I wanted to miss

23 Excursion

nothing. I wanted to go as slow as possible; those moments that we were outside the prison had to stretch as long as days and hours and years; oh, we hadn't to go at more than a snail's pace. And I saw to it that we didn't. The warder could shout his head off. This dreadful ecstasy had to linger.

I have never in my life, before or since, beheld a scene as entrancing in its splendour as what I viewed from that dusty road, that was impregnated with a heady fragrance – that dusty red road skirting the prison. I have seen Funchal from the sea; I have walked those cobbled roads, green with young grass-blades like sprinkled confetti, and I couldn't see what there was in Madeira to thrill the tourists, who all said, 'Oh,' and 'Oh,' as though it was paradise. And I have seen middle-aged men standing in St James' Park and looking over the bridge at the part of London on the other side of Whitehall, with the early light of a summer morning on it: and I wondered what they saw in it. And the Paris boulevards, and in Brussels, the Avenue Louise, and all sorts of other places and scenes – and among them, not least, the Hex River mountains from the train-window. I have seen lots of sights – since that day when I walked out of the back-gate of the prison, to go and put up that bracket at the guard-post. And all those sights have left me cold.

I don't think that even love has had for me the warmth and the beauty and the deep-drawn delight that came to me on that road, red with perfumed dust, skirting the prison. Love. Well, I was young. And I was in love with the whole world. And life had not yet been made sick for me through the poison of introspection. And so I walked slowly in spite of the discipline-warder's bellowings, in order to miss nothing, in order that this incredible joy that had come to me suddenly and undeservedly, should fill my entire being, dropping rose-petals on the places where my shoulders were bruised.

It was a dream-world that I walked into. For four years I had been dreaming of a moment such as this was. I was outside. It was all *world*. I was walking along a road where free people walked – men and women and children: and, above all, women. Sunlight and shadow and distance played queer tricks with my eyes. Because I had been confined within cramped walls for four years, my eyes were unable to accommodate themselves to the majesty of distance. To be able to see far away – fruit-trees a long way off, for instance, and a white-washed fence at the bottom of the road: all these things were very beautiful. They were invested with the magic of strangeness. I was in a painted world, queerly different from what I had expected the outside to be. I had so forgotten common things, that when I saw a couple of fowls in a back-yard I stopped and stared at them in an unspeakable joy.

For four years I had only memories of what the world was really like. And what I saw now, distance and hues, and pale lights and patches of grass: they no longer corresponded with my ideas about them. They were quite different from my memories of them. And they were even more lovely than I had expected them to be.

For years I had dreamt of the world. I had tried, in the nights when I had lain awake, to recall that gaudy lost world that I had known up to the time when I was twenty. And I saw now that it was less brightly-coloured than I had pictured it to be. But I was not disappointed. On the contrary, this pallid reality was something infinitely more exquisite than my black and scarlet visionings of it had been.

We got to the guard-post much too soon. But before we entered it a woman and a girl came past: the wife and daughter of a warder. And they didn't look at us of course. Because this was on the prison reserve, where they lived; and so they were used to seeing convicts.

But I stared at them, at this woman and girl. I couldn't look at them enough, I had to see them, and I had to remember. I had to remember everything about them, every detail of how they looked, and what they felt like. I had to remember everything about what that divine moment of their nearness did to my senses, and every single detail of their faces and their bodies and their eyes and their dresses, and the folds in their frocks, and the crinkles in the woman's legs, at the back of her knees, and the way their bodies swayed when they walked, and the way their light, summery dresses fluttered in the breeze when they walked. Above all, I had to remember that sublime impact on my soul, on my blood, of their having passed close to me. I must not forget that feeling of thick silence that was fragrant with the inside of them.

For I had to remember all that when I was locked up again. I had to treasure it all up; not a drop of it was to be spilt; and I did, as a matter of fact, succeed in keeping that memory vivid for at least a year after that – perhaps even longer.

That woman's dress was short. I hadn't expected that. How was I to know that women's fashions had undergone so much change during the four years in which I was shut away from the sound and the sight of all women? And the little girl's frock was a washed-out sort of blue. I don't mean that the colour really was washed out of course, it was only that I had expected the colours of materials to be more startling-hued than what they actually were. And I knew, instantly, that those really were the colours of the outside world, the colours of trees and the colours of dresses. I knew immediately that that girl wasn't wearing a faded dress. It was only that I had, during the years, come to imagine, in waking dreams of the outside world, that there was a brilliance about those things of living and the acts of living which was not really there.

But, of course, this pallor only enhanced the incredible miracle of the life that people live. It made the mystery all the more refined. The glitter was all the more alluring because it was subdued. Life was washed out, faded. So its attractiveness was a haunted thing. The outside world was deadly artistry.

After the bracket had been nailed into place, the convict who went with me having made holes in the wall with the cold chisel in the places where I showed him – mine being the higher-up job of hammering in the plugs and securing the bracket – we went back along the road we had come. But this time the convict who had come with me joined with the warder in making us hurry up. For it was getting on towards lunch-time, and my convict-colleague was hungry. He was only a short-timer; so in the walk between the guard-post and the back-gate of the prison there was little novelty for him.

But this time I didn't mind hurrying. I had already seen so much. I had a whole world of things to remember in the days to come. I had been allowed into fairy-land. I had thrilled to the earth and its beauty and its secrets. The faces and the figures of that woman and girl had not come up to my expectations in respect of the dark loveliness that I had come to associate with woman. But their beauty seemed all the more ethereal

23 Excursion

because it was not held fast in swift contours and vivid colouring. And their beauty had become all the more intangible because it had made contact with my senses not as spirit but as clay. Paradise was so much nearer to me than the soil, during those years of my dreaming of the outside world. And what there was of clay in that girl and woman was a thing of far greater mystery to me than their quality of soul.

Reality was more trancelike than a vision, more breath-taking than any dream.

During the many months that followed, of my sojourning inside the walls, that saunter along the dusty road was a warm and luscious memory for me. It was an excursion into realms of gaudy adventure where my sight had been dazzled with shining fresh flowers and my ears had been filled with the sound of old gold. And life had been broken open like a ripe pomegranate, and tropical fronds had bent low in laughter, and spring had exulted in the stillness of young growth.

I had tiptoed down the corridors of ancient palaces, richly arrassed and niched with armorial bearings; my footsteps had wandered through sacred groves. And I would look at my feet, alone in my cell for many nights thereafter; and I would think that these feet, shod in these same boots, had walked down that road, once, and had got red dust on them, had walked in the same dust in which people of the outside world had walked, in which that girl and that woman had walked. And thinking like that I would not feel cut off from the world at all. For my boots were tangible proof that I was one with the earth and with life; proof – that any court of law would accept – that I belonged with people.

And, of course, the immediate effect of my adventure in Avalon was that my dreamings of the outside world became again exotic things of black and scarlet, heavy with perfumes, low-hung with the night. In my visionings the world outside the prison was invested with more vivid colours than ever before ...

(Only the other day I passed that same spot again, by car. After an interval of twenty years. And the red road had been tarred. And I saw then that the whole distance we had walked, the distance from the back-gate to the guard-post, which still stood there on the corner – with the bracket still in place, no doubt, for I had nailed it in solid – was less than a hundred yards.)

24

Like Mother Used to Make

(1949)

Shirley Jackson

David Turner, who did everything in small quick movements, hurried from the bus stop down the avenue toward his street. He reached the grocery on the corner and hesitated; there had been something. Butter, he remembered with relief; this morning, all the way up the avenue to his bus stop, he had been telling himself butter, don't forget butter coming home tonight, when you pass the grocery remember butter. He went into the grocery and waited his turn, examining the cans on the shelves. Canned pork sausage was back, and corned-beef hash. A tray full of rolls caught his eye, and then the woman ahead of him went out and the clerk turned to him.

'How much is butter?' David asked cautiously.

'Eighty-nine,' the clerk said easily.

'Eighty-nine?' David frowned.

'That's what it is,' the clerk said. He looked past David at the next customer.

'Quarter of a pound, please,' David said. 'And a half-dozen rolls.'

Carrying his package home he thought, I really ought not to trade there any more; you'd think they'd know me well enough to be more courteous.

There was a letter from his mother in the mailbox. He stuck it into the top of the bag of rolls and went upstairs to the third floor. No light in Marcia's apartment, the only other apartment on the floor. David turned to his own door and unlocked it, snapping on the light as he came in the door. Tonight, as every night when he came home, the apartment looked warm and friendly and good; the little foyer, with the neat small table and four careful chairs, and the bowl of little marigolds against the pale green walls David had painted himself; beyond, the kitchenette, and beyond that, the big room where David read and slept and the ceiling of which was a perpetual trouble to him; the plaster was falling in one corner and no power on earth could make it less noticeable. David consoled himself for the plaster constantly with the thought that perhaps if he had not taken an apartment in an old brownstone the plaster would not be falling, but then, too, for the money he paid he could not have a foyer and a big room and a kitchenette, anywhere else.

He put his bag down on the table and put the butter away in the refrigerator and the rolls in the breadbox. He folded the empty bag and put it in a drawer in the kitchenette. Then he hung his coat in the hall closet and went into the big room, which he called his living-room, and lighted the desk light. His word for the room, in his own mind, was 'charming.' He had always been partial to yellows and browns, and he had painted the desk and the bookcases and the end tables himself, had even painted the walls, and had hunted around the city for the exact tweedish tan drapes he had in mind. The room satisfied him: the rug was a rich dark brown that picked up the darkest thread in the drapes, the furniture was almost yellow, the cover on the studio couch and the lampshades were orange. The rows of plants on the window sills gave the touch of green the room needed; right now David was looking for an ornament to set on the end table, but he had his heart set on a low translucent green bowl for more marigolds, and such things cost more than he could afford, after the silverware.

He could not come into this room without feeling that it was the most comfortable home he had ever had; tonight, as always, he let his eyes move slowly around the room, from couch to drapes to bookcase, imagined the green bowl on the end table, and sighed as he turned to the desk. He took his pen from the holder, and a sheet of the neat notepaper sitting in one of the desk cubbyholes, and wrote carefully: 'Dear Marcia, don't forget you're coming for dinner tonight. I'll expect you about six.' He signed the note with a 'D' and picked up the key to Marcia's apartment which lay in the flat pencil tray on his desk. He had a key to Marcia's apartment because she was never home when her laundryman came, or when the man came to fix the refrigerator or the telephone or the windows, and someone had to let them in because the landlord was reluctant to climb three flights of stairs with the pass key. Marcia had never suggested having a key to David's apartment, and he had never offered her one; it pleased him to have only one key to his home, and that safely in his own pocket; it had a pleasant feeling to him, solid and small, the only way into his warm fine home.

He left his front door open and went down the dark hall to the other apartment. He opened the door with his key and turned on the light. This apartment was not agreeable for him to come into; it was exactly the same as his: foyer, kitchenette, living-room, and it reminded him constantly of his first day in his own apartment, when the thought of the careful home-making to be done had left him very close to despair. Marcia's home was bare and at random; an upright piano a friend had given her recently stood crookedly, half in the foyer, because the little room was too narrow and the big room was too cluttered for it to sit comfortably anywhere; Marcia's bed was unmade and a pile of dirty laundry lay on the floor. The window had been open all day and papers had blown wildly around the floor. David closed the window, hesitated over the papers, and then moved away quickly. He put the note on the piano keys and locked the door behind him.

In his own apartment he settled down happily to making dinner. He had made a little pot roast for dinner the night before; most of it was still in the refrigerator and he sliced it in fine thin slices and arranged it on a plate with parsley. His plates were orange, almost the same color as the couch cover, and it was pleasant to him to arrange a salad, with the lettuce on the orange plate, and the thin slices of cucumber. He put coffee on to cook, and sliced potatoes to fry, and then, with his dinner cooking agreeably and the window open to lose the odor of the frying potatoes, he set lovingly to arranging his table. First, the tablecloth, pale green, of course. And the two fresh green napkins. The orange plates and the precise cup and saucer at each place. The plate of rolls in the center, and the odd salt and pepper shakers, like two green frogs. Two glasses – they came from the five-and-ten, but they had thin green bands around them – and finally, with great care, the silverware. Gradually, tenderly, David was buying himself a complete set of silverware; starting out modestly with a service for two, he had added to it until now he had well over a service for four, although not quite a service for six, lacking salad forks and soup spoons. He had chosen a sedate, pretty pattern, one that would be fine with any sort of table setting, and each morning he gloried in a breakfast that started with a shining silver spoon for his grapefruit, and had a compact butter knife for his toast and a solid heavy knife to break his eggshell, and a fresh silver spoon for his coffee, which he sugared with a particular spoon meant only for sugar. The silverware lay in a tarnish-proof box on a high shelf all to itself, and David lifted it down carefully to take out a service for two. It made a lavish display set out on the table – knives, forks, salad forks, more forks for the pie, a spoon to each place, and the special serving pieces – the sugar spoon, the large serving spoons for the potatoes and the salad, the fork for the meat, and the pie fork. When the table held as much silverware as two people could possibly use he put the box back on the shelf and stood back, checking everything and admiring the table, shining and clean. Then he went into his living-room to read his mother's letter and wait for Marcia.

The potatoes were done before Marcia came, and then suddenly the door burst open and Marcia arrived with a shout and fresh air and disorder. She was a tall handsome girl with a loud voice, wearing a dirty raincoat, and she said, 'I didn't forget, Davie, I'm just late as usual. What's for dinner? You're not mad, are you?'

David got up and came over to take her coat. 'I left a note for you,' he said.

'Didn't see it,' Marcia said. 'Haven't been home. Something smells good.'

'Fried potatoes,' David said. 'Everything's ready.'

'Golly.' Marcia fell into a chair to sit with her legs stretched out in front of her and her arms hanging. 'I'm tired,' she said. 'It's cold out.'

'It was getting colder when I came home,' David said. He was putting dinner on the table, the platter of meat, the salad, the bowl of fried potatoes. He walked quietly back and forth from the kitchenette to the table, avoiding Marcia's feet. 'I don't believe you've been here since I got my silverware,' he said.

Marcia swung around to the table and picked up a spoon. 'It's beautiful,' she said, running her finger along the pattern. 'Pleasure to eat with it.'

'Dinner's ready,' David said. He pulled her chair out for her and waited for her to sit down.

Marcia was always hungry; she put meat and potatoes and salad on her plate without admiring the serving silver, and started to eat enthusiastically. 'Everything's beautiful,' she said once. 'Food is wonderful, Davie.'

'I'm glad you like it,' David said. He liked the feel of the fork in his hand, even the sight of the fork moving up to Marcia's mouth.

Marcia waved her hand largely. 'I mean everything,' she said, 'furniture, and nice place you have here, and dinner, and everything.'

'I *like* things this way,' David said.

'I know you do.' Marcia's voice was mournful. 'Someone should teach me, I guess.'

'You *ought* to keep your home neater,' David said. 'You ought to get curtains at least, and keep your windows shut.'

'I never remember,' she said. 'Davie, you are the most *wonderful* cook.' She pushed her plate away, and sighed.

David blushed happily. 'I'm glad you like it,' he said again, and then he laughed. 'I made a pie last night.'

'A pie.' Marcia looked at him for a minute and then she said, 'Apple?'

David shook his head, and she said, 'Pineapple?' and he shook his head again, and, because he could not wait to tell her, said, 'Cherry.'

'My *God*!' Marcia got up and followed him into the kitchen and looked over his shoulder while he took the pie carefully out of the breadbox. 'Is this the first pie you ever made?'

'I've made two before,' David admitted, 'but this one turned out better than the others.'

She watched happily while he cut large pieces of pie and put them on other orange plates, and then she carried her own plate back to the table, tasted the pie, and made wordless gestures of appreciation. David tasted his pie and said critically, 'I think it's a little sour. I ran out of sugar.'

'It's perfect,' Marcia said. 'I always loved a cherry pie really *sour*. This isn't sour enough, even.'

David cleared the table and poured the coffee, and as he was setting the coffeepot back on the stove Marcia said, 'My doorbell's ringing.' She opened the apartment door and listened, and they could both hear the ringing in her apartment. She pressed the buzzer in David's apartment that opened the downstairs door, and far away they could hear heavy footsteps starting up the stairs. Marcia left the apartment door open and came back to her coffee. 'Landlord, most likely,' she said. 'I didn't pay my rent again.' When the footsteps reached the top of the last staircase Marcia yelled, 'Hello?' leaning back in her chair to see out the door into the hall. Then she said, 'Why, Mr Harris.' She got up and went to the door and held out her hand. 'Come in,' she said.

'I just thought I'd stop by,' Mr Harris said. He was a very large man and his eyes rested curiously on the coffee cups and empty plates on the table. 'I don't want to interrupt your dinner.'

'*That's* all right,' Marcia said, pulling him into the room. 'It's just Davie. Davie, this is Mr Harris, he works in my office. This is Mr Turner.'

'How do you do,' David said politely, and the man looked at him carefully and said, 'How do you do?'

'Sit down, sit down,' Marcia was saying, pushing a chair forward. 'Davie, how about another cup for Mr Harris?'

'Please don't bother,' Mr Harris said quickly, 'I just thought I'd stop by.'

While David was taking out another cup and saucer and getting a spoon down from the tarnish-proof silverbox, Marcia said, 'You like homemade pie?'

'Say,' Mr Harris said admiringly, 'I've forgotten what homemade pie *looks* like.'

'Davie,' Marcia called cheerfully, 'how about cutting Mr Harris a piece of that pie?'

Without answering, David took a fork out of the silverbox and got down an orange plate and put a piece of pie on it. His plans for the evening had been vague; they had involved perhaps a movie if it were not too cold out, and at least a short talk with Marcia about the state of her home; Mr Harris was settling down in his chair and when David put the pie down silently in front of him he stared at it admiringly for a minute before he tasted it.

'Say,' he said finally, 'this is certainly some pie.' He looked at Marcia. 'This is really *good* pie,' he said.

'You like it?' Marcia asked modestly. She looked up at David and smiled at him over Mr Harris' head. 'I haven't made but two, three pies before,' she said.

David raised a hand to protest, but Mr Harris turned to him and demanded, 'Did you ever eat any better pie in your life?'

'I don't think Davie liked it much,' Marcia said wickedly, 'I think it was too sour for him.'

'I *like* a sour pie,' Mr Harris said. He looked suspiciously at David. 'A cherry pie's *got* to be sour.'

'I'm glad you like it, anyway,' Marcia said. Mr Harris ate the last mouthful of pie, finished his coffee, and sat back. 'I'm sure glad I dropped in,' he said to Marcia.

David's desire to be rid of Mr Harris had slid imperceptibly into an urgency to be rid of them both; his clean house, his nice silver, were not meant as vehicles for the kind of fatuous banter Marcia and Mr Harris were playing at together; almost roughly he took the coffee cup away from the arm Marcia had stretched across the table, took it out to the kitchenette and came back and put his hand on Mr Harris' cup.

'Don't bother, Davie, honestly,' Marcia said. She looked up, smiling again, as though she and David were conspirators against Mr Harris. 'I'll do them all tomorrow, honey,' she said.

'Sure,' Mr Harris said. He stood up. 'Let them wait. Let's go in and sit down where we can be comfortable.'

Marcia got up and led him into the living-room and they sat down on the studio couch. 'Come on in, Davie,' Marcia called.

The sight of his pretty table covered with dirty dishes and cigarette ashes held David. He carried the plates and cups and silverware into the kitchenette and stacked them in the sink and then, because he could not endure the thought of their sitting there any longer, with the dirt gradually hardening on them, he tied an apron on and began to wash them carefully. Now and then, while he was washing them and drying them and putting them away, Marcia would call to him, sometimes, 'Davie, what *are* you doing?' or, 'Davie, won't you stop all that and come sit down?' Once she said, 'Davie, I don't want you to wash all those dishes,' and Mr Harris said, 'Let him work, he's happy.'

David put the clean yellow cups and saucers back on the shelves – by now, Mr Harris' cup was unrecognizable; you could not tell, from the clean rows of cups, which one he had used or which one had been stained with Marcia's lipstick or which one had held David's coffee which he had finished in the kitchenette – and finally, taking the tarnish-proof box down, he put the silverware away. First the forks all went together into the little grooves which held two forks each – later, when the set was complete, each groove would hold four forks – and then the spoons, stacked up neatly one on top of another in their own grooves, and the knives in even order, all facing the same way, in the special tapes in the lid of the box. Butter knives and serving spoons and the pie knife all went into their own places, and then David put the lid down on the lovely shining set and put the box back on the shelf. After wringing out the dishcloth and hanging up the dish towel and taking off his apron he was through, and he went slowly into the living-room. Marcia and Mr Harris were sitting close together on the studio couch, talking earnestly.

'My *father's* name was James,' Marcia was saying as David came in, as though she were clinching an argument. She turned around when David came in and said, 'Davie, you were so nice to do all those dishes yourself.'

'That's all right,' David said awkwardly. Mr Harris was looking at him impatiently.

'I should have helped you,' Marcia said. There was a silence, and then Marcia said, 'Sit down, Davie, won't you?'

David recognized her tone; it was the one hostesses used when they didn't know what else to say to you, or when you had come too early or stayed too late. It was the tone he had expected to use on Mr Harris.

'James and I were just talking about …' Marcia began and then stopped and laughed. 'What *were* we talking about?' she asked, turning to Mr Harris.

'Nothing much,' Mr Harris said. He was still watching David.

'Well,' Marcia said, letting her voice trail off. She turned to David and smiled brightly and then said, 'Well,' again.

Mr Harris picked up the ashtray from the end table and set it on the couch between himself and Marcia. He took a cigar out of his pocket and said to Marcia, 'Do you mind cigars?' and when Marcia shook her head he unwrapped the cigar tenderly and bit off the end. 'Cigar smoke's good for plants,' he said thickly, around the cigar, as he lighted it, and Marcia laughed.

David stood up. For a minute he thought he was going to say something that might start, 'Mr Harris, I'll thank you to ...' but what he actually said, finally, with both Marcia and Mr Harris looking at him, was, 'Guess I better be getting along, Marcia.'

Mr Harris stood up and said heartily, 'Certainly have enjoyed meeting you.' He held out his hand and David shook hands limply.

'Guess I better be getting along,' he said again to Marcia, and she stood up and said, 'I'm sorry you have to leave so soon.'

'Lots of work to do,' David said, much more genially than he intended, and Marcia smiled at him again as though they were conspirators and went over to the desk and said, 'Don't forget your key.'

Surprised, David took the key of her apartment from her, said good night to Mr Harris, and went to the outside door.

'Good night, Davie honey,' Marcia called out, and David said 'Thanks for a simply *wonderful* dinner, Marcia,' and closed the door behind him.

He went down the hall and let himself into Marcia's apartment; the piano was still awry, the papers were still on the floor, the laundry scattered, the bed unmade. David sat down on the bed and looked around. It was cold, it was dirty, and as he thought miserably of his own warm home he heard faintly down the hall the sound of laughter and the scrape of a chair being moved. Then, still faintly, the sound of his radio. Wearily, David leaned over and picked up a paper from the floor, and then he began to gather them up one by one.

25

The Lagoon

(1951)

Janet Frame

At low tide the water is sucked back into the harbour and there is no lagoon, only a stretch of dirty grey sand shaded with dark pools of sea-water where you may find a baby octopus if you are lucky, or the spotted orange old house of a crab or the drowned wreckage of a child's toy boat. There is a bridge over the lagoon where you may look down into the little pools and see your image tangled up with sea-water and rushes and bits of cloud. And sometimes at night there is an under-water moon, dim and secret.

All this my grandmother told me, my Picton grandmother who could cut supple-jack and find kidney fern and make a track through the thickest part of the bush. When my grandmother died all the Maoris at the Pa came to her funeral, for she was a friend of the Maoris, and her mother had been a Maori princess, very beautiful they said, with fierce ways of loving and hating.

See the lagoon, my grandmother would say. The dirty lagoon, full of drifting wood and seaweed and crabs' claws. It is dirty and sandy and smelly in summer. I remember we used to skim round, white stones over the water, and catch tiddlers in the little creek near by, and make sand castles on the edge, this is my castle we said, you be Father I'll be Mother and we'll live here and catch crabs and tiddlers for ever.

I liked my grandmother to talk about the lagoon. And when we went for a holiday to Picton where Grandma lived I used to say Grandma tell me a story. About the Maori Pa. About the old man who lived down the Sounds and had a goat and a cow for friends. About the lagoon. And my grandmother would tell me stories of the Sounds and the Pa and herself when she was young. Being a girl and going out to work in the rich people's houses. But the lagoon never had a proper story, or if it had a proper story my grandmother never told me.

See the water she would say. Full of seaweed and crabs' claws. But I knew that wasn't the real story and I didn't find out the real story till I was grown-up and Grandma had died and most of the old Maoris were gone from the Pa, and the old man and the cow and the goat were forgotten.

I went for a holiday in Picton. It was a long journey by train and I was glad at the end of it to see the green and blue town that I remembered from childhood, though it was smaller of course and the trees had shrunk and the hills were tiny.

I stayed with an aunt and uncle. I went for launch rides round the harbour and I went for picnics with summery people in floral frocks and sun hats, and kids in print frocks, or khaki shorts if they were boys, especially if they were boys with fathers in the army. We took baskets with fruit and sandwiches, not tomato for tomato goes damp though some like it damp, and threepences in the pocket for ice-creams. There were races for the kiddies and some for the men and women, and afterwards a man walked round the grounds throwing lollies in the air. They were great days out picnicking in the Sounds with the Maoris singing and playing their ukeleles, but they didn't sing the real Maori songs, they sang "You are My Sunshine" and "South of the Border". And then it got dark and the couples came back from the trees and the launches were got ready and everybody went back singing, with the babies crying because they were tired and sunburnt and bitten by sandflies. Sandflies are the devil everybody said, but they were great days for the kiddies.

Perhaps I liked the new Picton, I don't know. If there were things I hadn't noticed before there were also things gone that I thought would be there for ever. The two gum trees that I called the two ladies were gone or if they were there I couldn't find them, and the track over the Domain Hill wasn't there. We used to climb up and watch the steamer coming in from the Straits. And there was gorse mixed up with the bush, and the bush itself didn't hold the same fear, even with its secret terrible drippings and rustlings that go on for ever.

There were more people in the town too. The Main Trunk Line brings more tourists, my aunt said. There were people everywhere, lying on the beach being burned or browned by the sun and sea, people whizzing round the harbour in motor-boats like the pop-pop boats we used to whizz round in the bath on Christmas morning. People surf-riding, playing tennis, fishing in the Straits, practising in skiffs for the Regatta. People.

But my grandmother wasn't there to show me everything and tell me stories. And the lagoon was dirtier than ever. See the lagoon said my aunt. Full of drifting wood and seaweed and crabs' claws. We could see the lagoon from the kitchen window. We were looking at photographs that day, what silly clothes people wore in those days. There was Grandma sitting on the verandah with her knitting, and there was my great grandmother, the Maori princess with her big brown eyes, and her lace dress on that her husband bought her, handmade lace said my aunt, he loved her till he met that woman from Nelson, men are crazy sometimes, but I suppose women are crazier.

– Is there a story, I said. I was a child again, Grandma tell me about ...

My aunt smiled. She guesses things sometimes.

– The sort of story they put in *Truth*, she said. On the morning of the tragedy witness saw defendant etc. etc. Your great grandmother was a murderess. She drowned her husband, pushed him in the lagoon. I suppose the tide was high, I don't know. They would call it The Woman From Nelson ... she mused. They would have photos. But then

25 The Lagoon

nobody knew, only the family. Everybody thought he had had one over the eight and didn't know where he was going.

My aunt drew aside the curtain and peered out. She reminded me of the women in films who turn to the window in an emotional moment, but the moment wasn't emotional nor was my aunt.

– It's an interesting story, she said. I prefer Dostoevsky to *Truth*.

The water was brown and shining and to the right lay the dark shadow of the Domain Hill. There were kids playing on the edge, Christopher Robins with sand between the toes, sailing toy warships and paddling with bare feet in the pools.

– Grandmother never told me, I said.

Again my aunt smiled. The reason (she quoted) one talks farthest from the heart is the fear that it may be hurt.

And then my aunt dropped the curtain across the window and turned to the photographs again.

Was it my aunt speaking or was it my grandmother or my great grandmother who loved a white lace dress?

At low tide there is no lagoon. Only a stretch of dirty grey sand. I remember we used to skim thin, white stones over the water and catch tiddlers in the little creek near by and make sand castles, this is my castle we said you be Father I'll be Mother and we'll live here and catch crabs and tiddlers for ever ...

26

The Flying Machine

(1953)

Ray Bradbury

In the year AD 400, the Emperor Yuan held his throne by the Great Wall of China, and the land was green with rain, readying itself toward the harvest, at peace, the people in his dominion neither too happy nor too sad.

Early on the morning of the first day of the first week of the second month of the new year, the Emperor Yuan was sipping tea and fanning himself against a warm breeze when a servant ran across the scarlet and blue garden tiles, calling, 'Oh, Emperor, Emperor, a miracle!'

'Yes,' said the Emperor, 'the air *is* sweet this morning.'

'No, no, a miracle!' said the servant, bowing quickly.

'And this tea is good in my mouth, surely that is a miracle.'

'No, no, Your Excellency.'

'Let me guess then – the sun has risen and a new day is upon us. Or the sea is blue. *That* now is the finest of all miracles.'

'Excellency, a man is flying!'

'What?' The Emperor stopped his fan.

'I saw him in the air, a man flying with wings. I heard a voice call out of the sky, and when I looked up, there he was, a dragon in the heavens with a man in its mouth, a dragon of paper and bamboo, coloured like the sun and the grass.'

'It is early,' said the Emperor, 'and you have just wakened from a dream.'

'It is early, but I have seen what I have seen! Come, and you will see it too.'

'Sit down with me here,' said the Emperor. 'Drink some tea. It must be a strange thing, if it is true, to see a man fly. You must have time to think of it, even as I must have time to prepare myself for the sight.'

They drank tea.

'Please,' said the servant at last, 'or he will be gone.'

The Emperor rose thoughtfully. 'Now you may show me what you have seen.'

They walked into a garden, across a meadow of grass, over a small bridge, through a grove of trees, and up a tiny hill.

'There!' said the servant.

The Emperor looked into the sky.

And in the sky, laughing so high that you could hardly hear him laugh, was a man; and the man was clothed in bright papers and reeds to make wings and a beautiful yellow tail, and he was soaring all about like the largest bird in a universe of birds, like a new dragon in a land of ancient dragons.

The man called down to them from high in the cool winds of morning, 'I fly, I fly!'

The servant waved to him. 'Yes, yes!'

The Emperor Yuan did not move. Instead he looked at the Great Wall of China now taking shape out of the farthest mist in the green hills, that splendid snake of stones which writhed with majesty across the entire land. That wonderful wall which had protected them for a timeless time from enemy hordes and preserved peace for years without number. He saw the town nestled to itself by a river and a road and a hill, beginning to waken.

'Tell me,' he said to his servant, 'has anyone else seen this flying man?'

'I am the only one, Excellency,' said the servant, smiling at the sky, waving.

The Emperor watched the heavens another minute and then said, 'Call him down to me.'

'Ho, come down, come down! The Emperor wishes to see you!' called the servant, hands cupped to his shouting mouth.

The Emperor glanced in all directions while the flying man soared down the morning wind. He saw a farmer, early in his fields, watching the sky, and he noted where the farmer stood.

The flying man alit with a rustle of paper and a creak of bamboo reeds. He came proudly to the Emperor, clumsy in his rig, at last bowing before the old man.

'What have you done?' demanded the Emperor.

'I have flown in the sky, Your Excellency,' replied the man.

'What *have* you done?' said the Emperor again.

'I have just told you!' cried the flier.

'You have told me nothing at all.' The Emperor reached out a thin hand to touch the pretty paper and the birdlike keel of the apparatus. It smelled cool, of the wind.

'Is it not beautiful, Excellency?'

'Yes, too beautiful.'

'It is the only one in the world!' smiled the man. 'And I am the inventor.'

'The *only* one in the world?'

'I swear it!'

'Who else knows of this?'

'No-one. Not even my wife, who would think me mad with the sun. She thought I was making a kite. I rose in the night and walked to the cliffs far away. And when the morning breezes blew and the sun rose, I gathered my courage, Excellency, and leaped from the cliff. I flew! But my wife does not know of it.'

'Well for her, then,' said the Emperor. 'Come along.'

They walked back to the great house. The sun was full in the sky now, and the smell of the grass was refreshing. The Emperor, the servant, and the flier paused within the huge garden.

The Emperor clapped his hands. 'Ho, guards!'

The guards came running.

'Hold this man.'

The guards seized the flier.

'Call the executioner,' said the Emperor.

'What's this!' cried the flier, bewildered. 'What have I done?' He began to weep, so that the beautiful paper apparatus rustled.

'Here is the man who has made a certain machine,' said the Emperor, 'and yet asks us what he has created. He does not know himself. It is only necessary that he create, without knowing why he has done so, or what this thing will do.'

The executioner came running with a sharp silver axe. He stood with his naked, large-muscled arms ready, his face covered with a serene white mask.

'One moment,' said the Emperor. He turned to a nearby table upon which sat a machine that he himself had created. The Emperor took a tiny golden key from his own neck. He fitted this key to the tiny, delicate machine and wound it up. Then he set the machine going.

The machine was a garden of metal and jewels. Set in motion, birds sang in tiny metal trees, wolves walked through miniature forests, and tiny people ran in and out of sun and shadow, fanning themselves with miniature fans, listening to the tiny emerald birds, and standing by impossibly small but tinkling fountains.

'Is it not beautiful?' said the Emperor. 'If you asked me what I have done here, I could answer you well. I have made birds sing, I have made forests murmur, I have set people to walking in this woodland, enjoying the leaves and shadows and songs. That is what I have done.'

'But, oh, Emperor!' pleaded the flier, on his knees, the tears pouring down his face. 'I have done a similar thing! I have found beauty. I have flown on the morning wind. I have looked down on all the sleeping houses and gardens. I have smelled the sea and even *seen* it, beyond the hills, from my high place. And I have soared like a bird; oh, I cannot say how beautiful it is up there, in the sky, with the wind about me, the wind blowing me here like a feather, there like a fan, the way the sky smells in the morning! And how free one feels! *That* is beautiful, Emperor, that is beautiful too!'

'Yes,' said the Emperor sadly, 'I know it must be true. For I felt my heart move with you in the air and I wondered: What is it like? How does it feel? How do the distant pools look from so high? And how my houses and servants? Like ants? And how the distant towns not yet awake?'

'Then spare me!'

'But there are times,' said the Emperor, more sadly still, 'when one must lose a little beauty if one is to keep what little beauty one already has. I do not fear you, yourself, but I fear another man.'

'What man?'

'Some other man who, seeing you, will build a thing of bright papers and bamboo like this. But the other man will have an evil face and an evil heart, and the beauty will be gone. It is this man I fear.'

'Why? Why?'

'Who is to say that someday just such a man, in just such an apparatus of paper and reed, might not fly in the sky and drop huge stones upon the Great Wall of China?' said the Emperor.

No-one moved or said a word.

'Off with his head,' said the Emperor.

The executioner whirled his silver axe.

'Burn the kite and the inventor's body and bury their ashes together,' said the Emperor.

The servants retreated to obey.

The Emperor turned to his hand-servant, who had seen the man flying. 'Hold your tongue. It was all a dream, a most sorrowful and beautiful dream. And that farmer in the distant field who also saw, tell him it would pay him to consider it only a vision. If ever the word passes around, you and the farmer die within the hour.'

'You are merciful, Emperor.'

'No, not merciful,' said the old man. Beyond the garden wall he saw the guards burning the beautiful machine of paper and reeds that smelled of the morning wind. He saw the dark smoke climb into the sky. 'No, only very much bewildered and afraid.' He saw the guards digging a tiny pit wherein to bury the ashes. 'What is the life of one man against those of a million others? I must take solace from that thought.'

He took the key from its chain about his neck and once more wound up the beautiful miniature garden. He stood looking out across the land at the Great Wall, the peaceful town, the green fields, the rivers and streams. He sighed. The tiny garden whirred its hidden and delicate machinery and set itself in motion; tiny people walked in forests, tiny foxes loped through sun-speckled glades in beautiful shining pelts, and among the tiny trees flew little bits of high song and bright blue and yellow colour, flying, flying, flying in that small sky.

'Oh,' said the Emperor, closing his eyes, 'look at the birds, look at the birds!'

27

The Cricket Match

(1957)

Sam Selvon

The time when the West Indies cricket eleven come to England to show the Englishmen the finer points of the game, Algernon was working in a tyre factory down by Chiswick way, and he lambast them English fellars for so.

'That is the way to play the game,' he tell them, as the series went on and West Indies making some big score and bowling out them English fellars for duck and thing, 'you thought we didn't know how to play the game, eh? That is cricket, lovely cricket.'

And all day he singing a calypso that he make up about the cricket matches that play, ending up by saying that in the world of sport, is to wait until the West Indies report.

Well in truth and in fact, the people in this country believe that everybody who come from the West Indies at least like the game even if they can't play it. But you could take it from me that it have some tests that don't like the game at all, and among them was Algernon. But he see a chance to give the Nordics tone and he get all the gen on the matches and players, and come like an authority in the factory on cricket. In fact, the more they ask him the more convinced Algernon get that perhaps he have the talent of a Walcott in him only waiting for a chance to come out.

They have a portable radio hide away from the foreman and they listening to the score every day. And as the match going on you should hear Algernon: 'Yes, lovely stroke,' and 'That should have been a six,' and so on. Meanwhile, he picking up any round object that near to hand and making demonstration, showing them how Ramadhin does spin the ball.

'I bet you used to play a lot back home,' the English fellars tell him.

'Who, me?' Algernon say. 'Man, cricket is breakfast and dinner where I come from. If you want to learn about the game you must go down there. I don't want to brag,' he say, hanging his head a little, 'but I used to live next door to Ramadhin, and we used to teach one another the fine points.'

But what you think Algernon know about cricket in truth? The most he ever play was in the street, with a bat make from a coconut branch, a dry mango seed for ball, and

27 The Cricket Match

a pitchoil tin for wicket. And that was when he was a boy, and one day he get lash with the mango seed and since that time he never play again.

But all day long in the factory, he and another West Indian fellar name Roy getting on as if they invent the game, and the more the West Indies eleven score, the more they getting on. At last a Englisher name Charles, who was living in the suburbs, say to Algernon one morning:

'You chaps from the West Indies are really fine cricketers. I was just wondering ... I play for a side where I live, and the other day I mentioned you and Roy to our captain, and he said why don't you organize an eleven and come down our way one Saturday for a match? Of course,' Charles went on earnestly, 'we don't expect to be good enough for you, but still, it will be fun.'

'Oh,' Algernon say airily, 'I don't know. I uses to play in first-class matches, and most of the boys I know accustom to a real good game with strong opposition. What kind of pitch you have?'

'The pitch is good,' Charles say. 'Real English turf.'

Algernon start to hedge. He scratch his head. He say, 'I don't know. What you think about the idea, Roy?'

Roy decide to hem and leave Algernon to get them out of the mooch. He say, 'I don't know, either. It sound like a good idea, though.'

'See what you can do,' Charles say, 'and let me know this week.'

Afterwards in the canteen having elevenses Roy tell Algernon: 'You see what your big mouth get us into.'

'*My* big mouth!' Algernon say. 'Who it is say he bowl four top bats for duck one after the other in a match in Queen's Park oval in Port of Spain? Who it is say he score two hundred and fifty not out in a match against Jamaica?'

'Well to tell you the truth Algernon,' Roy say, now that they was down to brass tacks, 'I ain't play cricket for a long time. In fact, I don't believe I could still play.'

'Me too, boy,' Algernon say. 'I mean, up here in England you don't get a chance to practise or anything. I must be out of form.'

They sit down there in the canteen cogitating on the problem.

'Anyway,' Roy say, 'it look as if we will have to hustle an eleven somehow. We can't back out of it now.'

'I studying,' Algernon say, scratching his head. 'What about Eric, you think he will play?'

'You could ask him, he might. And what about Williams? And Wilky? And Heads? Those boys should know how to play.'

'Yes, but look at trouble to get them! Wilky working night and he will want to sleep. Heads is a man you can't find when you want. And Williams – I ain't see him for a long time, because he owe me a pound and he don't come my way these days.'

'Still,' Roy say, 'we will have to manage to get a side together. If we back out of this now them English fellars will say we are only talkers. You better wait for me after work this evening, and we will go around by some of the boys and see what we could do.'

That was the Monday, and the Wednesday night about twelve of the boys get together in Algernon room in Kensal Rise, and Algernon boiling water in the kettle and making tea while they discuss the situation.

'Algernon always have big mouth, and at last it land him in trouble.'

'Cricket! I never play in my life!'

'I uses to play a little "pass-out" in my days, but to go and play against a English side! Boy, them fellars like this game, and they could play, too!'

'One time I hit a ball and it went over a fence and break a lady window and ...'

'All right, all right, ease up on the good old days, the problem is right now. I mean, we have to rally.'

'Yes, and then when we go there everybody get bowl for duck, and when them fellars batting we can't get them out. Not me.'

But in the end, after a lot of blague and argument, they agree that they would go and play.

'What about some practice?' Wilky say anxiously. Wilky was the only fellar who really serious about the game.

'Practice!' Roy say. 'It ain't have time for that. I wonder if I could still hold a bat?' And he get up and pick up a stick Algernon had in the corner and begin to make stance.

'Is not that way to hold a bat, stupid. Is so.'

And there in Algernon room the boys begin to remember what they could of the game, and Wilky saying he ain't playing unless he is captain, and Eric saying he ain't playing unless he get pads because one time a cork ball nearly break his shinbone, and a fellar name Chips pull a cricket cap from his back pocket and trying it on in front a mirror.

So everything was arranged in a half-hearted sort of way. When the great day come, Algernon had hopes that they might postpone the match, because only eight of the boys turn up, but the English captain say it was a shame for them to return without playing, that he would make his side eight, too.

Well that Saturday on the village green was a historic day. Whether cold feet take the English side because of the licks the West Indies eleven was sharing at Lord's I can't say, but the fact is that they had to bowl first and they only coming down with some nice hop-and-drop that the boys lashing for six and four.

When Algernon turn to bat he walk out like a veteran. He bend down and inspect the pitch closely and shake his head, as if he ain't too satisfied with the condition of it but had to put up with it. He put on gloves, stretch out his hands as if he about to shift a heavy tyre in the factory, and take up the most unorthodox stance them English fellars ever did see. Algernon legs wide apart as if he doing the split and he have the bat already swing over his shoulder although the bowler ain't bowl yet. The umpire making sign to him that he covering the wicket but Algernon do as if he can't see. He make up his mind that he rather go for l.b.w. than for the stumps to fly.

No doubt an ordinary ball thrown with ease would have had him out in two-twos, but as I was saying, it look as if the unusual play of the boys have the Englishers in a quandary, and the bowler come down with a nice hop-and-drop that a baby couldn't miss.

Algernon close his eyes and he make a swipe at the ball, and he swipe so hard that when the bat collide the ball went right out of the field and fall in the road.

Them Englishers never see a stroke like that in their lives. All heads turn up to the sky watching the ball going.

Algernon feel like a king: only thing, when he hit the ball the bat went after it and nearly knock down a English fellar who was fielding silly-mid-on-square-leg.

Well praise the lord, the score was then sixty-nine and one set of rain start to fall and stop the match.

Later on, entertaining the boys in the local pub, the Englishers asking all sort of questions, like why they stand so and so and why they make such and such a stroke, and the boys talking as if cricket so common in the West Indies that the babies born either with a bat or a ball, depending on if it would be a good bowler or batsman.

'That was a wonderful shot,' Charles tell Algernon grudgingly. Charles still had a feeling that the boys was only talkers, but so much controversy raging that he don't know what to say.

'If my bat didn't fly out my hand,' Algernon say, and wave his hand in the air dramatically, as if to say he would have lost the ball in the other county.

'Of course, we still have to see your bowling,' the English captain say. 'Pity about the rain – usual English weather, you know.'

'Bowling!' Algernon echo, feeling as if he is a Walcott and a Valentine roll into one. 'Oh yes, we must come back some time and finish off the match.'

'What about next Saturday?' the captain press, eager to see the boys in action again, not sure if he was dreaming about all them wild swipe and crazy strokes.

'Sure, I'll get the boys together,' Algernon say.

Algernon say that, but it wasn't possible, because none of them wanted to go back after batting, frighten that they won't be able to bowl the Englishers out.

And Charles keep reminding Algernon all the time, but Algernon keep saying how the boys scatter about, some gone Birmingham to live, and others move and gone to work somewhere else, and he can't find them anywhere.

'Never mind,' Algernon tell Charles, 'next cricket season I will get a sharp eleven together and come down your way for another match. Now, if you want me to show you how I make that stroke ...'

28

The Blush

(1958)

Elizabeth Taylor

They were the same age – Mrs Allen and the woman who came every day to do the housework. 'I shall never have children now,' Mrs Allen had begun to tell herself. Something had not come true; the essential part of her life. She had always imagined her children in fleeting scenes and intimations; that was how they had come to her, like snatches of a film. She had seen them plainly, their chins tilted up as she tied on their bibs at meal-times; their naked bodies had darted in and out of the water-sprinkler on the lawn; and she had listened to their voices in the garden and in the mornings from their beds. She had even cried a little dreaming of the day when the eldest boy would go off to boarding-school; she pictured the train going out of the station; she raised her hand and her throat contracted and her lips trembled as she smiled. The years passing by had slowly filched from her the reality of these scenes – the gay sounds; the grave peace she had longed for; even the pride of grief.

She listened – as they worked together in the kitchen – to Mrs Lacey's troubles with her family, her grumblings about her grown-up son who would not get up till dinner-time on Sundays and then expected his mother to have cleaned his shoes for him; about the girl of eighteen who was a hairdresser and too full of dainty ways which she picked up from the women's magazines, and the adolescent girl who moped and glowered and answered back.

'My children wouldn't have turned out like that,' Mrs Allen thought, as she made her murmured replies. 'The more you do for some, the more you may,' said Mrs Lacey. But from gossip in the village which Mrs Allen heard, she had done all too little. The children, one night after another, for years and years, had had to run out for parcels of fish and chips while their mother sat in the Horse and Jockey drinking brown ale. On summer evenings, when they were younger, they had hung about outside the pub: when they were bored they pressed their foreheads to the window and looked in at the dark little bar, hearing the jolly laughter, their mother's the loudest of all. Seeing their faces, she would swing at once from the violence of hilarity to that of extreme annoyance and, although ginger-beer and packets of potato crisps would be handed out through the window, her anger went out with them and threatened the children as they ate and drank.

'And she doesn't always care who she goes there *with*,' Mrs Allen's gardener told her.

'She works hard and deserves a little pleasure – she has her anxieties,' said Mrs Allen, who, alas, had none.

She had never been inside the Horse and Jockey, although it was nearer to her house than the Chequers at the other end of the village where she and her husband went sometimes for a glass of sherry on Sunday mornings. The Horse and Jockey attracted a different set of customers – for instance, people who sat down and drank, at tables all round the wall. At the Chequers no one ever sat down, but stood and sipped and chatted as at a cocktail party, and luncheons and dinners were served, which made it so much more respectable: no children hung about outside, because they were all at home with their nannies.

Sometimes in the evenings – so many of them – when her husband was kept late in London, Mrs Allen wished that she could go down to the Chequers and drink a glass of sherry and exchange a little conversation with someone; but she was too shy to open the door and go in alone: she imagined heads turning, a surprised welcome from her friends, who would all be safely in married pairs; and then, when she left, eyes meeting with unspoken messages and conjecture in the air.

Mrs Lacey left her at midday and then there was gardening to do and the dog to be taken for a walk. After six o'clock, she began to pace restlessly about the house, glancing at the clocks in one room after another, listening for her husband's car – the sound she knew so well because she had awaited it for such a large part of her married life. She would hear, at last, the tyres turning on the soft gravel, the door being slammed, then his footsteps hurrying towards the porch. She knew that it was a wasteful way of spending her years – and, looking back, she was unable to tell one of them from another – but she could not think what else she might do. Humphrey went on earning more and more money and there was no stopping him now. Her acquaintances, in wretched quandaries about where the next term's school-fees were to come from, would turn to her and say cruelly: 'Oh, *you're* all right, Ruth. You've no idea what you are spared.'

And Mrs Lacey would be glad when Maureen could leave school and 'get out earning'. '"I've got my geometry to do," she says, when it's time to wash up the tea-things. "I'll geometry you, my girl," I said. "When I was your age, I was out earning."'

Mrs Allen was fascinated by the life going on in that house and the children seemed real to her, although she had never seen them. Only Mr Lacey remained blurred and unimaginable. No one knew him. He worked in the town in the valley, six miles away, and he kept himself to himself; had never been known to show his face in the Horse and Jockey. 'I've got my own set,' Mrs Lacey said airily. 'After all, he's nearly twenty years older than me. I'll make sure neither of my girls follow my mistake. "I'd rather see you dead at my feet," I said to Vera.' Ron's young lady was lucky; having Ron, she added. Mrs Allen found this strange, for Ron had always been painted so black; was, she had been led to believe, oafish, ungrateful, greedy and slow to put his hands in his pockets if there was any paying out to do. There was also the matter of his shoe-cleaning, for no young woman would do what his mother did for him – or said she did. Always, Mrs Lacey would sigh and say: 'Goodness me, if only I was their age and knew what I know now.'

She was an envious woman: she envied Mrs Allen her pretty house and her clothes and she envied her own daughters their youth. 'If I had your figure,' she would say to Mrs Allen. Her own had gone: what else could be expected, she asked, when she had had three children? Mrs Allen thought, too, of all the brown ale she drank at the Horse and Jockey and of the reminiscences of meals past which came so much into her conversations. Whatever the cause was, her flesh, slackly corseted, shook as she trod heavily about the kitchen. In summer, with bare arms and legs she looked larger than ever. Although her skin was very white, the impression she gave was at once colourful – from her orange hair and bright lips and the floral patterns that she always wore. Her red-painted toe-nails poked through the straps of her fancy sandals; turquoise-blue beads were wound round her throat.

Humphrey Allen had never seen her; he had always left for the station before she arrived, and that was a good thing, his wife thought. When she spoke of Mrs Lacey, she wondered if he visualised a neat, homely woman in a clean white overall. She did not deliberately mislead him, but she took advantage of his indifference. Her relationship with Mrs Lacey and the intimacy of their conversations in the kitchen he would not have approved, and the sight of those calloused feet with their chipped nail-varnish and yellowing heels would have sickened him.

One Monday morning, Mrs Lacey was later than usual. She was never very punctual and had many excuses about flat bicycle-tyres or Maureen being poorly. Mrs Allen, waiting for her, sorted out all the washing. When she took another look at the clock, she decided that it was far too late for her to be expected at all. For some time lately Mrs Lacey had seemed ill and depressed; her eyelids, which were chronically rather inflamed, had been more angrily red than ever and, at the sink or ironing-board, she would fall into unusual silences, was absent-minded and full of sighs. She had always liked to talk about the 'change' and did so more than ever as if with a desperate hopefulness.

'I'm sorry, but I was ever so sick,' she told Mrs Allen, when she arrived the next morning. 'I still feel queerish. Such heartburn. I don't like the signs, I can tell you. All I crave is pickled walnuts, just the same as I did with Maureen. I don't like the signs one bit. I feel I'll throw myself into the river if I'm taken that way again.'

Mrs Allen felt stunned and antagonistic. 'Surely not at your age,' she said crossly.

'You can't be more astonished than me,' Mrs Lacey said, belching loudly. 'Oh, pardon. I'm afraid I can't help myself.'

Not being able to help herself, she continued to belch and hiccough as she turned on taps and shook soap-powder into the washing-up bowl. It was because of this that Mrs Allen decided to take the dog for a walk. Feeling consciously fastidious and aloof she made her way across the fields, trying to disengage her thoughts from Mrs Lacey and her troubles; but unable to. 'Poor woman,' she thought again and again with bitter animosity.

She turned back when she noticed how the sky had darkened with racing, sharp-edged clouds. Before she could reach home, the rain began. Her hair, soaking wet, shrank into tight curls against her head; her woollen suit smelt like a damp animal. 'Oh, I am drenched,' she called out, as she threw open the kitchen door.

She knew at once that Mrs Lacey had gone, that she must have put on her coat and left almost as soon as Mrs Allen had started out on her walk, for nothing was done; the washing-up was hardly started and the floor was unswept. Among the stacked-up crockery a note was propped; she had come over funny, felt dizzy and, leaving her apologies and respects, had gone.

Angrily, but methodically, Mrs Allen set about making good the wasted morning. By afternoon, the grim look was fixed upon her face. 'How dare she?' she found herself whispering, without allowing herself to wonder what it was the woman had dared.

She had her own little ways of cosseting herself through the lonely hours, comforts which were growing more important to her as she grew older, so that the time would come when not to have her cup of tea at four-thirty would seem a prelude to disaster. This afternoon, disorganised as it already was, she fell out of her usual habit and instead of carrying the tray to the low table by the fire, she poured out her tea in the kitchen and drank it there, leaning tiredly against the dresser. Then she went upstairs to make herself tidy. She was trying to brush her frizzed hair smooth again when she heard the door bell ringing.

When she opened the door, she saw quite plainly a look of astonishment take the place of anxiety on the man's face. Something about herself surprised him, was not what he had expected. 'Mrs Allen?' he asked uncertainly and the astonishment remained when she had answered him.

'Well, I'm calling about the wife,' he said. 'Mrs Lacey that works here.'

'I was worried about her,' said Mrs Allen.

She knew that she must face the embarrassment of hearing about Mrs Lacey's condition and invited the man into her husband's study, where she thought he might look less out-of-place than in her brocade-smothered drawing-room. He looked about him resentfully and glared down at the floor which his wife had polished. With this thought in his mind, he said abruptly: 'It's all taken its toll.'

He sat down on a leather couch with his cap and his bicycle-clips beside him.

'I came home to my tea and found her in bed, crying,' he said. This was true. Mrs Lacey had succumbed to despair and gone to lie down. Feeling better at four o'clock, she went downstairs to find some food to comfort herself with; but the slice of dough-cake was ill-chosen and brought on more heartburn and floods of bitter tears.

'If she carries on here for a while, it's all got to be very different,' Mr Lacey said threateningly. He was nervous at saying what he must and could only bring out the words with the impetus of anger. 'You may or may not know that she's expecting.'

'Yes,' said Mrs Allen humbly. 'This morning she told me that she thought ...'

'There's no "thought" about it. It's as plain as a pikestaff.' Yet in his eyes she could see disbelief and bafflement and he frowned and looked down again at the polished floor.

Twenty years older than his wife – or so his wife had said – he really, to Mrs Allen, looked quite ageless, a crooked, bow-legged little man who might have been a jockey once. The expression about his blue eyes was like a child's: he was both stubborn and pathetic.

Mrs Allen's fat spaniel came into the room and went straight to the stranger's chair and began to sniff at his corduroy trousers.

'It's too much for her,' Mr Lacey said. 'It's too much to expect.'

To Mrs Allen's horror she saw the blue eyes filling with tears. Hoping to hide his emotion, he bent down and fondled the dog, making playful thrusts at it with his fist closed.

He was a man utterly, bewilderedly at sea. His married life had been too much for him, with so much in it that he could not understand.

'Now I know, I will do what I can,' Mrs Allen told him. 'I will try to get someone else in to do the rough.'

'It's the late nights that are the trouble,' he said. 'She comes in dog-tired. Night after night. It's not good enough. "Let them stay at home and mind their own children once in a while," I told her. "We don't need the money."'

'I can't understand,' Mrs Allen began. She was at sea herself now, but felt perilously near a barbarous, unknown shore and was afraid to make any movement towards it.

'I earn good money. For her to come out at all was only for extras. She likes new clothes. In the daytimes I never had any objection. Then all these cocktail parties begin. It beats me how people can drink like it night after night and pay out for someone else to mind their kids. Perhaps you're thinking that it's not my business, but I'm the one who has to sit at home alone till all hours and get my own supper and see next to nothing of my wife. I'm boiling over some nights. Once I nearly rushed out when I heard the car stop down the road. I wanted to tell your husband what I thought of you both.'

'My husband?' murmured Mrs Allen.

'What am I supposed to have, I would have asked him? Is she my wife or your sitter-in? Bringing her back at this time of night. And it's no use saying she could have refused. She never would.'

Mrs Allen's quietness at last defeated him and dispelled the anger he had tried to rouse in himself. The look of her, too, filled him with doubts, her grave, uncertain demeanour and the shock her age had been to him. He had imagined someone so much younger and – because of the cocktail parties – flighty. Instead, he recognised something of himself in her, a yearning disappointment. He picked up his cap and his bicycle-clips and sat looking down at them, turning them round in his hands. 'I had to come,' he said.

'Yes,' said Mrs Allen.

'So you won't ask her again?' he pleaded. 'It isn't right for her. Not now.'

28   The Blush

'No, I won't,' Mrs Allen promised and she stood up as he did and walked over to the door. He stooped and gave the spaniel a final pat. 'You'll excuse my coming, I hope.'

'Of course.'

'It was no use saying any more to her. Whatever she's asked, she won't refuse. It's her way.'

Mrs Allen shut the front door after him and stood in the hall, listening to him wheeling his bicycle across the gravel. Then she felt herself beginning to blush. She was glad that she was alone, for she could feel her face, her throat, even the tops of her arms burning, and she went over to a looking-glass and studied with great interest this strange phenomenon.

29

The Sacrificial Egg

(1959)

Chinua Achebe

Julius Obi sat gazing at his typewriter. The fat Chief Clerk, his boss, was snoring at his table. Outside, the gatekeeper in his green uniform was sleeping at his post. You couldn't blame him; no customer had passed through the gate for nearly a week. There was an empty basket on the giant weighing machine. A few palm-kernels lay desolately in the dust around the machine. Only the flies remained in strength.

Julius went to the window that overlooked the great market on the bank of the River Niger. This market, though still called Nkwo, had long spilled over into Eke, Oye, and Afo with the coming of civilization and the growth of the town into a big palm-oil port. In spite of this encroachment, however, it was still busiest on its original Nkwo day, because the deity who had presided over it from antiquity still cast her spell only on her own day – let men in their greed spill over themselves. It was said that she appeared in the form of an old woman in the centre of the market just before cock-crow and waved her magic fan in the four directions of the earth – in front of her, behind her, to the right and to the left – to draw to the market men and women from distant places. And they came bringing the produce of their lands – palm-oil and kernels, kola nuts, cassava, mats, baskets and earthenware pots; and took home many-coloured cloths, smoked fish, iron pots and plates. These were the forest peoples. The other half of the world who lived by the great rivers came down also – by canoe, bringing yams and fish. Sometimes it was a big canoe with a dozen or more people in it; sometimes it was a lone fisherman and his wife in a small vessel from the swift-flowing Anambara. They moored their canoe on the bank and sold their fish, after much haggling. The woman then walked up the steep banks of the river to the heart of the market to buy salt and oil and, if the sales had been very good, even a length of cloth. And for her children at home she bought bean cakes and mai-mai which the Igara women cooked. As evening approached, they took up their paddles again and paddled away, the water shimmering in the sunset and their canoe becoming smaller and smaller in the distance until it was just a dark crescent on the water's face and two dark bodies swaying forwards and backwards in it. Umuru then

The Sacrificial Egg

was the meeting place of the forest people who were called Igbo and the alien riverain folk whom the Igbo called Olu and beyond whom the world stretched in indefiniteness.

Julius Obi was not a native of Umuru. He had come like countless others from some bush village inland. Having passed his Standard Six in a mission school he had come to Umuru to work as a clerk in the offices of the all-powerful European trading company which bought palm-kernels at its own price and sold cloth and metalware, also at its own price. The offices were situated beside the famous market so that in his first two or three weeks Julius had to learn to work within its huge enveloping hum. Sometimes when the Chief Clerk was away he walked to the window and looked down on the vast anthill activity. Most of these people were not there yesterday, he thought, and yet the market had been just as full. There must be many, many people in the world to be able to fill the market day after day like this. Of course they say not all who came to the great market were real people. Janet's mother, Ma, has said so.

'Some of the beautiful young women you see squeezing through the crowds are not people like you or me but mammy-wota who have their town in the depths of the river,' she said. 'You can always tell them, because they are beautiful with a beauty that is too perfect and too cold. You catch a glimpse of her with the tail of your eye, then you blink and look properly, but she has already vanished in the crowd.'

Julius thought about these things as he now stood at the window looking down on the silent, empty market. Who would have believed that the great boisterous market could ever be quenched like this? But such was the strength of Kitikpa, the incarnate power of smallpox. Only he could drive away all those people and leave the market to the flies.

When Umuru was a little village, there was an age-grade who swept its market-square every Nkwo day. But progress had turned it into a busy, sprawling, crowded and dirty river port, a no-man's-land where strangers outnumbered by far the sons of the soil, who could do nothing about it except shake their heads at this gross perversion of their prayer. For indeed they had prayed – who will blame them – for their town to grow and prosper. And it had grown. But there is good growth and there is bad growth. The belly does not bulge out only with food and drink; it might be the abominable disease which would end by sending its sufferer out of the house even before he was fully dead.

The strangers who came to Umuru came for trade and money, not in search of duties to perform, for they had those in plenty back home in their village which was real home.

And as if this did not suffice, the young sons and daughters of Umuru soil, encouraged by schools and churches were behaving no better than the strangers. They neglected all their old tasks and kept only the revelries.

Such was the state of the town when Kitikpa came to see it and to demand the sacrifice the inhabitants owed the gods of the soil. He came in confident knowledge of the terror he held over the people. He was an evil deity, and boasted it. Lest he be offended those he killed were not killed but decorated, and no one dared weep for them. He put an end to the coming and going between neighbours and between villages. They said, 'Kitikpa is in that village,' and immediately it was cut off by its neighbours.

Julius was sad and worried because it was almost a week since he had seen Janet, the girl he was going to marry. Ma had explained to him very gently that he should no longer go to see them 'until this thing is over, by the power of Jehovah'. (Ma was a very devout Christian convert and one reason why she approved of Julius for her only daughter was that he sang in the choir of the CMS church.)

'You must keep to your rooms,' she had said in hushed tones, for Kitikpa strictly forbade any noise or boisterousness. 'You never know whom you might meet on the streets. That family has got it.' She lowered her voice even more and pointed surreptitiously at the house across the road whose doorway was barred with a yellow palm-frond. 'He has decorated one of them already and the rest were moved away today in a big government lorry.'

Janet walked a short way with Julius and stopped; so he stopped too. They seemed to have nothing to say to each other yet they lingered on. Then she said goodnight and he said goodnight. And they shook hands, which was very odd, as though parting for the night were something new and grave.

He did not go straight home, because he wanted desperately to cling, even alone, to this strange parting. Being educated he was not afraid of whom he might meet, so he went to the bank of the river and just walked up and down it. He must have been there a long time because he was still there when the wooden gong of the night-mask sounded. He immediately set out for home, half-walking and half-running, for night-masks were not a matter of superstition; they were real. They chose the night for their revelry because like the bat's their ugliness was great.

In his hurry he stepped on something that broke with a slight liquid explosion. He stopped and peeped down at the footpath. The moon was not up yet but there was a faint light in the sky which showed that it would not be long delayed. In this half-light he saw that he had stepped on an egg offered in sacrifice. Someone oppressed by misfortune had brought the offering to the crossroads in the dusk. And he had stepped on it. There were the usual young palm-fronds around it. But Julius saw it differently as a house where the terrible artist was at work. He wiped the sole of his foot on the sandy path and hurried away, carrying another vague worry in his mind. But hurrying was no use now; the fleet-footed mask was already abroad. Perhaps it was impelled to hurry by the threatening imminence of the moon. Its voice rose high and clear in the still night air like a flaming sword. It was yet a long way away, but Julius knew that distances vanished before it. So he made straight for the cocoyam farm beside the road and threw himself on his belly, in the shelter of the broad leaves. He had hardly done this when he heard the rattling staff of the spirit and a thundering stream of esoteric speech. He shook all over. The sounds came bearing down on him, almost pressing his face into the moist earth. And now he could hear the footsteps. It was as if twenty evil men were running together. Panic sweat broke all over him and he was nearly impelled to get up and run. Fortunately he kept a firm hold on himself … In no time at all the commotion in the air and on the earth – the thunder and torrential rain, the earthquake and flood – passed and disappeared in the distance on the other side of the road.

The next morning, at the office the Chief Clerk, a son of the soil spoke bitterly about last night's provocation of Kitikpa by the headstrong youngsters who had launched the noisy fleet-footed mask in defiance of their elders, who knew that Kitikpa would be enraged, and then ...

The trouble was that the disobedient youths had never yet experienced the power of Kitikpa themselves; they had only heard of it. But soon they would learn.

As Julius stood at the window looking out on the emptied market he lived through the terror of that night again. It was barely a week ago but already it seemed like another life, separated from the present by a vast emptiness. This emptiness deepened with every passing day. On this side of it stood Julius, and on the other Ma and Janet whom the dread artist decorated.

30

Action Will Be Taken *(An Action-Packed Story)*

(1966)

Heinrich Böll

Translated by Leila Vennewitz (1966)

Probably one of the strangest interludes in my life was the time I spent as an employee in Alfred Wunsiedel's factory. By nature I am inclined more to pensiveness and inactivity than to work, but now and again prolonged financial difficulties compel me – for pensiveness is no more profitable than inactivity – to take on a so-called job. Finding myself once again at a low ebb of this kind, I put myself in the hands of the employment office and was sent with seven other fellow-sufferers to Wunsiedel's factory, where we were to undergo an aptitude test.

The exterior of the factory was enough to arouse my suspicions: the factory was built entirely of glass brick, and my aversion to well-lit buildings and well-lit rooms is as strong as my aversion to work. I became even more suspicious when we were immediately served breakfast in the well-lit, cheerful coffee shop: pretty waitresses brought us eggs, coffee and toast, orange juice was served in tastefully designed jugs, goldfish pressed their bored faces against the sides of pale-green aquariums. The waitresses were so cheerful that they appeared to be bursting with good cheer. Only a strong effort of will – so it seemed to me – restrained them from singing away all day long. They were as crammed with unsung songs as chickens with unlaid eggs.

Right away I realized something that my fellow-sufferers evidently failed to realize: that this breakfast was already part of the test; so I chewed away reverently, with the full appreciation of a person who knows he is supplying his body with valuable elements. I did something which normally no power on earth can make me do: I drank orange juice on an empty stomach, left the coffee and egg untouched, as well as most of the toast, got up, and paced up and down in the coffee shop, pregnant with action.

As a result I was the first to be ushered into the room where the questionnaires were spread out on attractive tables. The walls were done in a shade of green that would have summoned the word 'delightful' to the lips of interior decoration enthusiasts. The room appeared to be empty, and yet I was so sure of being observed that I behaved as someone pregnant with action behaves when he believes himself unobserved: I ripped my pen impatiently from my pocket, unscrewed the top, sat down at the nearest table and pulled the questionnaire toward me, the way irritable customers snatch at the bill in a restaurant.

Question No. 1: Do you consider it right for a human being to possess only two arms, two legs, eyes, and ears?

Here for the first time I reaped the harvest of my pensive nature and wrote without hesitation: 'Even four arms, legs and ears would not be adequate for my driving energy. Human beings are very poorly equipped.'

Question No. 2: How many telephones can you handle at one time?

Here again the answer was as easy as simple arithmetic: 'When there are only seven telephones,' I wrote, 'I get impatient; there have to be nine before I feel I am working to capacity.'

Question No. 3: How do you spend your free time?

My answer: 'I no longer acknowledge the term free time – on my fifteenth birthday I eliminated it from my vocabulary, for in the beginning was the act.'

I got the job. Even with nine telephones I really didn't feel I was working to capacity. I shouted into the mouthpiece: 'Take immediate action!' or: 'Do something! – We must have some action – Action will be taken – Action has been taken – Action should be taken.' But as a rule – for I felt this was in keeping with the tone of the place – I used the imperative.

Of considerable interest were the noon-hour breaks, when we consumed nutritious foods in an atmosphere of silent good cheer. Wunsiedel's factory was swarming with people who were obsessed with telling you the story of their lives, as indeed vigorous personalities are fond of doing. The story of their lives is more important to them than their lives, you have only to press a button, and immediately it is covered with spewed-out exploits.

Wunsiedel had a right-hand man called Broschek, who had in turn made a name for himself by supporting seven children and a paralysed wife by working night-shifts in his student days, and successfully carrying on four business agencies, besides which he had passed two examinations with honours in two years. When asked by reporters: 'When do you sleep, Mr Broschek?' he had replied: 'It's a crime to sleep!'

Wunsiedel's secretary had supported a paralysed husband and four children by knitting, at the same time graduating in psychology and German history as well as breeding shepherd dogs, and she had become famous as a night-club singer where she was known as *Vamp Number Seven*.

Wunsiedel himself was one of those people who every morning, as they open their eyes, make up their minds to act. 'I must act,' they think as they briskly tie their bathrobe belts around them. 'I must act,' they think as they shave, triumphantly watching their beard hairs being washed away with the lather: these hirsute vestiges are the first daily sacrifices to their driving energy. The more intimate functions also give these people a sense of satisfaction: water swishes, paper is used. Action has been taken. Bread gets eaten, eggs are decapitated.

With Wunsiedel, the most trivial activity looked like action: the way he put on his hat, the way – quivering with energy – he buttoned up his overcoat, the kiss he gave his wife, everything was action.

When he arrived at his office he greeted his secretary with a cry of 'Let's have some action!' And in ringing tones she would call back: 'Action will be taken!' Wunsiedel then went from department to department, calling out his cheerful: 'Let's have some action!' Everyone would answer: 'Action will be taken!' And I would call back to him too, with a radiant smile, when he looked into my office: 'Action will be taken!'

Within a week I had increased the number of telephones on my desk to eleven, within two weeks to thirteen, and every morning on the streetcar I enjoyed thinking up new imperatives, or chasing the words *take action* through various tenses and modulations: for two whole days I kept saying the same sentence over and over again because I thought it sounded so marvellous: 'Action ought to have been taken'; for another two days it was: 'Such action ought not to have been taken.'

So I was really beginning to feel I was working to capacity when there actually was some action. One Tuesday morning – I had hardly settled down at my desk – Wunsiedel rushed into my office crying his 'Let's have some action!' But an inexplicable something in his face made me hesitate to reply, in a cheerful gay voice as the rules dictated: 'Action will be taken!' I must have paused too long, for Wunsiedel, who seldom raised his voice, shouted at me: 'Answer! Answer, you know the rules!' And I answered, under my breath, reluctantly, like a child who is forced to say: I am a naughty child. It was only by a great effort that I managed to bring out the sentence: 'Action will be taken,' and hardly had I uttered it when there really was some action: Wunsiedel dropped to the floor. As he fell he rolled over on to his side and lay right across the open doorway. I knew at once, and I confirmed it when I went slowly around my desk and approached the body on the floor: he was dead.

Shaking my head I stepped over Wunsiedel, walked slowly along the corridor to Broschek's office, and entered without knocking. Broschek was sitting at his desk, a telephone receiver in each hand, between his teeth a ballpoint pen with which he was making notes on a writing pad, while with his bare feet he was operating a knitting machine under the desk. In this way he helps to clothe his family. 'We've had some action,' I said in a low voice.

Broschek spat out the ballpoint pen, put down the two receivers, reluctantly detached his toes from the knitting machine.

'What action?' he asked.

'Wunsiedel is dead,' I said.

'No,' said Broschek.

'Yes,' I said, 'come and have a look!'

'No,' said Broschek, 'that's impossible,' but he put on his slippers and followed me along the corridor.

'No,' he said, when we stood beside Wunsiedel's corpse, 'no, no!' I did not contradict him. I carefully turned Wunsiedel over on to his back, closed his eyes, and looked at him pensively.

I felt something like tenderness for him, and realized for the first time that I had never hated him. On his face was that expression which one sees on children who obstinately refuse to give up their faith in Santa Claus, even though the arguments of their playmates sound so convincing.

'No,' said Broschek, 'no.'

'We must take action,' I said quietly to Broschek.

'Yes,' said Broschek, 'we must take action.'

Action was taken: Wunsiedel was buried, and I was delegated to carry a wreath of artificial roses behind his coffin, for I am equipped with not only a penchant for pensiveness and inactivity but also a face and figure that go extremely well with dark suits. Apparently as I walked along behind Wunsiedel's coffin carrying the wreath of artificial roses I looked superb. I received an offer from a fashionable firm of funeral directors to join their staff as a professional mourner. 'You are a born mourner,' said the manager, 'your outfit would be provided by the firm. Your face – simply superb!'

I handed in my notice to Broschek explaining that I had never really felt I was working to capacity there; that, in spite of the thirteen telephones, some of my talents were going to waste. As soon as my first professional appearance as a mourner was over I knew: This is where I belong, this is what I am cut out for.

Pensively I stand behind the coffin in the funeral chapel, holding a simple bouquet, while the organ plays Handel's *Largo*, a piece that does not receive nearly the respect it deserves. The cemetery café is my regular haunt; there I spend the intervals between my professional engagements, although sometimes I walk behind coffins which I have not been engaged to follow, I pay for flowers out of my own pocket and join the welfare worker who walks behind the coffin of some homeless person. From time to time I also visit Wunsiedel's grave, for after all I owe it to him that I discovered my true vocation, a vocation in which pensiveness is essential and inactivity my duty.

It was not till later that I realized I had never bothered to find out what was being produced in Wunsiedel's factory. I expect it was soap.

# 31

Woman from America

(1966)

Bessie Head

This woman from America married a man of our village and left her country to come and live with him here. She descended on us like an avalanche. People are divided into two camps: those who feel a fascinated love and those who fear a new thing.

Some people keep hoping she will go away one day, but already her big strong stride has worn the pathways of the village flat. She is everywhere about because she is a woman, resolved and unshakable in herself. To make matters worse or more disturbing she comes from the west side of America, somewhere near California. I gather from her conversation that people from the West are stranger than most people.

People of the West of America must be the most oddly beautiful people in the world; at least this woman from the West is the most oddly beautiful person I have ever seen. Every cross-current of the earth seems to have stopped in her and blended into an amazing harmony. She has a big dash of Africa, a dash of Germany, some Cherokee and heaven knows what else. Her feet are big and her body is as tall and straight and strong as a mountain tree. Her neck curves up high and her thick black hair cascades down her back like a wild and tormented stream. I cannot understand her eyes though, except that they are big, black, and startled like those of a wild free buck racing against the wind. Often they cloud over with a deep, intense, brooding look.

It takes a great deal of courage to become friends with a woman like that. Like everyone here, I am timid and subdued. Authority, everything can subdue me; not because I like it that way but because authority carries the weight of an age pressing down on life. It is terrible then to associate with a person who can shout authority down. Her shouting matches with authority are the terror and sensation of the village. It has come down to this. Either the woman is unreasonable or authority is unreasonable, and everyone in his heart would like to admit that authority is unreasonable. In reality, the rule is: If authority does not like you, then you are the outcast and humanity associates with you at their peril. So try always to be on the right side of authority, for the sake of peace, and please avoid the outcast. I do not say it will be like this forever. The whole world is crashing and interchanging itself and even remote bush villages in Africa are not to be left out!

It was inevitable though that this woman and I should be friends. I have an overwhelming curiosity that I cannot keep within bounds. I passed by the house for almost a month, but one cannot crash in on people. Then one day a dog they own had puppies, and my small son chased one of the puppies into the yard and I chased after him. Then one of the puppies became his and there had to be discussions about the puppy, the desert heat, and the state of the world and as a result of curiosity an avalanche of wealth has descended on my life. My small hut-house is full of short notes written in a wide sprawling hand. I have kept them all because they are a statement of human generosity and the wild carefree laugh of a woman who is as busy as women the world over about things women always entangle themselves in – a man, a home ... Like this ...

'Have you an onion to spare? It's very quiet here this morning and I'm all fagged out from sweeping and cleaning the yard, shaking blankets, cooking, fetching water, bathing children, and there's still the floor inside to sweep and dishes to wash ... it's endless!'

Sometimes too, conversations get all tangled up and the African night creeps all about and the candles are not lit and the conversation gets more entangled, intense; and the children fall asleep on the floor dazed by it all.

She is a new kind of American or even maybe will be a new kind of African. There isn't anyone here who does not admire her. To come from a world of chicken, hamburgers, TV, escalators, and whatnot to a village mud hut and a life so tough, where the most you can afford to eat is ground millet and boiled meat. Sometimes you cannot afford to eat at all. Always you have to trudge miles for a bucket of water and carry it home on your head. And to do all this with loud, ringing, sprawling laughter?

Black people in America care about Africa, and she has come here on her own as an expression of that love and concern. Through her, too, one is filled with wonder for a country that breeds individuals about whom, without and within, rushes the wind of freedom. I have to make myself clear, though. She is a different person who has taken by force what America will not give black people.

The woman from America loves both Africa and America, independently. She can take what she wants from both and say, 'Dammit'. It is a most strenuous and difficult thing to do.

32

The Man Who Wouldn't Get Up

(1966)

David Lodge

His wife was always the first to get up. As soon as the alarm rang she threw back the bedclothes, swung her legs to the floor and pulled on her dressing gown. Her self-discipline filled him with guilt and admiration.

'Now don't go lying in bed,' she said. 'I'm fed up with having your breakfast spoil.' He made no reply, feigning sleep. As soon as she had left the room he rolled over into the warm trough that her body had left in the mattress, and stretched luxuriously. It was the most sensually satisfying moment of his day, this stretch into a new, but warm part of the bed. But it was instantly impaired by the consciousness that he would soon have to get up and face the rest of the day.

He opened one eye. It was still dark, but the street-lamps cast a faint blue illumination into the room. He tested the atmosphere with his breath, and saw it turn to steam. Where one of the curtains was pulled back he could see that ice had formed on the inside of the window. In the course of the morning the ice would melt and the water would roll down to rot the paintwork on the window frame. Some of the water would trickle under the window frame where it would freeze again, jamming the window and warping the wood.

He closed his eye to shut out the painful vision of his house corroding and disintegrating around him. He couldn't, of course, suppress his knowledge of what was wrong with it – of what was wrong, for instance, with the room he lay in: the long jagged crack in the ceiling that ran like a sneer from the electric light fixture to the door, the tear in the lino near the chest of drawers, the cupboard door that hung open because the catch had gone, the wallpaper that bulged in patches where the damp had detached it from the wall, so that it seemed to breathe gently in and out with the opening and shutting of the door … He could not suppress his knowledge of all this, but while he was snug under the blankets, with his eyes shut tight, it was all somehow less oppressive, as if it had nothing to do with him personally.

It was only when he left the protection of the warm bed that he would stagger under the combined weight of dissatisfaction with his environment and despair of ever significantly improving it. And, of course, it wasn't just the bedroom. As he passed through the house the evidence of decay and disrepair would greet him at every turn: the dribbling tap in the bathroom, the broken banister on the staircase, the cracked window in the hall, the threadbare patch in the dining-room carpet that would be just a tiny bit bigger than yesterday. And it would be so cold, so cold. Icy draughts needling through keyholes, rattling the letter box, stirring the curtains.

And yet here, in bed, it was so warm and comfortable. The most luxuriously furnished, gas-fired centrally heated, double-glazed and insulated ideal home could not make him more warm and comfortable than he was at this moment.

His wife rattled the poker in the dining-room grate: the dull, metallic sounds were borne to every corner of the house through the water-pipes. It was the signal that breakfast was laid. From the room opposite his own Paul and Margaret, his two children, who had been playing in the cold and the gloom with the cheerful imperviousness to discomfort of the very young, issued boisterously on to the landing and thumped heavily down the stairs. The broken banister creaked menacingly. The dining-room door opened and slammed shut. From the kitchen he heard the distant clamour of cutlery and cooking utensils. He pulled the bedclothes more tightly round his head, muffling his ears and leaving only his nose and mouth free to breathe. He did not want to hear these sounds, harsh reminders of a harsh world.

When he looked beyond the immediate problem of getting up, of coping with the tiresome chores of washing, shaving, clothing and feeding his body, he saw no more inviting prospect before him: only the long walk to the bus stop through streets of houses exactly like his own, the long wait in line, the slow, juddering progress through the choked city streets, and eight hours' drudgery in a poky office which was, like his home, all full of broken things, discoloured, faded, chipped, scratched, grimy, malfunctioning things. Things which said as plainly as the interior of his house: this is your lot; try as hard as you like, but you will never significantly improve it; count yourself lucky if you can prevent it from deteriorating more rapidly.

He tried to gird his spirits preparatory to getting up by reminding himself how fortunate he was compared to many others. He forced his mind to dwell upon the sick and the dying, those in need, those in mental anguish. But the spectacle of human misery thus conjured up merely confirmed his helpless apathy. That others were able to bear these burdens with cheerful resignation gave him no encouragement: what hope had he of emulating them if his present discontents were enough to deprive his life of joy? What comfort was it that his present dreary existence was a fragile crust over an infinitely worse abyss into which he might plunge at any moment? The fact was, he no longer had any love of life. The thought pierced him with a kind of thrill of despair. I no longer love life. There is nothing in life which gives me pleasure any more. Except this: lying in bed. And the pleasure of this is spoiled because I know that I have got to get up. Well, then, why don't I just not get up? Because you've got to get up. You have a job. You have a family to support. Your wife has got up. Your children have got up. They have done their duty. Now you have to do yours. Yes, but it's easy for them. They still love life. I don't any more. I only love this: lying in bed.

He heard, through the wadding of bedclothes, the voice of his wife calling.

'George.' She called flatly, expressionlessly, ritualistically, not expecting an answer. He gave none, but turned over on to his other side, and stretched out his legs. His toes encountered an icy hot-water bottle at the foot of the bed and recoiled. He curled himself up into a foetal posture and withdrew his head completely under the bedclothes. It was warm and dark under the bedclothes, a warm dark cave. He inhaled the warm, fusty air with pleasure, and when it became dangerously deoxygenated he created cunning air-ducts in the bedclothes which admitted fresh air without light.

He heard very faintly his wife calling 'George'. More sharply, imperatively this time. It meant that his family had already consumed their corn-flakes and the bacon was cooked. Now the tension began to build between the longing to stay in bed and the urgency of rising. He contracted his limbs into a tighter coil and wriggled deeper into the mattress as he waited for the third summons.

'George!'

This meant he was now too late for breakfast – might with luck manage to swallow a cup of tea before he rushed out to catch his bus.

For what seemed like a long time, he held his breath. Then he suddenly relaxed and stretched out his limbs. He had decided. He would not get up. The secret was not to think of the consequences. Just to concentrate on the fact of staying in bed. The pleasure of it. The warmth, the comfort. He had free will. He would exercise it. He would stay in bed.

He must have dozed for a while. He was suddenly conscious of his wife in the room.

'It's a quarter past eight. Your breakfast's spoiled ... George ... are you getting up? ... George?' He detected a note of fear in her voice. Suddenly the bedclothes were lifted from his face. He pulled them back, annoyed that all his cunning air-vents had been disturbed.

'George, are you ill?' He was tempted to say, yes, I'm ill. Then his wife would tip-toe away, and tell the children to be quiet, their father was ill. And later she would light a fire in the bedroom and bring him a tray of tempting food. But that was the cowardly course; and the deception would only earn him, at the most, a day's respite from the life he hated. He was nourishing a grander, more heroic plan.

'No, I'm not ill,' he said through the bedclothes.

'Well, get up then, you'll be late for work.' He did not answer, and his wife left the room. He heard her banging about irritably in the bathroom, calling to the children to come and be washed. The lavatory cistern flushed and refilled noisily, the pipes whined and hummed, the children laughed and cried. Outside in the street footsteps hurried past on the pavement, cars wheezed, reluctant to start in the cold morning air, fired and moved away. He lay quiet under the bedclothes, concentrating, contemplating. Gradually he was able to eliminate all these noises from his consciousness. The way he had chosen was a mystical way.

***

32 The Man Who Wouldn't Get Up

The first day was the most difficult. His wife thought he was being merely idle and delinquent, and tried to make him get up by refusing to bring him any food. The fast caused him no great distress, however, and he stuck to his bed all day except for discreet, unobserved visits to the bathroom. When his wife retired that night she was angry and resentful. She complained because she hadn't been able to make the bed properly, and she held herself cold and rigid at the very edge of the mattress furthest from himself. But she was puzzled and guilty too, because he hadn't eaten. There was a note of pleading in her voice when she hoped he would have had enough of this silly nonsense by the next morning.

The next morning was much easier. He simply went off to sleep again as soon as the alarm had stopped ringing, untroubled by guilt or anxiety. It was blissful. Just to turn over and go to sleep again, knowing you weren't going to get up. Later, his wife brought him a breakfast tray and left it, wordlessly, on the floor beside his bed. His children came to the door of the bedroom and stared in at him while he ate. He smiled reassuringly at them.

In the afternoon, the doctor came, summoned by his wife. He marched breezily into the room and demanded, 'Well, now, what appears to be the trouble, Mr Barker?' 'No trouble, Doctor,' he replied gently.

The doctor gave him a brief examination and concluded: 'No reason at all why you shouldn't get out of bed, Mr Barker.' 'I know there isn't,' he replied. 'But I don't want to.'

The next day it was the vicar. The vicar begged him to think of his responsibilities as a husband and father. There were times, one knew only too well, when the struggle to keep going seemed too much to bear, when the temptation simply to give in became almost irresistible ... But that was not the true Christian spirit. 'Say not the struggle naught availeth ...'

'What about contemplative monks?' he asked. 'What about hermits, solitaries, column-squatters?'

Ah, but that kind of religious witness, though possibly efficacious in its own time, was not in harmony with modern spirituality. Besides, he could hardly claim that there was anything ascetic or penitential about his particular form of retreat from the world.

'It isn't all roses, you know,' he told the vicar.

And it wasn't. After seven days, he began to get bedsores. After a fortnight, he was too weak to walk unaided to the bathroom. After four weeks he remained permanently confined to his bed, and a nurse was employed to care for his bodily needs. He wasn't sure where the money was coming from to pay for the nurse, or indeed to maintain the house and his family. But he found that simply by not worrying about such problems, they solved themselves.

His wife had lost most of her resentment by now. Indeed he rather thought she respected him more than ever before. He was, he gathered, becoming something of a local, and even national, celebrity. One day a television camera was wheeled into his bedroom, and propped up on the pillows, holding the hand of his wife, he told his story to the viewing millions: how one cold morning he had suddenly realized that he no longer had any love of life, and his only pleasure was in lying in bed, and how he had taken the logical step of lying in bed for the rest of his life, which he did not expect to be protracted much longer, but every minute of which he was enjoying to the full.

After the television broadcast, the trickle of mail through the letter box became a deluge. His eyes were growing weak, and he relied on volunteers from the parish to help him with the correspondence.

Most of the letters pleaded with him to give life another chance, enclosing money or offers of lucrative employment. He declined the offers politely, and banked the money in his wife's name. (She used some of it to have the house redecorated; it amused him to watch the painters clambering about the bedroom; when they whitewashed the ceiling he covered his head with a newspaper.) There was a smaller, but to him more significant number of letters sending him encouragement and congratulations. 'Good luck to you, mate', said one of them, 'I'd do the same if I had the guts.' And another, written on the notepaper of a famous university, said: 'I deeply admire your witness to the intolerable quality of modern life and to the individual's inalienable right to opt out of it: you are an existentialist saint.' Though he wasn't clear about the meaning of all these words, they pleased him. Indeed, he had never felt so happy and so fulfilled as he did now.

And now, more than ever, he thought it would be sweet to die. Though his body was washed and fed and cared for, he felt vitality slowly ebbing away from it. He longed to put on immortality. It seemed as if he had solved not only the problem of life, but the problem of death too. There were times when the ceiling above his head became the canvas for some vision such as the old painters used to draw on the roofs of chapels: he seemed to see angels and saints peering down at him from a cloudy empyrean, beckoning him to join them. His body felt strangely weightless, as if only the bedclothes restrained it from rising into the air. Levitation! or even ... apotheosis! He fumbled with the blankets and sheets, but his limbs were weak. Then, with a supreme effort, he wrenched the bedclothes aside and flung them to the floor.

He waited, but nothing happened. He grew cold. He tried to drag the blankets back on to the bed, but the effort of throwing them off had exhausted him. He shivered. Outside it was getting dark. 'Nurse,' he called faintly; but there was no response. He called his wife, 'Margaret', but the house remained silent. His breath turned to steam on the cold air. He looked up at the ceiling, but there were no heads of angels and saints looking down: only a crack in the plaster that ran like a sneer from the door to the light fixture. And suddenly he realised what his eternity was to be. 'Margaret! Nurse!' he cried hoarsely. 'I want to get up! Help me up!'

But no one came.

33

A Very Desirable Residence

(1976)

P D James

During and after Harold Vinson's trial, at which I was a relatively unimportant prosecution witness, there was the usual uninformed, pointless and repetitive speculation about whether those of us who knew him would ever have guessed that he was a man capable of scheming to murder his wife. I was supposed to have known him better than most of the school staff, and my colleagues found it irritatingly self-righteous of me to be so very reluctant to be drawn into the general gossip about what, after all, was the school's major scandal in twenty years. 'You knew them both. You used to visit the house. You saw them together. Didn't you guess?' they insisted, obviously feeling that I had been in some way negligent, that I ought to have seen what was going on and prevented it. No, I never guessed; or, if I did, I guessed wrong. But they were perfectly right. I could have prevented it.

I first met Harold Vinson when I took up a post as junior art master at the comprehensive school where he taught mathematics to the senior forms. It wasn't too discouraging a place, as these teaching factories go. The school was centred on the old eighteenth-century grammar school, with some not-too-hideous modern additions, in a pleasant enough commuter town on the river about twenty miles south-east of London. It was a predominantly middle-class community, a little smug and culturally self-conscious, but hardly intellectually exciting. Still, it suited me well enough for a first post. I don't object to the middle class or their habitats; I'm middle class myself. And I knew that I was lucky to get the job. Mine is the usual story of an artist with sufficient talent but without enough respect for the fashionable idiocies of the contemporary artistic establishment to make a decent living. More dedicated men choose to live in cheap bedsitting rooms and keep on painting. I'm fussy about where and how I live so, for me, it was a diploma in the teaching of art and West Fairing Comprehensive.

It only took one evening in Vinson's home for me to realise that he was a sadist. I don't mean that he tormented his pupils. He wouldn't have been allowed to get away with it had he tried. These days the balance of power in the classroom has shifted with a vengeance and any tormenting is done by the children. No, as a teacher, he was surprisingly patient and conscientious, a man with real enthusiasm for his subject ('discipline' was the word he preferred to use, being something of an intellectual snob and given to academic jargon) with a surprising talent for communicating that enthusiasm to the children. He was a fairly rigid disciplinarian, but I've never found that children dislike firmness provided a master doesn't indulge in that mordant sarcasm which, by taking advantage of the children's inability to compete, is resented as particularly unfair. He got them through their examinations too. Say what you like, that's something middle-class kids and their parents appreciate. I'm sorry to have slipped into using the word 'kids', that modern shibboleth with its blend of condescension and sycophancy. Vinson never used it. It was his habit to talk about the alumni of the sixth. At first I thought it was an attempt at mildly pompous humour, but now I wonder. He wasn't really a humorous man. The rigid muscles of his face seldom cracked into a smile and when they did it was as disconcerting as a painful grimace. With his lean, slightly stooping figure, the grave eyes behind the horn-rimmed spectacles, the lines etched deeply from the nose to the corners of his unyielding mouth, he looked deceptively what we all thought he was – a middle-aged, disagreeable and not very happy pedant.

No, it wasn't his precious alumni whom he bullied and tyrannised over. It was his wife. The first time I saw Emily Vinson was when I sat next to her at Founder's Memorial Day, an archaic function inherited from the grammar school and regarded with such reverence that even those masters' wives who seldom showed their faces at the school felt obliged to make an appearance. She was, I guessed, almost twenty years younger than her husband, a thin, anxious-looking woman with auburn hair which had faded early and the very pale, transparent skin which often goes with that colouring. She was expensively and smartly dressed – too incongruously smartly for such a nondescript woman so that the ill-chosen, too-fashionable suit merely emphasised her frail ordinariness. But her eyes were remarkable, an unusual grey-green, huge and slightly exophthalmic under the arched narrow eyebrows. She seldom turned them on me, but when, from time to time, she gave me a swift elliptical glance it was as astounding as turning over an amateurish Victorian oil and discovering a Corot.

It was at the end of Founder's Memorial Day that I received my first invitation to visit them at their home. I found that they lived in some style. She had inherited from her father a small but perfectly proportioned Georgian house which stood alone in some two acres of ground with lawns slanting green down to the river. Apparently her father was a builder who had bought the house cheaply from its impoverished owner with the idea of demolishing it and building a block of flats. The planning authority had slapped on a preservation order just in time and he had died in weeks, no doubt from chagrin, leaving the house and its contents to his daughter. Neither Harold Vinson nor his wife seemed to appreciate their possession. He grumbled about the expense; she grumbled about the housework. The perfectly proportioned façade, so beautiful that it took the breath, seemed to leave them as unmoved as if they lived in a square brick box. Even the furniture, which had been bought with the house, was regarded by them with as little respect as if it were cheap reproduction. When at the end of my first visit I complimented Vinson on the spaciousness and proportions of the dining room he replied:

33   A Very Desirable Residence

'A house is only the space between four walls. What does it matter if they are far apart or close together, or what they are made of? You're still in a cage.' His wife was carrying the plates into the kitchen at the time and didn't hear him. He spoke so low that I scarcely heard him myself. I am not even sure now that I was meant to hear.

Marriage is both the most public and the most secret of institutions, its miseries as irritatingly insistent as a hacking cough, its private malaise less easily diagnosed. And nothing is so destructive as unhappiness to social life. No one wants to sit in embarrassed silence while his host and hostess demonstrate their mutual incompatibility and dislike. She could, it seemed, hardly open her mouth without annoying him. No opinion she expressed was worth listening to. Her small domestic chat – which was, after all, all she had – invariably provoked him by its banality so that he would put down his knife and fork with a look of patient resigned boredom as soon as, with a nervous preparatory glance at him, she would steel herself to speak. If she had been an animal, cringing away with that histrionic, essentially false look of piteous entreaty, I can see that the temptation to kick would be irresistible. And, verbally, Vinson kicked.

Not surprisingly they had few friends. Looking back it would probably be more true to say that they had no real friends. The only colleague of his who visited from the school, apart from myself, was Vera Pelling, the junior science teacher, and she, poor girl, was such an unattractive bore that there weren't many alternatives open to her. Vera Pelling is the living refutation of that theory so beloved, I understand, of beauty and fashion journalists in women's magazines that any woman if she takes the trouble can make something of her appearance. Nothing could be done about Vera's pig-like eyes and non-existent chin, and, reasonably enough, she didn't try. I am sorry if I sound harsh. She wasn't a bad sort. And if she thought that making a fourth with me at an occasional free supper with the Vinsons was better than eating alone in her furnished flat I suppose she had her reasons, as I had mine. I never remember having visited the Vinsons without Vera although Emily came to my flat on three occasions, with Harold's approval, to sit for her portrait. It wasn't a success. The result looked like a pastiche of an early Stanley Spencer. Whatever it was I was trying to capture, that sense of a secret life conveyed in the rare grey-green flash of those remarkable eyes, I didn't succeed. When Vinson saw the portrait he said:

'You were prudent, my boy, to opt for teaching as a livelihood. Although, looking at this effort, I would say that the choice was hardly voluntary.' For once I was tempted to agree with him.

Vera Pelling and I became oddly obsessed with the Vinsons. Walking home after one of their supper parties we would mull over the traumas of the evening like an old married couple perennially discussing the inadequacies of a couple of relatives whom we actively disliked but couldn't bear not to see. Vera was a tolerable mimic and would imitate Vinson's desiccated tones.

'My dear, I think that you recounted that not very interesting domestic drama last time we had supper together.'

'And what, my dear, have you been doing with yourself today? What fascinating conversation did you have with the estimable Mrs Wilcox while you cleaned the drawing room together?'

Really, confided Vera, tucking her arm through mine, it had become so embarrassing that it was almost enough to put her off visiting them. But not quite enough apparently. Which was why she, too, was at the Vinsons' on the night when it happened.

On the evening of the crime – the phrase has a stereotyped but dramatic ring which isn't inappropriate to what, look at it as you will, was no ordinary villainy – Vera and I were due at the school at 7 p.m. to help with the dress rehearsal of the school play. I was responsible for the painted backcloth and some of the props, and Vera for the make-up. It was an awkward time, too early for a proper meal beforehand and too late to make it sensible to stay on at school without some thought of supper, and when Emily Vinson issued through her husband an invitation to both Vera and me to have coffee and sandwiches at six o'clock it seemed sensible to accept. Admittedly, Vinson made it plain that the idea was his wife's. He seemed mildly surprised that she should wish to entertain us so briefly – insist on entertaining us was the expression he used. Vinson himself wasn't involved with the play. He never grudged spending his private time to give extra tuition in his own subject but made it a matter of rigid policy never to become involved in what he described as extramural divertissements appealing only to the regressed adolescent. He was, however, a keen chess player and on Wednesday evenings spent the three hours from nine until midnight at the local chess club, of which he was secretary. He was a man of meticulous habit and any school activity on a Wednesday evening would, in any case, have had to manage without him.

Every detail, every word spoken at that brief and unremarkable meal – dry ham sandwiches cut too thick and synthetic coffee – was recounted by Vera and me at the Crown Court so that it has always intrigued me that I can no longer visualise the scene. I know exactly what happened, of course. I can recall every word. It's just that I can no longer shut my eyes and see the supper table, the four of us seated there, imprinted in colours on the mind's eye. Vera and I said at the trial that both Vinsons seemed more than usually ill at ease, that Harold, in particular, gave us the impression that he wished we weren't there. But that could have been hindsight.

The vital incident, if you can call it that, happened towards the end of the meal. It was so very ordinary at the time, so crucial in retrospect. Emily Vinson, as if uneasily aware of her duties as hostess and of the unaccountable silence which had fallen on the table, made a palpable effort. Looking up with a nervous glance at her husband she said:

'Two such very nice and polite workmen came this morning – ' Vinson touched his lips with his paper serviette then crumpled it convulsively. His voice was unusually sharp as he broke in:

'Emily my dear, do you think you could spare us the details of your domestic routine this evening? I've had a particularly tiring day. And I am trying to concentrate my mind on this evening's game.' And that was all.

33 A Very Desirable Residence

The dress rehearsal was over by about nine o'clock, as planned, and I told Vera that I had left a library book at the Vinsons' and was anxious to pick it up on the way home. She made no objection. She gave the impression, poor girl, that she was never particularly anxious to get home. It was only a quarter of an hour's brisk walk to the house and, when we arrived, we saw at once that something was wrong. There were two cars, one with a blue light on the roof, and an ambulance parked unobtrusively but unmistakably at the side of the house. Vera and I glanced briefly at each other then ran to the front door. It was shut. Without ringing we dashed round to the side. The back door, leading to the kitchen quarters, was open. I had an immediate impression that the house was peopled with large men; two of them were in uniform. There was, I remember, a policewoman bending over the prone figure of Emily Vinson. And their cleaning woman, Mrs Wilcox, was there too. I heard Vera explaining to a plain-clothes policeman, obviously the senior man present, that we were friends of the Vinsons, that we had been there to supper only that evening. 'What's happened?' she kept asking. 'What's happened?' Before the police could answer, Mrs Wilcox was spitting it all out, eyes bright with self-important outrage and excitement. I sensed that the police wanted to get rid of her, but she wasn't so easily dislodged. And, after all, she had been first on the scene. She knew it all. I heard it in a series of disjointed sentences:

'Knocked on the head – terrible bruise – marks all over the parquet flooring where he dragged her – only just coming round now – human fiend – head resting on a cushion in the gas stove – the poor darling – came in just in time at nine twenty – always come to watch colour TV with her on Wednesday night – back door open as usual – found the note on the kitchen table.' The figure writhing on the floor, groaning and crying in a series of harsh grunting moans like an animal in travail, suddenly raised herself and spoke coherently.

'I didn't write it! I didn't write it!'

'You mean Mr Vinson tried to kill her?' Vera was incredulous, head turning from Mrs Wilcox to the watchful, inscrutable faces of the police. The senior officer broke in:

'Now Mrs Wilcox, I think it's time you went home. The ambulance is here. An officer will come along for your statement later this evening. We'll look after Mrs Vinson. There's nothing else for you to do.'

He turned to Vera and me. 'If you two were here earlier this evening, I'd like a word. We're fetching Mr Vinson now from his chess club. But if you two will just wait in the sitting room, please.'

Vera said, 'But if he knocked her unconscious and put her head in the gas oven, then why isn't she dead?'

It was Mrs Wilcox who replied, turning triumphantly as she was led out: 'The conversion, that's why. We're on natural gas from this morning. That North Sea stuff. It isn't poisonous. The two men from the Gas Board came just after nine o'clock.'

They were lifting Emily Vinson onto a stretcher now. Her voice came to us in a desperate wail.

'I tried to tell him. You remember? You heard him? I tried to tell him.'

***

The suicide note was one of the exhibits at Vinson's trial. A document examiner from the forensic science laboratory testified that it was a forgery, a clever forgery but not Mrs Vinson's writing. He couldn't give an opinion on whether it was the work of the husband, although it was certainly written on a page taken from a writing pad found in the desk in the sitting room. It bore no resemblance to the accused's normal writing. But, in his view, it hadn't been written by Mrs Vinson. He gave a number of technical reasons to support his opinion and the jury listened respectfully. But they weren't surprised. They knew that it hadn't been written by Mrs Vinson. She had stood in the witness box and told them so. And they were perfectly clear in their own minds who had written it.

There was other forensic evidence. Mrs Wilcox's 'marks all over the parquet flooring' were reduced to one long but shallow scrape, just inside the sitting-room door. But it was a significant scrape. It had been made by the heels of Emily Vinson's shoes. Traces of the floor polish which she used were found, not on the soles, but on the sides of the scraped heels and there were minute traces of her shoe polish in the scrape.

The fingerprint officer gave evidence. I hadn't realised until then that fingerprint experts are mostly civilians. It must be a dull job, that constant and meticulous examination of surfaces for the telltale composites and whirls. Hard on the eyes, I should think. In this case, the significance was that he hadn't found any prints. The gas taps had been wiped clean. I could see the jury physically perk up at the news. That was a mistake, all right. It didn't need the prosecution to point out that the taps should have shown Mrs Vinson's prints. She, after all, had cooked their last meal. A cleverer murderer would merely have worn gloves, smudging any existing prints but ensuring that he left none of his own. It had been an over-precaution to wipe the gas taps clean.

Emily Vinson – quiet, distressed but gallant, obviously reluctant to testify against her husband – was remarkably competent in the witness box. I hardly recognised her. No, she hadn't told her husband that she and Mrs Wilcox had arranged to watch the television together shortly after nine o'clock. Mrs Wilcox, who lived nearby, usually did come across to spend a couple of hours with her on Wednesday nights when Mr Vinson was at his chess club. No, she hadn't liked to tell Mr Vinson. Mr Vinson wasn't very fond of inviting people in. The message came over to the jury as clearly as if she had spelt it out – the picture of a downtrodden, unintellectual wife craving the human companionship which her husband denied her, guiltily watching a popular TV show with her cleaning woman at a time when she would be certain that her husband wouldn't catch them out. I glanced at his proud, unyielding mask, at the hands clutched over the edge of the dock, and imagined what he was thinking, what he would have said:

'Surely you have enough of domestic trivia and Mrs Wilcox's conversation – hardly exciting, I should have thought – without inviting her into your drawing room. The woman should know her place.'

The trial didn't take long. Vinson made no defence except to reiterate stubbornly, eyes fixed straight ahead, that he hadn't done it. His counsel did his best, but with the dogged persistence of a man resigned to failure, and the jury had the look of people glad to be faced, for once, with a clear-cut case they could actually understand. The verdict was inevitable. And the subsequent divorce hearing was even shorter. It isn't difficult to persuade a judge that your marriage has irretrievably broken down when your husband is serving a prison sentence for attempted murder.

Two months after the decree absolute we married and I took over the Georgian house, the river view, the Regency furniture. With the physical possessions, I knew exactly what I was getting. With my wife, I wasn't so sure. There had been something disturbing, even a little frightening, about the competence with which she had carried out my instructions. It hadn't, of course, been particularly difficult. We had planned it together during those sessions when I was painting her portrait. I had written and handed her the fake suicide note on the paper she had supplied a few days before our plans matured. We knew when the gas was due to be converted. She had, as instructed, placed the note on the kitchen table before scraping the heels of her shoes across the polished floor. She had even managed beautifully the only tricky part, to bang the back of her head sufficiently hard against the kitchen wall to raise an impressive bruise but not sufficiently hard to risk bungling the final preparations; the cushion placed in the bottom of the oven for the head, the gas tap turned on and then wiped clean with her handkerchief.

And who could have imagined that she was such a consummate actress? Sometimes, remembering that anguished animal cry of 'I tried to tell him … I tried to tell him', I wonder again what is going on behind those extraordinary eyes. She still acts, of course. I find it remarkably irritating, that habit she has particularly when we are in company, of turning on me that meek, supplicating, beaten-dog expression whenever I talk to her. It provokes unkindness. Perhaps it's intended to. I'm afraid I'm beginning to get rather a reputation for sadism. People don't seem to want to come to the house any more.

There is one solution, of course, and I can't pretend that I haven't pondered it. A man who has killed another merely to get his house isn't likely to be too fastidious about killing again. And it was murder; I have to accept that.

Vinson only served nine months of his sentence before dying in the prison hospital of what should have been an uncomplicated attack of influenza. Perhaps his job really was his life, and without his precious alumni the will to live snapped. Or perhaps he didn't choose to live with the memory of his wife's great betrayal. Beneath the petty tyranny, the impatience, the acerbity, there may have been love of a kind.

But the surest option is barred to me. A month ago Emily explained, meekly, like a child propounding a problem, and with a swift sidelong glance, that she had written a confession and left it with her solicitor.

'Just in case anything happens to me, darling.'

She explained that what we did to poor Harold is preying on her mind but that she feels better now that all the details are written down and she can be sure that, after her death, the truth will at last be known and Harold's memory cleared. She couldn't have made it more plain to me that it is in my interest to see that I die first.

I killed Harold Vinson to get the house; Emily, to get me. On the whole, she made the better bargain. In a few weeks I shall lose the house. Emily is selling it. After all, there's nothing I can do to stop her; the place belongs to her not me.

After we married I gave up the teaching post, finding it embarrassing to meet my colleagues as Emily's husband. It was not that anyone suspected. Why should they? I had a perfect alibi for the time of the crime. But I had a dream that, living in that perfection, I might become a painter after all. That was the greatest illusion of all.

So now they are taking down from the end of the drive the board which states 'This Desirable Residence for Sale'. Emily got a very good price for the house and the furniture. More than enough to buy the small but pretentious brick box on an executive estate in North London which will be my cage from now on. Everything is sold. We're taking nothing with us except the gas stove. But, as Emily pointed out when I remonstrated, why not? It's in perfectly good working order.

34

Sale

(1978)

Anita Desai

There they are, at the door now, banging. They had met him, written a note and made an appointment – and here they are, as a direct result of it all, rattling. He stands on the other side of the door, in the dusk-mottled room, fingering an unshaven chin and dropping cigarette butts on the floor which is already littered with them. There is a pause in the knocking. He hears their voices – querulous, impatient. He turns and silently goes towards the inner door that opens onto a passage. He pushes it ajar, quietly, holding his breath. At the end of the passage another door stands open: it is like a window or an alcove illuminated by the deep glow of the fire. There his wife sits, kneading dough in a brass bowl, with her head bowed so that her long hair broods down to her shoulders on either side of her heavy, troubled face. The red border of her sari cuts a bright gash through the still tableau. The child sits on the mat beside her, silent, absorbed in the mysteries of a long-handled spoon which he turns over with soft, wavering fingers that are unaccustomed to the unsympathetic steel. His head, too, is bowed so that his father, behind him, can see the small wisps of hair on the back of his neck. He looks at them, holding his breath till it begins to hurt his chest. Then the knocking is resumed and his wife, hearing it, raises her head. She sees him then, at the door, like a dog hanging about, wanting something, and immediately her nostrils flare. 'Can't you answer the door?' she cries. 'What's the matter with you? It must be them – this is your chance.' Startled, the child drops the spoon with a clatter. Quickly he shuts the door. Then he goes and opens the front door and lets them in.

'We were about to give up,' one man cries, laughing, and brings in his friend and also a woman, seeing whom the artist, who is not expecting her, finds himself dismayed and confused. A woman – therefore someone in league with his wife, he thinks, and stares at her lush, unreluctant face and the bright enamelled earrings that frame it. He is silent. The two men stare at him.

'You *were* expecting us, weren't you?' enquires the jovial man whom he had liked, once. 'We wrote – '

'Yes,' he murmurs. 'Oh yes, yes,' and stands there, on the threshold, with an empty match box in his hand, his face looking like a house from which ghosts had driven away all inhabitants.

Then the man introduces his wife. 'She also paints,' he says, 'and was so interested in seeing your pictures, I brought her along. You don't mind, do you?'

'No,' he says, gathering himself together with a laboured effort, and steps aside to let them in. Then it is they who are silent, staring in dismay at the shambles about them. There are pictures to look at, yes, but one lies on the floor with a bundle of rags and some cigarette stubs on it, another is propped up on a shelf with bottles of hair oil, clay toys and calendars before it, and others have drifted off the wooden divan into corners of the room, peering out from under old newspapers and dirty clothes. The artist watches them, wondering at the imbecility of their appearance as they huddle together and gape. 'Oh,' he says, recovering, 'the light,' and switches it on. It is unshaded and hangs low over the flat table at which he paints so that they are illuminated weirdly from the waist downwards, leaving their faces more confused with shadows than before. The woman is quickest to relax, to make herself known, to become acquainted. 'Ah,' she cries, hurrying to the shelf to pull out a picture. 'What are they?' she asks him, gazing first at the flowers that blaze across the dirty paper, then at him, coaxing him for their secret with an avidly enquiring look. 'Not cannas, not lotuses – what can they be?'

He smiles at her curiosity. 'Nothing,' he says. 'Not real flowers – just anything at all.'

'Really!' she exclaims, shaking her enamelled earrings. 'How wonderful to be able to imagine such forms, such colours. Look, Ram, aren't they pretty?' The two men become infected by her exaggerated attitude of relaxation. They begin to prowl about the room, now showing amusement at the litter which is, after all, only to be expected in an artist's studio, then crinkling their noses for, one has to admit, it *does* smell, and then showing surprised interest in the pictures of which they have come to select one for their home which is newly built and now to be furnished. What with the enthusiasm and thoroughness they bring to their task, the rags and grime of the studio are soon almost obliterated by the fanfare of colour that spills forth, a crazy whorl of them, unknown colours that cannot be named, spilling out of forms that cannot be identified. One cannot pinpoint any school, any technique, any style – one can only admit oneself in the presence of a continuous and inspired act of creation: so they tell themselves. The woman gives cry upon cry of excitement and turns again and again to the artist who stands watching them thoughtfully. 'But how did you get this colour? You must tell me because I paint – and I could never get anything like this. What is it?'

'Ahh, Naples Yellow,' he says, as if making a guess. 'No, but there is some orange in it too.'

'Ah yes, a little orange also.'

'And green?'

'Yes, a little perhaps.'

'No, but that special tinge – how did you get it? A little bit of white – or flesh pink? What is it? Ram, Ram, just look, isn't it pretty – this weird bird? I don't suppose it has a name?'

'No, no, it is not real. I am a city man, I know nothing about birds.'

'But you know everything about birds! And flowers. I suppose they *are* birds and flowers, all these marvellous things. And your paintings are full of them. How can it possibly be that you have never seen them?'

He has to laugh then – she is so artless, so completely without any vestige of imagination, and so completely unlike his wife. 'Look,' he says, suddenly buoyant, and points to the window. She has to stand on her toes to look out of the small aperture, through the bars, and then she gazes out with all the intentness she feels he expects of her, at the deep, smoke-ridden twilight wound around the ill-lit slum, the smoking heaps of dung-fires and the dark figures that sit and stand in it hopelessly. Like fog-horns, conch shells begin to blow as tired housewives summon up their flagging spirits for the always lovely, always comforting ritual of evening prayers. She tries to pierce the scene with her sharp eyes, trying to see what he sees in it, till she hears him laughing behind her with a cracked kind of hilarity. 'There you see – my birds and my flowers,' he tells her, clapping his hands as though enjoying a practical joke he has played on her. 'I see a tram – and that is my mountain. I see a letter-box – and that is my tree. Listen! Do you hear my birds?' He raises his hand and, with its gesture, ushers in the evening voices of children uttering those cries and calls peculiar to the time of parting, the time of relinquishing their games, before they enter their homes and disappear into sleep – voices filled with an ecstasy of knowledge, of sensation drawn to an apex, brought on by the realization of imminent departure and farewell: voices panicky with love, with lament, with fear and sacrifice.

The artist watches the three visitors and finds them attentive, puzzled. 'There,' he says, dropping his hand. 'There are my birds. I don't see them – but I hear them and imagine how they look. It is easy, no, when you can hear them so clearly?'

'You are a magician,' says the quiet man, shaking his head and turning to a crayon drawing of pale birds delicately stalking the shallows of a brooding sea. 'Look at these – I can't believe you haven't actually painted them on the spot.'

'No, I have not, but I do know the sea. You know, I am a fisherman! I should have been – my people are. How do you like this one of fishing boats? I used to see them coming in like this, in the evening, with the catch. And then my mother would cook one large one for dinner – oh, it was good, good!'

They all stand around him, smiling at this unexpected burst of childish exuberance. 'You paint from memory then?' enquires one, but the woman cries, 'You like fish? You must come and eat it at our house one day – I cook fish very well.'

'I will, I will,' he cries, scurrying about as though he were looking for something he had suddenly remembered he needed, hunting out seascapes for them to see, and more of the successful flowers. 'Oh, I will love that – to see this new house of yours and eat a meal cooked by you. Yes, I will come. Here, look, another one – a canal scene. Do you like it?

That is paddy growing there – it is so green …' Now he wants to turn out the entire studio for them, bring out his best. He chatters, they laugh. Pictures fall to the floor. Crayons are smeared, oils are smudged – but he does not mind. He does not even sign his pictures. When the woman pauses over a pastel that is blurred by some stroke of carelessness, he says, 'Oh that is nothing, I can touch it up. Do you see the blue? Do you like it? Yes, I will see your paintings and I will tell you plainly what I like and what I don't like, and you will appreciate anyway. Oh, I love fish …' Only now and then he grows aware of his wife, breathing heavily because of the weight of the child asleep on her arm, straining to hear at the door, frowning because she cannot understand, is not certain, is worried, worried to death … and then he draws down the corners of his mouth and is silent. But when a picture of curled flowers is brought to him, he stares at it till it comes into proper focus and explains it to them. 'Ah,' he says, 'I painted that long ago – for my son, when he was born. I wanted him to have flowers, flowers all about his bed, under his head, at his feet, everywhere. And I did not have any. I did not know of a garden from where I could get some. So I painted them. That is one of them. Ah yes, yes,' he smiles, and the three who watch him grow tender, sympathetic. The woman says, '*This* one? It is your son's? How lovely – how lucky.'

'No,' he cries loudly. 'I mean, you can have it. Do you like it? It is what you want for your new house?'

'Oh no,' she says softly and puts it away. 'You painted it for your child. I can't take it from him.'

The artist finds himself sweating and exhausted – he had not realized how he was straining himself. He has had nothing but tea and cigarettes since early that morning and there is no breath of air coming through the barred window. He wipes his face with his hand and blotches another crayon with his wet fingers as he picks it up and flings it away. 'Then what do you want?' he asks in a flat voice. 'What do you like? What do you want to have – a flower picture or a landscape?'

'Perhaps figures – people always make a room seem bright.'

'I don't paint figures,' he says shortly. 'You told me you wanted a landscape. Here they are – all sizes, big, small, medium; hills, seas, rivers; green, blue, yellow. Is there nothing you like?'

'Yes, yes,' they all assure him together, upset by his change of tone, and one holds up a picture at arm's length to admire it lavishly, another bends to shuffle through the pile on the table. But there are so many, they say, it is hard to choose. That is nothing, he says, *he* will choose for them. Oh no, they laugh, glancing to see if he is serious, for they have something very special in mind – something that will light up their whole house, become its focal point, radiate and give their home a tone, an atmosphere. No, not this one, not *quite* – it is lovely, but … Before he knows it, they are at the door, descending the stairs with one backward look at all the heroic mass of colour inside, saying goodbye. He rushes down the stairs after them, spreading out his arms. Their car stands under the lamp-post. He flings himself at the door, hangs on to it.

'There is not one you liked? I thought you had come to buy – you said – '

'Yes, we wanted to,' says the man whom he had liked, once. 'But not one of these. You see, we have something very special in mind, something quite extraordinary – '

'But – not one of those I showed you? I thought you liked them – you said – '

'I did, I did,' chirps the woman from the soft recesses of the back seat. 'Oh and those lovely flowers you painted for your son – *lucky* child!'

'You liked them? I will paint you another like it, just like it – '

'But we wanted a landscape really,' says the man. 'Something in those cool greys and whites. Perhaps a snow scene – now *that* would be something different.'

'Snow?' shouts the artist. 'I will paint snow. I will paint the Himalayas for you. How big do you want it? So big? So?'

'No, no,' they laugh. 'Not so big. That would be too expensive.'

'All right, smaller. I will paint it. By the end of the week you will have it.'

They laugh at his haste, his trembling, shrill excitement. 'But, my friend, have you ever seen snow?' enquires the jovial one, patting his arm.

'Ah!' he gives such a cry that it halts them in their movements of departure, to turn and see him spread out his arms till his fingers reach out of the smoke of the dung-fires and the dust of the unlit lanes, to reach out to the balm of ice and snow and isolation. 'I will paint such snow for you as you have never seen, as no one has ever painted. I can see it all, here,' and he taps his forehead with such emphasis that they smile – he is quite a comic. Or even a bit crazy. Drunk?

'Now, now, my friend,' says the man, patting his arm again. 'Don't be in a hurry about it. You paint it when you are in the mood. Then it will be good.'

'I am in the mood now,' he cries. 'I am always in the mood, don't you see? Tomorrow, tomorrow I will have it ready. I will bring it to your house. Give me the address!'

They laugh. The engine stutters to life and there is a metallic finality in the sound of the doors being shut. But he clings to the handle, thrusts his head in, his eyes blazing. 'And will you give me an advance?' he asks tensely. 'I need money, my friend. Can you give me an advance?'

The woman creeps away into a corner, wrapping herself closely in a white shawl. One man, in embarrassment, falls silent. The other laughs and puts his hands in his pockets, then draws them out to show they are empty. 'Brother, if I had some with me, I would give it to you – all of it – but since we only came to see, I didn't bring any. I'm sorry.'

'I need it.'

'Listen, when you bring the picture, I will give you something, even if I don't want it, I will give you something – in advance, for the one we will buy. But today, just now, I have nothing.'

The artist steps back to let them go. As they drive out of the lane and the smoke smudges and obscures the tail-lights, he hears his wife come out on the stairs behind him.

35

Land Deal

(1980)

Gerald Murnane

After a full explanation of what my object was, I purchased two large tracts of land from them – about 600,000 acres, more or less – and delivered over to them blankets, knives, looking-glasses, tomahawks, beads, scissors, flour, &c. &c., as payment for the land, and also agreed to give them a tribute, or rent, yearly.

John Batman, 1835

We certainly had no cause for complaint at the time. The men from overseas politely explained all the details of the contract before we signed it. Of course there were minor matters that we should have queried. But even our most experienced negotiators were distracted by the sight of the payment offered us.

The strangers no doubt supposed that their goods were quite unfamiliar to us. They watched tolerantly while we dipped our hands into the bags of flour, draped ourselves in blankets, and tested the blades of knives against the nearest branches. And when they left we were still toying with our new possessions. But what we marvelled at most was not their novelty. We had recognised an almost miraculous correspondence between the strangers' steel and glass and wool and flour and those metals and mirrors and cloths and foodstuffs that we so often postulated, speculated about, or dreamed of.

Is it surprising that a people who could use against stubborn wood and pliant grass and bloody flesh nothing more serviceable than stone – is it surprising that such a people should have become so familiar with the idea of metal? Each one of us, in his dreams, had felled tall trees with blades that lodged deep in the pale pulp beneath the bark. Any of us could have enacted the sweeping of honed metal through a stand of seeded grass or described the precise parting of fat or muscle beneath a tapered knife. We knew the strength and sheen of steel and the trueness of its edge from having so often called it into possible existence.

35 Land Deal

It was the same with glass and wool and flour. How could we not have inferred the perfection of mirrors – we who peered so often into rippled puddles after wavering images of ourselves? There was no quality of wool that we had not conjectured as we huddled under stiff pelts of possum on rainy winter evenings. And every day the laborious pounding of the women at their dusty mills recalled for us the richness of the wheaten flour that we had never tasted.

But we had always clearly distinguished between the possible and the actual. Almost anything was possible. Any god might reside behind the thundercloud or the waterfall, any faery race inhabit the land below the ocean's edge; any new day might bring us such a miracle as an axe of steel or a blanket of wool. The almost boundless scope of the possible was limited only by the occurrence of the actual. And it went without saying that what existed in the one sense could never exist in the other. Almost anything was possible except, of course, the actual.

It might be asked whether our individual or collective histories furnished any example of a possibility becoming actual. Had no man ever dreamed of possessing a certain weapon or woman and, a day or a year later, laid hold of his desire? This can be simply answered by the assurance that no one among us was ever heard to claim that anything in his possession resembled, even remotely, some possible thing he had once hoped to possess.

That same evening, with the blankets warm against our backs and the blades still gleaming beside us, we were forced to confront an unpalatable proposition. The goods that had appeared among us so suddenly belonged only in a possible world. We were therefore dreaming. The dream may have been the most vivid and enduring that any of us had known. But however long it lasted it was still a dream.

We admired the subtlety of the dream. The dreamer (or dreamers – we had already admitted the likelihood of our collective responsibility) had invented a race of men among whom possible objects passed as actual. And these men had been moved to offer us the ownership of their prizes in return for something that was itself not real.

We found further evidence to support this account of things. The pallor of the men we had met that day, the lack of purpose in much of their behaviour, the vagueness of their explanations – these may well have been the flaws of men dreamed of in haste. And, perhaps paradoxically, the nearly perfect properties of the stuffs offered to us seemed the work of a dreamer, someone who lavished on the central items of his dream all those desirable qualities that are never found in actual objects.

It was this point that led us to alter part of our explanation for the events of that day. We were still agreed that what had happened was part of some dream. And yet it was characteristic of most dreams that the substance of them seemed, at the time, actual to the dreamer. How, if we were dreaming of the strangers and their goods, were we able to argue against our taking them for actual men and objects?

We decided that none of us was the dreamer. Who, then, was? One of our gods, perhaps? But no god could have had such an acquaintance with the actual that he succeeded in creating an illusion of it that had almost deceived us.

There was only one reasonable explanation. The pale strangers, the men we had first seen that day, were dreaming of us and our confusion. Or, rather, the true strangers were dreaming of a meeting between ourselves and their dreamed-of selves.

At once, several puzzles seemed resolved. The strangers had not observed us as men observe one another. There were moments when they might have been looking through our hazy outlines towards sights they recognised more easily. They spoke to us with oddly raised voices and claimed our attention with exaggerated gestures as though we were separated from them by a considerable distance, or as though they feared we might fade altogether from their sight before we had served the purpose for which they had allowed us into their dream.

When had this dream begun? Only, we hoped, on that same day when we first met the strangers. But we could not deny that our entire lives and the sum of our history might have been dreamed by these people of whom we knew almost nothing. This did not dismay us utterly. As characters in a dream, we might have been much less at liberty than we had always supposed. But the authors of the dream encompassing us had apparently granted us at least the freedom to recognise, after all these years, the simple truth behind what we had taken for a complex world.

Why had things happened thus? We could only assume that these other men dreamed for the same purpose that we (dreamers within a dream) often gave ourselves up to dreaming. They wanted for a time to mistake the possible for the actual. At that moment, as we deliberated under familiar stars (already subtly different now that we knew their true origin), the dreaming men were in an actual land far away, arranging our very deliberations so that their dreamed-of selves could enjoy for a little while the illusion that they had acquired something actual.

And what was this unreal object of their dreams? The document we had signed explained everything. If we had not been distracted by their glass and steel that afternoon we would have recognised even then the absurdity of the day's events. The strangers wanted to possess the land.

Of course it was the wildest folly to suppose that the land, which was by definition indivisible, could be measured or parcelled out by a mere agreement among men. In any case, we had been fairly sure that the foreigners failed to see our land. From their awkwardness and unease as they stood on the soil, we judged that they did not recognise the support it provided or the respect it demanded. When they moved even a short distance across it, stepping aside from places that invited passage and treading on places that were plainly not to be intruded on, we knew that they would lose themselves before they found the real land.

Still, they had seen a land of some sort. That land was, in their own words, a place for farms and even, perhaps, a village. It would have been more in keeping with the scope of the dream surrounding them had they talked of founding an unheard-of city where they stood. But all their schemes were alike from our point of view. Villages or cities were all in the realm of possibility and could never have a real existence. The land would remain the land, designed for us yet, at the same time, providing the scenery for the dreams of a people who would never see either our land or any land they dreamed of.

35 Land Deal

What could we do, knowing what we then knew? We seemed as helpless as those characters we remembered from private dreams who tried to run with legs strangely nerveless. Yet if we had no choice but to complete the events of the dream, we could still admire the marvellous inventiveness of it. And we could wonder endlessly what sort of people they were in their far country, dreaming of a possible land they could never inhabit, dreaming further of a people such as ourselves with our one weakness, and then dreaming of acquiring from us the land which could never exist.

We decided, of course, to abide by the transaction that had been so neatly contrived. And although we knew we could never truly awake from a dream that did not belong to us, still we trusted that one day we might seem, to ourselves at least, to awake.

Some of us, remembering how after dreams of loss they had awakened with real tears in their eyes, hoped that we would somehow awake to be convinced of the genuineness of the steel in our hands and the wool round our shoulders. Others insisted that for as long as we handled such things we could be no more than characters in the vast dream that had settled over us – the dream that would never end until a race of men in a land unknown to us learned how much of their history was a dream that must one day end.

36

The Teddy-bears' Picnic

(1981)

William Trevor

'I simply don't believe it,' Edwin said. 'Grown-up people?'

'Well, grown-up now, darling. We weren't always grown-up.'

'But *teddy-bears*, Deborah?'

'I'm sure I've told you dozens of times before.'

Edwin shook his head, frowning and staring at his wife. They'd been married six months: he was twenty-nine, swiftly making his way in a stockbroker's office, Deborah was twenty-six and intended to continue being Mr Harridance's secretary until a family began to come along. They lived in Wimbledon, in a block of flats called The Zodiac. 23 The Zodiac their address was and friends thought the title amusing and lively, making jokes about Gemini and Taurus and Capricorn when they came to drinks. A Dane had designed The Zodiac in 1968.

'I'll absolutely tell you this,' Edwin said, 'I'm not attending this thing.'

'But darling –'

'Oh, don't be bloody silly, Deborah.'

Edwin's mother had called Deborah 'a pretty little thing', implying for those who cared to be perceptive a certain reservation. She'd been more direct with Edwin himself, in a private conversation they'd had after Edwin had said he and Deborah wanted to get married. 'Remember, dear,' was how Mrs Chalm had put it then, 'she's not always going to be a pretty little thing. This really isn't a very sensible marriage, Edwin.' Mrs Chalm was known to be a woman who didn't go in for cant when dealing with the lives of the children she had borne and brought up; she made no bones about it and often said so. Her husband, on the other hand, kept out of things.

Yet in the end Edwin and Deborah had married, one Tuesday afternoon in December, and Mrs Chalm resolved to make the best of it. She advised Deborah about this and that, she gave her potted plants for 23 The Zodiac, and in fact was kind. If Deborah had known about her mother-in-law's doubts she'd have been surprised.

'But we've always done it, Edwin. All of us.'

'All of who, for heaven's sake?'

'Well, Angela for one. And Holly and Jeremy of course.'

'*Jeremy*? My God!'

'And Peter. And Enid and Charlotte and Harriet.'

'You've never told me a word about this, Deborah.'

'I'm really sure I have.'

The sitting-room where this argument took place had a single huge window with a distant view of Wimbledon Common. The walls were covered with rust-coloured hessian, the floor with a rust-coloured carpet. The Chalms were still acquiring furniture: what there was, reflecting the style of The Zodiac's architecture, was in bent steel and glass. There was a single picture, of a field of thistles, revealed to be a photograph on closer examination. Bottles of alcohol stood on a glass-topped table, their colourful labels cheering that corner up. Had the Chalms lived in a Victorian flat, or a cottage in a mews, their sitting-room would have been different, fussier and more ornate, dictated by the architectural environment. Their choice of decor and furniture was the choice of newly-weds who hadn't yet discovered a confidence of their own.

'You mean you all sit round with your teddies,' Edwin said, 'having a picnic? And you'll still be doing that at eighty?'

'What d'you mean, eighty?'

'When you're eighty years of age, for God's sake. You're trying to tell me you'll still be going to this garden when you're stumbling about and hard of hearing, a gang of OAPs squatting out on the grass with teddy-bears?'

'I didn't say anything about when we're old.'

'You said it's a tradition, for God's sake.'

He poured some whisky into a glass and added a squirt of soda from a Sparklets syphon. Normally he would have poured a gin and dry vermouth for his wife, but this evening he felt too cross to bother. He hadn't had the easiest of days. There'd been an error in the office about the BAT shares a client had wished to buy, and he hadn't managed to have any lunch because as soon as the BAT thing was sorted out a crisis had blown up over sugar speculation. It was almost eight o'clock when he'd got back to The Zodiac and instead of preparing a meal Deborah had been on the telephone to her friend Angela, talking about teddy-bears.

Edwin was an agile young man with shortish black hair and a face that had a very slight look of a greyhound about it. He was vigorous and athletic, sound on the tennis court, fond of squash and recently of golf. His mother had once stated that Edwin could not bear to lose and would go to ruthless lengths to ensure that he never did. She had even remarked to her husband that she hoped this quality would not one day cause trouble, but her husband replied it was probably just what a stockbroker needed. Mrs Chalm had been thinking more of personal relationships, where losing couldn't be avoided. It was that she'd had on her mind when she'd had doubts about the marriage, for the doubts were not there simply because Deborah was a pretty little thing: it was the conjunction Mrs Chalm was alarmed about.

'I didn't happen to get any lunch,' Edwin snappishly said now. 'I've had a long unpleasant day and when I get back here –'

'I'm sorry, dear.'

Deborah immediately rose from among the rust-coloured cushions of the sofa and went to the kitchen, where she took two pork chops from a Marks and Spencer's carrier-bag and placed them under the grill of the electric cooker. She took a packet of frozen broccoli spears from the carrier-bag as well, and two Marks and Spencer's trifles. While typing letters that afternoon she'd planned to have fried noodles with the chops and broccoli spears, just for a change. A week ago they'd had fried noodles in the new Mexican place they'd found and Edwin said they were lovely. Deborah had kicked off her shoes as soon as she'd come into the flat and hadn't put them on since. She was wearing a dress with scarlet petunias on it. Dark-haired, with a heart-shaped face and blue eyes that occasionally acquired a bewildered look, she seemed several years younger than twenty-six, more like eighteen.

She put on water to boil for the broccoli spears even though the chops would not be ready for some time. She prepared a saucepan of oil for the noodles, hoping that this was the way to go about frying them. She couldn't understand why Edwin was making such a fuss just because Angela had telephoned, and put it down to his not having managed to get any lunch.

In the sitting-room Edwin stood by the huge window, surveying the tops of trees and, in the distance, Wimbledon Common. She must have been on the phone to Angela for an hour and a half, probably longer. He'd tried to ring himself to say he'd be late but each time the line had been engaged. He searched his mind carefully, going back through the three years he'd known Deborah, but no reference to a teddy-bears' picnic came to him. He'd said very positively that she had never mentioned it, but he'd said that in anger, just to make his point: reviewing their many conversations now, he saw he had been right and felt triumphant. Of course he'd have remembered such a thing, any man would.

Far down below, a car turned into the wide courtyard of The Zodiac, a Rover it looked like, a discreet shade of green. It wouldn't be all that long before they had a Rover themselves, even allowing for the fact that the children they hoped for would be arriving any time now. Edwin had not objected to Deborah continuing her work after their marriage, but family life would naturally be much tidier when she no longer could, when the children were born. Eventually they'd have to move into a house with a garden because it was natural that Deborah would want that, and he had no intention of disagreeing with her.

'Another thing is,' he said, moving from the window to the open doorway of the kitchen, 'how come you haven't had a reunion all the years I've known you? If it's an annual thing –'

'It isn't an annual thing, Edwin. We haven't had a picnic since 1975 and before that 1971. It's just when someone feels like it, I suppose. It's just a bit of fun, darling.'

'You call sitting down with teddy-bears a bit of fun? Grown-up people?'

'I wish you wouldn't keep on about grown-ups. I know we're grown-ups. That's the whole point. When we were little we all vowed –'

'Jesus Christ!'

He turned and went to pour himself another drink. She'd never mentioned it because she knew it was silly. She was ashamed of it, which was something she would discover when she grew up a bit.

'You know I've got Binky,' she said, following him to where the drinks were and pouring herself some gin. 'I've told you hundreds of times how I took him everywhere. If you don't like him in the bedroom I'll put him away. I didn't know you didn't like him.'

'I didn't say that, Deborah. It's completely different, what you're saying. It's private for a start. I mean, it's your teddy-bear and you've told me how fond you were of it. That's completely different from sitting down with a crowd of idiots –'

'They're not idiots, Edwin, actually.'

'Well, they certainly don't sound like anything else. D'you mean Jeremy and Peter are going to arrive clutching teddy-bears and then sit down on the grass pretending to feed them biscuit crumbs? For God's sake, Jeremy's a medical *doctor*!'

'Actually, nobody'll sit on the grass because the grass will probably be damp. Everyone brought rugs last time. It's really because of the garden, you know. It's probably the nicest garden in South Bucks, and then there're the Ainley-Foxletons. I mean, they do so love it all.'

He'd actually been in the garden, and he'd once actually met the Ainley-Foxletons. One Saturday afternoon during his engagement to Deborah there had been tea on a raised lawn. Laburnum and broom were out, a mass of yellow everywhere. Quite pleasant old sticks the Ainley-Foxletons had been, but neither of them had mentioned a teddy-bears' picnic.

'I think she did as a matter of fact,' Deborah mildly insisted. 'I remember because I said it hadn't really been so long since the last one – eighteen months ago would it be when I took you to see them? Well, 1975 wasn't all that long before that, and she said it seemed like aeons. I remember her saying that, I remember "aeons" and thinking it just like her to come out with a word people don't use any more.'

'And you never thought to point out the famous picnic site? For hours we walked round and round that garden and yet it never occurred to you –'

'We didn't walk round and round. I'm sorry you were bored, Edwin.'

'I didn't say I was bored.'

'I know the Ainley-Foxletons can't hear properly and it's a strain, but you said you wanted to meet them –'

'I didn't say anything of the kind. You kept telling me about these people and their house and garden, but I can assure you I wasn't crying out to meet them in any way whatsoever. In fact, I rather wanted to play tennis that afternoon.'

'You didn't say so at the time.'

'Of course I didn't say so.'

'Well, then.'

'What I'm trying to get through to you is that we walked round and round that garden even though it had begun to rain. And not once did you say, "That's where we used to have our famous teddy-bears' picnic."'

'As a matter of fact I think I did. And it isn't famous. I wish you wouldn't keep on about it being famous.'

Deborah poured herself more gin and added the same amount of dry vermouth to the glass. She considered it rude of Edwin to stalk about the room just because he'd had a bad day, drinking himself and not bothering about her. If he hadn't liked the poor old Ainley-Foxletons he should have said so. If he'd wanted to play tennis that afternoon he should have said so too.

'Well, be all that as it may,' he was saying now, rather pompously in Deborah's opinion, 'I do not intend to take part in any of this nonsense.'

'But everybody's husband will, and the wives too. It's only fun, darling.'

'Oh, do stop saying it's fun. You sound like a half-wit. And something's smelling in the kitchen.'

'I don't think that's very nice, Edwin. I don't see why you should call me a half-wit.'

'Listen, I've had an extremely unpleasant day –'

'Oh, do stop about your stupid old day.'

She carried her glass to the kitchen with her and removed the chops from beneath the grill. They were fairly black, and serve him right for upsetting her. Why on earth did he have to make such a fuss, why couldn't he be like everyone else? It was something to giggle over, not take so seriously, a single Sunday afternoon when they wouldn't be doing anything anyway. She dropped a handful of noodles into the hot oil, and then a second handful.

In the sitting-room the telephone rang just as Edwin was squirting soda into another drink. 'Yes?' he said, and Angela's voice came lilting over the line, saying she didn't want to bother Debbie but the date had just been fixed: June 17th. 'Honestly, you'll split your sides, Edwin.'

'Yes, all right, I'll tell her,' he said as coldly as he could. He replaced the receiver without saying goodbye. He'd never cared for Angela, patronizing kind of creature.

Deborah knew it had been Angela on the telephone and she knew she would have given Edwin the date she had arranged with Charlotte and Peter, who'd been the doubtful ones about the first date, suggested by Jeremy. Angela had said she was going to ring back with this information, but when the Chalms sat down to their chops and broccoli spears and noodles Edwin hadn't yet passed the information on.

'Christ, what are these?' he said, poking at a brown noodle with his fork and then poking at the burnt chop.

'The little things are fried noodles, which you enjoyed so much the other night. The larger thing is a pork chop, which wouldn't have got overcooked if you hadn't started an argument.'

'Oh, for God's sake!'

He pushed his chair back and stood up. He returned to the sitting-room and Deborah heard the squirting of the soda syphon. She stood up herself, followed him to the sitting-room and poured herself another gin and vermouth. Neither of them spoke. Deborah returned to the kitchen and ate her share of the broccoli spears. The sound of television came from the sitting-room. 'Listen, buster, you give this bread to the hit or don't you?' a voice demanded. 'O.K., I give the bread,' a second voice replied.

They'd had quarrels before. They'd quarrelled on their honeymoon in Greece for no reason whatsoever. They'd quarrelled because she'd once left the ignition of the car turned on, causing a flat battery. They'd quarrelled because of Enid's boring party just before Christmas. The present quarrel was just the same kind of thing, Deborah knew: Edwin would sit and sulk, she'd wash the dishes up feeling miserable, and he'd probably eat the chop and the broccoli when they were cold. She couldn't blame him for not wanting the noodles because she didn't seem to have cooked them correctly. Then she thought: what if he doesn't come to the picnic, what if he just goes on being stubborn, which he could be when he wanted to? Everyone would know. 'Where's Edwin?' they would ask, and she'd tell some lie and everyone would know it was a lie, and everyone would know they weren't getting on. Only six months had passed, everyone would say, and he wouldn't join in a bit of fun.

But to Deborah's relief that didn't happen. Later that night Edwin ate the cold pork chop, eating it from his fingers because he couldn't manage to stick a fork into it. He ate the cold broccoli spears as well, but he left the noodles. She made him tea and gave him a Danish pastry and in the morning he said he was sorry.

'So if we could it would be lovely,' Deborah said on her office telephone. She'd told her mother there was to be another teddy-bears' picnic, Angela and Jeremy had arranged it mainly, and the Ainley-Foxletons would love it of course, possibly the last they'd see.

'My dear, you're always welcome, as you know.' The voice of Deborah's mother came all the way from South Bucks, from the village where the Ainley-Foxletons' house and garden were, where Deborah and Angela, Jeremy, Charlotte, Harriet, Enid, Peter and Holly had been children together. The plan was that Edwin and Deborah should spend the weekend of June 17th with Deborah's parents, and Deborah's mother had even promised to lay on some tennis for Edwin on the Saturday. Deborah herself wasn't much good at tennis.

'Thanks, Mummy,' she managed to say just as Mr Harridance returned from lunch.

'No, spending the whole weekend actually,' Edwin informed his mother. 'There's this teddy-bear thing Deborah has to go to.'

'What teddy-bear thing?'

Edwin went into details, explaining how the children who'd been friends in a South Bucks village nearly twenty years ago met from time to time to have a teddy-bears' picnic because that was what they'd done then.

'But they're adults surely now,' Mrs Chalm pointed out.

'Yes, I know.'

'Well, I hope you have a lovely time, dear.'

'Delightful, I'm sure.'

'It's odd when they're adults, I'd have thought.'

Between themselves, Edwin and Deborah did not again discuss the subject of the teddy-bears' picnic. During the quarrel Edwin had felt bewildered, never quite knowing how to proceed, and he hoped that on some future occasion he would be better able to cope. It made him angry when he wasn't able to cope, and the anger still hung about him. On the other hand, six months wasn't long in a marriage which he hoped would go on for ever: the marriage hadn't had a chance to settle into the shape that suited it, any more than he and Deborah had had time to develop their own taste in furniture and decoration. It was only to be expected that there should be problems and uncertainty.

As for Deborah, she knew nothing about marriages settling into shape: she wasn't aware that rules and tacit understandings, arrangements of give and take, were what made marriage possible when the first gloss had worn off. Marriage for Deborah was the continuation of a love affair, and as yet she had few complaints. She knew that of course they had to have quarrels.

They had met at a party. Edwin had left a group of people he was listening to and had crossed to the corner where she was being bored by a man in computers. 'Hello,' Edwin just said. All three of them were eating plates of paella.

Finding a consideration of the past pleasanter than speculation about the future, Deborah often recalled that moment: Edwin's sharp face smiling at her, the computer man discomfited, a sour taste in the paella. 'You're not Fiona's sister?' Edwin said, and when ages afterwards she'd asked him who Fiona was he confessed he'd made her up. 'I shouldn't eat much more of this stuff,' he said, taking the paella away from her. Deborah had been impressed by that: she and the computer man had been fiddling at the paella with their forks, both of them too polite to say that there was something the matter with it. 'What do you do?' Edwin said a few minutes later, which was more than the computer man had asked.

In the weeks that followed they told one another all about themselves, about their parents and the houses they'd lived in as children, the schools they'd gone to, the friends they'd made. Edwin was a daring person, he was successful, he liked to be in charge of things. Without in any way sounding boastful, he told her of episodes in his childhood, or risks taken at school. Once he'd dismantled the elderly music master's bed, causing it to collapse when the music master later lay down on it. He'd removed the carburettor from some other master's car, he'd stolen an egg-beater from an ironmonger's shop. All of them were dares, and by the end of his schooldays he had acquired the reputation of being fearless: there was nothing, people said, he wouldn't do.

It was easy for Deborah to love him, and everything he told her, self-deprecatingly couched, was clearly the truth. But Deborah in love naturally didn't wonder how this side of Edwin would seem in marriage, nor how it might develop as Edwin moved into middle age. She couldn't think of anything nicer than having him there every day, and in no way did she feel let down on their honeymoon in Greece or by the couple of false starts they made with flats before they eventually ended up in 23 The Zodiac. Edwin went to his office every day and Deborah went to hers. That he told her more about share prices than she told him about the letters she typed for Mr Harridance was because share prices were more important. It was true that she would often have quite liked to pass on details of this or that, for instance of the correspondence with Flitts, Hay and Co concerning nearly eighteen thousand defective chair castors. The correspondence was interesting because it had continued for two years and had become vituperative. But when she mentioned it Edwin just agreeably nodded. There was also the business about Miss Royal's scratches, which everyone in the office had been conjecturing about: how on earth had a woman like Miss Royal acquired four long scratches on her face and neck between five-thirty one Monday evening and nine-thirty the following morning? 'Oh yes?' Edwin had said, and gone on to talk about the Mercantile Investment Trust.

Deborah did not recognize these telltale signs. She did not remember that when first she and Edwin exchanged information about one another's childhoods Edwin had sometimes just smiled, as if his mind had drifted away. It was only a slight disappointment that he didn't wish to hear about Flitts, Hay and Co, and Miss Royal's scratches: no one could possibly get into a state about things like that. Deborah saw little significance in the silly quarrel they'd had about the teddy-bears' picnic, which was silly itself of course. She didn't see that it had had to do with friends who were hers and not Edwin's; nor did it occur to her that when they really began to think about the decoration of 23 The Zodiac it would be Edwin who would make the decisions. They shared things, Deborah would have said: after all, in spite of the quarrel they were going to go to the teddy-bears' picnic. Edwin loved her and was kind and really rather marvellous. It was purely for her sake that he'd agreed to give up a whole weekend.

So on a warm Friday afternoon, as they drove from London in their Saab, Deborah was feeling happy. She listened while Edwin talked about a killing a man called Dupree had made by selling out his International Asphalt holding. 'James James Morrison Morrison Weatherby George Dupree,' she said.

'What on earth's that?'

'It's by AA Milne, the man who wrote about Pooh Bear. Poor Pooh!'

Edwin didn't say anything.

'Jeremy's is called Pooh.'

'I see.'

In the back of the car, propped up in a corner, was the blue teddy-bear called Binky which Deborah had had since she was one.

The Teddy-bears' Picnic 36

The rhododendrons were in bloom in the Ainley-Foxletons' garden, late that year because of the bad winter. So was the laburnum Edwin remembered, and the broom, and some yellow azaleas. 'My dear, we're so awfully glad,' old Mrs Ainley-Foxleton said, kissing him because she imagined he must be one of the children in her past. Her husband, tottering about on the raised lawn which Edwin also remembered from his previous visit, had developed the shakes. 'Darlings, Mrs Bright has ironed our tablecloth for us!' Mrs Ainley-Foxleton announced with a flourish.

She imparted this fact because Mrs Bright, the Ainley-Foxletons' charwoman, was emerging at that moment from the house, with the ironed tablecloth over one arm. She carried a tray on which there were glass jugs of orange squash and lemon squash, a jug of milk, mugs with Beatrix Potter characters on them, and two plates of sandwiches that weren't much larger than postage stamps. She made her way down stone steps from the raised lawn, crossed a more extensive lawn and disappeared into a shrubbery. While everyone remained chatting to the Ainley-Foxletons – nobody helping to lay the picnic out because that had never been part of the proceedings – Mrs Bright reappeared from the shrubbery, returned to the house and then made a second journey, her tray laden this time with cakes and biscuits.

Before lunch Edwin had sat for a long time with Deborah's father in the summerhouse, drinking. This was something Deborah's father enjoyed on Sunday mornings, permitting himself a degree of dozy inebriation which only became noticeable when two bottles of claret were consumed at lunch. Today Edwin had followed his example, twice getting to his feet to refill their glasses and during the course of lunch managing to slip out to the summerhouse for a fairly heavy tot of whisky, which mixed nicely with the claret. He could think of no other condition in which to present himself – with a teddy-bear Deborah's mother had pressed upon him – in the Ainley-Foxletons' garden. 'Rather you than me, old chap,' Deborah's father had said after lunch, subsiding into an armchair with a gurgle. At the last moment Edwin had quickly returned to the summerhouse and had helped himself to a further intake of whisky, drinking from the cap of the Teacher's bottle because the glasses had been collected up. He reckoned that when Mrs Ainley-Foxleton had kissed him he must have smelt like a distillery, and he was glad of that.

'Well, here we are,' Jeremy said in the glade where the picnic had first taken place in 1957. He sat at the head of the tablecloth, cross-legged on a tartan rug. He had glasses and was stout. Peter at the other end of the tablecloth didn't seem to have grown much in the intervening years, but Angela had shot up like a hollyhock and in fact resembled one. Enid was dumpy, Charlotte almost beautiful; Harriet had protruding teeth, Holly was bouncy. Jeremy's wife and Peter's wife, and Charlotte's husband – a man in Shell – all entered into the spirit of the occasion. So did Angela's husband, who came from Czechoslovakia and must have found the proceedings peculiar, everyone sitting there with a teddy-bear that had a name. Angela put a record on Mrs Ainley-Foxleton's old wind-up gramophone. 'Oh, don't go down to the woods today,' a voice screeched, 'without consulting me.' Mr and Mrs Ainley-Foxleton were due to arrive at the scene later, as was the tradition. They came with chocolates apparently, and bunches of buttercups for the teddy-bears.

'Thank you, Edwin,' Deborah whispered while the music and the song continued. She wanted him to remember the quarrel they'd had about the picnic; she wanted him to know that she now truly forgave him, and appreciated that in the end he'd seen the fun of it all.

'Listen, I have to go to the lav,' Edwin said. 'Excuse me for a minute.' Nobody except Deborah seemed to notice when he ambled off because everyone was talking so, exchanging news.

The anger which had hung about Edwin after the quarrel had never evaporated. It was in anger that he had telephoned his mother, and further anger had smacked at him when she'd said she hoped he would have a lovely time. What she had meant was that she'd told him so: marry a pretty little thing and before you can blink you're sitting down to tea with teddy-bears. You're a fool to put up with rubbish like this was what Deborah's father had meant when he'd said rather you than me.

Edwin did not lack brains and he had always been aware of it. It was his cleverness that was still offended by what he considered to be an embarrassment, a kind of gooey awfulness in an elderly couple's garden. At school he had always hated anything to do with dressing up, he'd even felt awkward when he'd had to read poetry aloud. What Edwin admired was solidity: he liked Westminster and the City, he liked trains moving smoothly, suits and clean shirts. When he'd married Deborah he'd known – without having to be told by his mother – that she was not a clever person, but in Edwin's view a clever wife was far from necessary. He had seen a future in which children were born and educated, in which Deborah developed various cooking and housekeeping skills, in which together they gave nice dinner parties. Yet instead of that, after only six months, there was this grotesque absurdity. Getting drunk wasn't a regular occurrence with Edwin: he drank when he was angry, as he had on the night of the quarrel.

Mr Ainley-Foxleton was pottering about with his stick on the raised lawn, but Edwin took no notice of him. The old man appeared to be looking for something, his head poked forward on his scrawny neck, bespectacled eyes examining the grass. Edwin passed into the house. From behind a closed door he could hear the voices of Mrs Ainley-Foxleton and Mrs Bright, talking about buttercups. He opened another door and entered the Ainley-Foxletons' dining-room. On the sideboard there was a row of decanters.

Edwin discovered that it wasn't easy to drink from a decanter, but he managed it none the less. Anger spurted in him all over again. It seemed incredible that he had married a girl who hadn't properly grown up. None of them had grown up, none of them desired to belong in the adult world, not even the husbands and wives who hadn't been involved in the first place. If Deborah had told him about any of it on that Sunday afternoon when they'd visited this house he wondered even if he would have married her.

Yet replacing the stopper of the decanter between mouthfuls in case anyone came in, Edwin found it impossible to admit that he had made a mistake in marrying Deborah: he loved her, he had never loved anyone else, and he doubted if he would ever love anyone else in the future. Often in an idle moment, between selling and buying in the office, he thought of her, seeing her in her different clothes and sometimes without any clothes at all. When he returned to 23 The Zodiac he sometimes put his arms around her and would not let her go until he had laid her gently down on their bed. Deborah thought the world of him, which was something she often said.

In spite of all that it was extremely annoying that the quarrel had caused him to feel out of his depth. He should have been able to sort out such nonsense within a few minutes; he deserved his mother's jibe and his father-in-law's as well. Even though they'd only been married six months, it was absurd that since Deborah loved him so he hadn't been able to make her see how foolish she was being. It was absurd to be standing here drunk.

The Ainley-Foxletons' dining-room, full of silver and polished furniture and dim oil paintings, shifted out of focus. The row of decanters became two rows and then one again. The heavily carpeted floor tilted beneath him, falling away to the left and then to the right. Deborah had let him down. She had brought him here so that he could be displayed in front of Angela and Jeremy and Charlotte, Harriet, Holly, Enid, Peter, and the husbands and the wives. She was making the point that she had only to lift her little finger, that his cleverness was nothing compared with his love for her. The anger hammered at him now, hurting him almost. He wanted to walk away, to drive the Saab back to London and when Deborah followed him to state quite categorically that if she intended to be a fool there would have to be a divorce. But some part of Edwin's anger insisted that such a course of action would be an admission of failure and defeat. It was absurd that the marriage he had chosen to make should end before it had properly begun, due to silliness.

Edwin took a last mouthful of whisky and replaced the glass stopper. He remembered another social occasion, years ago, and he was struck by certain similarities with the present one. People had given a garden party in aid of some charity or other which his mother liked to support, to which he and his brother and sister, and his father, had been dragged along. It had been an excruciatingly boring afternoon, in the middle of a heatwave. He'd had to wear his floppy cotton hat, which he hated, and an awful tan-coloured summer suit, made of cotton also. There had been hours and hours of just standing while his mother talked to people, sometimes slowly giving them recipes, which they wrote down. Edwin's brother and sister didn't seem to mind that; his father did as he was told. So Edwin had wandered off, into a house that was larger and more handsome than the Ainley-Foxletons'. He had poked about in the downstairs rooms, eaten some jam he found in the kitchen, and then gone upstairs to the bedrooms. He'd rooted around for a while, opening drawers and wardrobes, and then he'd climbed a flight of uncarpeted stairs to a loft. From here he'd made his way out on to the roof. Edwin had almost forgotten this incident and certainly never dwelt on it, but with a vividness that surprised him it now returned.

He left the dining-room. In the hall he could still hear the voices of Mrs Ainley-Foxleton and Mrs Bright. Nobody had bothered with him that day; his mother, whose favourite he had always been, was even impatient when he said he had a toothache. Nobody had noticed when he'd slipped away. But from the parapet of the roof everything had been different. The faces of the people were pale, similar dots, all gazing up at him. The colours of the women's dresses were confused among the flowers. Arms waved frantically at him; someone shouted, ordering him to come down.

On the raised lawn the old man was still examining the grass, his head still poked down towards it, his stick prodding at it. From the glade where the picnic was taking place came a brief burst of applause, as if someone had just made a speech. '... today's the day the teddy-bears have their picnic,' sang the screeching voice, faintly.

A breeze had cooled Edwin's sunburnt arms as he crept along the parapet. He'd sensed his mother's first realization that it was he, and noticed his brother's and his sister's weeping. He had seen his father summoned from the car where he'd been dozing. Edwin had stretched his arms out, balancing like a tightrope performer. All the boredom, the tiresome heat, the cotton hat and suit, were easily made up for. Within minutes it had become his day.

'Well, it's certainly the weather for it,' Edwin said to the old man.

'Eh?'

'The weather's nice,' he shouted. 'It's a fine day.'

'There's fungus in this lawn, you know. Eaten up with it.' Mr Ainley-Foxleton investigated small black patches with his stick. 'Never knew there was fungus here,' he said.

They were close to the edge of the lawn. Below them there was a rockery full of veronica and sea-pinks and saponaria. The rockery was arranged in a semicircle, around a sundial.

'Looks like fungus there too,' Edwin said, pointing at the larger lawn that stretched away beyond this rockery.

'Eh?' The old man peered over the edge, not knowing what he was looking for because he hadn't properly heard. 'Eh?' he said again, and Edwin nudged him with his elbow. The stick went flying off at an angle, the old man's head struck the edge of the sundial with a sharp, clean crack. 'Oh, don't go down to the woods today,' the voice began again, drifting through the sunshine over the scented garden. Edwin glanced quickly over the windows of the house in case there should be a face at one of them. Not that it would matter: at that distance no one could see such a slight movement of an elbow.

They ate banana sandwiches and egg sandwiches, and biscuits with icing on them, chocolate cake and coffee cake. The teddy-bears' snouts were pressed over the Beatrix Potter mugs, each teddy-bear addressed by name. Edwin's was called Tomkin.

'Remember the day of the thunderstorm?' Enid said, screwing up her features in a way she had – like a twitch really, Edwin considered. The day he had walked along the parapet might even have been the day of the thunderstorm, and he smiled because somehow that was amusing. Angela was smiling too, and so were Jeremy and Enid, Charlotte, Harriet and Holly, Peter and the husbands and the wives. Deborah in particular was smiling.

When Edwin glanced from face to face he was reminded of the faces that had gazed up at him from so far below, except that there'd been panic instead of smiles.

'Remember the syrup?' Angela said. 'Poor Algernon had to be given a horrid bath.'

'Wasn't it Horatio, surely?' Deborah said.

'Yes, it was Horatio,' Enid confirmed, amusingly balancing Horatio on her shoulder.

'Today's the day the teddy-bears have their picnic,' suddenly sang everyone, taking a lead from the voice on the gramophone. Edwin smiled and even began to sing himself. When they returned to Deborah's parents' house the atmosphere would be sombre. 'Poor old chap was overlooked,' he'd probably be the one to explain, 'due to all that fuss.' And in 23 The Zodiac the atmosphere would be sombre also. 'I'm afraid you should get rid of it,' he'd suggest, arguing that the blue teddy-bear would be for ever a reminder. Grown up a bit because of what had happened, Deborah would of course agree. Like everything else, marriage had to settle into shape.

Charlotte told a story of an adventure her Mikey had had when she'd taken him back to boarding-school, how a repulsive girl called Agnes Thorpe had stuck a skewer in him. Holly told of how she'd had to rescue her Percival from drowning when he'd toppled out of a motor-boat. Jeremy wound up the gramophone and the chatter jollily continued, the husbands and wives appearing to be as delighted as anyone. Harriet said how she'd only wanted to marry Peter and Peter how he'd determined to marry Deborah. 'Oh, don't go down to the woods today,' the voice began again, and then came Mrs Ainley-Foxleton's scream.

Everyone rushed, leaving the teddy-bears just anywhere and the gramophone still playing. Edwin was the first to bend over the splayed figure of the old man. He declared that Mr Ainley-Foxleton was dead, and then took charge of the proceedings.

37

My Father Writes to My Mother

(1985)

Assia Djebar

Translated by Dorothy S Blair (1993)

Whenever my mother spoke of my father, she, in common with all the women in her town, simply used the personal pronoun in Arabic corresponding to 'him'. Thus, every time she used a verb in the third person singular which didn't have a noun subject, she was naturally referring to her husband. This form of speech was characteristic of every married woman, from fifteen to sixty, with the proviso that in later years, if the husband had undertaken the pilgrimage to Mecca, he could be given the title of 'Hajj'.

Everybody, children and adults, especially girls and women, since all important conversations took place among the womenfolk, learnt very quickly to adapt to this rule whereby a husband and wife must never be referred to by name.

After she had been married for a few years, my mother gradually learnt a little French. She was able to exchange a few halting words with the wives of my father's colleagues who had, for the most part, come from France and, like us, lived with their families in the little block of flats set aside for the village teachers.

I don't know exactly when my mother began to say, '*My husband* has come, *my husband* has gone out ... I'll ask *my husband*,' etc. Although my mother did make rapid progress in the language, in spite of taking it up fairly late in life, I can still hear the evident awkwardness in her voice betrayed by her laboured phraseology, her slow and deliberate enunciation at that time. Nevertheless, I can sense how much it cost her modesty to refer to my father directly in this way.

It was as if a floodgate had opened within her, perhaps in her relationship with her husband. Years later, during the summers we spent in her native town, when chatting in Arabic with her sisters or cousins, my mother would refer to him quite naturally by his first name, even with a touch of superiority. What a daring innovation! Yes, quite unhesitatingly – I was going to say, unequivocally – in any case, without any of the usual euphemisms and verbal circumlocutions. When her aunts and elderly female relations were present, she would once more use the traditional formalities, out of respect for them; such freedom of language would have appeared insolent and incongruous to the ears of the pious old ladies.

37 My Father Writes to My Mother

Years went by. As my mother's ability to speak French improved, while I was still a child of no more than twelve, I came to realise an irrefutable fact: namely that, in the face of all these womenfolk, my parents formed a couple. One thing was an even greater source of pride in me: when my mother referred to any of the day-to-day incidents of our village life – which in our city relatives' eyes was very backward – the tall figure of my father – my childhood hero – seemed to pop up in the midst of all these women engaged in idle chit-chat on the age-old patios to which they were confined.

My father, no one except my father; none of the other women ever saw fit to refer to their menfolk, their masters who spent the day outside the house and returned home in the evening, taciturn, with eyes on the ground. These nameless uncles, cousins, relatives by marriage, were for us an unidentifiable collection of individuals to all of whom their spouses alluded impartially in the masculine gender.

With the exception of my father ... My mother, with lowered eyes, would calmly pronounce his name 'Tahar' – which, I learned very early, meant 'The Pure' – and even when a suspicion of a smile flickered across the other women's faces or they looked half ill at ease, half indulgent, I thought that a rare distinction lit up my mother's face.

These harem conversations ran their imperceptible course: my ears only caught those phrases which singled my mother out above the rest. Because she always made a point of bringing my father's name into these exchanges, he became for me still purer than his given name betokened.

***

One day something occurred which was a portent that their relationship would never be the same again – a commonplace enough event in any other society, but which was unusual to say the least with us: in the course of an exceptionally long journey away from home (to a neighbouring province, I think), my father wrote to my mother – yes, to my mother!

He sent her a postcard, with a short greeting written diagonally across it in his large, legible handwriting, something like 'Best wishes from this distant region' or possibly, 'I am having a good journey and getting to know an unfamiliar region' etc. and he signed it simply with his first name. I am sure that, at the time, he himself would not have dared add any more intimate formula above his signature, such as 'I am thinking of you', or even less, 'Yours affectionately'. But, on the half of the card reserved for the address of the recipient, he had written 'Madame' followed by his own surname, with the possible addition – but here I'm not sure – of 'and children', that is to say we three, of whom I, then about ten years old, was the eldest ...

The radical change in customs was apparent for all to see: my father had quite brazenly written his wife's name, in his own handwriting, on a postcard which was going to travel from one town to another, which was going to be exposed to so many masculine eyes, including eventually our village postman – a Muslim postman to boot – and, what is more, he had dared to refer to her in the western manner as 'Madame So-and-So ...', whereas, no local man, poor or rich, ever referred to his wife and children in any other way than by the vague periphrasis: 'the household'.

So, my father had 'written' to my mother. When she visited her family she mentioned this postcard, in the simplest possible words and tone of voice, to be sure. She was about to describe her husband's four or five days' absence from the village, explaining the practical problems this had posed: my father having to order the provisions just before he left, so that the shopkeepers could deliver them every morning; she was going to explain how hard it was for a city woman to be isolated in a village with very young children and cut off in this way ... But the other women had interrupted, exclaiming, in the face of this new reality, this almost incredible detail:

'He wrote to you, *to you*?'

'He wrote his wife's name and the postman must have read it? Shame! ...'

'He could at least have addressed the card to his son, for the principle of the thing, even if his son is only seven or eight!'

My mother did not reply. She was probably pleased, flattered even, but she said nothing. Perhaps she was suddenly ill at ease, or blushing from embarrassment; yes, her husband had written to her, in person! ... The eldest child, the only one who might have been able to read the card, was her daughter: so, daughter or wife, where was the difference as far as the addressee was concerned?

'I must remind you that I've learned to read French now!'

This postcard was, in fact, a most daring manifestation of affection. Her modesty suffered at that very moment that she spoke of it. Yet, it came second to her pride as a wife, which was secretly flattered.

***

The murmured exchanges of these segregated women struck a faint chord with me, as a little girl with observing eyes. And so, for the first time, I seem to have some intuition of the possible happiness, the mystery in the union of a man and a woman.

My father had dared 'to write' to my mother. Both of them referred to each other by name, which was tantamount to declaring openly their love for each other, my father by writing to her, my mother by quoting my father henceforward without false shame in all her conversations.

38

Smoke

(1986)

Ila Mehta

Translated by Sima Sharma (1986)

Ba comes back this evening by the five o'clock train. Shubha glanced at her watch. It was only four o'clock, still some time to go. A vast sea of overpowering emptiness engulfed her being. Nothing left to do. Nothing ... except wait.

Her hands wandered over the books lying on the table and picked one up. It was a fat book written in English, on women's health problems and their treatments. It opened with the picture of a naked woman, bared in vivid detail, sketched with dexterity. For clinical purposes only, of course!

She slammed it shut, pushed it back and walked out of the room onto the open balcony. She stood still. The oppressive, tormenting afternoon was still astride the earth, its heat permeating every nook and cranny. 'Like my own emptiness,' she thought. 'Not a hollow neutral vacuum but this leaden emptiness, opaque and solid.'

'The russet evening shall wax but a few moments only. And then all will be dark again.' A wan smile on her lips, Shubha stepped back into the room.

Just half past four. Driving her car towards the station, Dr Shubha scolded herself, 'You're becoming neurotic, Shubha. The sun itself looks like a dark blot to you.'

Suddenly her belly tightened. Was everything shipshape for Ba's homecoming? All details seen to? Like unwinding a reel of film, she went over the house slowly, room by room, in her mind's eye. Nothing amiss. All in order. Each corner had been cleaned with care. But suppose? ... Well – her practice and the clinic really left her with no time to spare. Her mother-in-law knew it well. And those few snatched private moments, well, forget it. It's just as well Ba did not know.

Swiftly, suddenly, a cold shiver rose from the pit of her stomach to her throat, with a chilling reminder – the picture! The photograph of Subodh had been left undusted, with the dirty gray string of dried flowers hanging around it. She had forgotten to place a fresh wreath. And with it remained Bapuji's photograph, too. Ba would of course go straight up to them, first thing on coming home.

38 Smoke

Framed in dry dead petals, Subodh's face smiled unmoving in black and white – like the printed picture of Krishna on last year's Diwali card, chucked on top of a heap of discarded papers.

Shubha gripped the steering wheel hard.

The ashtray beside the telephone – had it been cleaned? Often, ever so often in these past few days, she had sat there smoking as she talked over the telephone. Suppose Ba were to ask why we needed an ashtray at all in our house? What then? Oh God! There was no time now to turn back to the house. She parked the car and went into the station.

The train arrived on time. The luggage was stacked into the car. Shubha slid behind the wheel and started the engine and Ba got in beside her. Inching her way through milling crowds, sounding the horn intermittently, slamming the brakes on at traffic lights, she drove homeward. The driving, the traffic and the tortuous progress, she had grown used to it all now and could manage mechanically.

Ba talked. As she talked, the fatigue of the journey was shot through with the lively satisfaction that lit her face. Crisply, rapidly, Ba went about recounting the little happenings and family gossip, as she always did. Like the clickety-clack of needles knitting all the inconsequential details into the common tale of the extended Indian family. Aunt, nephew, cousin, grandmother, crisscrossing relatives gathered together to celebrate or to mourn.

The car ran on. It had to run on. Ba's words flitted out of the window like dry leaves swept along by the afternoon breeze. Shubha was quiet. Her thoughts hovered round that ashtray near the telephone – cigarette ash wafting in the air.

Home at last. Pressing the horn twice to summon a servant, Shubha ran up the stairs, not even waiting for Ba to alight. She went straight to the telephone. No ashtray there. Damn it! She herself had put it away into the cupboard this morning.

Ba came in and headed straight for the photographs. Bapuji and Subodh smiled through the film of dust. Only four months after Shubha had stepped in as a bride, father and son had died together in a road accident.

A crystal bowl decked with fresh young blossoms had once dashed to the floor and shattered. Since then, like the myriad splinters of glass, were the moments of life: each to be picked up, one at a time, and one by one to be put away.

Ba carefully cleaned the photographs, knelt down and touched her head to the floor. Rising she turned to Shubha, and on a faintly reproachful note asked, 'My dear, how did so much dust gather? Surely you remembered the fresh flowers and obeisance every day?'

One could make excuses – of a patient being ill, of visits to be paid. But words failed Shubha. She walked slowly out of the room.

Outside, she stood leaning against the rails of the balcony. Ba, she thought, must now be busy washing and bathing. At once she was seized with an irrepressible urge. The small space between thumb and finger throbbed palpably.

She went back to the room. Ba would take a long time in her bath. She pulled the packet out with an impatient hand and lit a cigarette, taking in the first few drags hungrily. Oh God. Just to quell the restless thirst of hours ...

One cigarette smoked, she lit another from its end. This too must be finished before Ba came out. She stood there and inhaled the smoke, deep and steady.

But how long can this go on? How long can the act be kept secret from her mother-in-law? There was the clinic, of course, where she could smoke. But Ba might just walk in there too, one day.

The sound of the bathroom door being unlatched broke her reverie. She flung the cigarette away, turned her head and peered. No, Ba was not yet back. She drew a long breath and sank down on the cane sofa.

Life. How it stretched interminably. How inexorably the seconds tick away. No might in the world can give them a shove and push them back. Time ...

A wave of exhaustion swept over her all at once. As if she had been plodding miles, carrying a heavy load. Now she only wanted to sit, just sit with a cigarette dangling from her listless hand.

'Don't you have to go to the clinic today?' Ba's voice reached out to her.

'I'm going,' she answered, and snapped her purse shut. But she remained rooted to the sofa. The prospect of the clinic was depressing.

The faces that waited for her there would be dismal, every one of them, some bereft of all hope. To think of them was to enter that gray realm. 'I cannot eat a morsel, doctor.' 'A fever of 100 degrees since yesterday.' 'The swellings on the feet have not gone down.' Some throats riddled with swollen glands, some tumors destined to live or to die, a ceaseless tug-of-war and unending complaints.

She heaved a sigh and just as she was about to rise and leave, Ba came in. Seeing Shubha still sitting, she drew up the cane chair opposite and sat down.

'Shubha, the wedding was really great fun, very enjoyable. Oh dear, we – now let's see, how many years since I last saw a wedding? Your wedding, of course, and after that – oh well. But Mama was hurt that you did not attend. I explained to him of course. She is a doctor, I said. She has a commitment to her patients. Far be it from me to come in the way of her duty. What do you say? Isn't that so?'

An answer. One must say something now. Ba was waiting for a response. That is how it should be – some give-and-take, some conversation. Without these mundane exchanges, a home would freeze into one of those two dimensional stills. Her voice, pitched a shade too high, broke the lengthening pause. 'How did Indu look as a bride? Was she dressed heavily for the occasion?'

'Yes indeed, dear. They had called in one of these makeup artists, you know. A full hundred rupees she charged! But Indu looked like a doll.'

Ba pulled herself up a bit and continued, 'You know Shubha, it really makes me laugh. These modern girls are all just dolls, mere dolls. Not a jot of idealism, noble thoughts or sensibilities.'

Shubha gazed out in silence as the evening spread its shadow over the earth. She looked into the falling darkness.

'Come, now. You'll be late for work,' Ba said. Shubha rose to her feet. Clutching the balustrade firmly in hand, she walked down the steps and out of the house. She started the car but after a moment switched off the engine. She would walk to the clinic today, she decided. It was only a short distance and she was in no mood to drive.

At the clinic, she found a large number of patients waiting for her. She took them all in at a glance. At the end of the line sat a man, neatly dressed, middle-aged. Their eyes met. An enigmatic smile played on his lips as he said, 'I've been waiting for you for ever so long.'

Shubha reacted with a start. It was not the words or voice so much, but the smile that was disquieting. A shiver of fear. As if this man could read her mind, as if he knew all, inside out.

She turned her eyes away in haste. She sat erect in her chair and answered, a trifle too loudly, a trifle too crisply, 'Sorry, I have been delayed a bit.'

One after another the patients came up to her. Some were advised to consult a specialist, for some an X-ray, for others merely an aspirin. It was all so routine. And the eyes of the man at the end of the queue somehow radiated strength to her – enhancing her capabilities, her insight, and her confidence. Yet there was that undercurrent of irritability, a weariness, an overwhelming desire just to let go!

She glanced at him. His smile hurt her, chased her about like some little whirligig, a sparkler that children light on festival nights which scatters a shower of thrill and fear round and round in its zigzag trail.

Most of the patients had departed. It was his turn now – the last one. A cigarette. The urgent need to smoke welled up in her. Her fingers pulled out a cigarette from her purse. The man sprang up and lit it with his own lighter.

'Thank you.'

He then sat down in the chair opposite her.

'Latika has been unwell since yesterday. Doctor, would you please come?'

His voice now struck dread, like his haunting smile. His words, so mildly spoken, were a confident invitation. Beneath the words lay the unspoken phrases: 'I know ... I know it all ... Everything.'

She stood up and said, 'Yes, let's go. We shall watch for a day or two and then maybe call in a specialist.'

He picked up Shubha's black bag, walked ahead to his car and held the door open for her. A moment's pause, then Shubha got into the front seat. He closed the door with care, walked round and got in beside her, behind the wheel.

Latika was of course not yet as well as she ought to be, but, even so, her condition did not quite merit a house call. Still, Shubha spent a long evening at their house. The long-ailing spinster and her bachelor brother together managed to keep the evening scintillating. She sat for a long time with the brother and sister, savoring the easy flow of conversation: the simple chatter that bounces off the walls of a house giving it the dimensions of a home. The fear of that smile had now vanished. Skeins of laughter and companionship spun a shimmering cocoon around her.

'Doctor, stay and eat with us,' begged Latika. Shubha sprang up with a start and looked at her watch. Nine-thirty! Ba waited at home for her. She had returned.

'No thank you – it's late. Some other time.' She stood up.

'I had no idea of your taste in these things. I have a number of imported brands – cigarettes as well as drinks,' he said.

'Oh, no! It's only occasional ...' Murmuring, she crossed to the telephone, called the clinic, told the compounder to close for the day. She felt agitated, scared. She had lingered too long – the laughter, the jokes – for no good reason on earth. Life. She felt alive, and yet dreaded the very touch of life, afraid to come alive.

He drove her home in his car. Lifting her black bag in his hand, he offered to carry it upstairs. But she took it from him with a 'No, thank you.'

He did not move, but looked at her and said softly, 'Will you not come again, unless my sister is ill? Won't you come over just to see us? We have really enjoyed your visit. You see, we are quite alone.'

She could no longer stand there. Mumbling a formal 'Yes, of course,' she quickly climbed the steps.

A cloud of sweet incense hit her at the door. She entered the living room and saw the two photographs of Subodh and Bapuji draped with thick garlands of flowers. A bunch of incense sticks burned before them. The air hung heavy with the sweet scent. Ba sat on the floor facing the pictures, reciting the Gita.

Softly, Shubha crossed over to her room, put down her purse and taking the cigarette packet out, tucked it away into the cupboard. She washed her hands and face and rinsed her mouth with antiseptic. When she returned to the living room Ba had finished her recitation and was spooning the food onto the plates.

'I had to call on a patient. It got late,' she said and sat down to eat.

Ba's hand stopped still in midair. Shubha jumped up and prostrated herself before Subodh's photograph. Subodh was smiling at her – a distant lifeless smile framed by fresh voluptuous blossoms.

As they ate, Ba began to talk again. Shubha barely heard her. Her thoughts, her being were still in Latika's house. The faint whiff of aftershave lotion, light laughter. 'You see, we are quite alone.' His words, his eyes ...

'We are quite alone.' She heard the words distinctly again and looked up, startled. It was Ba talking to her.

'I told your Mama, "Do not worry for us, brother. What if we are quite alone? I and my dear Shubha, we are quite apart from others."'

Shubha looked down at her plate as she ate.

Ba spoke on: 'Mama was all too full of praise, dear. "Shubha is indeed a saint," he said. "Her life is like an incense stick. It burns itself to release its fragrance into the world."'

Suddenly, Ba's voice ceased. Shubha looked up at her mother-in-law. A deep frown knitting her brow, Ba stared steadily into the corner opposite. She got up and walked over, and picked up something from the floor.

'Shubha, what is this?' Ba's voice cracked. Like hard dry earth. The barren sunbaked earth cracks, willy-nilly, along deep jagged fissures.

With thin trembling fingers Ba held up the burnt-out stub of a cigarette.

39

Fishing

(1987)

Patricia Grace

While the others were out getting paua and kina, Ria fished. She'd picked ngakihi off the sea rocks, then taken the line and bait to a place where there was weed. The waves were green there – not heavy, and not breaking until right on shore. On shore they broke, tracking up over the stones.

She thumbed ngakihi out of their shells and baited the hooks, then unwound some of the line and walked to the edge of the water, whirling the traces. She cast, and the line shot out, dropping close to the weed.

From where she sat she could see the others, some out diving off the dinghy to pick kina off the sea bed, others snorkelling about amongst the rocks getting paua. That was the way the younger ones liked to do things, yet she knew if they'd waited until the tide was down they could've walked out and got all the paua they needed, in water that was just knee deep.

Further out past the divers, the children were jumping off Chicken Rock, struggling in the breaking waves and climbing up again. In the shallow water younger children were pushing a log about, and babies paddled and played, watched by mothers who really wanted to be getting kina and paua, or out jumping off Chicken Rock. If she'd stayed there with them she would've watched the kids and given her nieces a break. But today she'd decided to go off on her own and fish.

There were a few tugs on her line and then the biting stopped. She began to pull in, knowing that the bait would be gone, bringing the line in swiftly so the sinker wouldn't snag. Ngakihi was soft bait but would have to do until the water was shallow enough for her to get paua. She baited up and cast the line again – not straight, not far, but the spot was worth a try.

Looking back she could see the old man sitting under the big umbrella. He would be watching, thinking about the place, thinking about how he knew the shape of the sea bed right there. She knew he would like to have told someone about when the crayfish were thick, about when you could, at this time of the year, have looked down from the hills and seen the large red mass moving shoreward, which was crayfish coming in. She would have listened to him tell about how they'd pulled the weed aside with long-handled spears to find the crayfish that had backed themselves into narrow cracks in the rocks. The old man liked the umbrella.

Out on Chicken Rock the children were facing out to sea, waving. There was the sound of a motor, and then a boat came into sight and began weaving its way in. She couldn't see clearly but knew it would be her cousin May, with her husband and their family, coming to catch what could be the last good tide of the summer. The boat stopped close to shore and the children got out, then it rode out again to where May and Maru would set their nets.

The fish were biting all right, but she wasn't hooking them. She pulled in and baited up again.

Now the kids out on the rock were calling, looking shoreward this time. They would be tired by now, wanting someone to bring the dinghy out to get them. She watched as someone rowed out and nosed the boat up against the big rock. The children climbed down to be taken ashore, too exhausted and too hungry to swim for it. They were soon back on shore, running everywhere picking up sticks. They wouldn't be given bread until the wood had been gathered. Not long after that she saw smoke rising against the backdrop of cliffs. The divers were wading in with full bags.

At low tide she went to look for paua. There were several there on the stones and she collected three. She washed and shelled the smallest one, intending to eat it. Then she decided she wouldn't eat until she had caught her fish. She wouldn't eat, and she wouldn't go back to drink tea. Knowing that her line would snag in such shallow water, she lay down, sheltering where the stones had piled, and waited for the tide to flow again.

For some time there was little activity in the incoming tide. Then suddenly the fish were there again, biting and pulling, and she knew it was just a matter of time.

It was colder now but the kids were back in the water again – the mothers too, getting their chance at last. Cassie was helping the old man up to the car, wanting to get him home before the cold set in. The old man liked being able to come there by car.

By the time she caught her fish it was late afternoon. It was a small fish, but she was satisfied. All she'd hoped for was to catch one fish on this, the last good day of summer. She took it down to the water's edge where she cleaned and scaled it.

Then she knew there was something else for her to do, because how could you be really sure of coming there again next summer? And why should you come if you didn't let the place know you? It wasn't enough just to hold at the end of a line. The mothers were right about needing to go beyond the shore.

She walked out into the half-tide and let herself gradually into the water. She squatted for a while with her skirt floating up about her, then she pushed forward and down, pulling herself along the stony sea bed for as long as her breath lasted. When she came to the larger rocks where the weed grew thickly, she stood and pushed her way through. Once in the clear water again she lay on her back, letting herself go the way the water moved her. It was a familiar place, and she knew she could lie there like that quite safely.

Fishing 39

She lay there for a long time watching the sky redden as the sun went down.

Back on shore she picked up her line and the little fish, and walked quickly back to where the others were sitting round the fire, or getting ready to go for the nets.

They were amused at her one little fish, that it had taken her most of the day to catch. She knew they were wondering why she would spend all day on her own, without food, then come back wet and cold with just one little fish, especially when she knew there would be plenty of fish once the nets were brought in.

But it was her cousin May who said to her, as though they were picking up a conversation that could have begun years before, 'Because if you don't, it's like you won't any more. It's like if you sit under the umbrella once, then that's it. You have to still know, and you have to do enough ... to carry you over. You have to be in there because you don't want to be just waiting by the edge.'

40

The Fire Eater's Return

(1988)

Earl Lovelace

In the half light of the night his smile came out like the desperate grimace of a hungry, big-headed grey cat, something between a snarl and a smile, and for a moment I could not tell whether his intention was to entreat or to attack. I shifted my body so as to be sideways to him so I could parry his blow or launch my own counter-offensive if he intended to be hostile. The smile broadened. It was Blues.

Blues no longer exuded his usual air of grandeur. His face had a bleached, grey look, like he wasn't getting enough sleep or proper food to eat. And though he was still neat, with his shirt tucked into his trousers and his sleeves buttoned down at the wrist, his chest had caved in, and the sparkle had gone out of his eyes.

'God, I glad to see you!' he said.

Seeing me looking at him, he reached for the camouflage of a smile; but, I could see behind that smile that Blues had come face to face with a most formidable reality, and his optimism that he would conquer the world of the city with his own cunning and charm and his pretence at gentility had finally run out.

'This is my lady,' he said, indicating the woman at his side. I had been so focused on Blues that I had not made any connection between him and the woman who had followed him as he dodged his way through the traffic to cross the street.

I now looked into a beautiful, ravished face with large, beady eyes of a frightening intensity. Her thin body was folded in a long, African-print dress and her small head was wrapped in a headtie of the same cloth. 'I am Santo,' I said.

She made no attempt to shake my hand, and she mumbled something and moved a little closer to Blues.

'I didn't get your name,' I said.

'Ayesha,' she said, with such surprising hostility that I wondered what wrong I had done her.

I remembered then that I had seen her with Blues at Carnival. It was the Tuesday. The last band had left the Savannah stage where it had gone to be judged for Band of the Year competition. Around the Savannah the disc jockeys were belting out calypsos over their sound systems. Young people were assembling for their last lap, their last dance. Parents were taking children home. On the street were strewn bits of costume, suddenly superfluous for masqueraders. A sword there, a cape of a Ghengis Khan warrior, the headpiece of a Viking, a pair of wings of an angel, a warrior's lance, a devil's tail. Blues had apparently collected from these bits and pieces and made himself a costume and he was rushing with his costume into the band, moving with a frenzied reckless dancing, in one hand a lance, the other hand keeping the Viking's headpiece securely on his head. His angel's wings sticking out from beneath his arms. And he was going, going with a ferocious energy. In the half-light of the fading evening, I caught a glimpse of his face from where I was standing. There was no humour on it. It was a tortured mask with his grin. The sole of one shoe had come loose and was flapping and it gave to his otherwise frenzied display a sort of pathetic and awesome sadness. Authentic masqueraders cleared the way for him. In fact, he cleared his own way, and those glimpsing this madness, feeling the brush of his wings and fearing danger from his lance, got out of his way. Behind him, running to keep up with him was this same woman, dressed in the same clothes. I suspect she was trying to restrain him. But he wasn't taking her on. From where I stood I saw Blues plunge himself into the band and plough his way through with his irresistible and absolutely frightening and intimidating frenzy. No one tried to stop him. The whole thing lasted perhaps not a minute and I stood and watched it. I thought of rushing forward and restraining him. I thought Blues had gone mad. If he saw me then, if he saw that I had seen him in this way, the shame would kill him. But it was more than that. In my cowardice I hid from him. I was sure that something violent would take place. Next day I looked at the newspapers to see if they had reported the incident. There was nothing.

Now he was here before me.

'Well, let's go and have a beer,' I said. 'It's years I aint see you.'

'Yes. Let's go and siddown somewhere. Where?' He looked at me for guidance. And in that look, I saw for the first time since knowing Blues a look of defeat, of surprise, of disappointment, of someone let down and ashamed.

We went to an upstairs place right there on Independence Square and he was the first to sit down, dropping into his chair like a weight sinking into a river.

'Sit down,' he said to Ayesha and she drew her chair close to his and sat down.

'How's things?' I asked. It was really a formality.

'Hard,' he said. 'Things hard. Things not good. They say they have a recession, they have to lay off people ...'

'Why you don't get a job for him?' Ayesha said accusingly. 'You's a big editor.'

'Ayesha,' Blues said, lifting his voice tiredly. 'What you going on with that for?'

'But, you want a job,' she said. 'And he is your friend. Your big friend.'

Blues was speaking almost to himself, his voice was so low, 'I was working with Atlas Security. You working in this job. You have to stand up whole day. You can't sit down.

40 The Fire Eater's Return

You have to be there to watch everybody, to look at everything. And what I there for. I have this gun on my waist. I have this gun and you know it have times when I say to myself, why you don't stick up the cashier. Why you don't rob the bank.'

'And you spending money so free with your big friends. Always so free with money,' Ayesha said, accusingly.

And Blues: 'Is not the money alone. Is everything. Is life. Is how Kelly dead. How in the revolution he go up on the Hills and how they bring him down with his head blown away. Kelly was there in Cunaripo playing good good football. He was nearly as good as Berris, you know. And what he get shoot for? People don't even remember him. Is the love, Santo. Is how people don't care.'

'And all this time you spending money like you have money,' Ayesha said, addressing him. She turned to me, 'You never wonder where he getting money from? You see him spending, carrying girls to the beach, going and sit down in restaurant. You was his friend. You never tell him nothing?'

'So what I protecting with that gun?' I ask. 'So I give them they gun and their uniform otherwise any day I would stick up the bank.'

The waitress came around for our order.

'What you having?' I asked Ayesha.

She looked dumbly at me.

'You not taking a beer?' Blues asked her.

'No. I don't want no beer.'

'What you want?'

'I don't want nothing.'

I looked at Blues.

'Don't worry with her, eh Santo.' And, to Ayesha, 'Ayesha, Santo is my friend, from Cunaripo. Is nearly twenty years I know him. Is a long time. I learn a lot from him.'

'So, you see what he come to,' Ayesha said to me. 'You was his model. You know he take you for his model. He was trying to follow you.'

'I will take a guinness,' Blues said.

'And bring a beer for me. A guinness and a beer,' I said to the waitress.

'Ayesha,' Blues pleaded. He was sort of embarrassed for me. 'Ayesha, is twenty years I know Santo.'

'And you think Santo know you?' She was addressing me now. 'You know Blues? Blues like to be a big man, a big gentleman. Blues like people to like him. He want to be somebody. He spend his money free. He don't complain. Nobody don't ever think about him. Is just his hard luck now. You meet and you drink and you talk. You know anything about Blues? And he live in a dream, he live in a dream. And is not until somebody go mad or kill somebody that you half wake up and see that that is where it was going all the time.'

'Ayesha, I tired tell you. Don't talk that talk.' But Ayesha was on her way to the bathroom.

'I know its rough,' I said.

'They beat me, Santo.' There was a timbre of surprise in his voice. 'I come in town. I come to this city. I was never lazy. I was always doing something.'

I knew Blues was desperate. I had seventy dollars on me. I gave him fifty. He just put it in his pocket without saying anything. I took out my cigarettes and gave him one. I lit it for him.

We were both smoking silently when Ayesha returned.

'Take something,' I begged her.

She took a pull off Blues' cigarette. She still didn't want to have anything to do with me.

'Don't worry with Ayesha, you know,' Blues said. 'She does say anything. She have a hot mouth. Look, I tell her. I say, Girl, if anybody is to blame for anything is me. Is me.' He struck his chest. 'I can't blame anybody else. Is just that, that I thought I did know how to live. You know what I mean, Santo? I don't want no set of things, she neither. We don't want no set of things, eh, Ayesha.'

Ayesha took one of his hands. 'Let's go,' she said. 'We going.' She began to get up.

'I play the arse a lot too, you know,' Blues said, with his first smile for the evening.

'Yes,' I said, with my own smile. I was thinking of his performance, of his affectation. I was thinking of his coming down here in the city, the masquerade, Attila, the women.

'No.' Ayesha screamed. 'No.' She really was intent on opposing me. 'No. You didn't play the arse more than anybody. You was stupid, but you wasn't more stupid than anybody. You wanted to be a gentleman.'

'Yes, I thought it was so easy. The clothes, the walk, I had everything. I thought I was fooling them,' Blues said. 'They was the ones fooling me. I was the fool.'

'People have to find their own truth,' I said. 'Everybody.'

'You shoulda tell him that long ago,' Ayesha said. 'Why you didn't tell him that?'

'People have to live their own life,' I said.

'Why you didn't tell him that this was shit? He was watching you.'

Blues was watching me now.

'I suppose that I was a believer too,' I said.

Nobody said anything.

'Give me an orange juice,' Ayesha said.

Neither Blues nor I said anything lest we rouse Ayesha who sat like a trigger sipping the orange juice.

'About the job,' I said, when we were ready to leave, 'I don't know what they will have. But, come and see me sometime next week. That will give me some time to see if I could see somebody who know somebody who you could talk to for a job. Make sure and come, you know. Ayesha, see that he come.'

'Okay. And thanks,' he said, talking about the money. 'You save my life today.'

But, no. I did not save his life.

Blues did not turn up the next week as I expected him to. I saw him about a month later as I was coming out of the newsroom. He looked a bit better but wasted, hard. He was wearing a long African dress over his trousers. A silver bracelet was on his wrist and his head was bound with a red cloth. He was wearing sandals. Ayesha walked a few paces behind him. He looked very serious, and he was bowing to everyone on the way. 'Peace Brother. Peace and love. Peace sister.'

'I thought you say you would come to see me,' I said.

'The black race is under threat. They are stealing our dreams, our rhythms. Santo,' he said seriously, 'you have to stop sleeping. What you doing with yourself? You have to get out the rat race. People have to care, Santo. People have to care about people.'

'Where you going now? Come, let's take a beer.'

'Sorry. I have to go to the Square. I preach there. I counsel the sufferers.'

'And you, how do you live, man?'

'We take up a collection. A few dollars to buy candles, get something to eat.'

'Okay, then. Next time.'

Then, a few months ago he came into the office of the newsroom of *The Standard*. He was dressed in leopard-skin tights, his head was bound with a single golden band across his forehead, a bar of iron on his shoulder. He looked greying, paunchy. Ayesha was with him. She had some handbills. She was in the same costume of the African woman. She was handing out the handbills, things that they had written up and had xeroxed.

THE RETURN OF THE IRON MAN
FIRE EATING, BOTTLE DANCING AND OTHER OCCULT ACTIVITIES
GRAND DEMONSTRATION IN WOODFORD SQUARE
ADMISSION FREE. GIVE WHAT YOU CAN AFFORD

He wanted me to write a story on him. It was a big thing he was planning. All the newspapers will be there, he said. He had spoken to television, the radio stations. The Bomb will be there. He wanted me to do a story on him so that it would appear on the day of the event and he wanted me to send a cameraman to cover it.

'It will be the greatest thing in Port of Spain,' he said.

Ayesha stood silent watching him, watching me.

I took the details of the show and I wrote the story. I had a lot of questions, however.

Twenty years ago Blues came to Port of Spain with an acrobatic troupe from Cunaripo, bottle dancing and eating fire. Today he returns this time to Woodford Square to give the public a treat with his superhuman feats, defying pain and banishing suffering.

I wrote the story and gave it to the editor. He didn't publish it. Another story on him appeared in one of the weekly papers. It made Blues look comical. My story would have given a better perspective on Blues.

That Friday morning he came to the office, he and Ayesha.

'I see the *Evening News* write something. *The Express* had something. But, nothing from *The Standard*.'

'Your friend,' Ayesha said, sardonically.

'I write the story, but they didn't use it.'

'You sending somebody today? Why you don't come and cover it? I see your name on all kindsa articles. If you cover it, people bound to read it.'

'Okay,' I said. 'Okay. Look. Today is parliament. I have to cover the budget debate. That is my assignment. I don't know if I will be able to get away. But, I promise you, I will get a photographer and a reporter to come. It's a promise.'

'Okay,' he said and shook hands. 'I sorry we aint have time for a beer. But, with these things you have to go and see bout everything for yourself.'

'So you stop preaching, or what?'

'Santo, the world today is gimmick. People want something more spectacular than words, something more grand. Faith needs spectacle.' The words had popped out of him spontaneously, even he seemed surprised by them, and impressed.

When he and Ayesha left, the reporters in the newsroom were giggling. 'Santo, you have some real strange friends.'

When I came back from covering parliament that evening, Gordon, the fellar who I had asked to cover the Blues story for me said to me, 'You know I have something to tell you. But what it is slip me.' He was hurrying out of the newsroom. His wife was waiting on him. 'Oh, I know now,' he called out from the doorway. 'You remember that crazy fellar, your friend who was in the newsroom this morning with that thin African woman. Well, he catch himself afire in the square.'

'How you mean catch himself afire?'

'You know these fire eaters does pour some gasolene in their mouth and then light a match and blow out fire. Well it look like this fellar wanted to be so spectacular. Is like he drink a whole pint of gas and when he light it, poof! Was a ball of blazing fire. If you see the great picture Chandler get of it. Want to see it?'

I didn't want to see it.

'That wasn't the fellar you had a story on sometime last week?' the editor asked.

'Yes, I gave it in. But you didn't use it.'

'Well, we running it.'

Next day they had my story in the paper with pictures of Blues with flames pouring out of his mouth and they had a big headline: THE RETURN OF THE FIRE EATER and below that, The Fire Eater Eats His Last.

41

The Secret of My Youth

(1990)

Mimoza Ahmeti

She had a rather curious name. They called her Eyes. I don't know whether she was given the name at birth, the time at which our parents give us names without taking our wishes into consideration, or whether she acquired it as a result of her big eyes. Whatever the case may be, it is true that those eyes of hers had a sense of perception much keener than normal people could possibly imagine.

I had avoided those eyes for a long time. I could not help feeling a shudder down my spine when I heard someone whisper that her eyes sometimes underwent a perilous disfigurement. Quite normal people, for instance, had complained that they had seen themselves reflected in her eyes as a drop of water. Other people, serious, respectable and admired individuals, had found themselves not reflected, but grotesquely mutilated in her eyes.

No, I certainly did not want to see myself transformed into a monster in the eyes of a girl.

I had taken a decision. Whatever should happen, I was resolved not to let myself be captured by her eyes. But ... I had taken this decision before ever being seen by them. And, indeed, I was seen by them. Every time I try to avoid something, it homes in on me. Now there is nothing I desire more than to be captured by those two eyes, and this time totally.

I am presently convinced that everything beautiful on earth is an exception, an 'anomaly' of sorts, towards which everything normal or average is attracted, in contradiction to its nature. Yes, and those all-possessing eyes could do nothing other in the essence of their activity than to constitute an 'anomaly'. They offered a precise reflection. Yes, I realize there is an element of illusion in most human reflections. It is perhaps for this reason that knowledge as a process is so long and infinite whereas human existence is so short and ephemeral. Because the reflection in her eyes was so precise, many people were confused by them.

They were the most marvellous eyes I have ever seen in my whole life, the meeting of physical beauty and functional perfection. When I praised her eyes, that is, when I told her I loved her, she replied simply, 'My eyes were not always like that. Experience has made them the way they are.' She had never spoken to me of the particular quality of her glance. Perhaps she regarded it as a matter of course. And for her, it was one. But not for me.

I did not understand that when she observed something, a city, a flower or a face, for example, a certain space in her eyes remained empty. The objects she observed did not always fill her eyes. It could very well happen that any object, however big it might seem, would leave a void in her eyes. This unoccupied space in her eyes she often filled with blue sky or with dreams of the future. Such was her life.

I did not realize either that I was one of the rare human beings (though I doubt very much that I was alone in this capacity) to fill almost all the space in her eyes with my reflection. Almost. But almost is not the same as completely. There was a bit of space left over, a little bit of space, indeed so little that, had she wanted to, she could have filled that little corner with the reflection of a tree or a bird in the spring. But, then, total bliss would have been beyond reach. It was only when her eyes were filled with the person reflected in them, only when no space was left over in them, that bliss could be attained. It was a strange game played between her eyes and her brain. Only now am I beginning to understand why she gazed so long at the sky. It filled her eyes. She loved it.

I allowed my happiness to be jeopardized, the happiness of the two of us. I was incomplete. There was something missing in me, something that created a void, a tiny unfilled hole in the corner of her eye, but it was room enough for a reflection, and by no means the most unusual of reflections: the boon of happiness.

I could not understand, and I thought a lot about it later, why a girl with big, bright eyes should have made such a sacrifice. Perhaps it came about since, though I was incomplete, I was the most complete of all the incomplete persons she had known up to then. I was almost 'the one' destined for her eyes. I was not completely 'the one', but almost. Do you understand now? Is it not terrible? It was simply a question of a little tiny something missing, but something which jeopardized everything.

And so she sacrificed herself. I did not realize that she was constantly reducing the size of her eyes solely to rid herself of that little hole which was always left over beside my reflection. If only she had told me, if only she had mentioned the problem, I would have done battle with myself and, why not, done battle with the others to grow in her eyes, or at least to become sufficient. What a shame! I was insufficient, and I did not even know it!

I did not realize that she was reducing the size of her eyes for my sake. I noticed nothing to begin with. Perhaps she had not started reducing their size at the start, since she was waiting for me to grow, to become 'big'. It was later, when she had given up all hope of my growing, that I spotted the wrinkle in the corner of her eye, a fold in the muscle under the skin which disturbed me somehow.

The days passed. Her eyes became more and more disturbing for me, not in their beauty, but in the way she used them. They had withered, had decreased in size. And all the time, my love had withered and decreased in size. They were not the same two eyes I had caught a glimpse of at the start, eyes which people, both young and old, would

41 The Secret of My Youth

gossip about at length. For me they had fallen into a morass of normality. Even worse. They had become devoid of all beauty. Deceptive eyes. That is the impression they made on me.

Anger began to take form within my breast. It looked as if she were making fun of me. And anyway, what significance could my love possibly have without her eyes? My words of reproach turned into insult. I could not understand why she put up with me. Her patience made me believe that I was right. I did not realize, as I now do, how rare, how extremely rare people were who could fill her eyes. I had attributed this rarity to my virtue. How ridiculous! She seemed to realize this and therefore put up with me. I was not 'the one', but I was 'almost the one' ... So she put up with me.

The more I reproached her, the more patience she showed, and the more her eyes withered and wrinkled, the more their glance grew faint. Finally one evening I seized her by the shoulders and shook her in rage: 'You're lying, you're lying,' I cried out. 'You have ugly eyes, the ugliest eyes I have ever seen. Leave me alone! I've had enough!'

She was stupefied. As I shouted, her eyes slowly opened. To my surprise, they grew big and bright, penetrating and pure, just as they had been when I saw them for the first time, when ... they were still free of me. I don't know why, but I was now speechless, something stuck in my throat like a bone.

She gave no reply. She departed with eyes revived as I stood there benumbed by what I had done. No, not by what I had done. In reality, I was overwhelmed by the metamorphosis in her eyes. For one moment, a flash of lightning had illuminated the dark clouds of my doubts, a flash which proved lethal to my hardly profound conviction that I had been the cause of the withering and shrinking of her eyes, the most beautiful eyes on earth.

I called her name several times over. You will never believe how hard it was for me to call her by her name: 'Hey, Eyes. Come back, Eyes!'

But it was in vain. She did not return. Having turned her eyes away from me, I regained the place that I deserved in them. Soon thereafter my happiness dissipated. I had been almost complete, but not complete. I was insufficient. The game played between her eyes and her brain was now interrupted.

She had no intention of returning. There was to be no more bliss. Perhaps there never had been. She had created it with hard work by wearing out, indeed by damaging, her eyes. Bliss is the only thing that we have still not learned to appreciate when it is bestowed upon us. A weakness? Perhaps. But because of it, I still feel human in my suffering. I suffer to become sufficient, to become perhaps something more.

Some people say that bliss is impossible, unreal. But I got very close and I know what it is, even though I did not succeed in mastering it. I believe that I can do it, though. I want to take possession of bliss! Let them laugh at me all they want (laughing at someone else is often nothing more than a painful reflection of our own impotence). I want to attain the impossible. I want to be complete. I want to fill those eyes to the full. To attain total bliss.

This is the secret of my youth. One more reason for living.

42

The Light on the Sea

(1993)

John Wickham

Two elderly women were sitting in the room with their backs to the sea when I stepped through the front door. They were sitting at opposite ends of the room, which was large enough, but looked even larger because it was so sparsely furnished: three or four chairs in dully grey upholstery and a table or two, but no flowers on them and no pictures on the walls. I said, 'Good Morning,' and they looked in my direction, blinking but not speaking. I guessed that they could not make me out with my figure silhouetted against the bright light of the doorway and they must have been a trifle alarmed at my sudden appearance. I stepped further into the room and then they spoke, both of them together and both of them pleasantly, as if they were glad to see me, although they had never seen me before.

I asked whether there was a Mr Farley in the house and they both shook their heads and looked as if they were sorry for my sake that there was no Mr Farley to offer me. Then one of them said that, perhaps if I went downstairs, someone might be able to tell me, because the truth was that they didn't really know the names of all the guests. Both of them brightened up at this and one of them got out of her chair to show me where the staircase was. I told her that she needn't have bothered, but she came with me all the same, anxious to help.

At the bottom of the stairs, an old man, gaunt, bony-faced, with thin white hair, was sitting at a small table which was covered with a check tablecloth frayed at the edges. A small yellow plastic bowl was before him and he was staring at its contents with an expression of disgust amounting to revulsion. With a silver teaspoon, he began to stir an egg yolk which had separated from its accompanying white, and he let the yellow viscous liquid drip off the spoon back into the bowl and emitted a series of heavy, forlorn sighs. He was quite unaware of my presence and paid not the slightest attention to me. Opposite the table, a door opened on a kitchen, and as I pushed my head inside the room, a woman in a blue apron looked up from what she was doing and I asked her whether she had a Mr Farley living there. She wiped her hands in her apron and told me that she would go to let him know that he had a visitor.

42　The Light on the Sea

The white-haired old man at the table was still sighing and stirring the yellow mess in his bowl while I waited. Another woman, whom I had not seen before, came out of the kitchen and stopped by the old man's table and asked him, solicitously, I thought, whether there was something wrong with his egg. The question irritated him and it was clear that his irritation puzzled the woman. There was nothing wrong with the egg, so far as she could see. And, indeed, from where I stood, the egg, as an egg, seemed perfectly good. But what the woman could not understand was that the old man's disgust had nothing to do with the egg, as an egg.

'Oh, my God,' he half-muttered, half-whispered. 'Look at this.' He rapped the plastic bowl with his spoon and then tilted it as if he would empty it of its yellow contents. 'But look at this, couldn't you …?' But words failed him, and with something like a mixture of resolve and resignation, he plunged the spoon into the bowl and raised it to his mouth. But his hand was trembling and the spoon, when it reached his mouth, was empty. And still the woman was watching him, concerned and, it seemed to me, anxious to help, could not understand what was wrong.

Mr Farley came forward to see me. He was wearing a scarlet dressing gown and deep red carpet slippers, and he smiled broadly when I moved out of the light of the doorway and he was able to see me. I had taken some fruit for him, a hand of bananas, a pawpaw and a shaddock, and when he took the bag from me, he smiled even more. He sat in a chair beside the bed and motioned me to make myself comfortable on the bed.

'I am so glad to see you,' he said.

I told him that I had been wondering how he was getting on. I had heard only a few days before that he had gone into the home.

'I am as well as an old man can be,' he said, and grinned broadly.

I had known Mr Farley ever since I was a child; he had taught me in my first class at the elementary school and I was fond of him in a pitying sort of way. He was not a good teacher of small boys: he could not keep them in order and did not really try to, and I used to feel sorry for him when the boys teased him by asking silly questions which he took seriously and to which he always tried to give considered replies. I never understood how he could not see through the questions. He never lost his temper and I used often to be angry with him, because he didn't seem to see how ineffectual he was.

It did not surprise me that Mr Farley never succeeded in his career, never became talked about but always remained a kind of butt, outside the swim of things, a harmless figure of fun. Until one evening, at his invitation, some of us who had already graduated from his class, went to his house to look at his pictures.

He lived near our school in an old house set back from the main road to town and behind what seemed to us a thick forest of trees – breadfruit, sugar apple, hog plum, soursop. The possibilities of such a house and such a forest were enormous to us, and Mr Farley immediately went up in our estimation.

That afternoon we sat around a room full of dark mahogany furniture – what-not, an old sideboard with a lion's head carved on its back panel and an assortment of rocking chairs. An old oil lamp stood on the sideboard. The room smelt of dust and mildew, but it was cosy. Mr Farley gave us lemonade and sweet biscuits, and when we had finished eating, he brought some of his pictures for us to look at: water colours and a few oils and some sketches in ink.

I did not like the sketches and remember thinking that they were childish; the outlines were weak. But the water colours were like Mr Farley himself, muted and shy. Some of them were of the sea, which he made look like an inland lake of quiet dappled water. He took us into a dark cellar under the house where hundreds of canvases were stacked carelessly on the floor around the walls. It was too dark to see them very clearly, but many of them looked as if they consisted only of shapes randomly arranged. In a way, they were frightening, like creatures bred of the dark shadows of the cellar and never seeing the light. I was glad to escape back up the stairs and into the relative brightness of the parlour.

Now, as I sat on his bed, I thought: how like a child he is! He was babbling with excitement at being visited, like a child given a present. I asked him if he remembered the afternoon when a group of us visited him and he showed us his pictures, but he had forgotten. It was too long ago, I suppose. And I asked him if he still painted and what had become of the pictures. Had he sold them?

'Oh,' he said, 'I left them behind at the house when I came here.' He dismissed them as if they were part of something he had discarded and would prefer to forget; there had been so many pictures in the cellar, hundreds of them, and I was tempted to ask him to let me go and look at them. Who could tell? There might be a masterpiece lurking in that gloom, waiting to be discovered. I could not believe that he had left them behind, just like that. I asked him what he planned to do with them.

'Nothing,' he said. 'They weren't any good.' He did not sound regretful but, rather, relieved, as if he had rid himself of a great, unbearable burden at last.

I asked him, 'Did you think when you were young, that you would ever come to a life without painting – a canvas and brushes and paints?'

He answered simply. 'It was always only a hope, never a conviction. But hope sustained until …' His voice trailed away as if he no longer remembered the sequence of events.

The bare, poorly-furnished room was without books or pictures, uncurtained, with only a single window through which the morning sunlight poured bright and undiluted, a spare bed across the width of the room in a far corner, no flowers and the ceiling stained brown with water from the floor above. Yet, while I was saddened by the bare and loveless look of the room and the lonely figures of the other members of the household, the two old women in the living room and the gaunt man in the kitchen sighing over his egg as he recalled better days, as I thought about the terrible loneliness to which old age had sentenced them, I had to accept that Mr Farley was cheerful. Perhaps it was because he had never had a family; he had always been lonely and this state was not new to him. He was smiling when he began to speak.

'All those pictures,' he said, 'and, believe me, I never felt as if I had ever finished a single one of them. There was always something to be done to complete every one. So I never had any satisfaction. I would put it aside, meaning to go back and finish it, but

I was never able to. Another picture would come to mind and crowd the last effort and failure out, and I never looked at that last one again; I was never able to remember what I wanted to paint.'

'It must have been like a nightmare,' I said, 'or a series of nightmares, never being able to recall the vision that started the picture.'

'Frustration it was, and confusion. That's what it was. I am glad for this peace now.' And he looked around the room, the bare and cheerless room, like a child welcoming an open space where he could run and romp.

'How do you spend your time now?' It was, all of a sudden, important for me to know.

'I look at the sea,' he said, so solemnly that I thought he was making fun of the question. But he wasn't.

'You know,' he said, 'I never knew what light was. All those years behind those trees in that dark house. The light used to trickle through the leaves, only trickle, never flow. Mark you, I used to like it, I didn't complain. I thought the gloom was pleasant. But I never knew what light was.'

'And how did you come to find out, to see the light?' I asked.

'I was lucky. When my sister died, there was no one to look after things; I had never learned to cook. My friend told me about this place. The moment I saw it, with the light on the sea, I knew that I was not going back to that dark house.'

'So you just upped and left your pictures and the furniture and everything?'

'It was easy and, besides, what was there to wait for? They look after me very well here, the girls are kind and they leave me alone, which is a kindness. Do you understand how being left alone can be a real kindness? And, now, look, you have come to see me. You never came to the old house.'

'Don't you feel lonely here?'

'No, not lonelier than I have always felt. I have never been what you could call gregarious. And I never get tired of looking at the sea.'

He laughed, and I said goodbye and told him that I would come soon to see him again.

'When you came,' he said, 'I was going to have a shower.' He clutched his dressing gown with a dramatic gesture, like Gielgud clutching his toga in Julius Caesar. I never thought that he had such panache in his make-up. As he spoke, he was making his way to the bathroom, and by the time I reached the door and looked back to see what he was doing, he had already put me out of his mind.

When I stepped outside the front door, I found one of the old ladies pulling dry yellow leaves off a hibiscus bush in the untidy garden. She was so intent on what she was doing that she did not even reply when I said goodbye.

The bright Sunday morning glistened and the sea sparkled vast and wide and flat to the horizon.

43

New York Day Women

(1995)

Edwidge Danticat

Today, walking down the street, I see my mother. She is strolling with a happy gait, her body thrust toward the DON'T WALK sign and the yellow taxicabs that make forty-five-degree turns on the corner of Madison and Fifty-seventh Street.

I have never seen her in this kind of neighborhood, peering into Chanel and Tiffany's and gawking at the jewels glowing in the Bulgari windows. My mother never shops outside of Brooklyn. She has never seen the advertising office where I work. She is afraid to take the subway, where you may meet those young black militant street preachers who curse black women for straightening their hair.

Yet, here she is, my mother, who I left at home that morning in her bathrobe, with pieces of newspapers twisted like rollers in her hair. My mother, who accuses me of random offenses as I dash out of the house.

Would you get up and give an old lady like me your subway seat? In this state of mind, I bet you don't even give up your seat to a pregnant lady.

My mother, who is often right about that. Sometimes I get up and give my seat. Other times, I don't. It all depends on how pregnant the woman is and whether or not she is with her boyfriend or husband and whether or not *he* is sitting down.

As my mother stands in front of Carnegie Hall, one taxi driver yells to another, 'What do you think this is, a dance floor?'

My mother waits patiently for this dispute to be settled before crossing the street.

In Haiti when you get hit by a car, the owner of the car gets out and kicks you for getting blood on his bumper.

My mother who laughs when she says this and shows a large gap in her mouth where she lost three more molars to the dentist last week. My mother, who at fifty-nine, says dentures are okay.

43   New York Day Women

You can take them out when they bother you. I'll like them. I'll like them fine.

Will it feel empty when Papa kisses you?

Oh no, he doesn't kiss me that way anymore.

My mother, who watches the lottery drawing every night on channel 11 without ever having played the numbers.

A third of that money is all I would need. We would pay the mortgage, and your father could stop driving that taxicab all over Brooklyn.

I follow my mother, mesmerized by the many possibilities of her journey. Even in a flowered dress, she is lost in a sea of pinstripes and gray suits, high heels and elegant short skirts, Reebok sneakers, dashing from building to building.

My mother, who won't go out to dinner with anyone.

If they want to eat with me, let them come to my house, even if I boil water and give it to them.

My mother, who talks to herself when she peels the skin off poultry.

Fat, you know, and cholesterol. Fat and cholesterol killed your aunt Hermine.

My mother, who makes jam with dried grapefuit peel and then puts in cinnamon bark that I always think is cockroaches in the jam. My mother, whom I have always bought household appliances for, on her birthday. A nice rice cooker, a blender.

I trail the red orchids in her dress and the heavy faux leather bag on her shoulders. Realizing the ferocious pace of my pursuit, I stop against a wall to rest. My mother keeps on walking as though she owns the sidewalk under her feet.

As she heads toward the Plaza Hotel, a bicycle messenger swings so close to her that I want to dash forward and rescue her, but she stands dead in her tracks and lets him ride around her and then goes on.

My mother stops at a corner hot-dog stand and asks for something. The vendor hands her a can of soda that she slips into her bag. She stops by another vendor selling sundresses for seven dollars each. I can tell that she is looking at an African print dress, contemplating my size. I think to myself, Please Ma, don't buy it. It would be just another thing I would bury in the garage or give to Goodwill.

Why should we give to Goodwill when there are so many people back home who need clothes? We save our clothes for the relatives in Haiti.

Twenty years we have been saving all kinds of things for the relatives in Haiti. I need the place in the garage for an exercise bike.

You are pretty enough to be a stewardess. Only dogs like bones.

This mother of mine, she stops at another hot-dog vendor's and buys a frankfurter that she eats on the street. I never knew that she ate frankfurters. With her blood pressure, she shouldn't eat anything with sodium. She has to be careful with her heart, this day woman.

I cannot just swallow salt. Salt is heavier than a hundred bags of shame.

She is slowing her pace, and now I am too close. If she turns around, she might see me. I let her walk into the park before I start to follow again.

My mother walks toward the sandbox in the middle of the park. There a woman is waiting with a child. The woman is wearing a leotard with biker's shorts and has small weights in her hands. The woman kisses the child good-bye and surrenders him to my mother, then she bolts off, running on the cemented stretches in the park.

The child given to my mother has frizzy blond hair. His hand slips into hers easily, like he's known her for a long time. When he raises his face to look at my mother, it is as though he is looking at the sky.

My mother gives this child the soda that she bought from the vendor on the street corner. The child's face lights up as she puts in a straw in the can for him. This seems to be a conspiracy just between the two of them.

My mother and the child sit and watch the other children play in the sandbox. The child pulls out a comic book from a knapsack with Big Bird on the back. My mother peers into his comic book. My mother, who taught herself to read as a little girl in Haiti from the books that her brothers brought home from school.

My mother, who has now lost six of her seven sisters in Ville Rose and has never had the strength to return for their funerals.

Many graves to kiss when I go back. Many graves to kiss.

She throws away the empty soda can when the child is done with it. I wait and watch from a corner until the woman in the leotard and biker's shorts returns, sweaty and breathless, an hour later. My mother gives the woman back her child and strolls farther into the park.

I turn around and start to walk out of the park before my mother can see me. My lunch hour is long since gone. I have to hurry back to work. I walk through a cluster of joggers, then race to a *Sweden Tours* bus. I stand behind the bus and take a peek at my mother in the park. She is standing in a circle, chatting with a group of women who are taking other people's children on an afternoon outing. They look like a Third World Parent – Teacher Association meeting.

I quickly jump into a cab heading back to the office. Would Ma have said hello had she been the one to see me first?

As the cab races away from the park, it occurs to me that perhaps one day I would chase an old woman down a street by mistake and that old woman would be somebody else's mother, who I would have mistaken for mine.

Day women come out when nobody expects them.

Tonight on the subway, I will get up and give my seat to a pregnant woman or a lady about Ma's age.

My mother, who stuffs thimbles in her mouth and then blows up her cheeks like Dizzy Gillespie while sewing yet another Raggedy Ann doll that she names Suzette after me.

I will have all these little Suzettes in case you never have any babies, which looks more and more like it is going to happen.

My mother who had me when she was thirty-three – *l'âge du Christ* – at the age that Christ died on the cross.

That's a blessing, believe you me, even if American doctors say by that time you can make retarded babies.

My mother, who sews lace collars on my company softball T-shirts when she does my laundry.

Why, you can't look like a lady playing softball?

My mother, who never went to any of my Parent – Teacher Association meetings when I was in school.

You're so good anyway. What are they going to tell me? I don't want to make you ashamed of this day woman. Shame is heavier than a hundred bags of salt.

A Village after Dark

(2001)

Kazuo Ishiguro

There was a time when I could travel England for weeks on end and remain at my sharpest – when, if anything, the travelling gave me an edge. But now that I am older I become disoriented more easily. So it was that on arriving at the village just after dark I failed to find my bearings at all. I could hardly believe I was in the same village in which not so long ago I had lived and come to exercise such influence.

There was nothing I recognized, and I found myself walking forever around twisting, badly lit streets hemmed in on both sides by the little stone cottages characteristic of the area. The streets often became so narrow I could make no progress without my bag or my elbow scraping one rough wall or another. I persevered nevertheless, stumbling around in the darkness in the hope of coming upon the village square – where I could at least orient myself – or else of encountering one of the villagers. When after a while I had done neither, a weariness came over me, and I decided my best course was just to choose a cottage at random, knock on the door, and hope it would be opened by someone who remembered me.

I stopped by a particularly rickety-looking door, whose upper beam was so low that I could see I would have to crouch right down to enter. A dim light was leaking out around the door's edges, and I could hear voices and laughter. I knocked loudly to ensure that the occupants would hear me over their talk. But just then someone behind me said, 'Hello.'

I turned to find a young woman of around twenty, dressed in raggedy jeans and a torn jumper, standing in the darkness a little way away.

'You walked straight past me earlier,' she said, 'even though I called to you.'

'Did I really? Well, I'm sorry. I didn't mean to be rude.'

'You're Fletcher, aren't you?'

'Yes,' I said, somewhat flattered.

'Wendy thought it was you when you went by our cottage. We all got very excited. You were one of that lot, weren't you? With David Maggis and all of them.'

'Yes,' I said, 'but Maggis was hardly the most important one. I'm surprised you pick him out like that. There were other, far more important figures.' I reeled off a series of names and was interested to see the girl nodding at each one in recognition. 'But this must have all been before your time,' I said. 'I'm surprised you know about such things.'

'It was before our time, but we're all experts on your lot. We know more about all that than most of the older ones who were here then. Wendy recognized you instantly just from your photos.'

'I had no idea you young people had taken such an interest in us. I'm sorry I walked past you earlier. But you see, now that I'm older, I get a little disoriented when I travel.'

I could hear some boisterous talk coming from behind the door. I banged on it again, this time rather impatiently, though I was not so eager to bring the encounter with the girl to a close.

She looked at me for a moment, then said, 'All of you from those days are like that. David Maggis came here a few years ago. In '93, or maybe it was '94. He was like that. A bit vague. It must get to you after a while, travelling all the time.'

'So Maggis was here. How interesting. You know, he wasn't one of the really important figures. You mustn't get carried away with such an idea. Incidentally, perhaps you could tell me who lives in this cottage.' I thumped the door again.

'The Petersons,' the girl said. 'They're an old house. They'll probably remember you.'

'The Petersons,' I repeated, but the name meant nothing to me.

'Why don't you come to our cottage? Wendy was really excited. So were the rest of us. It's a real chance for us, actually talking to someone from those days.'

'I'd very much like to do that. But first of all I'd better get myself settled in. The Petersons, you say.'

I thumped the door again, this time quite ferociously. At last it opened, throwing warmth and light out into the street. An old man was standing in the doorway. He looked at me carefully, then asked, 'It's not Fletcher, is it?'

'Yes, and I've just got into the village. I've been travelling for several days.'

He thought about this for a moment, then said, 'Well, you'd better come in.'

I found myself in a cramped, untidy room full of rough wood and broken furniture. A log burning in the fireplace was the only source of light, by which I could make out a number of hunched figures sitting around the room. The old man led me to a chair beside the fire with a grudgingness that suggested it was the very one he had just vacated. Once I sat down, I found I could not easily turn my head to see my surroundings or the others in the room. But the warmth of the fire was very welcome, and for a moment I just stared into its flames, a pleasant grogginess drifting over me. Voices came from behind me, inquiring if I was well, if I had come far, if I was hungry, and I replied as best I could, though I was aware that my answers were barely adequate. Eventually, the questions ceased, and it occurred to me that my presence was creating a heavy awkwardness, but I was so grateful for the warmth and the chance to rest that I hardly cared.

Nonetheless, when the silence behind me had gone unbroken for several minutes, I resolved to address my hosts with a little more civility, and I turned in my chair. It was then, as I did so, that I was suddenly seized by an intense sense of recognition. I had chosen the cottage quite at random, but now I could see that it was none other than the very one in which I had spent my years in this village. My gaze moved immediately to the far corner – at this moment shrouded in darkness – to the spot that had been *my* corner, where once my mattress had been and where I had spent many tranquil hours browsing through books or conversing with whoever happened to drift in. On summer days, the windows, and often the door, were left open to allow a refreshing breeze to blow right through. Those were the days when the cottage was surrounded by open fields and there would come from outside the voices of my friends, lazing in the long grass, arguing over poetry or philosophy. These precious fragments of the past came back to me so powerfully that it was all I could do not to make straight for my old corner then and there.

Someone was speaking to me again, perhaps asking another question, but I hardly listened. Rising, I peered through the shadows into my corner, and could now make out a narrow bed, covered by an old curtain, occupying more or less the exact space where my mattress had been. The bed looked extremely inviting, and I found myself cutting into something the old man was saying.

'Look,' I said, 'I know this is a bit blunt. But, you see, I've come such a long way today. I really need to lie down, close my eyes, even if it's just for a few minutes. After that, I'm happy to talk all you like.'

I could see the figures around the room shifting uneasily. Then a new voice said, rather sullenly, 'Go ahead then. Have a nap. Don't mind us.'

But I was already picking my way through the clutter toward my corner. The bed felt damp, and the springs creaked under my weight, but no sooner had I curled up with my back to the room than my many hours of travelling began to catch up with me. As I was drifting off, I heard the old man saying, 'It's Fletcher, all right. God, he's aged.'

A woman's voice said, 'Should we let him go to sleep like that? He might wake in a few hours and then we'll have to stay up with him.'

'Let him sleep for an hour or so,' someone else said. 'If he's still asleep after an hour, we'll wake him.'

At this point, sheer exhaustion overtook me.

It was not a continuous or comfortable sleep. I drifted between sleep and waking, always conscious of voices behind me in the room. At some point, I was aware of a woman saying, 'I don't know how I was ever under his spell. He looks such a ragamuffin now.'

In my state of near-sleep, I debated with myself whether these words applied to me or, perhaps, to David Maggis, but before long sleep engulfed me once more.

When I next awoke, the room appeared to have grown both darker and colder. Voices were continuing behind me in lowered tones, but I could make no sense of the conversation. I now felt embarrassed at having gone to sleep in the way I had, and for a few further moments remained motionless with my face to the wall. But something about me must have revealed that I was awake, for a woman's voice, breaking off from the general conversation, said, 'Oh, look, look.' Some whispers were exchanged, then I heard the sound of someone coming toward my corner. I felt a hand placed gently on my shoulder, and looked up to find a woman kneeling over me. I did not turn my body sufficiently to see the room, but I got the impression that it was lit by dying embers, and the woman's face was visible only in shadow.

'Now, Fletcher,' she said. 'It's time we had a talk. I've waited a long time for you to come back. I've thought about you often.'

I strained to see her more clearly. She was somewhere in her forties, and even in the gloom I noticed a sleepy sadness in her eyes. But her face failed to stir in me even the faintest of memories.

'I'm sorry,' I said. 'I have no recollection of you. But please forgive me if we met some time ago. I do get very disoriented these days.'

'Fletcher,' she said, 'when we used to know one another, I was young and beautiful. I idolized you, and everything you said seemed like an answer. Now here you are, back again. I've wanted to tell you for many years that you ruined my life.'

'You're being unfair. All right, I was mistaken about a lot of things. But I never claimed to have any answers. All I said in those days was that it was our duty, all of us, to contribute to the debate. We knew so much more about the issues than the ordinary people here. If people like us procrastinated, claiming we didn't yet know enough, then who was there to act? But I never claimed I had the answers. No, you're being unfair.'

'Fletcher,' she said, and her voice was oddly gentle, 'you used to make love to me, more or less every time I wandered in here to your room. In this corner, we did all kinds of beautifully dirty things. It's odd to think how I could have once been so physically excited by you. And here you're just a foul-smelling bundle of rags now. But look at me – I'm still attractive. My face has got a bit lined, but when I walk in the village streets I wear dresses I've made specially to show off my figure. A lot of men want me still. But you, no woman would look at you now. A bundle of stinking rags and flesh.'

'I don't remember you,' I said. 'And I've no time for sex these days. I've other things to worry about. More serious things. Very well, I was mistaken about a lot in those days. But I've done more than most to try and make amends. You see, even now I'm travelling. I've never stopped. I've travelled and travelled trying to undo what damage I may once have caused. That's more than can be said of some others from those days. I bet Maggis, for instance, hasn't worked nearly as hard to try and put things right.'

The woman was stroking my hair.

'Look at you. I used to do this, run my fingers through your hair. Look at this filthy mess. I'm sure you're contaminated with all sorts of parasites.' But she continued slowly to run her fingers through the dirty knots. I failed to feel anything erotic from this, as perhaps she wished me to do. Rather, her caresses felt maternal. Indeed, for a moment it was as though I had finally reached some cocoon of protectiveness, and I began once more to feel sleepy. But suddenly she stopped and slapped me hard on the forehead.

'Why don't you join the rest of us now? You've had your sleep. You've got a lot of explaining to do.' With that she got up and left.

For the first time, I turned my body sufficiently to survey the room. I saw the woman making her way past the clutter on the floor, then sitting down in a rocking chair by the fireplace. I could see three other figures hunched around the dying fire. One I recognized to be the old man who had opened the door. The two others – sitting together on what looked like a wooden trunk – seemed to be women of around the same age as the one who had spoken to me.

The old man noticed that I had turned, and he indicated to the others that I was watching. The four of them proceeded to sit stiffly, not speaking. From the way they did this, it was clear that they had been discussing me thoroughly while I was asleep. In fact, as I watched them I could more or less guess the whole shape their conversation had taken. I could see, for instance, that they had spent some time expressing concern for the young girl I had met outside, and about the effect I might have on her peers.

'They're all so impressionable,' the old man would have said. 'And I heard her inviting him to visit them.'

To which, no doubt, one of the women on the trunk would have said, 'But he can't do much harm now. In our time, we were all taken in because all his kind – they were young and glamorous. But these days the odd one passing through from time to time, looking all decrepit and burned out like that – if anything, it goes to demystify all that talk about the old days. In any case, people like him have changed their position so much these days. They don't know themselves what they believe.'

The old man would have shaken his head. 'I saw the way that young girl was looking at him. All right, he looks a pitiful mess over there just now. But once his ego's fed a little, once he has the flattery of the young people, sees how they want to hear his ideas, then there'll be no stopping him. It'll be just like before. He'll have them all working for his causes. Young girls like that, there's so little for them to believe in now. Even a stinking tramp like this could give them a purpose.'

Their conversation, all the time I slept, would have gone something very much like that. But now, as I observed them from my corner, they continued to sit in guilty silence, staring at the last of their fire. After a while, I rose to my feet. Absurdly, the four of them kept their gazes averted from me. I waited a few moments to see if any of them would say anything. Finally, I said, 'All right, I was asleep earlier, but I've guessed what you were saying. Well, you'll be interested to know I'm going to do the very thing you feared. I'm going this moment to the young people's cottage. I'm going to tell them what to do with all their energy, all their dreams, their urge to achieve something of lasting good in this world. Look at you, what a pathetic bunch. Crouching in your cottage, afraid to do anything, afraid of me, of Maggis, of anyone else from those times. Afraid to do anything in the world out there, just because once we made a few mistakes. Well, those young people haven't yet sunk so low, despite all the lethargy you've been preaching at them down the years. I'll talk to them. I'll undo in half an hour all of your sorry efforts.'

'You see,' the old man said to the others. 'I knew it would be this way. We ought to stop him, but what can we do?'

I crashed my way across the room, picked up my bag, and went out into the night.

The girl was still standing outside when I emerged. She seemed to be expecting me and with a nod began to lead the way.

The night was drizzly and dark. We twisted and turned along the narrow paths that ran between the cottages. Some of the cottages we passed looked so decayed and crumbling that I felt I could destroy one of them simply by running at it with all my weight.

The girl kept a few paces ahead, occasionally glancing back at me over her shoulder. Once she said, 'Wendy's going to be so pleased. She was sure it was you when you went past earlier. By now, she'll have guessed she was right, because I've been away this long, and she'll have brought the whole crowd together. They'll all be waiting.'

'Did you give David Maggis this sort of reception, too?'

'Oh, yes. We were really excited when he came.'

'I'm sure he found that very gratifying. He always had an exaggerated sense of his own importance.'

'Wendy says Maggis was one of the interesting ones, but that you were, well, important. She thinks you were really important.'

I thought about this for a moment.

'You know,' I said, 'I've changed my mind on very many things. If Wendy's expecting me to say all the things I used to all those years ago, well, she's going to be in for a disappointment.'

The girl did not seem to hear this, but continued to lead me purposefully through the clusters of cottages.

After a little while, I became aware of footsteps following a dozen or so paces behind us. At first, I assumed this was just some villager out walking and refrained from turning round. But then the girl halted under a street lamp and looked behind us. I was thus obliged also to stop and turn. A middle-aged man in a dark overcoat was coming toward us. As he approached, he held out his hand and shook mine, though without smiling.

'So,' he said, 'you're here.'

I then realized I knew the man. We had not seen each other since we were ten years old. His name was Roger Button, and he had been in my class at the school I had attended for two years in Canada before my family returned to England. Roger Button and I had not been especially close, but, because he had been a timid boy, and because he, too, was from England, he had for a while followed me about. I had neither seen nor heard from him since that time. Now, as I studied his appearance under the street lamp, I saw the years had not been kind to him. He was bald, his face was pocked and lined, and there was a weary sag to his whole posture. For all that, there was no mistaking my old classmate.

'Roger,' I said, 'I'm just on my way to visit this young lady's friends. They've gathered together to receive me. Otherwise I'd have come and looked you up straightaway. As it was, I had it in my mind as the next thing to do, even before getting any sleep tonight. I was just thinking to myself, However late things finish at the young people's cottage, I'll go and knock on Roger's door afterward.'

'Don't worry,' said Roger Button as we all started to walk again. 'I know how busy you are. But we ought to talk. Chew over old times. When you last saw me – at school, I mean – I suppose I was a rather feeble specimen. But, you know, that all changed when I got to fourteen, fifteen. I really toughened up. Became quite a leader type. But you'd long since left Canada. I always wondered what would have happened if we'd come across each other at fifteen. Things would have been rather different between us, I assure you.'

As he said this, memories came flooding back. In those days, Roger Button had idolized me, and in return I had bullied him incessantly. However, there had existed between us a curious understanding that my bullying him was all for his own good; that when, without warning, I suddenly punched him in the stomach on the playground, or when, passing him in the corridor, I impulsively wrenched his arm up his back until he started to cry, I was doing so in order to help him toughen up. Accordingly, the principal effect such attacks had on our relationship was to keep him in awe of me. This all came back to me as I listened to the weary-looking man walking beside me.

'Of course,' Roger Button went on, perhaps guessing my train of thought, 'it might well be that if you hadn't treated me the way you did I'd never have become what I did at fifteen. In any case, I've often wondered how it would have been if we'd met just a few years later. I really was something to be reckoned with by then.'

We were once again walking along the narrow twisted passages between cottages. The girl was still leading the way, but she was now walking much faster. Often we would only just manage to catch a glimpse of her turning some corner ahead of us, and it struck me that we would have to keep alert if we were not to lose her.

'Today, of course,' Roger Button was saying, 'I've let myself go a bit. But I have to say, old fellow, you seem to be in much worse shape. Compared with you, I'm an athlete. Not to put too fine a point on it, you're just a filthy old tramp now, really, aren't you? But, you know, for a long time after you left I continued to idolize you. Would Fletcher do this? What would Fletcher think if he saw me doing that? Oh, yes. It was only when I got to fifteen or so that I looked back on it all and saw through you. Then I was very angry, of course. Even now, I still think about it sometimes. I look back and think, Well, he was just a thoroughly nasty so-and-so. He had a little more weight and muscle at that age than I did, a little more confidence, and he took full advantage. Yes, it's very clear, looking back, what a nasty little person you were. Of course, I'm not implying you still are today. We all change. That much I'm willing to accept.'

'Have you been living here long?' I asked, wishing to change the subject.

'Oh, seven years or so. Of course, they talk about you a lot around here. I sometimes tell them about our early association. "But he won't remember me," I always tell them. "Why would he remember a skinny little boy he used to bully and have at his beck and call?" Anyway, the young people here, they talk about you more and more these days. Certainly, the ones who've never seen you tend to idealize you the most. I suppose you've come back to capitalize on all that. Still, I shouldn't blame you. You're entitled to try and salvage a little self-respect.'

We suddenly found ourselves facing an open field, and we both halted. Glancing back, I saw that we had walked our way out of the village; the last of the cottages were some distance behind us. Just as I had feared, we had lost the young woman; in fact, I realized we had not been following her for some time.

At that moment, the moon emerged, and I saw we were standing at the edge of a vast grassy field – extending, I supposed, far beyond what I could see by the moon.

Roger Button turned to me. His face in the moonlight seemed gentle, almost affectionate.

'Still,' he said, 'it's time to forgive. You shouldn't keep worrying so much. As you see, certain things from the past will come back to you in the end. But then we can't be held accountable for what we did when we were very young.'

'No doubt you're right,' I said. Then I turned and looked around in the darkness. 'But now I'm not sure where to go. You see, there were some young people waiting for me in their cottage. By now they'd have a warm fire ready for me and some hot tea. And some home-baked cakes, perhaps even a good stew. And the moment I entered, ushered in by that young lady we were following just now, they'd all have burst into applause. There'd be smiling, adoring faces all around me. That's what's waiting for me somewhere. Except I'm not sure where I should go.'

Roger Button shrugged. 'Don't worry, you'll get there easily enough. Except, you know, that girl was being a little misleading if she implied you could walk to Wendy's cottage. It's much too far. You'd really need to catch a bus. Even then, it's quite a long journey. About two hours, I'd say. But don't worry, I'll show you where you can pick up your bus.'

With that, he began to walk back toward the cottages. As I followed, I could sense that the hour had got very late and my companion was anxious to get some sleep. We spent several minutes walking around the cottages again, and then he brought us out into the village square. In fact, it was so small and shabby it hardly merited being called a square; it was little more than a patch of green beside a solitary street lamp. Just visible beyond the pool of light cast by the lamp were a few shops, all shut up for the night. There was complete silence and nothing was stirring. A light mist was hovering over the ground.

Roger Button stopped before we had reached the green and pointed.

'There,' he said. 'If you stand there, a bus will come along. As I say, it's not a short journey. About two hours. But don't worry, I'm sure your young people will wait. They've so little else to believe in these days, you see.'

'It's very late,' I said. 'Are you sure a bus will come?'

'Oh, yes. Of course, you may have to wait. But eventually a bus will come.' Then he touched me reassuringly on the shoulder. 'I can see it might get a little lonely standing out here. But once the bus arrives your spirits will rise, believe me. Oh, yes. That bus is always a joy. It'll be brightly lit up, and it's always full of cheerful people, laughing and joking and pointing out the window. Once you board it, you'll feel warm and comfortable, and the other passengers will chat with you, perhaps offer you things to eat or drink. There may even be singing – that depends on the driver. Some drivers encourage it, others don't. Well, Fletcher, it was good to see you.'

We shook hands, then he turned and walked away. I watched him disappear into the darkness between two cottages.

I walked up to the green and put my bag down at the foot of the lamppost. I listened for the sound of a vehicle in the distance, but the night was utterly still. Nevertheless, I had been cheered by Roger Button's description of the bus. Moreover, I thought of the reception awaiting me at my journey's end – of the adoring faces of the young people – and felt the stirrings of optimism somewhere deep within me.

45

The Clean Slate

(2001)

Hilary Mantel

About eleven o'clock this morning – after the nurses had 'tidied her up' as they put it, and she'd fixed her eye make-up – I sat down by my mother's bed and coaxed her to do the family tree with me. Considering how self-centred she is, it worked out surprisingly well. She would like to write 'VERONICA' in the centre of the paper and strike lines of force running outwards from herself. But (although she thinks this would give you an accurate picture of the world) she does have a grasp on how these things are done. She has seen the genealogy of the Kings and Queens of England, their spurious portraits glowing by their names, stamp-sized and in stained-glass colours; their plaits of flaxen hair, their crude medieval crowns with gems like sucked sweets.

She has seen these, in the books she pretends to read. So she understands that you can also do a family tree for us, the poor bloody infantry.

The pictures by the names will be equally spurious. A woman once told me that there was no family so poor, when the last century ended, that they didn't have their photographs taken. It might be true. In that case, somebody burned ours.

I began this enterprise because I wanted to find out something about my ancestors who lived in the drowned village. I thought it might provide a reason for my fear of water – one I could use to make people feel bad, when they advise me that swimming is good exercise for a person of my age. Then again, I thought it might be a topic I could turn into cash. I could go to Dunwich, I thought, and write about a village that slipped into the sea. Or to Norfolk, to talk to people who have mortgaged houses on the edge of cliffs. I could work it up into a feature for the Sunday press. They could send a photographer, and we could balance on the cliff edge at Overstrand, just one rusting wire between us and infinite blue light.

But Veronica was not interested in the submerged. She twitched at the ribbons at her bosom – still firm, by the way – and eased herself irritably against the pillows. The veins in her hands stood out, as if she had sapphires and wore them beneath the skin.

She hardly listened to my questions, and said in a huffy way, 'I really can't tell you much about all that, I'm afraid.'

The people from the drowned village were on her father's side of the family, and were English. Veronica was interested in matriarchies, in Irish matriarchies, and in reliving great moments in the life of matriarchies by repeating the same old stories: the jokes that have lost their punchlines, the retorts and witty snubs that have come unfastened from their origins. Perhaps I shouldn't blame her, but I do. I distrust anecdote. I like to understand history through figures and percentages of these figures, through knowing the price of coal and the price of corn, and the price of a loaf in Paris on the day the Bastille fell. I like to be free, so far as I can, from the tyranny of interpretation.

The village of Derwent began to sink beneath the water in the winter of 1943. This was years before I was born. The young Veronica was no doubt forming up thoughts of what children she would have, and how she would make them turn out. She had white skin and green eyes and dyed her hair red with patent formulations. It didn't really matter what man she married, he was only a vehicle for her dynastic ambitions.

Veronica's mother – my maternal grandmother – was called Agnes. She came from a family of twelve. Don't worry, I won't give you a rundown on each one of them. I couldn't, if I wanted to. When I ask Veronica to help me fill in the gaps, she obliges with some story that relates to herself, and then hints – if I try to bring her back to the subject – that there are some things best left unsaid. 'There was more to that episode than was ever divulged,' she would say. I did find out a few facts about the previous generation: none of them cheerful. That one brother went to prison (willingly) for a theft committed by another. That one sister had a child who died unchristened within minutes of birth. She was a daughter whose existence flickered briefly somewhere between the wars; she has no name, and her younger brother to this very day does not know of her existence. Not really a person: more like a negative that was never developed.

The village of Derwent didn't die of an accident, but of a policy. Water was needed by the urban populations of Manchester, Sheffield, Nottingham and Leicester. And so in 1935 they began to build a dam across the River Derwent. Ladybower was the dam's name.

When Derwent was flooded it was already flattened, already deserted. But when I was a child I didn't know this. I understood that the people themselves had left before the flood, but I imagined them going about their daily work till the last possible moment: listening out for a warning, something like an air-raid siren, and then immediately dropping whatever it was they were doing. I saw them shrugging into their stout woollen coats – buttoning in the children, tickling smiling chins – and picking up small suitcases and brown paper parcels, trudging with resigned Derbyshire faces to meeting points on the corner. I saw them laying down their knitting in mid-stitch, throwing a pea-pod half shelled into the colander: folding away the morning paper with a phrase half read, an ellipsis that would last their lifetimes.

***

'Leicester, did you say?' Veronica beamed at me. 'Your Uncle Finbar was last seen in Leicester. He had a market stall.'

I shuffled my hospital armchair forward, across the BUPA contract carpet. 'Your uncle,' I said. 'That's my great-uncle.'

'Yes.' She can't think why I quibble: what's hers is mine.

'What was he selling?'

'Old clothes.' Veronica chuckled knowingly. 'So it was said.'

I didn't rise to her bait. All I want from her is some dates. She likes to make mysteries and imply she has secret knowledge. She won't say which year she was born and has told a blatant lie about her age to the admissions people, which could of course jeopardize her insurance claim. Also, I am conjoined to the same insurance scheme, and they might begin to wonder about me if they ever compare files and see that by their records my mother is only ten years older than me.

A man once told me that you can date women by looking at the backs of their knees. That delta of soft flesh and broken veins, he swore, it is the only thing that cannot lie.

'They were a wild lot,' Veronica said. 'Your uncles. They were,' she said, 'you must remember, Irishmen.'

No, they weren't. Irish, yes, I concede. But not wild, not nearly wild enough. They drank when they had money and prayed when they had none. They worked in the steamy heat of mills and when they knocked off shift and stepped outside, the cold gnawed through their clothes and cracked their bones like crazed china. You would have thought they would have bred, but they didn't. Some had no children at all, others had just one. These only children were precious, wouldn't you think? But one failed to marry, and another spent much of his life in an asylum.

So far, so good: what sort of family do you expect me to come from? All-singing, all-dancing? You'd just know they'd be tubercular, probably syphilitic, certifiably insane, dyslexic, paralytic, circumcised, circumscribed, victims of bad pickers in identity parades, mangled in industrial machinery, decapitated by forklift trucks, dental cripples, sodomites, sent blind by measles, riddled with asbestosis and domiciled downwind of Chernobyl. I assume you've read my new novel, *The Clean Slate*. I was working on the first draft at the time I decided to tackle Veronica. I had the theory that our family was bent on erasing itself, through divorce, elective celibacy and a series of gynaecological catastrophes. 'But I had children,' Veronica said, bewildered. 'I had you, didn't I?' Yes, Miss Bedjacket, you bet you did.

Probably the one thing you couldn't guess would be that I come from the drowned village. As a child I could hardly realize it myself. There is such a thing as portent-overload. Of course, I had the whole thing wrong. I misunderstood, and was prone to believe any rubbish people put my way.

Suppose that in Pompeii they had been given an alert: time, but not much of it. They would have left – what – their oil jars, their weaving shuttles, their vessels of wine, dashed and dripping? I can't really picture it. I have never been to Italy. Suppose they had taken the warning and cleared out. That was how I thought Derwent would be: a Pompeii, a *Marie Celeste*.

I thought that the waters would rise, at first inch by inch, and creep under each closed door. And then swill about, aimless for a while, contained by linoleum. The first thing to go would be the little striped mats that people dotted about in those days. They were cheap things that would go sodden quickly. Beneath the lino would be stone flags. They would hold the water, like some denying stepmother, in a chilly embrace: it would be the work of a generation, to wear them down ...

And so, thwarted, the water rises, like daughters or peasants denied, and plunges hungry fingers into the cupboards where the sugar and the flour is kept. The colander, resting on the stone sink, goes floating, the water recirculating through its holes. The half-shelled pea-pods bob, and eggcups, pans and chamber pots join the flotilla, as the water rises to the window sills. A street's worth of tea brews itself. Cakes of soap twirl twelve feet in the air, as if God were taking His Saturday soak. Gabbling like gossips on a picnic, the water surges, each hour higher by a foot, riser by riser creeping up the stairs and washing about the private items of Derbyshire persons, about their crisply ironed bloomers floating free of lavender presses: the lapping of wavelets hemming their plain knee-bands with lace. The flannel bedsheets are soaked, and the woollen blankets press on the mattresses like the weight of sodden sin: till the mad gaiety of the waters takes them over, and buoys them up in the finest easy style. The beds go sailing, tub chairs are coracles; the yellowed long johns with their attached vests wave arms and legs, cut free from conjugal arrangements, and swim like Captain Webb for liberty and France.

This was what I imagined. I thought some upriver valve was eased, and the flood began.

But in fact, the Ladybower dam was downvalley from Derwent village. There was no flood. Derwent died by drips. The rain fell and was bottled. The streams flowed and were contained. Ladybower closed her downstream valves and gradually the valley filled, in the course of nature, from the hillside streams and the precipitation of Pennine cloud bursts. It filled slowly: as tears, if you cried enough, would fill a bowl.

Veronica is old now. She does and does not understand this. She could always entertain what they call 'discontinuities'. That is to say, slippages in time or sense, breaches between cause and effect. She can also entertain big fat sweating lies, usually told either to mystify people or to make her look good. I cannot tell you how many times she has misled me. I take the map of the Derwent valley to the light. I look back at her in the bed. I am sorry to say it – I wish I could say something else – but the plan of the reservoirs looks very like a diagrammatic representation of the female reproductive tract. Not a detailed one: just the kind you might give to medical students in their first year, or children who persist in enquiring. One ovary is the Derwent reservoir, the other is Hogg Farm. This second branch descends by Underbank to Cocksbridge. The other branch descends by Derwent Hall, past the school and the church, through the drowned village of Ashopton to the

45 The Clean Slate

neck of the womb itself, at Ladybower House and Ladybower Wood: from there, to the Yorkshire Bridge weir, and the great world beyond.

What I know now is this: they demolished the village before they flooded it. Stone by stone it was smashed. They waited till the vicar had died before they knocked down the vicarage. I think of Derwent Hall and the shallow river that ran beside it, the packhorse bridge and the bridle path. They knocked down the hall and sold what they could. The drawing-room floor – oak boards – went for £40. The oak panelling was sold at 2s and 6d per square foot.

The village of Derwent had a church, St James & St John. There was a silver patten and an ancient font which the heathens at the hall had once used as a flowerpot. There was a sundial, and four bells, and 284 bodies buried in the churchyard. Nowhere could be found to take in these homeless bones, and the Water Board decided to bury them on land of its own. But the owner of the single house in the neighbourhood raised such objections that the project was called off. It seemed they would have to go under the water, the dead men of Derwent.

But the churchyard at Bamford offered to house them, at the last push. They were exhumed one by one and their condition recorded – 'complete skeleton', together with the nature of the subsoil, the state of the coffin and the depth at which they were found. The Water Board paid £500 and it was all settled up. A bishop said prayers.

Through 1944, the water rose steadily. By June 1945, only a pair of stone gateposts and the spire of the church could be seen.

When I was a child, people would tell me AS A FACT that in hot summers, the church spire would rise above the waters, eerie and desolate under the burning sun.

This is also untrue.

The church tower was blown up, in 1947. I have a photograph of it, blasted, crumbling, in the very act of joining the ruins below. But even if I showed this to Veronica, she wouldn't believe me. She'd only say I was persecuting her. She doesn't care for evidence, she seems to say. She has her own versions of the past, and her own way of protecting them.

Sometimes, to pass her time, Veronica knits something. I say 'something' because I'm not sure if it has a future as a garment, or if she'll be wearing it anywhere out of here. She has a way of working her elbows that points her needles straight at me. When the nurse comes in she drops her weapons in the fold of the sheets and smiles, nicey-nice.

Every Saturday night, in the village where Veronica grew up, the English fought the Irish, at a specified street, called Waterside. As a child I used to play on this desolate spot. Bullrushes, reeds, swamps. (Be home for half past seven, Veronica always said.) I expect they were not serious fights. More like minuets with broken bottles. After all, next Saturday night they would have to do it all over again.

No; it was the Derbyshire people who were the wild bunch, in my opinion. Two brothers used to go around the pubs and advertise each other: my brother here will fight, run, leap, play cricket or sing, against any man in this county. The cricketer destroyed his career by felling the umpire with a blow in his only first-class match. Another brother, making his way home by moonlight, manslaughtered a person, tossed him over a wall and took ship for America. Another walked the bridle path from Glossop to Derwent in the company of a man who described himself as a doctor, but was later discovered to be an escaped and homicidal lunatic.

I like to imagine cross-connections. Perhaps this 'doctor' was my psychotic Irish relative who was committed to a madhouse. I tried to run my theory past Veronica, and see if the dates fitted at all. She said she knew nothing about the bridle path, nothing about a lunatic. I was about to take her up on it when a nurse put her head around the door and said, 'The doctor's here.' I had to stand in the corridor. 'Coffee?' some moron said, gesturing to two inches of sludge on a warm-plate. I just ignored the question. I put my head on the clear, clean plaster of the wall, which was painted in a neutral shade, like thought.

After a time, a doctor came out and stood by my elbow. He did a big act of ahem to attract my attention and when I continued to rest my head on the restful plaster he percussed my shoulder till I looked around. He was a short, irate, grey-haired man. He was smaller than me, in fact, and trying to impart news of some sort, almost certainly bad. As I write, the average height of an Englishwoman is a hair's breadth below 5′5″. I barely scrape 5′3″, and yet I tower over Veronica. A tear stings my eye. *So small.* Within the space of a breath, I witness myself: tear is processed, ticked, and shed.

The Ladybower Reservoir has a surface area of 504 acres. Its perimeter is thirteen miles approximately. Its maximum depth is 135 feet. One hundred thousand tons of concrete were used in its building, and one million tons of earth. I am suspicious of these round figures, as I am sure you are. But can I offer them to you, as a basis for discussion? When people talk of 'burying the past', and 'all water under the bridge', these are the kind of figures they are trading in.

46

The American Embassy

(2002)

Chimamanda Ngozi Adichie

She stood in line outside the American embassy in Lagos, staring straight ahead, barely moving, a blue plastic file of documents tucked under her arm. She was the forty-eighth person in the line of about two hundred that trailed from the closed gates of the American embassy all the way past the smaller, vine-encrusted gates of the Czech embassy. She did not notice the newspaper vendors who blew whistles and pushed *The Guardian*, *Thenews*, and *The Vanguard* in her face. Or the beggars who walked up and down holding out enamel plates. Or the ice-cream bicycles that honked. She did not fan herself with a magazine or swipe at the tiny fly hovering near her ear. When the man standing behind her tapped her on the back and asked, 'Do you have change, *abeg*, two tens for twenty naira?' she stared at him for a while, to focus, to remember where she was, before she shook her head and said, 'No.'

The air hung heavy with moist heat. It weighed on her head, made it even more difficult to keep her mind blank, which Dr Balogun had said yesterday was what she would have to do. He had refused to give her any more tranquilizers because she needed to be alert for the visa interview. It was easy enough for him to say that, as though she knew how to go about keeping her mind blank, as though it was in her power, as though she invited those images of her son Ugonna's small, plump body crumpling before her, the splash on his chest so red she wanted to scold him about playing with the palm oil in the kitchen. Not that he could even reach up to the shelf where she kept oils and spices, not that he could unscrew the cap on the plastic bottle of palm oil. He was only four years old.

The man behind her tapped her again. She jerked around and nearly screamed from the sharp pain that ran down her back. Twisted muscle, Dr Balogun had said, his expression awed that she had sustained nothing more serious after jumping down from the balcony.

'See what that useless soldier is doing there,' the man behind her said.

She turned to look across the street, moving her neck slowly. A small crowd had gathered. A soldier was flogging a bespectacled man with a long whip that curled in the air before it landed on the man's face, or his neck, she wasn't sure because the man's hands were raised as if to ward off the whip. She saw the man's glasses slip off and fall. She saw the heel of the soldier's boot squash the black frames, the tinted lenses.

'See how the people are pleading with the soldier,' the man behind her said. 'Our people have become too used to pleading with soldiers.'

She said nothing. He was persistent with his friendliness, unlike the woman in front of her who had said earlier, 'I have been talking to you and you just look at me like a moo-moo!' and now ignored her. Perhaps he was wondering why she did not share in the familiarity that had developed among the others in the line. Because they had all woken up early – those who had slept at all – to get to the American embassy before dawn; because they had all struggled for the visa line, dodging the soldiers' swinging whips as they were herded back and forth before the line was finally formed; because they were all afraid that the American embassy might decide not to open its gates today, and they would have to do it all over again the day after tomorrow since the embassy did not open on Wednesdays, they had formed friendships. Buttoned-up men and women exchanged newspapers and denunciations of General Abacha's government, while young people in jeans, bristling with savoir faire, shared tips on ways to answer questions for the American student visa.

'Look at his face, all that bleeding. The whip cut his face,' the man behind her said.

She did not look, because she knew the blood would be red, like fresh palm oil. Instead she looked up Eleke Crescent, a winding street of embassies with vast lawns, and at the crowds of people on the sides of the street. A breathing sidewalk. A market that sprung up during the American embassy hours and disappeared when the embassy closed. There was the chair-rental outfit where the stacks of white plastic chairs that cost one hundred naira per hour decreased fast. There were the wooden boards propped on cement blocks, colorfully displaying sweets and mangoes and oranges. There were the young people who cushioned cigarette-filled trays on their heads with rolls of cloth. There were the blind beggars led by children, singing blessings in English, Yoruba, pidgin, Igbo, Hausa when somebody put money in their plates. And there was, of course, the makeshift photo studio. A tall man standing beside a tripod, holding up a chalk-written sign that read EXCELLENT ONE-HOUR PHOTOS, CORRECT AMERICAN VISA SPECIFICATIONS. She had had her passport photo taken there, sitting on a rickety stool, and she was not surprised that it came out grainy, with her face much lighter-skinned. But then, she had no choice, she couldn't have taken the photo earlier.

Two days ago she had buried her child in a grave near a vegetable patch in their ancestral hometown of Umunnachi, surrounded by well-wishers she did not remember now. The day before, she had driven her husband in the boot of their Toyota to the home of a friend, who smuggled him out of the country. And the day before that, she hadn't needed to take a passport photo; her life was normal and she had taken Ugonna to school, had bought him a sausage roll at Mr Biggs, had sung along with Majek Fashek on her car radio. If a fortune-teller had told her that she, in the space of a few days, would no longer recognize her life, she would have laughed. Perhaps even given the fortune-teller ten naira extra for having a wild imagination.

'Sometimes I wonder if the American embassy people look out of their window and enjoy watching the soldiers flogging people,' the man behind her was saying. She wished he would shut up. It was his talking that made it harder to keep her mind blank, free of Ugonna. She looked across the street again; the soldier was walking away now, and even from this distance she could see the glower on his face. The glower of a grown man who could flog another grown man if he wanted to, when he wanted to. His swagger was as flamboyant as that of the men who four nights ago broke her back door open and barged in.

Where is your husband? Where is he? They had torn open the wardrobes in the two rooms, even the drawers. She could have told them that her husband was over six feet tall, that he could not possibly hide in a drawer. Three men in black trousers. They had smelled of alcohol and pepper soup, and much later, as she held Ugonna's still body, she knew that she would never eat pepper soup again.

Where has your husband gone? Where? They pressed a gun to her head, and she said, 'I don't know, he just left yesterday,' standing still even though the warm urine trickled down her legs.

One of them, the one wearing a black hooded shirt who smelled the most like alcohol, had eyes that were startlingly bloodshot, so red they looked painful. He shouted the most, kicked at the TV set. *You know about the story your husband wrote in the newspaper? You know he is a liar? You know people like him should be in jail because they cause trouble, because they don't want Nigeria to move forward?*

He sat down on the sofa, where her husband always sat to watch the nightly news on NTA, and yanked at her so that she landed awkwardly on his lap. His gun poked her waist. *Fine woman, why you marry a troublemaker?* She felt his sickening hardness, smelled the fermentation on his breath.

Leave her alone, the other one said. The one with the bald head that gleamed, as though coated in Vaseline. *Let's go.*

She pried herself free and got up from the sofa, and the man in the hooded shirt, still seated, slapped her behind. It was then that Ugonna started to cry, to run to her. The man in the hooded shirt was laughing, saying how soft her body was, waving his gun. Ugonna was screaming now; he never screamed when he cried, he was not that kind of child. Then the gun went off and the palm oil splash appeared on Ugonna's chest.

'See oranges here,' the man in line behind her said, offering her a plastic bag of six peeled oranges. She had not noticed him buy them.

She shook her head. 'Thank you.'

'Take one. I noticed that you have not eaten anything since morning.'

She looked at him properly then, for the first time. A nondescript face with a dark complexion unusually smooth for a man. There was something aspirational about his crisp-ironed shirt and blue tie, about the careful way he spoke English as though he feared he would make a mistake. Perhaps he worked for one of the new-generation banks and was making a much better living than he had ever imagined possible.

'No, thank you,' she said. The woman in front turned to glance at her and then went back to talking to some people about a special church service called the American Visa Miracle Ministry.

'You should eat, oh,' the man behind her said, although he no longer held out the bag of oranges.

She shook her head again; the pain was still there, somewhere between her eyes. It was as if jumping from the balcony had dislodged some bits and pieces inside her head so that they now clattered painfully. Jumping had not been her only choice, she could have climbed onto the mango tree whose branch reached across the balcony, she could have dashed down the stairs. The men had been arguing, so loudly that they blocked out reality, and she believed for a moment that maybe that popping sound had not been a gun, maybe it was the kind of sneaky thunder that came at the beginning of harmattan, maybe the red splash really was palm oil, and Ugonna had gotten to the bottle somehow and was now playing a fainting game even though it was not a game he had ever played. Then their words pulled her back. *You think she will tell people it was an accident? Is this what Oga asked us to do? A small child! We have to hit the mother. No, that is double trouble. Yes. No, let's go, my friend!*

She had dashed out to the balcony then, climbed over the railing, jumped down without thinking of the two storeys, and crawled into the dustbin by the gate. After she heard the roar of their car driving away, she went back to her flat, smelling of the rotten plantain peels in the dustbin. She held Ugonna's body, placed her cheek to his quiet chest, and realized that she had never felt so ashamed. She had failed him.

'You are anxious about the visa interview, *abi*?' the man behind her asked.

She shrugged, gently, so as not to hurt her back, and forced a vacant smile.

'Just make sure that you look the interviewer straight in the eye as you answer the questions. Even if you make a mistake, don't correct yourself, because they will assume you are lying. I have many friends they have refused, for small-small reasons. Me, I am applying for a visitor's visa. My brother lives in Texas and I want to go for a holiday.'

He sounded like the voices that had been around her, people who had helped with her husband's escape and with Ugonna's funeral, who had brought her to the embassy. Don't falter as you answer the questions, the voices had said. Tell them all about Ugonna, what he was like, but don't overdo it, because every day people lie to them to get asylum visas, about dead relatives that were never even born. Make Ugonna real. Cry, but don't cry too much.

'They don't give our people immigrant visas anymore, unless the person is rich by American standards. But I hear people from European countries have no problems getting visas. Are you applying for an immigrant visa or a visitor's?' the man asked.

'Asylum.' She did not look at his face; rather, she felt his surprise.

'Asylum? That will be very difficult to prove.'

She wondered if he read *The New Nigeria*, if he knew about her husband. He probably did. Everyone supportive of the pro-democracy press knew about her husband, especially because he was the first journalist to publicly call the coup plot a sham, to write a story accusing General Abacha of inventing a coup so that he could kill and jail his opponents. Soldiers had come to the newspaper office and carted away large numbers of that edition in a black truck; still, photocopies got out and circulated throughout Lagos – a neighbor had seen a copy pasted on the wall of a bridge next to posters announcing church crusades and new films. The soldiers had detained her husband for two weeks and broken the skin on his forehead, leaving a scar the shape of an L. Friends had gingerly touched the scar when they gathered at their flat to celebrate his release, bringing bottles of whiskey. She remembered somebody saying to him, *Nigeria will be well because of you*, and she remembered her husband's expression, that look of the excited messiah, as he talked about the soldier who had given him a cigarette after beating him, all the while stammering in the way he did when he was in high spirits. She had found that stammer endearing years ago; she no longer did.

'Many people apply for asylum visa and don't get it,' the man behind her said. Loudly. Perhaps he had been talking all the while.

'Do you read *The New Nigeria*?' she asked. She did not turn to face the man, instead she watched a couple ahead in the line buy packets of biscuits; the packets crackled as they opened them.

'Yes. Do you want it? The vendors may still have some copies.'

'No. I was just asking.'

'Very good paper. Those two editors, they are the kind of people Nigeria needs. They risk their lives to tell us the truth. Truly brave men. If only we had more people with that kind of courage.'

It was not courage, it was simply an exaggerated selfishness. A month ago, when her husband forgot about his cousin's wedding even though they had agreed to be wedding sponsors, telling her he could not cancel his trip to Kaduna because his interview with the arrested journalist there was too important, she had looked at him, the distant, driven man she had married, and said, 'You are not the only one who hates the government.' She went to the wedding alone and he went to Kaduna, and when he came back, they said little to each other; much of their conversation had become about Ugonna, anyway. You will not believe what this boy did today, she would say when he came home from work, and then go on to recount in detail how Ugonna had told her that there was pepper in his Quaker Oats and so he would no longer eat it, or how he had helped her draw the curtains.

'So you think what those editors do is bravery?' She turned to face the man behind her.

'Yes, of course. Not all of us can do it. That is the real problem with us in this country, we don't have enough brave people.' He gave her a long look, righteous and suspicious, as though he was wondering if she was a government apologist, one of those people who criticized the pro-democracy movements, who maintained that only a military government would work in Nigeria. In different circumstances, she might have told him of her own journalism, starting from university in Zaria, when she had organized a rally to protest General Buhari's government's decision to cut student subsidies. She might have told him how she wrote for the *Evening News* here in Lagos, how she did the story on the attempted murder of the publisher of *The Guardian*, how she had resigned when she finally got pregnant, because she and her husband had tried for four years and she had a womb full of fibroids.

She turned away from the man and watched the beggars make their rounds along the visa line. Rangy men in grimy long tunics who fingered prayer beads and quoted the Koran; women with jaundiced eyes who had sickly babies tied to their backs with threadbare cloth; a blind couple led by their daughter, blue medals of the Blessed Virgin Mary hanging around their necks below tattered collars. A newspaper vendor walked over, blowing his whistle. She could not see *The New Nigeria* among the papers balanced on his arm. Perhaps it had sold out. Her husband's latest story, 'The Abacha Years So Far: 1993 to 1997,' had not worried her at first, because he had written nothing new, only compiled killings and failed contracts and missing money. It was not as if Nigerians did not already know these things. She had not expected much trouble, or much attention, but only a day after the paper came out, BBC radio carried the story on the news and interviewed an exiled Nigerian professor of politics who said her husband deserved a Human Rights Award. *He fights repression with the pen, he gives a voice to the voiceless, he makes the world know.*

Her husband had tried to hide his nervousness from her. Then, after someone called him anonymously – he got anonymous calls all the time, he was that kind of journalist, the kind who cultivated friendships along the way – to say that the head of state was personally furious, he no longer hid his fear; he let her see his shaking hands. Soldiers were on their way to arrest him, the caller said. The word was, it would be his last arrest, he would never come back. He climbed into the boot of the car minutes after the call, so that if the soldiers asked, the gateman could honestly claim not to know when her husband had left. She took Ugonna down to a neighbor's flat and then quickly sprinkled water in the boot, even though her husband told her to hurry, because she felt somehow that a wet boot would be cooler, that he would breathe better. She drove him to his coeditor's house. The next day, he called her from Benin Republic; the coeditor had contacts who had sneaked him over the border. His visa to America, the one he got when he went for a training course in Atlanta, was still valid, and he would apply for asylum when he arrived in New York. She told him not to worry, she and Ugonna would be fine, she would apply for a visa at the end of the school term and they would join him in America. That night, Ugonna was restless and she let him stay up and play with his toy car while she read a book. When she saw the three men burst in through the kitchen door, she hated herself for not insisting that Ugonna go to bed. If only …

'Ah, this sun is not gentle at all. These American Embassy people should at least build a shade for us. They can use some of the money they collect for visa fee,' the man behind her said.

Somebody behind him said the Americans were collecting the money for their own use. Another person said it was intentional to keep applicants waiting in the sun. Yet another laughed. She motioned to the blind begging couple and fumbled in her bag for a twenty-naira note. When she put it in the bowl, they chanted, 'God bless you, you will have money, you will have good husband, you will have good job,' in Pidgin English and then in Igbo and Yoruba. She watched them walk away. They had not told her, 'You will have many good children.' She had heard them tell that to the woman in front of her.

The embassy gates swung open and a man in a brown uniform shouted, 'First fifty on the line, come in and fill out the forms. All the rest, come back another day. The embassy can attend to only fifty today.'

'We are lucky, *abi?*' the man behind her said.

She watched the visa interviewer behind the glass screen, the way her limp auburn hair grazed the folded neck, the way green eyes peered at her papers above silver frames as though the glasses were unnecessary.

'Can you go through your story again, ma'am? You haven't given me any details,' the visa interviewer said with an encouraging smile. This, she knew, was her opportunity to talk about Ugonna.

She looked at the next window for a moment, at a man in a dark suit who was leaning close to the screen, reverently, as though praying to the visa interviewer behind. And she realized that she would die gladly at the hands of the man in the black hooded shirt or the one with the shiny bald head before she said a word about Ugonna to this interviewer, or to anybody at the American embassy. Before she hawked Ugonna for a visa to safety.

Her son had been killed, that was all she would say. Killed. Nothing about how his laughter started somehow above his head, high and tinkly. How he called sweets and biscuits 'breadie-breadie.' How he grasped her neck tight when she held him. How her husband said that he would be an artist because he didn't try to build with his LEGO blocks but instead he arranged them, side by side, alternating colors. They did not deserve to know.

'Ma'am? You say it was the government?' the visa interviewer asked.

'Government' was such a big label, it was freeing, it gave people room to maneuver and excuse and re-blame. Three men. Three men like her husband or her brother or the man behind her on the visa line. Three men.

'Yes. They were government agents,' she said.

'Can you prove it? Do you have any evidence to show that?'

'Yes. But I buried it yesterday. My son's body.'

'Ma'am, I am sorry about your son,' the visa interviewer said. 'But I need some evidence that you know it was the government. There is fighting going on between ethnic groups, there are private assassinations. I need some evidence of the government's involvement and I need some evidence that you will be in danger if you stay on in Nigeria.'

She looked at the faded pink lips, moving to show tiny teeth. Faded pink lips in a freckled, insulated face. She had the urge to ask the visa interviewer if the stories in *The New Nigeria* were worth the life of a child. But she didn't. She doubted that the visa interviewer knew about pro-democracy newspapers or about the long, tired lines outside the embassy gates in cordoned-off areas with no shade where the furious sun caused friendships and headaches and despair.

'Ma'am? The United States offers a new life to victims of political persecution but there needs to be proof ...'

A new life. It was Ugonna who had given her a new life, surprised her by how quickly she took to the new identity he gave her, the new person he made her. 'I'm Ugonna's mother,' she would say at his nursery school, to teachers, to parents of other children. At his funeral in Umunnachi, because her friends and family had been wearing dresses in the same Ankara print, somebody had asked, 'Which one is the mother?' and she had looked up, alert for a moment, and said, 'I'm Ugonna's mother.' She wanted to go back to their ancestral hometown and plant ixora flowers, the kind whose needle-thin stalks she had sucked as a child. One plant would do, his plot was so small. When it bloomed, and the flowers welcomed bees, she wanted to pluck and suck at them while squatting in the dirt. And afterwards, she wanted to arrange the sucked flowers side by side, like Ugonna had done with his LEGO blocks. That, she realized, was the new life she wanted.

At the next window, the American visa interviewer was speaking too loudly into his microphone, "I'm not going to accept your lies, sir!'

The Nigerian visa applicant in the dark suit began to shout and to gesture, waving his see-through plastic file that bulged with documents. 'This is wrong! How can you treat people like this? I will take this to Washington!' until a security guard came and led him away.

'Ma'am? Ma'am?'

Was she imagining it, or was the sympathy draining from the visa interviewer's face? She saw the swift way the woman pushed her reddish-gold hair back even though it did not disturb her, it stayed quiet on her neck, framing a pale face. Her future rested on that face. The face of a person who did not understand her, who probably did not cook with palm oil, or know that palm oil when fresh was a bright, bright red and when not fresh, congealed to a lumpy orange.

She turned slowly and headed for the exit.

'Ma'am?' she heard the interviewer's voice behind her.

She didn't turn. She walked out of the American embassy, past the beggars who still made their rounds with enamel bowls held outstretched, and got into her car.

47

Nietverloren

(2002)

J M Coetzee

For as long as he could remember, from when he was first allowed to roam by himself out in the veld, out of sight of the farmhouse, he was puzzled by it: a circle of bare, flat earth ten paces across, its periphery marked with stones, a circle in which nothing grew, not a blade of grass.

He thought of it as a fairy circle, a circle where fairies came at night to dance by the light of the tiny sparkling rods that they carried in the picturebooks he read, or perhaps by the light of glowworms. But in the picturebooks the fairy circle was always in a clearing in a forest, or else in a glen, whatever that might be. There were no forests in the Karoo, no glens, no glowworms; were there even fairies? What would fairies do with themselves in the daytime, in the stunned heat of summer, when it was too hot to dance, when even the lizards took shelter under stones? Would the fairies have enough sense to hide under stones too, or would they lie panting among the thornbushes, longing for England?

He asked his mother about the circle. Is it a fairy circle, he demanded? It can only be a fairy circle, she replied. He was not convinced.

They were visitors on the farm, though not particularly welcome visitors. They visited because they were family, and family were always entitled to visit. This particular visit had stretched on month after month: his father was away in the war, fighting the Italians, and they had nowhere else to go. He could have asked his grandmother what the circle was, but his grandmother never went into the veld, saw no sense in walking for the sake of walking. She would never have laid eyes on the circle, it was not the kind of thing that interested her.

The war ended; his father returned with a stiff little military moustache and a dapper, upright stride. They were back on the farm; he was walking with him in the veld. When they came to the circle, which he no longer called a fairy circle since he no longer believed in fairies, his father casually remarked, 'Do you see that? That's the old threshing floor. That's where they used to thresh, in the old days.'

47

Thresh: not a word he knew, but whatever it meant, he did not like it. Too much like *thrash*. *Get a thrashing*: that was what happened to boys when they were naughty. *Naughty* was another word he drew back from. He did not want to be around when words like that were spoken.

Threshing turned out to be something one did with flails. There was a picture of it in the encyclopedia: men in funny old-fashioned clothes beating the ground with sticks with what look like bladders tied to them.

'But what are they *doing*?' he asked his mother.

'They are flailing the wheat,' she replied.

'What is flailing?'

'Flailing is threshing. Flailing is beating.'

'But *why*?'

'To separate the kernels of wheat from the chaff,' she explained.

Flailing the wheat: it was all beyond him. Was he being asked to believe that once upon a time men used to beat wheat with bladders out in the veld? What wheat? Where did they get wheat to beat?

He asked his father. His father was vague. The threshing happened when he was small, he said; he was not paying attention. He was small, then he went away to boarding school; when he came back they were no longer threshing, perhaps because the drought killed the wheat, the drought of 1929 and 1930 and 1931, on and on, year after year.

That was the best his father could offer: not a fairy circle but a threshing floor, until the great drought came; then just a patch of earth where nothing grew. There the story rested for thirty years. After thirty years, back on the farm on what turned out to be his final visit, the story came up again, or if not the story in full then enough of it for him to be able to fill in the gaps. He was paging through photographs from the old days when he came upon a photograph of two young men with rifles, off on a hunt. In the background, not supposed to be part of the photograph, were two donkeys yoked together, and a man in tattered clothes, also not supposed to be in the picture, one hand on the yoke, squinting toward the camera from under his hat.

He peered more closely. Surely he recognised the site! Surely that was the threshing floor! The donkeys and their leader, captured in mid-stride sometime in the 1920s, were on the threshing floor, treading the wheat with their hooves, separating the grains from the chaff. If the photograph could come to life, if the two grinning young men were to pick up their rifles and disappear over the rim of the picture, he would at last have it before him, the whole mysterious business of threshing. The man with the hat, and the two donkeys, would resume their tread round and round the threshing floor, a tread that would, over the years, compact the earth so tightly that nothing would ever grow there. They would trample the wheat, and the wind – the wind that always blows in the Karoo, from horizon to horizon – would lift the chaff and whirl it away; the grain that was left behind would be gathered up and picked clean of straw and pebbles and ground small, ground to the finest flour, so that bread could be baked in the huge old wood-burning oven that used to dominate the farm kitchen.

But where did the wheat come from that the donkeys so patiently trod, donkeys dead now these many years, their bones cast out and picked clean by ants?

The wheat, it turned out (this was the outcome of a long investigation, and even then he could not be sure if what he heard was true), was grown right here, on the farm, on what in the old days must have been cultivated land but has now reverted to bare veld. An acre of land had been given over to the growing of wheat, just as there had been an acre given over to pumpkin and squash and watermelon and sweetcorn and beans. Every day, from a dam that was just a pile of stones now, farmhands used to irrigate the acres; when the kernels turned brown, they reaped the wheat by hand, with sickles, bound it in sheaves, carted it to the threshingfloor, threshed it, then ground it to flour (he searched everywhere for the grinding stones, without success). From the bounty of those two acres the table was stocked not only of his grandfather but of all the families who worked for him. There were even cows kept, for milk, and pigs to eat the scraps.

So all those years ago this had been a self-sufficient farm, growing all its needs; and all the other farms in the neighbourhood, this vast, sparsely peopled neighbourhood, were self-sufficient too, more or less – farms where nothing grows any more, where no ploughing or sowing or tilling or reaping or threshing takes place, farms which have turned into vast grazing grounds for sheep, where farmers sit huddled over computers in darkened rooms calculating their profit and loss on sheepswool and lambsflesh.

Hunting and gathering, then pastoralism, then agriculture: those, he had been taught as a child, were the three stages in the ascent of man from savagery, an ascent whose end was not yet in sight. Who would have believed that there were places in the world where in the space of a century or two man would graduate from stage one to stage two to stage three and then regress to stage two. This Karoo, looked upon today as a desert on which flocks of ungulates barely clung to life, was not too long ago a region where hopeful farmers planted in the thin, rocky soil seeds brought from Europe and the New World, pumped water out of the artesian basin to keep them alive, subsisted on their fruits: a region of small, scattered peasant farmers and their labourers, independent, almost outside the money economy.

What put an end to it? No doubt the Great Drought disheartened many and drove them off the land. And no doubt, as the artesian basin was depleted over the years, they had to drill deeper and deeper for water. And of course who would want to break his back growing wheat and milling flour and baking bread when you had only to get in a car and drive for an hour to find a shop with racks and racks of ready-baked bread, to say nothing of pasteurised milk and frozen meat and vegetables?

Still, there was a larger picture. What did it mean for the land as a whole, and the conception the land had of itself, that huge tracts of it should be sliding back into prehistory? In the larger picture, was it really better that families who in the old days lived on the land by the sweat of their brow should now be mouldering in the windswept townships of Cape Town? Could one not imagine a different history and a different social order in which the Karoo was reclaimed, its scattered sons and daughters reassembled, the earth tilled again?

Bill and Jane, old friends from the United States, have arrived on a visit. Starting in the north of the country, they have driven in a hired car down the east coast; now the plan is that all four of them will drive from Cape Town to Johannesburg. The route, which runs for hundreds of miles through the Karoo, is not one that he likes. For reasons of his own he finds it depressing. But these are special friends, this is what they want to do, he does not demur.

'Didn't you say your grandfather had a farm in the Karoo?' says Bill. 'Do we pass anywhere near there?'

'It's not in the family anymore,' he replies. It is a lie. The farm is in the hands of his cousin Constant. Furthermore it does not take much of a detour off the Cape Town–Johannesburg road to get there. But he does not want to see the farm again, and what it has become, not in this life.

They leave Cape Town late in the day, spend the first night in Matjiesfontein at the Lord Milner Hotel, where they are served dinner by waitresses in floral dresses and frilled Victorian caps. He and his wife sleep in the Olive Schreiner Room, their friends in the Baden Powell Room. On the walls of the Olive Schreiner room are watercolours of Karoo scenes ('Crossing the Drift', 'Karoo Sunset'), photographs of cricketers: the Royal Fusiliers team of 1899, burly, moustachioed young Englishmen, come to die for their queen in a faroff land, some of them buried not far away.

The next morning they leave early. For hours they drive through empty scrubland ringed by flat-topped hills. Outside Richmond they stop for gas. Jane picks up a pamphlet. 'Nietverloren,' it says. 'Visit an old-style Karoo farm, experience old-style grace and simplicity. Only 15 km from Richmond on the Graaff–Reinet road. Luncheons 12–2.'

They follow the signs to Nietverloren. At the turnoff a young man in a beret and khaki shirt scrambles to open the gate for them, stands to attention and salutes as they drive through.

The farmhouse, gabled in Cape Dutch style, brilliantly whitewashed, stands on an outcrop of rock overlooking fields and orchards. They are greeted at the door by a smiling young woman. 'I'm Velma, I'm your hostess,' she says, with a light, pleasing Afrikaans accent. They are the only guests thus far.

For lunch they are served leg of lamb and roast potatoes, braised baby carrots with raisins, roast pumpkin with cinnamon, followed by custard pie, *melktert*. 'It's what we call *boerekos*,' explains Velma, their hostess: 'farm cuisine. Everything grown on the farm.'

'And the bread?' he asks. 'Do you grow your own wheat, and thresh it and all the rest?'

Velma laughs lightly 'Good heavens no, we don't go as far back as that. But our bread is baked here in our kitchen, in our wood-fired oven, just like in the old days, as you will see on the tour.'

47 Nietverloren

They exchange glances. 'I'm not sure we have time for a tour,' he says. 'How long does it take?'

'The tour is in two parts. First my husband takes you around the farm in the four-wheel drive. You see sheep-shearing, you see wool-sorting; if there are children they get to play with the lambs – the lambs are very cute. Then we've got a little museum, you can see all the grades of wool and the sheep-shearing instruments from the old days and the clothes people wore. Then I take you on a tour of the house, you see everything – the kitchen, which we have restored just as it used to be, and the bathroom, the old bathroom with the hip bath and the furnace, all just like in the old days, and everything else. Then you can relax, and at four o'clock we offer you tea.'

'And how much is that?'

'For the tour and the tea together it is seventy-five rands per person.'

He glances at Bill, at Jane. They are the guests, they must decide. Bill shakes his head. 'It sounds fascinating, but I just don't think we have the time. Thank you, Velma.'

They drive back through the orchard – grapevines, oranges, apricots heavy on the bough – past a pair of languid-eyed Jersey cows with calves by their side.

'Remarkable what they grow, considering how dry it is,' says Jane.

'The soil is surprisingly fertile,' he says. 'With enough water you could grow anything here. It could be a paradise.'

'But – ?'

'But it makes no economic sense. The only crop it makes sense to farm nowadays is people. The tourist crop. Places like Nietverloren are the only farms, if you can call them that, left in the Karoo: time-bubble, theme-park farms. The rest are just sheep ranches. There is no reason for the owners to live on them. They might as well be managed out of the cockpit of a helicopter. As in some cases they are. More enterprising landowners have gone back even further in time. They have got rid of the sheep and restocked their farms with game – antelope, zebra – and brought in hunters from overseas, from Germany and the US. A thousand rand for an eland, two thousand for a kudu. You shoot the animal, they mount the horns for you, you take them home with you on the plane. Trophies. The whole thing is called the safari experience, or sometimes just the African experience.'

'You sound bitter.'

'The bitterness of defeated love. I used to love this land. Then it fell into the hands of the entrepreneurs, and they gave it a makeover and a face-lift and put it on the market. This is the only future you have in South Africa, they told us: to be waiters and whores to the rest of the world. I want nothing to do with it.'

A look passes between Bill and Jane. 'I'm sorry,' murmurs Jane.

Jane is sorry. He is sorry. All of them are a bit sorry, and not only for his outburst. Even Velma back on Nietverloren must be sorry for the charade she has to go through day after day, and the girls in their Victorian getup back in the hotel in Matjiesfontein: sorry and ashamed. A light grade of sorriness sits over the whole country, like cloud, like mist. But there is nothing to be done about it, nothing he can think of.

48

The Universal Story

(2003)

Ali Smith

There was a man dwelt by a churchyard.

Well, no, okay, it wasn't always a man; in this particular case it was a woman. There was a woman dwelt by a churchyard.

Though, to be honest, nobody really uses that word nowadays. Everybody says cemetery. And nobody says dwelt any more. In other words:

There was once a woman who lived by a cemetery. Every morning when she woke up she looked out of her back window and saw –

Actually, no. There was once a woman who lived by – no, in – a second-hand bookshop. She lived in the flat on the first floor and ran the shop which took up the whole of downstairs. There she sat, day after day, among the skulls and the bones of second-hand books, the stacks and shelves of them spanning the lengths and breadths of the long and narrow rooms, the piles of them swaying up, precarious like rootless towers, towards the cracked plaster of the ceiling. Though their bent or riffled or still chaste spines had been bleached by years of anonymous long-gone light, each of them had been new once, bought in a bookshop full of the shine of other new books. Now each was here, with too many possible reasons to guess at when it came to the question of how it had ended up sunk in the bookdust which specked the air in which the woman, on this winter's day, sat by herself, sensing all round her the weight of it, the covers shut on so many millions of pages that might never be opened to light again.

The shop was down a side street off the centre of a small rural village which few tourists visited in the summer and in which business had slowed considerably since 1982, the year the Queen Mother, looking frail and holding her hat on her head with one hand because of the wind, had cut the ribbon on the bypass which made getting to the city much quicker and stopping in the village quite difficult. Then the bank had closed and eventually the post office. There was a grocer's but most people drove to the supermarket six miles away. The supermarket also stocked books, though hardly any.

48 The Universal Story

Occasionally someone would come into the second-hand bookshop looking for something he or she had heard about on the radio or read about in the papers. Usually the woman in the shop would have to apologize for not having it. For instance, it was February now. Nobody had been into the shop for four days. Occasionally a bookish teenage girl or boy, getting off the half-past four school bus which went between the village and the town, used to push, shy, at the door of the shop and look up with the kind of delight you can see even from behind in the shoulders and back and the angle of head of a person looking up at the endless promise of books. But this hadn't happened for a while.

The woman sat in the empty shop. It was late afternoon. It would be dark soon. She watched a fly in the window. It was early in the year for flies. It flew in veering triangles then settled on *The Great Gatsby* by F Scott Fitzgerald to bask in what late winter sun there was.

Or – no. Wait:

There was once a fly resting briefly on an old paperback book in a second-hand bookshop window. It had paused there in a moment of warmth before launching back into the air, which it would do any second now. It wasn't any special or unusual kind of fly or a fly with an interesting species name – for instance, a robber fly or an assassin fly, a bee fly or a thick-headed fly, a dance fly, a dagger fly, a snipe fly or a down-looker fly. It wasn't even a stout or a cleg or a midge. It was a common house fly, a *Musca domesticus linnaeus*, of the diptera family, which means it had two wings. It stood on the cover of the book and breathed air through its spiracles.

It had been laid as an egg less than a millimetre long in a wad of manure in a farmyard a mile and a half away and had become a legless maggot feeding off the manure it had been laid in. Then, because winter was coming, it had wriggled by sheer muscle contraction nearly a hundred and twenty feet. It had lain dormant for almost four months in the grit round the base of a wall under several feet of stacked hay in the barn. In a spell of mild weather over the last weekend it had broken the top off the pupa and pulled itself out, a fly now, six millimetres long. Under an eave of the barn it had spread and dried its wings and waited for its body to harden in the unexpectedly springlike air coming up from the Balearics. It had entered the rest of the world through a fly-sized crack in the roof of the barn that morning then zigzagged for over a mile looking for light, warmth and food. When the woman who owned the shop had opened her kitchen window to let the condensation out as she cooked her lunch, it had flown in. Now it was excreting and regurgitating, which is what flies do when they rest on the surfaces of things.

To be exact, it wasn't an it, it was a female fly, with a longer body and red slitted eyes set wider apart than if she had been a male fly. Her wings were each a thin, perfect, delicately veined membrane. She had a grey body and six legs, each with five supple joints, and she was furred all over her legs and her body with minuscule bristles. Her face was striped velvet-silver. Her long mouth had a sponging end for sucking up liquid and for liquefying solids like sugar or flour or pollen.

She was sponging with her proboscis the picture of the actors Robert Redford and Mia Farrow on the cover of the Penguin 1974 edition of *The Great Gatsby*. But there was little there really of interest, as you might imagine, to a house fly which needs urgently to feed and to breed, which is capable of carrying over one million bacteria and transmitting everything from common diarrhoea to dysentery, salmonella, typhoid fever, cholera, poliomyelitis, anthrax, leprosy and tuberculosis; and which senses that at any moment a predator will catch her in its web or crush her to death with a fly-swat or, if she survives these, that it will still any moment now simply be cold enough to snuff out herself and all ten of the generations she is capable of setting in motion this year, all nine hundred of the eggs she will be capable of laying given the chance, the average twenty days of life of an average common house fly.

No. Hang on. Because:

There was once a 1974 Penguin edition of F Scott Fitzgerald's classic American novel *The Great Gatsby* in the window of a quiet second-hand bookshop in a village that very few people visited any more. It had a hundred and eighty-eight numbered pages and was the twentieth Penguin edition of this particular novel – it had been reprinted three times in 1974 alone; this popularity was partly due to the film of the novel which came out that year, directed by Jack Clayton. Its cover, once bright yellow, had already lost most of its colour before it arrived at the shop. Since the book had been in the window it had whitened even more. In the film-still on it, ornate in a twenties-style frame, Robert Redford and Mia Farrow, the stars of the film, were also quite faded, though Redford was still dapper in his golf cap and Farrow, in a very becoming floppy hat, suited the sepia effect that the movement of sun and light on the glass had brought to her quite by chance.

The novel had first been bought for 30p (6/-) in 1974 in a Devon bookshop by Rosemary Child who was twenty-two and who had felt the urge to read the book before she saw the film. She married her fiancé Roger two years later. They mixed their books and gave their doubles to a Cornwall hospital. This one had been picked off the hospital library trolley in Ward 14 one long hot July afternoon in 1977 by Sharon Patten, a fourteen-year-old girl with a broken hip who was stuck in bed in traction and bored because Wimbledon was over. Her father had seemed pleased at visiting hour when he saw it on her locker and though she'd given up reading it halfway through she kept it there by the water jug for her whole stay and smuggled it home with her when she was discharged. Three years later, when she didn't care any more what her father thought of what she did, she gave it to her schoolfriend David Connor who was going to university to do English, telling him it was the most boring book in the world. David read it. It was perfect. It was just like life is. Everything is beautiful, everything is hopeless. He walked to school quoting bits of it to himself under his breath. By the time he went up north to university in Edinburgh two years later, now a mature eighteen-year-old, he admired it, as he said several times in the seminar, though he found it a little adolescent and believed the underrated *Tender Is the Night* to be Fitzgerald's real masterpiece. The tutor, who every year had to mark around a hundred and fifty abysmal first-year essays on *The Great Gatsby*, nodded sagely and gave him a high pass in his exam. In 1985, having landed a starred first and a job in personnel management, David sold all his old literature course books to a girl called Mairead for thirty pounds. Mairead didn't like English – it had no proper answers – and decided to do economics instead. She sold them all again, making a lot more money than David had. *The Great Gatsby* went for £2.00, six times its original price, to a first-year student called Gillian Edgbaston. She managed never to read it and left it on the shelves of the rented house she'd been living in when she moved out in 1990. Brian Jackson, who owned the rented house, packed it in a box which sat behind the freezer in his garage for five years. In 1995 his mother, Rita, came to visit and while he was tidying out his garage she found it in the open box, just lying there on the gravel in his driveway. *The Great Gatsby*! she said. She hadn't read it for years. He remembers her reading it that summer, it was two summers before she died, and her feet were up on the sofa and her head was deep in the book. She had a whole roomful of books at home. When she died in 1997 he boxed them all up and gave them to a registered charity. The registered charity checked through them for what was valuable and sold the rest on in auctioned boxes of thirty miscellaneous paperbacks, a fiver per box, to second-hand shops all over the country.

The woman in the quiet second-hand bookshop had opened the box she bought at auction and had raised her eyebrows, tired. Another *Great Gatsby*.

The Great Gatsby. F Scott Fitzgerald. Now a Major Picture. The book was in the window. Its pages and their edges were dingy yellow because of the kind of paper used in old Penguin Modern Classics; by nature these books won't last. A fly was resting on the book now in the weak sun in the window.

But the fly suddenly swerved away into the air because a man had put his hand in among the books in the window display in the second-hand bookshop and was picking the book up.

Now:

There was once a man who reached his hand in and picked a second-hand copy of F Scott Fitzgerald's *The Great Gatsby* out of the window of a quiet second-hand bookshop in a small village. He turned the book over as he went to the counter.

How much is this one, please? he asked the grey-looking woman.

She took it from him and checked the inside cover.

That one's £1, she said.

It says thirty pence here on it, he said, pointing to the back.

That's the 1974 price, the woman said.

The man looked at her. He smiled a beautiful smile. The woman's face lit up.

But, well, since it's very faded, she said, you can have it for fifty.

Done, he said.

Would you like a bag for it? she asked.

No, it's okay, he said. Have you any more?

Any more Fitzgerald? the woman said. Yes, under F. I'll just – .

No, the man said. I mean, any more copies of *The Great Gatsby*.

You want another copy of *The Great Gatsby*? the woman said.

I want all your copies of it, the man said, smiling.

The woman went to the shelves and found him four more copies of *The Great Gatsby*. Then she went through to the storeroom at the back of the shop and checked for more.

Never mind, the man said. Five'll do. Two pounds for the lot, what do you say?

His car was an old Mini Metro. The back seat of it was under a sea of different editions of *The Great Gatsby*. He cleared some stray copies from beneath the driver's seat so they wouldn't slide under his feet or the pedals while he was driving and threw the books he'd just bought over his shoulder on to the heap without even looking. He started the engine. The next second-hand bookshop was six miles away, in the city. His sister had called him from her bath two Fridays ago. James, I'm in the bath, she'd said. I need F Scott Fitzgerald's *The Great Gatsby*.

F what's the what? he'd said.

She told him again. I need as many as possible, she said.

Okay, he'd said.

He worked for her because she paid well; she had a grant.

Have you ever read it? she asked.

No, he'd said. Do I have to?

So we beat on, she'd said. Boats against the current. Borne back ceaselessly into the past. Get it?

What about petrol money, if I'm supposed to drive all over the place looking for books? he'd said.

You've got five hundred quid to buy five hundred books. You get them for less, you can keep the change. And I'll pay you two hundred on top for your trouble. Boats against the current. It's perfect, isn't it?

And petrol money? he'd said.

I'll pay it, she'd sighed.

Because:

There was once a woman in the bath who had just phoned her brother and asked him to find her as many copies of *The Great Gatsby* as possible. She shook the drips off the phone, dropped it over the side on to the bathroom carpet and put her arm back into the water quick because it was cold.

She was collecting the books because she made full-sized boats out of things boats aren't usually made out of. Three years ago she had made a three-foot-long boat out of daffodils which she and her brother had stolen at night from people's front gardens all over town. She had launched it, climbing into it, in the local canal. Water had come up round her feet almost immediately, then up round her knees, her thighs, till she was midriff-deep in icy water and daffodils floating all round her, unravelled.

But a small crowd had gathered to watch it sink and the story had attracted a lot of local and even some national media attention. Sponsored by Interflora, which paid enough for her to come off unemployment benefit, she made another boat, five feet long and out of mixed flowers, everything from lilies to snowdrops. It also sank, but this time was filmed for an arts project, with her in it, sinking. This had won her a huge arts commission to make more unexpected boats. Over the last two years she had made ten- and twelve-footers out of sweets, leaves, clocks and photographs and had launched each one with great ceremony at a different UK port. None of them had lasted more than eighty feet out to sea.

The Great Gatsby, she thought in the bath. It was a book she remembered from her adolescence and as she'd been lying in the water fretting about what to do next so her grant wouldn't be taken away from her it had suddenly come into her head.

It was perfect, she thought, nodding to herself. So we beat on. The last line of the book. She ducked her shoulders under the water to keep them warm.

And so, since we've come to the end already:

The seven-foot boat made of copies of *The Great Gatsby* stuck together with waterproof sealant was launched in the spring in the port of Felixstowe.

The artist's brother collected over three hundred copies of *The Great Gatsby* and drove between Wales and Scotland doing so. It is still quite hard to buy a copy of *The Great Gatsby* second-hand in some of the places he visited. It cost him a hundred and eighty-three pounds fifty exactly. He kept the change. He was also a man apt to wash his hands before he ate, so was unharmed by any residue left by the fly earlier in the story on the cover of the copy he bought in the quiet second-hand bookshop.

This particular copy of *The Great Gatsby*, with the names of some of the people who had owned it inked under each other in their different handwritings on its inside first page – Rosemary Child, Sharon Patten, David Connor, Rita Jackson – was glued into the prow of the boat, which stayed afloat for three hundred yards before it finally took in water and sank.

The fly which had paused on the book that day spent that evening resting on the light fitting and hovering more than five feet above ground level. This is what flies tend to do in the evenings. This fly was no exception.

The woman who ran the second-hand bookshop had been delighted to sell all her copies of *The Great Gatsby* at once, and to such a smiling young man. She replaced the one which had been in the window with a copy of Dante's *The Divine Comedy* and as she was doing so she fanned open the pages of the book. Dust flew off. She blew more dust off the top of the pages then wiped it off her counter. She looked at the book dust smudged on her hand. It was time to dust all the books, shake them all open. It would take her well into the spring. Fiction, then non-fiction, then all the sub-categories. Her heart was light. That evening she began, at the letter A.

The woman who lived by a cemetery, remember, back at the very beginning? She looked out of her window and she saw – ah, but that's another story.

And lastly, what about the first, the man we began with, the man dwelt by a churchyard?

He lived a long and happy and sad and very eventful life, for years and years and years, before he died.

Golden Boys

(2008)

Shih-Li Kow

Two years ago, when Wei Seng told me that he was getting married in Melbourne, I had shrunk to the size of a mouse. He said, 'We're signing the marriage papers at the registry office and I'm back in the office the next day. There's no reason for you to fly eight hours just for that and our apartment is too small for both of you.' I could have slept in the pocket of his shirt if he let me.

After he hung up, I had repeated to my husband: A wedding banquet in Melbourne costs one year's salary. Hotels are expensive. Air tickets too.

My husband said, 'Lousy excuses. He don't want us at his wedding. He din't want us at his graduation and now he don't want two old chicken sellers to spoil his party.' He hawked up the words like phlegm. 'We got only one son and not even a tea ceremony? The boy make me lose face.'

I said, 'The boy knows what he's doing. He got his own plans.'

'You always defend the boy. *Teew* Melbourne. We can arrange a wedding dinner here in the school hall. Twenty tables already enough for everybody. Tell him come home. Bring a suit. Bring the girl. What's so difficult?'

'You yourself talk to him. If you want this, want that, you yourself call him and tell him.'

My husband – people call him Kentucky Chan – did not. Father and son could not talk without quarrelling. Wei Seng hated being called Kentucky Chan's son. Once, when he was seven or so, he had come home from school crying. Someone had said that he was birthed in a Kentucky Fried Chicken restaurant with a mascot cockerel for a father. But my husband liked the name that started as a joke in the wet market. He said nobody else had a name like it.

Although it pained me that there was to be no tea ceremony, to forego the wedding banquet was a relief. I imagined my husband in Kentucky Chan mode, drinking too much and laughing too loudly; *yamseng* toasts like a shouting contest between old men who top up their VSOPs before the third course is served; the karaoke gang singing

Teresa Teng and Jackie Cheung oldies until they are dragged off the stage. It would have been a long wait for the alcohol to run out and the night to end.

Wei Seng is coming home today, this fourth day of the Chinese New Year. My golden boy. He is himself the father of a boy now. I have not seen him in person for four years. I worry about accidents on the highway. The new roads might confuse him in the dark. I worry about how much he has changed and what his wife will think of me. I worry. At the same time, anticipation floats me almost off the floor.

I wipe down sauce bottles and condiment jars in the kitchen. In the living room, my husband watches an action movie. He turns up the sound over the noise of the rain; his hearing is not what it used to be. Every now and then, gunshot bangs and loud music fill the house. On the table, dinner is cold. I have laid out steamed white chicken, yams and pork belly, braised mushrooms on broccoli. Soup is on the stove; rice is keeping warm. We wait.

I put down the tea towel and look at my hands. I have big knuckles and bumpy veins that go up to my forearms. They are not womanly hands. When my niece married, I went to a salon to get my hair styled. In the photographs, my hair swept elegantly across my forehead but my face was like a man's. When my husband saw me in my mail order cheongsam, he said, 'You look like a jackfruit in a paper bag.'

Beauty creams, collagen drinks, detox teas, YouTube make-up tutorials, hair dyes, dresses, tai chi, four-day three-night holidays once a year. They cannot undo the coarseness sunk into the body from forty years of graceless toil: getting up every day before cockcrow, packing sleepy chickens into wire cages, shouting above the market din, slitting so many scrawny throats, and tearing out so many handfuls of hot, wet feathers and innards. Day after day until the day my husband put down his knife and declared that it was enough. Maybe my husband was right. Maybe Wei Seng does not want a jackfruit of a mother and a father named after fried chicken in his shiny, new life. I worry and wipe the cutlery.

When Wei Seng walks through our door, at last, it is as if all the lights have come on in our house. I hug him. I laugh. I start to cry. The vacuum of past years sucks in his presence. All the should-haves rush in. I should have hugged him more as a child, should have celebrated and not sulked when he came in third in class in Form Five, should have quietly closed the door when I caught him masturbating, should never, never have let my husband beat him into working at the chicken stall. He was too good for the wet market. Maybe he is even too good for me.

Wei Seng kisses me on the cheek and removes my arms from around him. 'Later, Ma, later. Didn't you hear me honk?' He wipes the rain from his face with his hand. 'Quick. Get me an umbrella and a torch light. Black like hell outside and raining waterfalls.'

I fetch the new umbrella that was a present from Mrs Sim next door. Her son has a job in Kuala Lumpur printing logos and he brings her things like umbrellas and shopping bags when he comes home. Wei Seng only gives us money. Money is always better than umbrellas, Melbourne is better than KL. One faraway son is better than none at all.

With the umbrella in one hand and a torch light in the other, Wei Seng steps out into the rain, cursing.

My husband says, 'Cry what, woman. Who died?'

'Alright, alright.' I wipe away my tears. 'He's tired and wet. Not yet one foot in our house and he's already grumpy.'

'Why you din't hear his car? You always say you can hear better than me.'

'Alright, my fault. The rain is also my fault. Please shut up now.'

Wei Seng comes back with his wife and child under his umbrella. My own mother used to say: a pair of new testicles and a little mushroom stem in the family is the best form of good fortune. My husband is smiling. I see all the sparse pegs of teeth in his doughy gums. He should close his mouth before a cockroach flies in.

Wei Seng says, 'Ti Yen, my parents.'

'Nice to meet you, Mr Chan, Mrs Chan. Noah, say hello to Grandma and Grandpa.' She does not call us Ma and Pa like Wei Seng. We have not had a wedding tea ceremony.

The child slides off his mother's lap, toddles to the television and picks up the toy my husband bought last week.

'Noah, say "Thank you".'

'Uh you,' says the child to the plastic rocket. 'Oom oom.'

My husband says, 'Oom oom. Clever boy, Noah Chan.'

For the next two hours, I scurry back and forth between the kitchen, dining table, and bedroom. I fetch slippers and towels. I serve bowls of hot rice and soup while Wei Seng and his family fuss and arrange themselves until all are showered, fed, and installed in our room with the double bed. When the house is finally quiet and there is nothing else to fetch or find or wash, I retire to Wei Seng's old room. My husband is on the single bed. I roll out a mattress on the floor.

'No-ah Chan,' he whispers, 'sounds like a no luck name.'

'Shut up. I am tired to death.'

'The boy don't talk. Something's not right. Did you look at him properly? He's not normal.'

I switch off the lights and say, 'Shut up. Shut up.'

The thought that I have tried to evade the whole evening catches up. I try not to multiply the number of years, the days in a year, and the number of chickens slaughtered and eviscerated in a day. How many chicken lives have passed through the hands of Kentucky Chan and me? Tens of thousands, maybe even hundreds of thousands. I fall asleep dreaming of Noah doing sums and eating feathers with his slack mouth.

In the morning, I find Wei Seng unloading things from the car. The morning is cool and clean, rinsed with yesterday's rain.

'You rented this car from the airport?' I squeeze his shoulders with both hands and thump his back. He feels solid and strong.

'No, it belongs to Ti Yen's family.'

'You had reunion dinner with her family first?'

'Yes, Ma. With her two sisters in KL. They picked us up from the airport and we rested for a few days before driving here. Don't complain, please, we're here now.'

'I'm not complaining. I wish you had more time. We haven't seen you for so many years. Now, there's your wife and the boy to talk to. The boy …'

'He has Down Syndrome, Ma. You should have noticed it already.'

My guilt solidifies into something barbed and real. The third generation pays the price for the previous two, either the price of wrongdoings or of lives lived too frivolously. It's true. There is always a price. The chicken business was inherited from my husband's father and during the months that I was pregnant, I had taken all the precautions. I turned my face away from my husband killing the chickens at the market. I freed birds and fish as atonement. I put money into collection boxes for orphanages as insurance against bad luck. When Wei Seng arrived, perfect and unmarked by even a mole, I had rejoiced. I thought that karma had skipped him, but it has not. It has given him this child as a debt to bear instead.

I say, 'Poor boy. Poor, poor boy.'

'Don't say that, Ma, especially to my wife. It is not uncommon, and we go for classes to learn how to manage. We're OK but I would like you to help with Noah.'

'Yes, sure. I can babysit the boy. You take your wife and drive her around town. Show her all the old places.' I mean his old school, the market where our chicken stall used to be, the lakes, his childhood fishing spots, the river, and the food stalls under the yellow flame tree. Those places are full of memories for him.

'No, Ma. I mean full time. Come to Melbourne and live with us.'

'Melbourne? But you said your flat is too small.'

'You can share Noah's room until we get a bigger place. We need your help. I was promoted last month, and if I do well, I'll make partner in the firm. It's a big thing for me. Ti Yen travels a lot for her business and we don't want a stranger for a live-in nanny when she's travelling and I'm working late. We want someone we can trust with Noah. Pa can take care of himself for a few years.'

'A few years! This is too sudden, Seng. Are you going to talk to your Pa?'

'I can't talk to him. You know I'll end up leaving the house if I do. Decide for yourself, Ma. For once, decide for yourself.' He takes out a highchair and a plastic potty from the car. 'I'm going to drive out with my wife to see if we can get a hotel room in town. Last night was uncomfortable. All those mosquitoes. You really should get someone to clean up the backyard. Maybe I'll look for a grasscutter. We won't be long. The boy's milk is on the table in case he wakes up.'

I put a kettle to boil. At the Heaven God altar outside the main door, I top up the red oil in the shot glass, float a fresh wick on the oil, and strike a match to light the wick. I light a coil of incense with the flame. I change the tea in the three red plastic teacups. I do the same at the Goddess of Mercy altar in the living room and the Earth God altar on the floor. Each time, I use exactly three matches. If it's the first or fifteenth of every lunar month, I also light a pair of red candles at every altar. Then I load the laundry into the washing machine, sweep the floor, and mop the kitchen and living room. This is what I do every morning.

When he wakes, my husband will check on our rabbits; feed the few chickens we still have; search for eggs in the grass; and inspect our guava, papaya, mango, and jackfruit trees. If there are new fruits, he will make newspaper bags to tie around the fruits to save them from squirrels. Then he will get on his motorcycle and ride to the coffee shop next to the market for morning tea with his friends. If it is the first or fifteenth of the lunar month, I will ask him to buy three stalks of chrysanthemum from the flower seller for the altars. This is what he does every morning.

Since we stopped selling chickens, this is what we do every morning.

While the washing machine churns, I make a thermos of kopi-o and sit down to a breakfast of cream crackers. I think of Australia. In Melbourne, I will not have altars and gods. Our chicken business, our house, the altars, and the gods were handed down by my father-in-law. Although I upkeep the altars, they are not really mine. They are Chan family gods who became my responsibility when I married. I don't know if the gods recognise me as anything but the caretaker maid who cleans their altars. I sip my kopi-o which is a little bitter.

The child wails in the bedroom, startling me. I grab the bottle of milk warming in a bowl of hot water.

'Hello, Noah boy.' He takes the bottle and plops back onto the pillow, sucking and staring at me. I tuck a bolster under his little arms and he lets me rub his head. Sweet child. Any other child waking up in a strange house with a stranger would have screamed the roof down.

I think of Melbourne, Seng, and this child. What, then, will happen to Kentucky Chan if I were to leave? We have little to say to each other these days. We are not like the Sims next door who go for walks holding hands. I don't know what they talk about on their walks; their lives are as dull as ours, but Mrs Sim would not leave her husband on his own. Maybe she still has a girl's love for her husband. I can't say the same for myself.

I hold the child's feet. 'I'm sorry it had to be you.' He smiles and kicks playfully. Sweet child. Innocent love is easy to reciprocate.

When Wei Seng returns, he says, 'We went to have a look at the rest house by the river. I thought we could get a room with air-conditioning. The place is filthy, even the lobby stinks of cockroach and damp carpet.'

My husband says, 'Next year, we book you a room in the bungalow guest house on the hill. Got four-star rating on Tripadvisor.'

Wei Seng looks at me and I press my lips together.

His wife says, 'Next year, we'll be in Australia for the new year. My family will join us there.' She is sharp-eyed and quick, like a small, quiet predator. She does not seem like a woman who would agree to a one-hour marriage in an office. Maybe Wei Seng had lied about his wedding celebrations.

49   Golden Boys

I busy myself with lunch. I blanch noodles, boil shrimp wontons in yesterday's chicken soup, slice leftover braised mushroom and pork, drizzle sesame oil and soya sauce, sprinkle spring onions and pepper, and serve up four plates.

Wei Seng's wife says, 'Yummy, yummy, Noah. Grandma made us some really yummy noodles.' I suspect I am being flattered into becoming an unpaid live-in nanny and cook. If she were my daughter, I would not feel manipulated. If I had a daughter, I would have been with her from the time her labour pains started.

Wei Seng eats with such a good appetite I fill up just watching him eat.

After lunch, we play blackjack and gin rummy. The child and his mother amuse themselves with the rabbits outside. They chase our chickens around the house. I hear her repeating words: papaya, bird, flower, chicken, rabbit, tree, leaf. They sound happy. I wait for Wei Seng to bring up the matter of Melbourne. He does not and I lose all my chips.

I cook dinner: pork curry with potatoes, pomfret steamed with salted spinach and sour plum, sweet potato leaves with *sambal belacan*, lotus root soup with pork bones. Some days, all I think about is what I have in the refrigerator and what to cook. The child is fed rice in soup, just like Seng was at that age. Sweet child. If I go to Melbourne, I will cook for them. I am sure there are no slaughterhouses in their supermarkets. The meat there would be lifeless and clean of guilt.

My husband eats with his eyes on the television screen. The hosts of a Hong Kong variety show keep up a stream of talk; auspicious words gush out of their mouths like gibberish. My husband says, 'Day after tomorrow is the seventh day of new year.'

After a while, Wei Seng says, 'Seventh day? Are you thinking of *yee sang*? I'll go get some tomorrow.'

My husband grunts 'Yes.' Even now, he does not know how to talk to his son. I wish he would switch off the television. Television chatter in the house is the sound of people who have nothing left to say to each other.

He is not a bad man, my husband. He has worked hard. When his father became bedridden, he paid a small fortune for a day nurse to clean and feed the old man. Every Qing Ming, he trims the overgrown grass around his parents' grave, repaints the faded names on the tombstones with gold paint, lays out offerings of the old man's favourite food, and burns a big heap of paper money. Wei Seng saw all this growing up. A son's filial piety does not have to be earned. The loyalty of son to father is an obligation. Wei Seng should have learnt that growing up. His father is not a bad man. Long ago, Kentucky Chan too was his father's golden boy.

The gilt falls off soon enough. I recall the time he and that chickenfeed salesgirl carried on behind my back. Everyone in the market had known about it. I was made a fool, but I should not dredge it up now. The matter was buried long ago. When I think about that pale, thin girl who did not fight – she only wanted her sales targets, not the man – I must also remember the lover that I had. My husband and I are even. In fact, more than even; it is in my favour that Kentucky never found out about my cheating. He never will.

Golden Boys 49

I toss an imaginary coin: heads grandchild or tails husband, mother or wife, wife or grandmother, cook or nanny, stay here or go there. The coin hovers in the air like a dragonfly, deciding where to land.

The next morning, I see my husband and the child by the rabbit hut under the guava trees. He hauls up a rabbit by the ears. The child holds the rabbit's forepaw and my husband moves the paw up and down in a handshake. He says, 'Hello, Noah, how are you? My name is Tootoo.'

The child squeals in delight, 'Tootoo, Tootoo.'

'Wah, see this fat-fat one. We tell Grandma to cook it in ginger and garlic, OK?'

Our rabbits grow fast as long as the dogs stay away. Sometimes, if a pack of dogs spooks them, one or two will die with their red eyes open. Caged for too long, their heart shrinks until a loud bark is as dangerous as a knife. They cannot be eaten when they die like that, their flesh poisoned by fear.

Wei Seng comes up to me with a big, red lantern. 'A bit late for the new year but better late than never.' His wife holds up another.

Wei Seng goes up on a stool. I hand him hooks, string, and tassels. He says, 'Ma, do you have your passport ready?'

'I have a passport. I went to Koh Samui last year. But I haven't spoken to your Pa yet.'

'Please do it. We can fly back together.'

'Better that I speak to him when you're not here. He will catch fire, you know him. He's been grumbling for years about a wedding banquet. He keeps talking about shark's fin soup and tea ceremonies.'

'Tell you what, Ma,' Wei Seng grins and for a split second, he looks thirteen or fourteen, like a boy wrangling for permission to go fishing after his examinations. 'You agree to Melbourne, I'll agree to a big dinner before we leave. You can invite anyone you like. Invite all the aunties and uncles from the market. My wife and I will do the tea ceremony, right Ti Yen?'

His wife says, smiling, 'No shark's fin soup, though. If we keep eating them, there'll be none left.'

I say, 'Yes, all the shark's fin in the soup is gelatine nowadays. No more sharks in the sea.' Maybe they all grew legs and walk on land now, their words sweet and their mouths full of teeth. I look at the lanterns. A dinner invitation will make up for the pitying looks I have to endure when people see the child.

A shrill scream comes from the backyard. The child must have fallen, slipped down the slope hidden by the undergrowth. I follow Wei Seng and his wife to the backyard as fast as my body will let me. When I get there, I see him crying in his mother's arms, muttering and swinging his head between his fists.

The child's mother says to my husband, 'How could you do this? What jungle are we in? Savages!' She carries the sobbing child into the house.

Kentucky Chan is squatting by the water tap next to the drain. His knees are folded up by his shoulders and his hands move in a basin between his feet. He is washing a thing that looks like a foetus. Tootoo the rabbit is lunch.

'What? A rabbit only, what,' he says.

'Pa! They're not used to this. All this blood. The boy thinks the rabbits are your pets.'

'Old fool,' I say.

My husband tosses a handful of entrails into a bin. 'One call me a savage. One call me a fool. Damn women. Boys must start young. Like you when you were small, Seng. He won't cry after I show him a few more. Just wait and see. When I slaughter another one tomorrow, he won't cry.'

Wei Seng says, 'God! It's like our chicken days all over again. Haven't you stopped?'

'Our chicken days? Our chicken days sent you overseas. Our chicken days gave you master's degree. You forget where your good life came from.'

I add one rabbit to the tally of lives to account for. Wei Seng rushes into the house after his wife.

'Don't upset them,' I say. 'Don't quarrel, and don't touch any other rabbit.'

My rabbit is delicious – tender pieces cooked in a thick garlic and ginger sauce with a garnish of chives and black beans on the top. Wei Seng eats with relish. My cooking has ties that bind him still, but no compliments are passed at the table this time. The child's mother picks at some vegetables. The child eats a boiled egg and brown slop from a jar.

That night, we sit outdoors cracking sunflower seeds and peeling mandarin oranges. The matter of the rabbit is not brought up again. A breeze rolls around our front yard and keeps the mosquitoes away. The oranges give off a tang that smells like a new year. The child is asleep. His mother nibbles daintily. With every movement of her fingers, her diamond ring reflects light in silver needles.

Wei Seng tilts his face to the sky. It is a clear night and the stars are out. He is almost a stranger to me; the boy I raised feels like someone else of the same name. We are held together only by names on his birth certificate and the accumulated memory of his childhood years. I wonder whether he feels the loss of those years. I do not think so. He is still young. Time is not yet precious to him.

The next two days pass quickly and then it is time for Wei Seng to leave. There is a man with a noisy motor cutting the grass in our backyard. In the kitchen, there is a pile of groceries: rice, oil, noodles, sugar, salt, bottles of all the condiments that we use in the kitchen, cream crackers, kopi powder, toilet paper, soap powder, toiletries, prayer oil, incense coils, matches, mosquito coils, vitamins. Yesterday, Wei Seng went around the house making a shopping list of all our consumables and drove to the supermarket to get them. He says someone will come next week to install an air-conditioning unit in the room.

'You take care of yourselves. Pa, Ma,' Wei Seng says. 'Call if you need anything. Ma, think about what I said. I'll call you again. We leave for Melbourne in twelve days.'

He leaves two red packets and an envelope on the dining table. There is a lingering smell of their shampoos, soaps, and lotions around the house. Our bed that they slept in is rumpled. I can already feel the emptiness expanding, pressing on me.

'Money?' says my husband.

I look in the envelope. 'Yes, a lot. And an ATM card with the PIN number.'

'Enough for our funerals.'

'You first or me?'

He said, 'Of course me first. No need to even ask.' No need to ask. The good wife should know that she must outlive the husband. She must nurse the husband in sickness or old age till the end. The lucky spouse gets to die first, the dutiful one must do the work before she follows. It goes without saying.

The toy rocket is under the table. I pick it up and roll it in my big-knuckled hands: wife or grandmother, mother or wife, wife or lover, nanny or nurse, woman or jackfruit. The tossed coin in my head becomes a six-sided rolling dice.

I say, 'Do you remember all the bottles of brandy that we were saving for Seng's wedding? What if I could get Seng to agree to a wedding dinner before he flies back to Melbourne?'

The lanterns outside swing on their strings. The wind whips the tassels around in every which way. Toss the dice in the wind and it becomes a ball with my name. My own name and not the names I have answered to and collected like stones in my shoes.

50

Staying Behind

(2011)

Ken Liu

After the Singularity, most people chose to die.

The dead pity us and call us the *left behind*, as if we were unfortunate souls who couldn't get to a life raft in time. They cannot fathom the idea that we might *choose* to stay behind. And so, year after year, relentlessly, the dead try to steal our children.

***

I was born in Year Zero of the Singularity, when the first man Uploaded into a machine. The Pope denounced the 'Digital Adam'; the digerati celebrated; and everyone else struggled to make sense of the new world.

'We've always wanted to live forever,' said Adam Ever, the founder of Everlasting, Inc., and the first to go. In the form of a recording, his message was broadcast across the internet. 'Now we can.'

While Everlasting built its massive data center in Svalbard, nations around the world scrambled to decide if what happened there was murder. For every Uploaded man, there was a lifeless body left behind, the brain a bloody pulpy mess after the destructive scanning procedure. But what really happened to him, his essence, his – for lack of a better word – soul?

Was he now an artificial intelligence? Or was he still somehow human, with silicon and graphene performing the functions of neurons? Was it merely a hardware upgrade for consciousness? Or has he become a mere algorithm, a clockwork imitation of free will?

It began with the old and the terminally ill. It was very expensive. Then, as the price of admission lowered, hundreds, thousands, then millions lined up.

'Let's do it,' Dad said, when I was in high school. By then, the world was falling into chaos. Half the country was depopulated. Commodity prices plunged. The threat of war and actual war were everywhere: conquests, re-conquests, endless slaughter. Those who could afford it left on the next flight to Svalbard. Humanity was abandoning the world and destroying itself.

Mom reached out and held Dad's hand.

'No,' she said. 'They think they can cheat death. But they died the minute they decided to abandon the real world for a simulation. So long as there's sin, there must be death. It is the measure by which life gains meaning.'

She was a lapsed Catholic who nonetheless yearned for the certainty of the Church, and her theology always seemed to me a bit cobbled together. But she believed that there was a right way to live, and a right way to die.

***

While Lucy is away at school, Carol and I search her room. Carol looks through her closet for pamphlets, books, and other physical tokens of contact with the dead. I log on to Lucy's computer.

Lucy is strong-willed but dutiful. Ever since she was a little girl, I've been telling her that she must prepare to resist the temptations of the dead. Only she can assure the continuity of our way of life in this abandoned world. She listens to me and nods.

I want to trust her.

But the dead are very clever with their propaganda. In the beginning, they sometimes sent metallic gray drones over our towns, scattering leaflets filled with messages purporting to be from our loved ones. We burned the leaflets and shot at the drones, and eventually, they stopped coming.

Then they tried to come at us through the wireless links between the towns, the electronic lifeline that sustained those who stayed behind and kept our shrinking communities from being completely isolated from each other. We had to vigilantly watch the networks for their insidious tendrils, always seeking an opening.

Lately, their efforts have turned to the children. The dead may have finally given up on us, but they are grasping for the next generation, for our future. As her father, I have a duty to protect Lucy from that which she does not yet understand.

The computer boots up slowly. It's a miracle that I've managed to keep it running for so long, years past the obsolescence planned by its manufacturer. I've replaced every component in it, some multiple times.

I scan for a list of files recently created or modified by Lucy, emails received, web pages retrieved. Most are schoolwork or innocent chatter with friends. The inter-settlement network, such as it is, shrinks daily. It's difficult to keep the radio towers that link town to town powered and operating, with so many people each year dying and simply giving up. It used to be possible for us to communicate with friends as far away as San Francisco, the packets of data skipping from town to town in between like stones across a pond.

But now, only less than a thousand computers are still reachable from here, none farther away than Maine. Someday we won't be able to scavenge the components to keep the computers running anymore, and we'll regress even further into the past.

Carol is already done with her search. She sits down on Lucy's bed to watch me.

'That was fast,' I say.

She shrugs. 'We'll never find anything. If she trusts us, she'll talk to us. If she doesn't, then we won't find what she wants hidden.'

Lately, I've detected more such fatalistic sentiments in Carol. It's as though she's getting tired, not as committed to the cause. I find myself constantly striving to rekindle her faith.

'Lucy is still young,' I tell her, 'too young to understand what she would have to give up in exchange for the false promises of the dead. I know you hate this spying, but we're trying to save her life.'

Carol looks at me, and eventually she sighs and nods.

I check the image files for hidden data. I check the disk for links to deleted files that might hold secret codes. I scan the web pages, looking for code words offering false promises.

I sigh with relief. She's clean.

***

I don't much like leaving Lowell these days. The world outside our fence grows ever more harsh and dangerous. Bears have come back to eastern Massachusetts. Every year, the forest grows denser, closer to the town line. Some claim to have seen wolves roaming in the woods too.

A year ago, Brad Lee and I had to go to Boston to find spare parts for the town's generator, housed in the old mill by the Merrimack River. We carried shotguns, protection against both the animals and the vandals who still scurried in urban ruins, living off of the last of the canned food. The surface of Mass Ave., deserted for thirty years, was full of cracks, tufts of grass and shrubs peeking out from them. The harsh New England winters, wielding seeping water and prying ice, had chipped away at the tall buildings around us, their windowless shells crumbling and rusting in the absence of artificial heat and regular maintenance.

Coming around a corner downtown, we surprised two of them huddled around a fire, which they fed with books and papers taken from the bookstore nearby. Even vandals needed warmth, and maybe they also delighted in destroying what was left of civilization.

The two crouched and growled at us, but made no move as Brad and I pointed our guns at them. I remember their thin legs and arms, their dirty faces, their bloodshot eyes full of hate and terror. But mostly, I remember their wrinkled faces and white hair. *Even the vandals are growing old*, I thought. *And they have no children.*

Brad and I backed away carefully. I was glad we didn't have to shoot anyone.

***

The summer I was eight and Laura eleven, my parents took us on a road trip through Arizona, New Mexico, and Texas. We drove along old highways and side roads, a tour of the monumental beauty of the Western deserts, filled with nostalgic, desolate ghost towns.

As we passed through the Indian reservations – Navajo, Zuni, Acoma, Laguna – Mom wanted to stop at every roadside shop to admire the traditional pottery. Laura and I gingerly stepped through the aisles, careful not to break anything.

Back in the car, Mom let me handle a small pot that she had bought. I turned it over and over in my hands, examining the rough white surface, the neat, clean, black geometric designs, and the bold outline of the hunched-over flute player with feathers coming out of his head.

'Amazing, isn't it?' Mom said. 'This wasn't made on a potter's wheel. The woman coiled it by hand, using the same techniques that have been passed down for generations in her family. She even dug for the clay in the same places that her great-grandmother used. She's keeping alive an ancient tradition, a way of life.'

The pot suddenly felt heavy in my hands, as though I could sense the weight of its generations of memory.

'That's just a story to drum up business,' Dad said, glancing at me in the rearview mirror. 'But it would be even sadder if the story were true. If you're doing things the exact same way as your ancestors, then your way of life is dead, and you've become a fossil, a performance for the entertainment of tourists.'

'She was not performing,' Mom said. 'You have no sense of what's really important in life, what's worth holding on to. There's more to being human than *progress*. You're as bad as those Singularity zealots.'

'Please don't argue anymore,' Laura said. 'Let's just get to the hotel and sit by the pool.'

***

Jack, Brad Lee's son, is at the door. He's shy and awkward, even though he has been coming by our house for months. I've known him since he was a baby, like I know all the children in town. There are so few of them left. The high school, operating out of the old Whistler House, has only twelve students.

'Hello,' he mumbles, looking at the floor. 'Lucy and I need to work on our report.' I step aside to let him pass on his way upstairs to Lucy's room.

I don't need to remind him about the rules: door to the bedroom open, at least three of their four feet on the carpet at all times. I hear the indistinct sounds of their chatter and occasional laughter.

There is a kind of innocence to their courtship that was absent from my youth. Without the endless blast of cynical sexuality from TV and the real internet, children can stay children longer.

***

There weren't many doctors left near the end. Those of us who wanted to stay behind gathered into small communities, circling the wagons against the marauding bands of vandals who gorged themselves on pleasures of the flesh as the Uploaded left the physical world behind. I never got to finish college.

Mom lingered in her sickness for months. She was bedridden and drifted in and out of consciousness, her body pumped full of drugs that numbed her pain. We took turns sitting by her, holding her hand. When she had good days, temporary lulls of lucidity, there was only one topic of conversation.

'No,' Mom said, wheezing. 'You must promise me. This is important. I've lived a real life, and I will die a real death. I will *not* be turned into a recording. There are worse things than death.'

'If you Upload,' Dad said, 'you'll still have a choice. They can suspend your consciousness, or even erase it, if you don't like it after you try it. But if you don't Upload, you'll be gone forever. There's no room for regret or return.'

'If I do what you want,' Mom said, 'I will be gone. There is no way to come back to this, to the real world. I will not be simulated by a bunch of electrons.'

'Please stop,' Laura pleaded with Dad. 'You're hurting her. Why can't you leave her alone?'

Mom's moments of lucidity came further and further apart.

Then that night: waking up to the sound of the front door closing, looking outside the window to see the shuttle on the lawn, tumbling down the stairs.

They were carrying Mom into the shuttle on a stretcher. Dad stood by the door of the grey vehicle, only a little bigger than a van, Everlasting, Inc. painted on its side.

'Stop!' I shouted over the sound of the shuttle's engines.

'There's no time,' Dad said. His eyes were bloodshot. He hadn't slept for days. None of us had. 'They have to do it now before it's too late. I can't lose her.'

We struggled. He held me in a tight hug and wrestled me to the ground. 'It's *her* choice, not yours!' I screamed into his ear. He only held me tighter. I fought to free myself. 'Laura, stop them!'

Laura covered her eyes. 'Stop fighting, all of you! She would have wanted all of you to stop.'

I hated her for speaking as though Mom was already gone.

The shuttle closed its door and lifted into the air.

***

Dad left for Svalbard two days later. I refused to speak to him until the end.

'I'm going to join her now,' he said. 'Come as soon as you can.'

'You killed her,' I said. He flinched at the words, and I was glad.

***

Jack has asked Lucy to the prom. I'm pleased that the kids have decided to hold one. It shows that they are serious about keeping alive the stories and traditions they've heard from their parents, legends from a world they have only experienced vicariously in old videos and old pictures.

We struggle to maintain what we can of the life from before: put on old plays, read old books, celebrate the old holidays, sing old songs. We've had to give up so much. Old recipes have had to be adapted for limited ingredients, old hopes and dreams shrunken to fit within tightened horizons. But every deprivation has also brought us closer as a community, to hold on tighter to our traditions.

Lucy wants to make her own dress. Carol suggests that she look through her old dresses first. 'I have some formals left from when I was just a little older than you.'

Lucy is not interested. 'They're old,' she says.

'They're classic,' I tell her.

But Lucy is adamant. She cuts up her old dresses, curtains, scavenged tablecloths, and trades with the other girls for bits of fabric: silk, chiffon, taffeta, lace, plain cotton. She flips through Carol's old magazines, looking for inspiration.

Lucy is a good seamstress, far better than Carol. The children are all skilled in trades long thought obsolete in the world I grew up in: knitting, woodworking, planting and hunting. Carol and I had to rediscover and learn these things from books when we were already adults, adapting to a suddenly changed world. But for the children, it is all they have known. They are natives here.

All the students at the high school have spent the last few months doing research in the Textile History Museum, investigating the possibility of weaving our own cloth, preparing for a time when the decaying ruins of the cities would run out of usable clothes for us to salvage. There is some poetic justice in this: Lowell, which once rose on the back of the textile industry, must now rediscover those lost arts on our gentle slide back down the technology curve.

***

A week after Dad left, we received an email from Mom:

> I was wrong.
>
> Sometimes, I'm nostalgic and sad. I miss you, my children, and the world we left behind. But I'm ecstatic most of the time, often incredulous.
>
> There are hundreds of millions of us here, but there is no crowding. In this house there are countless mansions. Each of our minds inhabits its own world, and each of us has infinite space and infinite time.
>
> How can I explain it to you? I can only use the same words so many others have already used. In my old existence, I felt life but dimly and from a distance, cushioned, constrained, tied down by the body. But now I am free, a bare soul exposed to the full tides of eternal Life.
>
> How can speech compare to the intimacy of sharing with your father psyche to psyche? How can hearing about how much he loved me compare to actually feeling his love? To truly understand another person, to experience the texture of his mind – it is glorious.
>
> They tell me that this sensation is called hyperreality. But I don't care what it is called. I was wrong to cling so tightly to the comforts of an old shell made of flesh and blood. We, the real us, have always been patterns of electrons cascading across the abyss, the nothingness between atoms. What difference does it make if those electrons are in a brain or silicon chips?
>
> Life is sacred and eternal. But our old way of life was unsustainable. We demanded too much of our planet, of sacrifices made by every other living thing. I once thought that an unavoidable aspect of our existence, but it isn't. Now, with the oil tankers aground, the cars and trucks still, the fields fallow and factories silent, the living world that we had made almost extinct will return.
>
> Humanity is not a cancer of the planet. We simply needed to transcend the demands of our inefficient bodies, machines no longer adequate for their task. How many consciousnesses will now live in this new world, pure creatures of electric spirit and weightless thought? There are no limits.
>
> Come join us. We cannot wait to embrace you again.

Laura cried as she read it. But I felt nothing. This wasn't my mother speaking. The real Mom knew that what really mattered in life was the authenticity of this messy existence, the constant yearning for closeness to another despite imperfect understanding, the pain and suffering of our flesh.

She taught me that our mortality makes us human. The limited time given to each of us makes what we do meaningful. We die to make place for our children, and through our children a piece of us lives on, the only form of immortality that is real.

It is *this* world, the world we were meant to live in, that anchors us and demands our presence, not the imagined landscapes of a computed illusion.

This was a simulacrum of her, a recording of propaganda, a temptation into nihilism.

***

Carol and I met on one of my earliest scavenging trips. Her family had been hiding in the basement of their house on Beacon Hill. A gang of vandals found them and killed her father and brother. They were about to start on her when we showed up. I killed a man-shaped animal that day, and I'm not sorry about it.

We brought her back to Lowell, and though she was seventeen, for days, she clung to me and would not let me out of her sight. Even when sleeping, she wanted me to be there, holding her hand.

'Maybe my family made a mistake,' she said one day. 'We would have been better off if we had Uploaded. There's nothing but death left here now.'

I didn't argue with her. I let her follow me around as I went about my chores. I showed her how we were keeping the generator running, how we treated each other with respect, how we rescued old books and held on to old routines. There was still civilization in this world, kept alive like a flame. People did die, but people were also born. Life went on, sweet, joyful, authentic life.

Then one day, she kissed me.

'There's also you in this world,' she said. 'And that is enough.'

'No, not enough,' I said. 'We will also bring new life here.'

***

Tonight is the night.

Jack is at the door. He looks good in that tuxedo. It's the same one I wore to my prom. They'll play the same songs too, pumping the music from an old laptop and speakers on their last legs.

Lucy is splendid in her dress: white with black print, cut in a simple pattern, but very elegant. The skirt is wide and full-length, draping gracefully to the floor. Carol did her hair, curls with a hint of glitter. She looks glamorous, with a hint of childish playfulness.

I take pictures with a camera, one that still mostly works.

I wait until I'm sure I have my voice under control. 'You have no idea how glad I am to see young people dancing, the way we used to.'

She kisses me on the cheek. 'Goodbye, Dad.' There are tears in her eyes. And that makes everything go blurry for me again.

Carol and Lucy embrace for a moment. Carol wipes her eyes. 'You're all set.'

'Thanks, Mom.'

Then Lucy turns to Jack. 'Let's go.'

Jack will take her to the Lowell Four Seasons on his bicycle. It's the best that can be done since we've been without gasoline for many years. Lucy gingerly settles onto the top tube, sitting sideways, one hand holding her dress up. Jack wraps her in his arms protectively as he grabs the handles. And they are off, wobbling down the street.

'Have fun,' I yell after them.

***

Laura's betrayal was the hardest to take.

'I thought you were going to help me and Carol with the baby,' I said.

'What kind of world is this to bring a child into?' Laura said.

'And you think things will be better if you go there, where there are no children, no new life?'

'We've tried to keep this going for fifteen years, and every year it becomes harder and harder to believe in this charade. Maybe we were wrong. We should adapt.'

'It's only a charade when you've lost faith,' I said.

'Faith in what?'

'In humanity, in our way of life.'

'I don't want to fight our parents anymore. I just want us to be together again, a family.'

'Those *things* aren't our parents. They are imitation algorithms. You've always wanted to avoid conflict, Laura. But some conflicts cannot be avoided. Our parents died when Dad lost faith, when he couldn't resist the false promises made by machines.'

At the end of the road into the woods was a little clearing, grassy, full of wildflowers. A shuttle was waiting in the middle. Laura stepped into the open door.

Another life lost.

***

The children have permission to stay out until midnight. Lucy had asked me not to volunteer as a chaperone, and I complied, conceding her this bit of space for the night.

Carol is restless. She tries to read but she's been on the same page for an hour.

'Don't worry.' I try to comfort her.

She tries to smile at me, but she can't hide her anxiety. She looks up past my shoulder at the clock on the living room wall.

I glance back too. 'Doesn't it feel later than eleven?'

'No,' Carol says. 'Not at all. I don't know what you mean.'

Her voice is too eager, almost desperate. There's a hint of fear in her eyes. She's close to panicking.

I open the door of the house and step into the dark street. The sky has grown clearer over the years, and many more stars are now visible. But I'm looking for the Moon. It's not in the right place.

I come back into the house and go into the bedroom. My old watch, one that I no longer wear because there are so few occasions when being on time matters, is in the nightstand drawer. I pull it out. It's almost one in the morning. Someone had tampered with the living room clock.

Carol stands in the door to the bedroom. The light is behind her so I can't see her face.

'What have you done?' I ask. I'm not angry, just disappointed.

'She can't talk to you. She doesn't think you'll listen.'

Now the anger rises in me like hot bile.

'Where are they?'

Carol shakes her head, saying nothing.

I remember the way Lucy said goodbye to me. I remember the way she walked carefully out to Jack's bike, holding up her voluminous skirt, a skirt so wide that she could hide anything under it, a change of clothing and comfortable shoes for the woods. I remember Carol saying, 'You're all set.'

'It's too late,' Carol says. 'Laura is coming to pick them up.'

'Get out of the way. I have to save her.'

'Save her for what?' Carol is suddenly furious. She does not move. 'This is a play, a joke, a re-enactment of something that never was. Did you go to your prom on a *bicycle*? Did you play only songs that your parents listened to when they were kids? Did you grow up thinking that scavenging would be the only profession? Our way of life is long gone, dead, finished!

'What will you have her do when this house falls apart in thirty years? What will she do when the last bottle of aspirin is gone, the last steel pot rusted through? Will you condemn her and her children to a life of picking through our garbage heaps, sliding down the technology ladder year after year until they've lost all the progress made by the human race in the last five thousand years?'

I don't have time to debate her. Gently, but firmly, I put my hands on her shoulders, ready to push her aside.

'I will stay with you,' Carol says. 'I will always stay with you because I love you so much that I'm not afraid of death. But she is a child. She should have a chance for something new.'

Strength seems to drain from my arms. 'You have it backwards.' I look into her eyes, willing her to have faith again. 'Her life gives our lives meaning.'

Her body suddenly goes limp, and she sinks to the floor, sobbing silently.

'Let her go,' Carol says, quietly. 'Just let her go.'

'I can't give up,' I tell Carol. 'I'm human.'

***

I pump the pedals furiously once I'm past the gate in the fence. The cone of light cast by the flashlight jumps around as I try to hold it against the handlebars. But I know this road into the woods well. It leads to the clearing where Laura once stepped into that shuttle.

Bright light in the distance, and the sound of engines revving up.

I take out my gun and fire a few shots into the air.

The sound of the engines dies down.

I emerge into the opening in the woods, under a sky full of bright, cold, pinprick stars. I jump off the bike and let it fall by the side of the path. The shuttle is in the middle of the clearing. Lucy and Jack, now in casual clothes, stand in the open doorway of the shuttle.

'Lucy, sweetheart, come back out of there.'

'Dad, I'm sorry. I'm going.'

'No, you are not.'

An electronic simulation of Laura's voice comes out of the shuttle's speakers. 'Let her go, brother. She deserves to have a chance to see what you refuse to see. Or, better yet, come with us. We've all missed you.'

I ignore her, *it*. 'Lucy, there is no future there. What the machines promise you is not real. There are no children there, no hope, only a timeless, changeless, simulated existence as fragments of a machine.'

'We have children now,' the copy of Laura's voice says. 'We've figured out how to create children of the mind, natives of the digital world. You should come and meet your nephews and nieces. *You* are the one clinging to a changeless existence. This is the next step in our evolution.'

'You can experience nothing when you are not human.' I shake my head. I shouldn't take its bait and debate a machine.

'If you leave,' I tell Lucy, 'you'll die a death with no meaning. The dead will have won. I can't let that happen.'

I raise my gun. The barrel points at her. I will not lose my child to the dead.

Jack tries to step in front of her, but Lucy pushes him away. Her eyes are full of sorrow, and the light from inside the shuttle frames her face and golden hair like an angel.

Suddenly I see how much she looks like my mother. Mom's features, having passed through me, have come alive again on my daughter. This is how life is meant to be lived. Grandparents, parents, children, each generation stepping out of the way of the next, an eternal striving towards the future, to progress.

I think about how Mom's choice was taken away from her, how she was not allowed to die as a human, how she was devoured by the dead, how she became a part of their ceaselessly looping, mindless recordings. My mother's face, from memory, is superimposed onto the face of my daughter, my sweet, innocent, foolish Lucy.

I tighten my grip on the gun.

'Dad,' Lucy says, calmly, her face as steady as Mom's all those years ago. 'This is *my* choice. Not yours.'

***

It's morning by the time Carol steps into the clearing. Warm sunlight through the leaves dapples the empty circle of grass. Dewdrops hang from the tips of the grass blades, in each a miniature, suspended, vision of the world. Birdsong fills the waking silence. My bike is still on the ground by the path where I left it.

Carol sits down by me without speaking. I put my arm around her shoulders and pull her close to me. I don't know what she's thinking, but it's enough for us to sit together like this, our bodies pressed together, keeping each other warm. There's no need for words. We look around at this pristine world, a garden inherited from the dead.

We have all the time in the world.

51

My Father's Head

(2014)

Okwiri Oduor

I had meant to summon my father only long enough to see what his head looked like, but now he was here and I did not know how to send him back.

It all started the Thursday that Father Ignatius came from Immaculate Conception in Kitgum. The old women wore their Sunday frocks, and the old men plucked garlands of bougainvillea from the fence and stuck them in their breast pockets. One old man would not leave the dormitory because he could not find his shikwarusi, and when I coaxed and badgered, he patted his hair and said: 'My God, do you want the priest from Uganda to think that I look like this every day?'

I arranged chairs beneath the avocado tree in the front yard, and the old people sat down and practised their smiles. A few people who did not live at the home came too, like the woman who hawked candy in the Stagecoach bus to Mathari North, and the man whose one-roomed house was a kindergarten in the daytime and a brothel in the evening, and the woman whose illicit brew had blinded five people in January.

Father Ignatius came riding on the back of a bodaboda, and after everyone had dropped a coin in his hat, he gave the bodaboda man 50 shillings and the bodaboda man said, 'Praise God,' and then rode back the way he had come.

Father Ignatius took off his coat and sat down in the chair that was marked, 'Father Ignatius Okello, New Chaplain', and the old people gave him the smiles they had been practising, smiles that melted like ghee, that oozed through the corners of their lips and dribbled onto their laps long after the thing that was being smiled about went rancid in the air.

Father Ignatius said, 'The Lord be with you', and the people said, 'And also with you', and then they prayed and they sang and they had a feast; dipping bread slices in tea and, when the drops fell on the cuffs of their woollen sweaters, sucking at them with their streamy, cinnamon tongues.

Father Ignatius' maiden sermon was about love: love your neighbour as you love yourself, that kind of self-deprecating thing. The old people had little use for love, and although they gave Father Ignatius an ingratiating smile, what they really wanted to know was what type of place Kitgum was, and if it was true that the Bagisu people were savage cannibals.

What I wanted to know was what type of person Father Ignatius thought he was, instructing others to distribute their love like this or like that, as though one could measure love on weights, pack it inside glass jars and place it on shelves for the neighbours to pick as they pleased. As though one could look at it and say, 'Now see: I have ten loves in total. Let me save three for my country and give all the rest to my neighbours.'

It must have been the way that Father Ignatius filled his mug – until the tea ran over the clay rim and down the stool leg and soaked into his canvas shoe – that got me thinking about my own father. One moment I was listening to tales of Acholi valour, and the next, I was stringing together images of my father, making his limbs move and his lips spew words, so that in the end, he was a marionette and my memories of him were only scenes in a theatrical display.

Even as I showed Father Ignatius to his chambers, cleared the table, put the chairs back inside, took my purse, and dragged myself to Odeon to get a matatu to Uthiru, I thought about the millet-coloured freckle in my father's eye, and the 50-cent coins he always forgot in his coat pockets, and the way, each Saturday morning, men knocked on our front door and said things like, 'Johnson, you have to come now; the water pipe has burst and we are filling our glasses with shit,' and, 'Johnson, there is no time to put on clothes even; just come the way you are. The maid gave birth in the night and flushed the baby down the toilet.'

Every day after work, I bought an ear of street-roasted maize and chewed it one kernel at a time, and, when I reached the house, I wiggled out of the muslin dress and wore dungarees and drank a cup of masala chai. Then I carried my father's toolbox to the bathroom. I chiselled out old broken tiles from the wall, and they fell onto my boots, and the dust rose from them and exploded in the flaring tongues of fire lapping through chinks in the stained glass.

This time, as I did all those things, I thought of the day I sat at my father's feet and he scooped a handful of groundnuts and rubbed them between his palms, chewed them, and then fed the mush to me. I was of a curious age then: old enough to chew with my own teeth, yet young enough to desire that hot, masticated love, love that did not need to be indoctrinated or measured in cough-syrup caps.

The Thursday Father Ignatius came from Kitgum, I spent the entire night on my stomach on the sitting-room floor, drawing my father. In my mind I could see his face, see the lines around his mouth, the tiny blobs of light in his irises, the crease at the part where his ear joined his temple. I could even see the thick line of sweat and oil on his shirt collar, the little brown veins that broke off from the main stream of dirt and ran down on their own.

I could see all these things, yet no matter what I did, his head refused to appear within the borders of the paper. I started off with his feet and worked my way up and in the end my father's head popped out of the edges of the paper and onto scuffed linoleum and plastic magnolias and the wet soles of bathroom slippers.

I showed Bwibo some of the drawings. Bwibo was the cook at the old people's home, with whom I had formed an easy camaraderie.

'My God!' Bwibo muttered, flipping through them. 'Simbi, this is abnormal.'

The word 'abnormal' came out crumbly, and it broke over the sharp edge of the table and became clods of loam on the plastic floor covering. Bwibo rested her head on her palm, and the bell sleeves of her cream-coloured caftan swelled as though there were pumpkins stacked inside them.

I told her what I had started to believe, that perhaps my father had had a face but no head at all. And even if my father had had a head, I would not have seen it: people's heads were not a thing that one often saw. One looked at a person, and what one saw was their face: a regular face-shaped face, that shrouded a regular head-shaped head. If the face was remarkable, one looked twice. But what was there to draw one's eyes to the banalities of another's head? Most times when one looked at a person, one did not even see their head there at all.

Bwibo stood over the waist-high jiko, poured cassava flour into a pot of bubbling water and stirred it with a cooking oar. 'Child,' she said, 'how do you know that the man in those drawings is your father? He has no head at all, no face.'

'I recognize his clothes. The red corduroys that he always paired with yellow shirts.'

Bwibo shook her head. 'It is only with a light basket that someone can escape the rain.'

It was that time of day when the old people fondled their wooden beads and snorted off to sleep in between incantations. I allowed them a brief, bashful siesta, long enough for them to believe that they had recited the entire rosary. Then I tugged at the ropes and the lunch bells chimed. The old people sat eight to a table, and with their mouths filled with ugali, sour lentils and okra soup, said things like, 'Do not buy chapati from Kadima's Kiosk – Kadima's wife sits on the dough and charms it with her buttocks,' or, 'Did I tell you about Wambua, the one whose cow chewed a child because the child would not stop wailing?'

In the afternoon, I emptied the bedpans and soaked the old people's feet in warm water and baking soda, and when they trooped off to mass I took my purse and went home.

The Christmas before the cane tractor killed my father, he drank his tea from plates and fried his eggs on the lids of coffee jars, and he retrieved his Yamaha drum-set from a shadowy, lizardy place in the back of the house and sat on the veranda and smoked and beat the drums until his knuckles bled.

One day he took his stool and hand-held radio and went to the veranda, and I sat at his feet, undid his laces and peeled off his gummy socks. He wiggled his toes about. They smelt slightly fetid, like sour cream.

My father smoked and listened to narrations of famine undulating deeper into the Horn of Africa, and, when the clock chimed eight o'clock, he turned the knob and listened to the death news. It was not long before his ears caught the name of someone he knew. He choked on the smoke trapped in his throat.

My father said: 'Did you hear that? Sospeter has gone! Sospeter, the son of Milkah, who taught Agriculture in Mirere Secondary. My God, I am telling you, everyone is going. Even me, you shall hear me on the death news very soon.'

I brought him his evening cup of tea. He smashed his cigarette against the veranda, then he slowly brought the cup to his lips. The cup was filled just the way he liked it, filled until the slightest trembling would have his fingers and thighs scalded.

My father took a sip of his tea and said: 'Sospeter was like a brother to me. Why did I have to learn of his death like this, over the radio?'

Later, my father lay on the fold-away sofa, and I sat on the stool watching him, afraid that, if I looked away, he would go too. It was the first time I imagined his death, the first time I mourned.

And yet it was not my father I was mourning. I was mourning the image of myself inside the impossible aura of my father's death. I was imagining what it all would be like: the death news would say that my father had drowned in a cesspit, and people would stare at me as though I were a monitor lizard trapped inside a manhole in the street. I imagined that I would be wearing my green dress when I got the news – the one with red gardenias embroidered in its bodice – and people would come and pat my shoulder and give me warm Coca Cola in plastic cups and say: 'I put my sorrow in a basket and brought it here as soon as I heard. How else would your father's spirit know that I am innocent of his death?'

Bwibo had an explanation as to why I could not remember the shape of my father's head.

She said: 'Although everyone has a head behind their face, some show theirs easily; they turn their back on you and their head is all you can see. Your father was a good man and good men never show you their heads; they show you their faces.'

Perhaps she was right. Even the day my father's people telephoned to say that a cane tractor had flattened him on the road to Shibale, no-one said a thing about having seen his head. They described the rest of his body with a measured delicacy: how his legs were strewn across the road, sticky and shiny with fresh tar, and how one foot remained inside his tyre sandal, pounding the pedal of his bicycle, and how cane juice filled his mouth and soaked the collar of his polyester shirt, and how his face had a patient serenity, even as his eyes burst and rolled in the rain puddles.

And instead of weeping right away when they said all those things to me, I had wondered if my father really had come from a long line of obawami, and if his people would bury him seated in his grave, with a string of royal cowries round his neck.

'In any case,' Bwibo went on, 'what more is there to think about your father, eh? That milk spilled a long time ago, and it has curdled on the ground.'

I spent the day in the dormitories, stripping beds, sunning mattresses, scrubbing PVC mattress pads. One of the old men kept me company. He told me how he came to spend his sunset years at the home – in August 1998 he was at the station waiting to board the evening train back home to Mombasa. When the bomb went off at the American Embassy, the police trawled the city and arrested every man of Arab extraction. Because he was 72 and already rapidly unravelling into senility, they dumped him at the old people's home, and he had been there ever since.

'Did your people not come to claim you?' I asked, bewildered.

The old man snorted. 'My people?'

'Everyone has people that belong to them.'

The old man laughed. 'Only the food you have already eaten belongs to you.'

Later, the old people sat in drooping clumps in the yard. Bwibo and I watched from the back steps of the kitchen. In the grass, ants devoured a squirming caterpillar. The dog's nose, a translucent pink doodled with green veins, twitched. Birds raced each other over the frangipani. One tripped over the power line and smashed its head on the moss-covered electricity pole.

Wasps flew low over the grass. A lizard crawled over the lichen that choked a pile of timber. The dog licked the inside of its arm. A troupe of royal butterfly dancers flitted over the row of lilies, their colourful gauze dancing skirts trembling to the rumble of an inaudible drumbeat. The dog lay on its side in the grass, smothering the squirming caterpillar and the chewing ants. The dog's nipples were little pellets of goat shit stuck with spit onto its furry underside.

Bwibo said, 'I can help you remember the shape of your father's head.'

I said, 'Now what type of mud is this you have started speaking?'

Bwibo licked her index finger and held it solemnly in the air. 'I swear, Bible red! I can help you and I can help you.'

Let me tell you: one day you will renounce your exile, and you will go back home, and your mother will take out the finest china, and your father will slaughter a sprightly cockerel for you, and the neighbours will bring some potluck, and your sister will wear her navy-blue PE wrapper, and your brother will eat with a spoon instead of squelching rice and soup through the spaces between his fingers.

And you, you will have to tell them stories about places not-here, about people that soaked their table napkins in Jik bleach and talked about London as though London were a place one could reach by hopping onto an Akamba bus and driving by Nakuru and Kisumu and Kakamega and finding themselves there.

You will tell your people about men that did not slit melons up into slices but split them into halves and ate each of the halves out with a spoon, about women that held each other's hands around street lamps in town and skipped about, showing snippets of grey Mother's Union bloomers as they sang:

> Kijembe ni kikali, param-param
>
> Kilikata mwalimu, param-param

You think that your people belong to you, that they will always have a place for you in their minds and their hearts. You think that your people will always look forward to your return.

Maybe the day you go back home to your people you will have to sit in a wicker chair on the veranda and smoke alone because, although they may have wanted to have you back, no-one really meant for you to stay.

My father was slung over the wicker chair on the veranda, just like in the old days, smoking and watching the hand-held radio. The death news rose from the radio, and it became a mist, hovering low, clinging to the cold glass of the sitting-room window.

My father's shirt flapped in the wind, and tendrils of smoke snapped before his face. He whistled to himself. At first the tune was a faceless, pitiful thing, like an old bottle that someone found on the path and kicked all the way home. Then the tune caught fragments of other tunes inside it, and it lost its free-spirited falling and rising.

My father had a head. I could see it now that I had the mind to look for it. His head was shaped like a butternut squash. Perhaps that was the reason I had forgotten all about it: it was a horrible, disconcerting thing to look at.

My father had been a plumber. His fingernails were still rimmed with dregs from the drainage pipes he tinkered about in, and his boots still squished with ugali from nondescript kitchen sinks. Watching him, I remembered the day he found a gold chain tangled in the fibres of someone's excrement, and he wiped the excrement off against his corduroys and sold the chain at Nagin Pattni, and that evening, hoisted high upon his shoulders, he brought home the red Greatwall television. He set it in the corner of the sitting room and said, 'Just look how it shines, as though it is not filled with shit inside.'

And every day I plucked a bunch of carnations and snipped their stems diagonally and stood them in a glass bowl and placed the glass bowl on top of the television so that my father would not think of shit while he watched the evening news.

I said to Bwibo, 'We have to send him back.'

Bwibo said, 'The liver you have asked for is the one you eat.'

'But I did not really want him back, I just wanted to see his head.'

Bwibo said, 'In the end, he came back to you and that should account for something, should it not?'

Perhaps my father's return accounted for nothing but the fact that the house already smelt like him – of burnt lentils and melting fingernails and the bark of bitter quinine and the sourness of wet rags dabbing at broken cigarette tips.

I threw things at my father: garlic, incense, salt, pork, and when none of that repelled him, I asked Father Ignatius to bless the house. He brought a vial of holy water, and he sprinkled it in every room, sprinkled it over my father. Father Ignatius said that I would need further protection, but that I would have to write him a cheque first.

One day I was buying roast maize in the street corner when the vendor said to me, 'Is it true what the vegetable-sellers are saying, that you finally found a man to love you but will not let him through your door?'

51 My Father's Head

That evening, I invited my father inside. We sat side by side on the fold-away sofa, and watched as a fly crawled up the dusty screen between the grill and the window glass. It buzzed a little as it climbed. The ceiling fan creaked, and it threw shadows across the corridor floor. The shadows leapt high and mounted doors and peered through the air vents in the walls.

The wind upset a cup. For a few seconds, the cup lay lopsided on the windowsill. Then it rolled on its side and scurried across the floor. I pulled at the latch, fastened the window shut. The wind grazed the glass with its wet lips. It left a trail of dust and saliva, and the saliva dribbled down slowly to the edge of the glass. The wind had a slobbery mouth. Soon its saliva had covered the entire window, covered it until the rosemary brushwood outside the window became blurry. The jacaranda outside stooped low, scratched the roof. In the next room, doors and windows banged.

I looked at my father. He was something at once strange and familiar, at once enthralling and frightening – he was the brittle, chipped handle of a ceramic tea mug, and he was the cold yellow stare of an owl.

My father touched my hand ever so lightly, so gently, as though afraid that I would flinch and pull my hand away. I did not dare lift my eyes, but he touched my chin and tipped it upwards so that I had no choice but to look at him.

I remembered a time when I was a little child, when I stared into my father's eyes in much the same way. In them I saw shapes: a drunken, talentless conglomerate of circles and triangles and squares. I had wondered how those shapes had got inside my father's eyes. I had imagined that he sat down at the table, cut out glossy figures from colouring books, slathered them with glue, and stuck them inside his eyes so that they made rummy, haphazard collages in his irises.

My father said, 'Would you happen to have some tea, Simbi?'

I brought some, and he asked if his old friend Pius Obote still came by the house on Saturdays, still brought groundnut soup and pumpkin leaves and a heap of letters that he had picked up from the post office.

I said, 'Pius Obote has been dead for four years.'

My father pushed his cup away. He said, 'If you do not want me here drinking your tea, just say so, instead of killing-killing people with your mouth.'

My father was silent for a while, grieving this man Pius Obote whose name had always made me think of knees banging against each other. Pius Obote used to blink a lot. Once, he fished inside his pocket for a biro and instead withdrew a chicken bone, still red and moist.

My father said to me, 'I have seen you. You have offered me tea. I will go now.'

'Where will you go?'

'I will find a job in a town far from here. Maybe Eldoret. I used to have people there.'

I said, 'Maybe you could stay here for a couple of days, Baba.'

52

The Nominee

(2018)

Curtis Sittenfeld

The journalist was born in 1964, which is to say she's seventeen years younger than I am. She has, starting in 1992, interviewed me several dozen times – she was at *The San Francisco Chronicle* when I met her, then moved to *The Washington Post*, and for the last eight years has been at *The New York Times* – and while we aren't friends, she reminds me of a neighbor or cousin; we didn't exactly choose each other, but we are ineluctably part of each other's lives.

What I appreciate about her is the blazing, undeniable intelligence that manifests itself in her ability, in our conversations, to recall minutiae from a transportation bill I sponsored in the Senate, or a 1994 speech I gave in Stockholm as First Lady; in her observations, appearing in her articles, of the perfect colorful detail from a state fair or pancake breakfast that I myself, sitting amidst it, missed; and in her snapping, spontaneous sense of humor. Once, at a signing ceremony for a greenhouse-gas-emissions law, when the president inadvertently referred to 'hair pollution' instead of 'air pollution,' my eyes landed on the journalist's, and I had to look away and bite my tongue. When we spoke after the ceremony, she began by saying, 'Like when you spill conditioner in the shower?' and I replied, 'I was actually thinking about a certain perm I got in the mid-eighties.'

The truth is that when she interviews me, I feel an alertness, a welcome kind of challenge, that's deeply satisfying. I've sometimes thought that the reason people who aren't particularly bright don't care for people who are is the hunch among the former that the latter speak to one another in code. Which we do: brain to brain, with an explanation-dispensing briskness, a shared understanding of subtext. I would never publicly admit this, least of all to her, but I believe the journalist is worthy of interviewing me in a way many kinder reporters are not.

What I care for least about the journalist is the sense of entitlement she demonstrates in small and large ways. Small: I never witness it, but according to my staff, she's a notorious pain about the logistics we've arranged for the press corps in a manner no print journalist from anywhere other than *The Times* would dare to be; she complains about which hotel room she's been assigned, or where she's sitting on the plane or bus.

Large: I believe she's quite sexist and either is blind to it or, more likely, sees herself as impervious, what with her fancy education, her cynicism, and her job at the cultural nexus of our post-everything society. Over and over, year in and year out, she asks me questions she'd never ask a man running for public office, a man elected to public office, a male senator or secretary of state or presidential candidate: Who designed the pantsuit I wore to the State of the Union? How has my husband influenced my foreign-policy views, stance on minimum wage, and opinion of vegans? Do I consider my marriage to be a good one? Is the country ready for a president who's also a grandmother? And always – always – some variation on this: Why do so many voters, even ones who admire my record, have difficulty connecting with me? Why do the American people find me fundamentally unlikable?

The journalist cushions her rhetoric. She says, *Some people say…* or *There's concern that…*, as if she is a mere observer of the questions' perpetuation. She then muses over the questions, and my responses, in her articles, which have become longer, less newsy, and more leisurely and reflective as she has achieved greater professional success. Granted, it is her editors who conjure the headlines and decide upon the accompanying art: a caricature of me with eyes and mouth opened so widely I look deranged, possibly about to devour a small child; or a photograph shot close up then magnified in such a way that every line on my face is a ravine, even beneath a visibly massive quantity of powdery foundation. However, I hold the journalist accountable for steering the packaging. The words in the headlines are someone else's, but it is she who has written the original sentences resulting in a magazine cover asking (with prominent bags beneath my eyes, no less), FRONTRUNNER FATIGUE?

At this point, I expect to be burned by the journalist. No matter how friendly our encounter, how personal, even, I will at best be irritated by what she writes. Years ago, when her child was a toddler, I found myself describing the bribing-with-Skittles method of toilet-training I'd used with my own daughter; a few days later, I read the journalist's borderline defamatory article about the controversial, and unprofitable, real-estate investments my husband and I had made in the late seventies. I might be irritated while recognizing that a piece does more harm than good, or I might be irritated *and* know it will lose me votes. Nevertheless, right now, in this moment, in July 2016, in Philadelphia, Pennsylvania, deep in the bowels of the Wells Fargo Center, in the minutes before I go onstage, she – the journalist – and the photographer accompanying her are the only media in the greenroom. My husband is here, our daughter and son-in-law and grandchildren, their nanny, many members of my campaign staff – my political director and communications director and media consultant and chief strategist, a handful of policy advisors – as well as my closest friends, among them my college roommate and the woman who was the second female partner at the law firm where, in 1979, I became the first. And of course our own photographer and videographer are here, the ones who chronicle the version of the narrative I not only prefer but believe to be true. Apart from the journalist and her photographer, however, there is no press.

'Madam Secretary,' the journalist says, 'how are you feeling?'

'I feel great,' I say. When I smile – my smile, of course, has been compared to that of a vulture and a hag, that of Lady Macbeth and Cruella de Vil and Joker from Batman – she smiles back.

'You've talked about this ad nauseam, obviously,' the journalist says, 'but now that it's really, officially happening – what's it like to be the first major party female nominee for president of the United States of America?'

I feel the way you felt at your high school graduation, I think. *It's anticlimactic. We've been marking time, waiting for this, since April 2015, right? Or since 2007? Or perhaps since 1992 or 1969 or 1789? But I also know some specific instant tonight will seize me, will catch me off-guard in spite of myself, and I'll be struck by the enormity of the situation and probably tear up, thereby launching a thousand articles about gender and crying.*

Aloud I say, 'I've been preparing for this moment for my entire life. I'm confident, I'm humbled, and I'm very optimistic about the future of our country.'

In 2002, when I was a senator and the journalist was at *The Washington Post*, she interviewed me in a hotel suite in San Francisco on a day on which I'd first traveled to meet the survivors of a tornado in Oklahoma and would spend the evening at a million-dollar fundraising dinner in Pacific Heights. In the suite's living room, we sat facing each other in armchairs a few feet apart; her recorder was set on a small round glass table to my left. Also in the room were my deputy chief of staff and two aides. My Secret Service agents stood outside the suite's exterior door.

The journalist has dark, short hair, and both of us were wearing pantsuits, mine navy and hers maroon (Ralph Lauren, though I'm speaking only for myself here). We'd been talking for about ten minutes, and my communications director had promised the journalist fifteen more, though I was prepared to go to twenty or even twentyfive.

'With regard to recent comments made by your colleagues on the Senate Armed Services Committee – ' she began, and then her torso pitched forward and she vomited partly onto her lap, partly onto the floor, and partly onto my lap. Although it happened quickly, some impulse had told me to cup my hands together, and a portion of her vomit, which was plentiful and dark tan in color, also landed in this ad hoc receptacle. (I've always suspected she'd recently eaten curried tuna salad; I have, since 2002, never eaten curried tuna salad.) The journalist raised her head, and her expression was so stricken – a bit of vomit clung to her lips – that truly, I felt far more concerned about her than me. 'Oh, my God,' she said, and her face had gone pale. 'I'm so sorry.'

'Well, I *am* a mother,' I said, 'so it's not the first time. Do you think there's more coming?' Already my deputy chief of staff had sprung up and was approaching us, but her revulsion was undisguised. She's one of the most competent people I've ever worked with; she's also squeamish, and I wondered if she might be the next to unleash the contents of her stomach.

'I can't believe I – ' the journalist was saying, but didn't complete the thought. Instead, again she said, 'I'm so sorry.'

52   The Nominee

'Are you staying in this hotel?' I asked.

The journalist nodded.

'Give her your room key,' I said and gestured to my deputy chief of staff. 'She'll get a change of clothes from your suitcase and bring it back here.' Unsteadily, the journalist passed off a key card – 'Room 318,' she called as my deputy hurried away – and, addressing my personal aide, I said, 'Please bring over a glass of water.' I stood, crossed the carpet, and entered the bathroom off the living room. Without closing the door, I scrubbed my hands; small brown chunks lodged in the drain. When I emerged, I asked the journalist, 'Do you need to lie down?'

I could see her hesitate – it's easy enough for one workhorse to recognize another, and I knew she wanted to continue the interview – and I said, 'Go into the bedroom. Put on a robe and rest on the bed, at least for a few minutes. All the linens can be changed tonight while I'm out.'

Still she hesitated – behind me, I heard my two aides murmuring to each other – and I extended my hand. The journalist grasped it as she stood, and I could feel her shakiness, a literal shakiness, as we walked arm in arm into the suite's bedroom in our vomit-bedecked pantsuits; the smell was disgusting, and later that night I ended up moving to a different suite altogether. I had never been this physically close to the journalist. I escorted her to the threshold of the bathroom inside the bedroom and asked, 'Shall I wait while you clean up?'

She shook her head, and when she spoke, some firmness had returned to her voice. 'I don't know what came over me.'

'I'll give you privacy,' I said. 'Take your time.'

'I'm not pregnant,' she said, and though I can't claim the thought hadn't crossed my mind, it was her very adamance that made me question the statement. She was at that time recently divorced and her son was in grade school. She didn't go on to have another baby, which, of course, is proof of nothing.

I began to close the bathroom door and she said, 'Wait.'

Our eyes met.

'I trust that this is all off the record,' she said, and even then it occurred to me that if the situation were reversed, she'd never have extended such a courtesy.

'You're in luck,' I said. 'Because I'm not a journalist.'

'How would a female president change other countries' perception of America?' the journalist asks in the Wells Fargo Center's greenroom. We stand next to a long table covered in a white cloth, beside the huge platter of sliced pineapple and strawberries; all around us are the hum and laughter of other conversations as well as the words and applause from the speech currently being delivered on the arena stage and broadcast on a TV on the greenroom wall.

I say, 'I imagine many countries will be pleased that we've caught up to a milestone they reached years ago.'

'And what might your presidency mean for women?'

'If elected, I'll proudly work on behalf of all Americans.'

'But it's no secret that you've always been a Rorschach test for people in terms of where they stand on issues like feminism and women in the workforce. Just as a symbol, you – '

I shake my head, interrupting her. 'Surely you realize that no one sees herself as a symbol?'

In 1957, my friend Carol Gurski's tenth birthday party took place at her house in Park Ridge, Illinois, a block away from where my own family lived. Six of us fifth-grade girls sat at the Gurskis' dining-room table eating cake, along with Carol's younger brother; her parents stood nearby. The subject of baseball arose – I was an ardent Cubs fan, despite their terrible record that year – and I said, 'Even if the White Sox are having a better season, Ernie Banks is clearly the best player on either team. If the Cubs build around him, they'll be good in time.'

Carol's father was across the table, behind Carol and facing me, and he smiled unpleasantly, in a way I had never previously recognized but have observed on a daily basis ever since. He said, 'You're awfully opinionated for a girl.'

And, really, there are so many other words people use to express the sentiment, but I always hear the echo of Bud Gurski.

When, in a 1995 speech in Beijing, I resisted pressure from both the White House and the Chinese government to tone down my declaration that human rights are inseparable from women's rights? *You're awfully opinionated for a girl.*

When I criticized the Taliban before everyone criticized the Taliban? *You're awfully opinionated for a girl.*

When I pushed for universal health care, a goal that turned out to be so controversial that my security detail required me for a time to wear a bulletproof vest in public? When I insisted, as secretary of state, on directly addressing with other governments the diplomatic damage wrought by the rash choices of the previous president? When I made that now-infamous crack about how I could have stayed home baking cookies and having teas? All those times, I was awfully, awfully opinionated.

During my tenure at the state department, I visited 112 countries, and much of what I did, in Pakistan and Russia, in Indonesia and Israel and Angola and El Salvador, was listen. Indeed, though I've failed at various times on various fronts, I've often thought that the bulk of my professional achievements have rested on two equally unsexy strengths: I am always willing to do my homework, and I am always willing to listen.

Also: I actually know, in a daily, granular way, what it's like to live in the White House, and the difference between thinking you know what it's like to live in the White House

52 The Nominee

and living in the White House is the difference between thinking you know what it's like to be a parent and being a parent.

Yes, I get it – the typical American voter possesses no more than fleeting familiarity with my résumé while feeling that he or she has been choking on my public image and my politics for almost twenty-five years. The typical American voter doesn't wish to share a beer with me.

I have my supporters, of course, and then some. But it's a bitter pill to swallow for those who aren't in that category: that the person most qualified to be the next president is an awfully opinionated girl.

Is the journalist's sexism attributable to the age difference between us, because she always took for granted her entry into the workforce? But surely she has experienced discrimination in the newsroom, at press conferences, on campaign planes and buses? Although she seems friendly with her male colleagues, sometimes her very jocularity suggests a compensating energy.

Is it because she was just nine years old when *Roe v Wade* was decided?

Is it because, while I grew up middle-class, she grew up rich? She's from Boston, I know, and she attended Choate and Yale.

Or is it because fundamentally, as a writer, she's a bystander instead of a participant?

We still are next to the greenroom's buffet, in this thicket of people I have known and mostly loved for many years. It's strange how much I feel and cannot say. Even stranger is how much I can say without being believed, without my words being considered anything other than hollow propaganda. The irony: I really *have* been preparing for this moment for my entire life. I actually *am* confident, humbled, and optimistic about the future of our country.

I plan to win the election in November, and I plan after that to win the reelection. I trust that Americans will become accustomed to a female president in much the way they became accustomed to a black one – in some cases enthusiastically and in others gracelessly. The thought of what will happen if I don't win, if my opponent somehow triumphs, is almost inconceivable, less for me personally than for our country. I am not exaggerating when I say it could be catastrophic; fortunately, I also don't believe it will occur.

Thus, it will likely be January 2025 when my presidency concludes. I will be seventy-seven years old, and the journalist sixty-one; we'll have known each other for more than three decades. And undoubtedly, before I return after so long to private life (Will I ever return to private life? Presumably not really, but such things are relative, and I might feel as if I have), the journalist and I will have one final encounter: my exit interview.

How delicious it will be to stop trying to *convince* people! To stop pretending that I don't hear the criticism, or that I don't care about it – there are, of course, ways in which I really don't hear it and really don't care about it, but neither can be entirely true so long as a heart still beats inside my chest. But it will be only after my long stretch in the public eye has concluded, after all my bids for quantifiable and unquantifiable approval, that I can be honest with the journalist and by extension with the American people.

The journalist will end my exit interview in the way she ends all interviews, which is by saying, 'Is there anything I should be asking you that I'm not?'

I cannot lie; more than once I've been tempted to say, *Do you remember when I caught your curried-tuna vomit in my hands? Because I do*. But the truth is that I had forgiven her even before she finished throwing up; that, at least, was out of her control. So, no. Such a question would be a waste.

Instead – I'll be casual, as if it's an afterthought – I'll say this: 'You've mentioned many times over the years that you find me unlikable. How do you think I find *you*?'

53

Hard to Say

(2020)

Sharon Morse

There's so much I don't remember about where I was born. Venezuela is just a few hazy scenes in my mind, so loosely tied together that they feel like dreams instead of memories. I don't remember my school, except for the sweet, smiling face of one of my preschool teachers. I don't remember our home, except for the balcony off the living room where I could feel the tropical breeze brush across my cheeks and whip my hair into a halo around my head. I don't even remember the language – my first language. It, too, got lost to the haze of dreamlike memories.

My sister remembers it all. She was ten when we moved – old enough for her memories to stay intact. I had my sixth birthday just after we got to the States.

I try not to get jealous as I walk into the kitchen to the sweet smell of cinnamon pancakes and the sound of Clarísa speaking Spanish on the phone with our grandmother. My sister laughs and asks how she and our grandfather are doing. I know enough Spanish to figure at least that out.

'Morning,' my mom says as I pull out a stool next to my sister.

'Morning,' I answer.

Clarí stands from her stool and walks to the other side of the kitchen, like the two words that Mom and I uttered are disrupting her enthralling conversation.

Mom slides a plate of cinnamon pancakes in front of me, swimming in butter. It's a tradition my mom has insisted on since my last day of kindergarten, when she accidentally knocked the cinnamon over and it went flying into the batter. We deemed it meant-to-be and carried on the tradition ever since. 'You know,' I say. 'I'm almost seventeen. You don't need to make me special last-day-of-school pancakes anymore.'

'I'll be making you last-day-of-school pancakes all the way through grad school, kid. Deal with it.'

I pop the top off the syrup bottle and pour it all over the pancakes. 'So, you're going to travel to wherever I'm attending college and make pancakes on a hot plate in my dorm room?'

Hard to Say 53

Mom raises an eyebrow. 'FedEx,' she says, dropping the pan into the sink. 'Or you can always go to school close enough to come home for pancakes, like your sister.'

I laugh as I cut into my pancakes, letting the syrup run down through the layers. 'Moms be crazy.'

'You laugh at me now,' she says, wiping down the countertop with a kitchen rag, 'but you're going to miss this when you're all grown up and I'm too old to trust around an open flame anymore.'

'Nah.' I pop a bite into my mouth, savoring the butter and cinnamon and maple syrup on my tongue. 'I'll put you in an old folks home way before that.'

'Valentina. Have a little respect for your mother.' Mom swats at me with the kitchen towel. 'At least make it a nice one – a retirement community for active seniors. With a pool for water aerobics.'

I laugh. 'Deal.'

Mom does that mom thing where she watches me like I'm going to grow up and leave the house if she dares to look away.

'I still have senior year, Mom. There will be more pancakes ahead of us.'

'I know.' She purses her lips and nods.

'Oh, God, are those tears?'

'No!' She hisses and turns away to start washing the dishes.

I cram another bite in my mouth and chew around my smile while Clarísa paces the length of the kitchen with the phone pressed to her ear. Her mouth moves a mile a minute in perfect Spanish.

Even though Spanish was my first language, now I have trouble piecing together even the most basic conversations. I can understand bits and pieces when someone speaks slow enough. But I can barely find a response with two hands and a flashlight unless it's sí, no, or gracias. It happened without even realizing it. One day it was just … gone. I can't even tell you when.

Dad shuffles into the kitchen and puts an arm around me, giving me a good squeeze along with a loud kiss to the top of my head. 'You ready for junior year to be over?'

I nod and swallow, my mouth full of pancakes. 'So ready.'

'History final today?' He sits on the stool next to me.

'And I have to turn in my final art project,' I say, nodding to the canvas on the kitchen table, a landscape of Texas bluebonnets and an old hill country barn to showcase perspective. I brought it home last night to work on the last few details.

'You'll nail that one, no problem. And I call dibs once it's graded. I want to hang it in my office.'

'Deal,' I say, smiling into my pancakes.

'Dad, Ita wants to talk to you.' My sister holds the phone out to him. Ita and Ito became my grandparents' names when Clarí was little and couldn't say Abuelita or Abuelito. Everyone thought it was adorable, so of course it stuck.

53 Hard to Say

Dad's smile falters as he grabs the phone. 'Hola, Mamá,' he says, but he walks toward his office before we can hear anything else.

'Is everything okay?' I push my plate toward my sister, and she takes my fork.

Clarí shoves a huge bite into her mouth. 'So good,' she mumbles to herself. 'I don't know,' she finally says when she's done chewing. 'I tried to ask how things were going, but she wouldn't tell me much other than the weather.'

I try to ignore the tightness in my chest. Clarísa's managed to stay close with our grandparents, but when you don't speak the same language anymore, staying close isn't so easy.

Clarísa sighs and runs a hand through her thick hair. She takes after Dad, with darker skin and hair. I try not to be jealous of that, too. My mom is beautiful, but Dad definitely has the good hair.

Dad's words float down the hallway, and we lean back on our stools, trying to hear more. He talks way too fast for me to pick up any of the words, but I can tell by his tone that something's up.

We both turn our heads to Mom, who starts tinkering around the kitchen, cleaning surfaces that are already clean.

'Mom, what's going on?' Clarísa asks.

Mom just shakes her head. 'Let your father tell you, okay?'

My sister and I look at each other as all sorts of scenarios run through my head. I search her eyes, wondering if I'll find the answers there, but it's clear that, whatever this is, Mom and Dad are shielding it from Clarí, too.

We both know the situation in Venezuela has been getting worse. We've all held our breath, waiting for tiny crumbs of updates from American news outlets. Over the past year I've followed some of the protests on Twitter – what I can make sense of with Google Translate, anyway. The worse the situation has gotten, the more the mainstream news has reported about it. Every time another update comes about the violence, the lack of food and medicine, the millions of people leaving the country daily, the strain it's putting on Colombia and Brazil, I can feel the tension in the house rising. It's in the set of my dad's shoulders, the tight smile on my mother's face, the hushed, late-night conversations in Spanish.

It's hard to imagine it's the same place where I would stand on that breezy balcony and watch the colorful birds fly by.

Dad shuffles into the kitchen, a smile on his face like nothing is wrong.

'Dad, what's going on?' Clarí's voice breaks and she swallows.

Dad sighs and runs a hand through his thick curls. 'Things in Caracas are … not good. You know already.'

I know that my parents have been sending money to my grandparents for several years. And I know that's why Clarí had to say no to half the schools she got into in favor of public, in-state tuition, and that there was no discussion of buying me a car on my sixteenth birthday like so many of my friends. But as things have gotten worse, sending money has turned into boxes full of grocery staples, basic household supplies, and finding an American doctor who could help us send Ito his heart medication.

'Is everything okay with Ito?' Clarí asks.

Dad nods and sits down on the stool next to mine. 'Everyone's fine. We just … have some news.' He turns on his stool to face us. 'Your mother and I have been working with an immigration lawyer for several months. After this election, we asked her to fast-track everything. We weren't sure if it would work out, so we wanted to wait until we knew for sure to tell you girls.'

'And?' Clarí asks.

'The lawyer called yesterday. We've got their visas.'

'They're coming to live here?' I ask, leaning on my elbows, like if I get closer to Dad, he'll have to tell me more. 'With us?'

Dad nods.

'When are they getting here?' Clarí asks.

'Day after tomorrow,' he answers. 'Plane tickets are already bought.'

Clarí's eyebrows practically retreat into her hairline. 'That's really soon.' But there's a lot in that sentence that she's not saying. Mainly, how long they've been hiding this from us.

'Where will they sleep?' I ask.

'In your room,' Mom answers. 'You can move your things into Clarísa's room, and you two can share while she's home for the summer.'

I nod. My room is bigger and the bathroom is attached. That's obviously where they should sleep. But Clarí and I have never shared a room. We haven't shared much, really. I love my sister, but we're not like TV sitcom sisters. We aren't really close, but we don't really fight, either. We're just … sisters. I've felt helpless for so long, watching my parents deal with this. At least I can do something to help.

'I can move my stuff after my last final today,' I say.

'I'll help,' Clarí adds.

'Are you going down there to help them move?' Ito and Ita are in their eighties now. There's no way they can pack up all their things by themselves.

Dad gets up from his stool and paces across the kitchen. 'A few years ago, it was pretty simple for a citizen to sponsor a family member, especially elderly parents. But these days it's … different.' I can tell there's more he wants to say. He clenches his fists at his sides like he's trying not to get worked up into an angry rant.

'What do you mean?' I ask.

'The lawyer recommended I don't go there right now.'

'But why? How are they going to move all their things?'

'Don't be so naive, Val,' Clarí says. 'Venezuela's on the travel ban list.'

53 Hard to Say

I slink back in my chair. 'I thought a judge blocked that?'

'Temporarily.' She pushes the rest of the pancakes across the counter. 'But they're still detaining all kinds of people at the airport for no reason.'

'But Dad has his citizenship now.'

'Hasn't stopped them from bothering anyone else.'

'Clarísa,' Dad says. 'Enough.'

I look back and forth from my sister to my dad. 'So, who's going to help them?' I ask, feeling more helpless than ever before. All our relatives in Venezuela moved back to Argentina, where Ita and Ito are originally from, several years ago. And most of our family friends have spread across the world. Everywhere from Miami to Lisbon to Singapore.

'No. They have to leave pretty much everything behind. Walk away from their home. Your sister is right. It won't be easy for them.'

'No,' I say as I poke at the last bite of pancake. 'I guess not.'

***

Mom nudges my shoulder in the middle of the night – at least it feels like the middle of the night. I groan and roll over in the new twin bed Mom got at Costco. We set it up yesterday, across the room from Clarí's. We didn't have time to prewash the sheets, so they still smell kind of like plastic.

'We're leaving for the airport,' Mom says in a whisper even though everyone in the house is now awake. 'We should be back in a couple hours.'

'A text message would have been sufficient,' Clarí whines.

'Oh, no,' Mom says. 'I want you girls up and dressed when we get back with your grandparents. You want them to arrive to two zombies just shuffling out of bed instead of their lovely granddaughters? What kind of welcome is that? Come on. Up.' Mom flips the lights on and we both groan. I throw my hand over my face, letting my eyes adjust.

'Evil, evil woman,' Clarí mutters, rolling back over.

'Uh huh,' Mom says, like she's proud to bear the name. 'Just get your butts up and throw on some decent clothes. No pajama pants.'

'Eeeevil.' Clarí kicks the covers off her bed, seemingly in protest.

I sit up and yawn. 'Do you need to pee?' I ask my sister.

'Yeah.'

'Well, go now. I'm going to take a shower.'

'No.'

'Okay, but once I get in there, you're gonna regret that you didn't go before I got in.'

'No,' she groans again.

'Suit yourself.' I stand up and make my way to the bathroom in the hallway that used to belong to just Clarí, but now is ours. I'd just go take one last shower in my bathroom, but it's pristine with a new shower curtain and everything. Mom will kill me if I mess it up.

Halfway through my shower, there's a bang on the door.

'I have to peeeeee!' My sister's voice rings out over the running water.

'What did I tell you?' I yell back. 'Go use Mom and Dad's!'

Sharing a bathroom is going to be so much fun.

***

The squeal out of my grandmother's mouth when we open the front door is so loud, I'm surprised the neighborhood dogs don't all start barking. She beckons to me and I can't help but run to her. She grabs my face with both her hands and searches my eyes. I smile as she talks to me; some I can understand, some I can't. Something about how I'm beautiful, and my guess is how grown-up I look. She hasn't laid eyes on me since I was little, so I'm sure it's as strange to her as it is to me. She squishes my cheeks again before crushing me to her chest, and I can't help but let out a laugh. I sink into her hug and breathe her in. She smells like peppermint and the stale cabin air of an airplane. And she's so thin that I worry my hug might crush her.

I get one more cheek squish and a kiss before she wipes her lipstick off of me. She turns to Clarí and does the same thing – sweet words and kisses until all her lipstick is on Clarí's cheeks instead of Ita's lips.

I turn to Ito to say hi and he gives me a shy smile. He looks so much older than the photos we have of him. His hair is whiter, and the skin around his eyes and mouth is more wrinkled and weathered. I lean in to give him a hug and he puts his long arms around me. He kisses the top of my head the way Dad always does and holds on just a little longer without saying anything. Ito is a man of few words. Right now that suits me just fine.

Dad tells us all to grab a suitcase – in Spanish, but with his gestures it's easy to understand what he's asking – as Mom leads my grandparents inside the house. I watch as Ita walks inside, keeping a hand on the underside of Ito's elbow, like he needs the stability. Dad says something I don't understand and points down at the threshold, and I realize he's telling them to watch their step.

After I set the last suitcase down in their closet, conversation in Spanish floats down the hallway from the kitchen and I follow the sound. When I walk in, Clarí is showing Ita around the kitchen, which Mom and Dad just updated a bit last year when all the nineties-era appliances started dying one by one. Ita runs her hand along the stove, saying

53 Hard to Say

something complimentary. She looks up at Dad and says something else, and everyone else laughs. I get from the way Dad looks half amused and half affronted that it must be a joke about him – his cooking I guess? But it's hard to know for sure.

***

My stomach growls as I walk into the kitchen, surveying a mess of flour and dishes.

'Your dad decided to help your grandmother make empanadas, so it's taking a while,' Mom says. 'Of course, it doesn't help that he's spent most of the time telling your abuela that she's doing everything wrong.'

I laugh. 'Isn't she the one who taught him how to make them?'

'Yes, but of course, he says he's perfected them over the years and so she should do it his way now. I swear, that man.' She says that every time Dad is being stubborn, which is at least once a day.

We finally sit down to eat in the dining room with a huge spread in front of us. There are empanadas as far as the eye can see. Dad informs me that the ones on the white platter are his and the ones on the platter with the flowers are Ita's and I'm to eat some of each and compare.

Mom bites her lip, visibly resisting the urge to say something. I catch her eye and she shakes her head, mouthing *I swear*.

They're both delicious, but the table erupts into arguments about which one they prefer. Or at least, I think that's what they're talking about. The conversation flies back and forth so fast that I barely catch a word.

Clarí jumps up and puts a napkin ring on Ita's head and she laughs. When I hear her say 'La reina,' I finally get the joke and laugh along with everyone else. Clarí has crowned her the queen of empanadas.

But it only gets harder to keep up after that. The conversation flows easily between everyone at the table, with laughter and raucous interruptions and gestures. Ito says something to Dad, then looks at me with a smirk on his face. Dad throws his head back and laughs right from his belly.

I look from Ito to Dad to try to figure out what they're saying about me. Clearly it's amusing. When I don't get a clue from them, I look to Mom, but she's laughing too.

Dad finally catches his breath and looks to me with tears in his eye from laughter. '¿Recuerdas ese viaje?' he asks me.

I blink and try to decode what he's asking me. If I remember something. But what?

'Of course you don't, you were so little,' he says, switching back to English for a second at my confused look. But then he switches right back, turning to Ito, and I'm back to not knowing what in the world anyone is talking about.

Hard to Say

I grab another empanada off the tray – one of Ita's, because they are better by a slim margin – and pick at the braided edge of the pastry as the conversation goes on around me.

***

I sleep in the next morning, because it's summer and I can. But when I go to get some cereal around noon, Ita and Clarí are in the kitchen. My sister is chopping something green while Ita gives her directions, motioning with her fingers to chop it in smaller pieces.

'What are y'all making?'

'Chimichurri,' she says without looking up. 'To go with dinner tonight.'

I walk across the kitchen and lean over to hug Ita.

'Buenos dias, Tinita,' she says, giving me a kiss on the cheek. Tinita was always her nickname for me, which makes me smile. Mom and Dad used to use it, but since we moved here, I preferred just Valentina or Val, so I'd asked them to stop. Now I kind of wish I hadn't.

'Buenos dias, Ita,' I tell her. I hope my pronunciation was okay. I'm trying to keep my mouth open more when I pronounce my vowels. I read that online somewhere. Hopefully it's not terrible advice, but it is the internet, so who knows.

I gesture to the pile of herbs Clarí is working on with Dad's best knife. 'Can't you just make that in the food processor?' Dad always does. Chimichurri is an Argentine sauce we keep around all the time; Dad probably makes a batch every week or so. I had to laugh when it started to become trendy and we suddenly saw it everywhere. But Dad says no one ever gets it right. That Texans always add cilantro.

Apparently he doesn't either, according to Ita.

Clarí shakes her head. 'Ita says that's, like, sacrilegious. Hand-chopped is the way to go.'

'Sí,' Ita responds. 'A mano.'

'She was mad that Dad doesn't have a mortar and pestle, but I think that's way too old-school for him.' Clarí laughs.

'Can I help?' I ask, but it looks like they're almost done.

'You can grab the oil.' Clarí nods toward the pantry.

I grab a couple of bottles, not knowing which one they want to use. To be honest, I never paid much attention when Dad was making it before. Cooking was always more Clarí's thing. 'Which one?' I ask.

Ita takes the bottles from me and inspects them. After taking a taste from each one, she settles on the olive oil and sets it next to the bowl already full of the chopped herbs, garlic, and red pepper flakes.

53 Hard to Say

Clarí scoops up the parsley and dumps it in the bowl. She asks Ita something in Spanish that I don't understand, and the two of them start talking. Their voices get louder, gestures more pronounced. They both take food pretty seriously.

'Mírame,' Ita says, pointing to the corner of her eye. Watch.

She perches the bottle of oil in one hand, thumb over the top to control the flow. With the other hand she begins to lightly stir the mixture as she slowly streams in the oil. It's just stirring, but she does it with flair. Like a *Top Chef* contestant sprinkling salt in the pan.

Clarí has more questions. And the two of them are off again on their intense foodie conversation. The more excited they get, the faster they talk. And the faster they talk, the less chance I have of picking up even a single word.

While they're distracted, I stick my finger in the bowl and then lick it.

It's good.

Better than Dad's.

I lick off the rest and forget about the cereal I came for. I just wipe my hand on a kitchen towel and go back to my room. The chatter continues in the kitchen. Ita and Clarí don't even notice I've gone.

***

'What crawled up your butt?' Clarí asks as she comes into the room. 'We were having fun and you just left.'

No, you were having fun, I don't say. 'Nothing.' I grab my clothes out of the drawer and try to stomp past her to take a shower, but she grabs me by the shoulder.

'Just tell me what you're mad about.' Clarí always wants to hash things out as soon as they come up. Doesn't she get that some of us like to stew in silence for a while?

I squeeze my eyes shut, trying to breathe through the lump rising up in my throat. 'Just let me by.'

'No.' She steps out wider to block the doorway.

'Ugh. Clarí. I really don't want to talk about this right now. Especially with you.'

'What does that mean?'

'It means you couldn't possibly understand what this is like for me. You and Ita are, like, best buds.'

'We were trying to include you. You're the one that walked off.'

'Well, you were doing a crappy job.'

Clarí doesn't have a clever retort to that one. She leans against the door frame and I take my chance to squeeze by her.

I finally let myself cry once I shut the bathroom door, hating that Clarí can probably hear me anyway. Of course she doesn't understand why I'm upset. She hasn't lost what

I've lost. She hasn't had to grieve for something she doesn't even remember having. I let the steam fill the tiny bathroom, fogging up the mirror while I hide away and let the water wash away the tears.

***

I wipe the sweat off my forehead as I walk in the back door. Walking over to my friend Amy's house in June was clearly a terrible idea. I always forget how hot ninety-something degrees is until summer comes around again. But I needed to be out of this house for a while, and I didn't feel like bugging Clarí for a ride after our fight yesterday.

When I step into the kitchen, Mom looks up from sorting through a bunch of plastic bags spread across the table. 'Oh, good. There you are.'

'I went to Amy's,' I say. 'What is all this?'

'Oh, I took Ita to the art supply store to get some things so she could paint.' She pulls a tube from one of the bags. 'We dug your easel out of the box under your bed,' Mom says. 'Hope you don't mind.'

I shake my head. 'No, it's fine.' I survey the stuff spread over the kitchen table. Mom even got out the old tablecloth I use when I paint at home.

My tabletop easel is set up, and there are several new canvases stacked on the counter. 'You guys didn't need to buy all this stuff. I have plenty of paint and brushes she can use.'

'Ita likes to use oil paint,' Mom says. 'She says that you don't use the same type of brushes for that.'

'Oh.' I guess that's true. I never thought of that. No one at school uses oils. Someone asked our teacher about them once, but she went on a tirade about the smell of turpentine, so no one ever asked again. Plus, from what I know about it, you have to wait a whole week for one layer of paint to dry so that you can work on top of it again.

I can't even wait all the way through a YouTube ad without hitting Skip.

Ita walks into the kitchen holding an old box. 'Come,' she says to me. 'Sit.'

'Me?' I point a finger to my chest. I look from Ita to Mom. The timing of all this – and the encouraging smile on Mom's face – makes me wonder if Clarí said something to Mom about my little meltdown yesterday.

'Sí.' She sits down at the table and opens the box. It's full of old pieces of paper. I sit beside her as she sifts through them all, not really searching for anything. Just looking. The box is full of beautiful images – magazine clippings of beautiful people or clothes or buildings, those *National Geographic*-type photos of animals or places. They're all really old, the paper crinkled and starting to yellow. She reaches a stack of photographs, and I recognize me and Clarí when we were little. Ita passes it to me with a smile.

'Que linda,' she says. How cute. She waits for me to look at the photo, then grabs hold of my cheek and gives it a pinch.

'Ita,' I laugh, brushing her hand away.

53   Hard to Say

A photo of a beach catches my eye as she sifts through the stack. I reach for it as Ita puts it down next to her and I know I remember this place. The way the palm trees lean in, surrounding a half-moon bay. And the color of the sand. Red. Almost like Texas dirt.

'That's Playa Colorada,' Mom says over my shoulder. I didn't even know she was standing there.

'It's in Venezuela?' I ask.

Ita nods. 'Sí.'

'I've been here before?' I ask, sure that I must have.

'Te acuerdas?' Do you remember?

'Sí. Me acuerdo,' I say, impressed at my on-the-fly conjugation. But I know we learned that one in junior high Spanish. 'Or, I think I do.'

Ita tells me the story, or starts to tell it to me, then switches to telling Mom. Her way of asking her to translate.

Mom tells me that we went there a few months before we moved to the States. That I had so much fun that day, I didn't want to leave. As she talks, some of the details start to fill in.

'I think I do remember. Clarí buried me in the sand …'

I look at Ita and she nods, smiling. Her smile makes me remember more than the beach. I remember the whole day. Playing with the other little kids, sitting with Ita in the hammock Dad strung up between the palm trees, Dad hacking away at a coconut, trying to get to the sweet water inside. Mom digging that giant hole in the sand so that Clarí could bury me up to my neck.

Ita digs through the rest of the photos, and there it is. A photo of just my head, sticking out of the red sand and Clarí holding the shovel with an evil grin.

Ita grabs the first photo from the tabletop. The one with the pretty palm trees. She says something to Mom, nodding to me.

'She wants you to paint this.'

'Me? I thought she was the one painting,' I say to Mom.

'I show you,' Ita says to me.

And she does. We start with the sky, blending blue and white into thin, wispy clouds on a sunny tropical day. The oil paints blend together so easily, and you can keep blending the colors even after you've spread them on the canvas. It takes some getting used to, but I love the feel of it.

After a while, I don't even notice how long, Mom leaves us on our own. The second I realize she's gone, my chest gets tight with worry. What if I have a question, or Ita asks me something and I don't understand? But after blending the reds and browns and yellows to mimic the bright color of the sand, I realize we don't actually need words right now. I pay attention to the way she changes the angle of her brush, and I watch as she shows me how to get the texture of the sand to translate onto the canvas.

The brushstrokes are their own language.

Reflection

(2021)

Silmy Abdullah

I am sitting mum, decked up and bejewelled. Golden drapes cascade down the wall behind me. Chandeliers hang from the ceiling like weighty earrings, sort of like the ones I am wearing today. My entourage of bridesmaids has just escorted me to the stage, dancing through the aisle, clapping to Bengali wedding songs.

My mother is in tears. Every now and then she wipes her eyes with tissue as she talks to a guest at a nearby table. I cannot hear them amid the blaring, obnoxious music, but I know exactly what the conversation entails, word for word. 'Don't cry, *Bhabi*,' the woman must have said. 'Today is a day of great happiness.' I also know what my mother will say next, 'My life is complete. My daughter has found her match.'

I graduated a few months ago with a master's from York University. I am twenty-five years old. They, meaning my suitors and their mothers, say my face is pretty, my smile particularly. I come from a good family, too, they tell me. But there is a slight limp in my left leg from polio, and this, they say, is a deal-breaker. Actually, they've never said it out loud. But each time I've looked into their eyes, I've seen the same descending cloud, a screen that shuts me out as soon as they notice my walk, tells me that I will never hear from them again. So, I've been told not to be picky. I should feel grateful to have any man who is magnanimous enough to sacrifice his desires to be with me. But I know it's the same for some of my friends, too. They've crossed the age of thirty and have three to four degrees. They, too, must not expect much, they are told.

My husband, Amir, is dashingly handsome. As he sits to my right on the velvet-cushioned seat, wearing his princely *sherwani* and turban, he blends in completely with the grandiosity of the night. He is tall with sharp, chiselled features, holds an MBA from the University of Toronto, and owns a townhouse in Ajax. 'You are so lucky, my dear!' my mother chanted the day he asked for my hand. A few coffee dates were all it took, just a few conversations that revealed nothing more than his current work projects and his childhood in Dhaka. He spoke little and smiled with reserve. But there was a tenderness in him that I could not deny. It irked me. Every time I think of that dreadful last date,

54 Reflection

when he asked me in his soft voice, his face expressionless, if I would marry him, I can feel the heat crawling under my skin all over again.

I had no reason to say no, since it was a yes from him. And turning down perfection wouldn't just make me look picky or ungrateful. It would stamp me as an arrogant fool and a downright jerk for the rest of my life. 'This is beyond our imagination!' my mother still repeats like a mantra. 'What an amazing guy, and just so nice.' Yes, the others were nice, too. The only difference – theirs was polite rejection, his was pitiful acceptance.

Our shoulders touch, and I cringe. My eyes sting as an army of cameras flash before me. The togetherness of me and my husband has just been captured, sealed, frozen in time. It did not seem like that even moments ago, when I signed the contract with my henna-covered hand and said, 'I accept' to the *Qazi*. I don't hold back the tears now. In that sense, Bengali brides are fortunate. We can cry without any restraint on our wedding day, easily releasing all kinds of suppressed agony under the guise of that one pain we have absolute permission to feel, the pain of leaving our parents. The lights keep firing at me like gunshots, and I look past defiantly, searching the crowd of five hundred guests for David.

David isn't Bengali. He has blond hair and cream-coloured skin. His eyes are blue, deep and mysterious like the sea. 'Your Canadian friend,' my mother calls him. I am never quite sure what bothers me more, her calling him 'Canadian' or my 'friend.' It is not her fault entirely. *Friend* is the safest label for a dead-end relationship, so this is how I introduced him to her, soon after I met him in my first year of graduate school. He could visit my house, chauffeur me to and from campus, we could work on assignments together, and in front of my mother we would always stand a safe distance apart from one another, not making much eye contact. It was the only way we could kiss without the worry of suspicion, sometimes inside his car at the university parking lot, other times in empty hallways, like curious, rebellious teenagers. For two years, we've been together, surreptitiously loving one another, though never talking about marriage. He didn't dare to bring it up, knowing that my mother would never forgive me for this betrayal, for dismissing all the struggles she has faced for me, raising me by herself after my father's passing, working night shifts at Walmart, imbibing cultural values in me against all odds in a Western country. For my sake, she refused to move out of our crumbling two-bedroom apartment in Bangla town, as if no dream existed beyond its rusted balcony railings and perpetually broken elevators. The one time I asked her to think about a house, she looked at me mockingly – arms crossed, eyebrows arched – and said to me, 'What good is a house if I can't secure your future? Every penny for your education, then for your marriage. After that, we'll see.'

Each time a man rejected me, it was David who sat through my grievances, patiently listening on the phone while I moved from crying and cursing to finally thanking my suitors for going away from me and my lover. Every time, he has comforted me with the same words, 'I love you. I always will.' I've never heard anything close to this from any of my suitors. In fact, I could see right through their masquerade of polite silences, laughing at me in their thoughts, repeating over and over again, 'You fool. What makes you think I will ever marry you?' And each time my mother brought another prospect, a

Bengali, thinking that he was the best possible match for me, I wanted to say to her, 'Will he love me like David?' I feel like screaming it today, into the microphone that sits on the podium. But I stay quiet. My struggles are nothing compared to my mother's. And for this reason, instead of eloping with David, I invite him as my friend, as a guest. He said nothing when I told him about Amir, except that I should go ahead with the marriage.

I think I see him.

My family friends, Sadaf and Saima, walk up on stage. They've just announced the ritual of *rusmat*, where bride and groom look at one another in the mirror, underneath the canopy of a glittery shawl, and declare what they see as they observe the image of their significant other. I quickly try to think of something. It has all been said and done. The husband usually says, 'I see the moon,' or 'I see my life.' When Saima was getting married, her husband, Ahmed said, 'The best thing that ever happened to me.' She said, her eyes full of truth, 'I see my best friend.'

Saima walks behind me and Amir and spreads a red-and-gold shawl over our heads. The weight of my sari, the pounds of gold around my neck, and the extra shawl over my head feel unbearable. I imagine myself standing in a garden with David, wearing a white gown and a dainty pair of earrings, facing him as he says, 'I do,' and comes close to kiss me.

Sadaf holds a mirror in front of me and Amir. 'What do you see?' she asks him.

Our eyes meet in the mirror, but I quickly glance away.

'My reflection,' Amir says, looking straight into the glass.

Saima and Sadaf break out in laughter.

'Come on, Mister, you gotta do better than that.'

When they ask me, I say the same thing, looking at myself.

My friends keep on laughing.

I was mistaken about David. It was someone else I saw in the crowd, a guest I don't know. I see him up close now. He has a different face – a rounder nose, a broader jawline, and eyes that are grey. My friends Halle and Beth join me at our special dinner table, reserved for the newlyweds and their closest friends and cousins. David is supposed to come with them. I want to ask them where he is, but my husband is right next to me. I scan the crowd one more time. The server brings a massive lamb roast, surrounded by lettuce sheets and discs of cucumber and tomato. It is placed at the centre, and my husband and I must hold the knife together to cut the meat. Another ritual. I check my phone to see if David has sent any texts, but there is nothing. I place my focus back on the knife. My husband holds it, too, as we run it through its chunky flesh. David is vegan. I wonder how he would react, watching me butcher a dead baby sheep all over again.

Two hours have passed since dinner. After sitting through a slew of dance performances by my friends and yet another photo marathon, it is time for me to leave the hall. My mother begins to howl. I, too, start to sob, this time feeling, for real, the grief of separating from her. I embrace her as tightly as I can, and relatives surround us in sympathy. Voices around me advise me to be strong. This is something David would never understand, the uncontrollable crying at the moment of the bride's departure. I remember him again. I take one last look around, as I prepare to exit through the main gate. Suddenly, pain shoots up my left leg. It feels heavy as I step outside. I suppress it so my husband does not have to hold me. Could it be possible David came for a little while and left, not wanting me to see him? Perhaps he did not want me to get weak? Maybe for this very reason, he did not come at all. In the car, I pull out my phone to see if there is a text message, saying, 'I love you. I always will.' *Nothing*. David's absence on this day, his detachment, doesn't make me think of him less. Instead, I long for him more desperately than ever. The softness of his voice. The woody smell of his cologne. The tender touch of his lips. I turn toward Amir. He's looking away, gazing indifferently out the window.

After hours of bright lights and loud music, the quiet in the hotel bedroom is unsettling. Ahmed carried our suitcases up to the room. Our friends who came with us to the hotel have left. I am in my nightgown, my wedding sari and veil laid against the chair, one of the few pieces of furniture in the minimalist room. Two lamps, dimly lit, flank the queen-sized bed. Magenta-red rose petals are scattered all over the white bedsheet. The large window is covered with white curtains that blow like apparitions above the air conditioner. While Amir uses the washroom, I take out my phone and charger. I cannot let it die. Before I can plug it in, Amir comes out, wearing his pyjamas.

'Muna, there is something I need to tell you,' he says as he hesitantly walks toward me.

Great. The jerk will now reveal his girlfriend. Or that he is gay. I knew it. He is too handsome. A part of me feels great relief. I can tell him about David. Then, we will be even.

'I didn't want to marry you, Muna,' he says. 'You deserve so much better than me.'

He pauses.

I have a bloody limp! What does he mean I deserve better?

'Go on,' I say.

I am prepared for the rejection. It was coming sooner or later. Compared to all my other suitors, he's kicked it up a notch. Instead of keeping silent and disappearing into thin air, he has separated me from David, then dressed his rejection in the 'it's not you, it's me' nonsense. *Sadistic bastard!*

He approaches the bed and sits beside me, at a distance where it's impossible for our bodies to touch accidentally. I feel safe, until he slowly begins to undo the buttons on his shirt. I am confused. I begin to feel a lump in my throat. I shift a little, turning my face away. After he takes off his shirt and places it on the bed, he raises his arms to pry off his undershirt. My heart starts to thump, my fists tighten as I clasp the bedsheet. I can feel the beads of sweat gathering on my neck. I want to shout and cry as loudly as I can. I cannot let this man touch me. *God, no!* I am glad my phone is close to me, on the bedside table.

'Muna, look at me, please,' he then says softly.

I finally turn my gaze toward him, and my palms release the sheet. I clasp my hands over my mouth as I stare at his bare upper body, the massive scars travelling from his right shoulder down to his chest and his right arm, wounds that have been etched deeply, stubbornly, into his skin.

'It was a kitchen accident,' he continues. 'I was heating a pan of oil to deep fry pakora. I bent down to pick up something from the floor. On my way back up … anyway, forget the details. It's a third-degree burn.'

I am unable to say anything more to Amir. I feel frozen.

'My mom and dad fell in love with you. They wouldn't let me tell you about this. But I was hoping you would say no to me anyway. I wouldn't mind. Everyone else did.

'You are free to decide, Muna,' he says as he puts his shirt back on and approaches the door.

'Where are you going?' I ask.

'I am going to see if they can give me another room.'

'Wait,' I call out to him. 'Please sleep here. We can talk tomorrow.'

Slowly, reluctantly, he comes back to the bed. As he starts to turn the lamps off, I stop him. 'Do you mind if we keep them on? I can't sleep in the dark.'

'Sure.'

He awkwardly slips into bed beside me, knocking over a glass of water he'd placed on the bedside table. The water splashes across his pillows. He jumps up, puts the glass back in position, and runs to the washroom. I follow him as he returns with a towel and presses it down on the pillows.

'Don't worry,' I tell him. 'Take one of mine.'

'What about you? Are you okay with one?'

'Yes, I'll be fine,' I lie to him. Since childhood, I have been used to sleeping with two pillows. He takes the pillow from my hand and adjusts it under his head. Lying on his back, he drapes his left arm over his face, covering his eyes. I can tell the light is keeping him awake. I rest my head on my pillow. I am not able to sleep, either. But for some reason, I am no longer making an effort to shut my eyes, to hurry into oblivion. I turn onto my side to face my husband. 'Tell me everything. How it happened.' He unfolds his arm and faces me. There are only a few inches between us. As he begins to speak, I gaze deep into his eyes, as clear as glass. Strange. I feel the urge to call him my friend, even though my mother is not here.

Hours have gone by. My head has shifted onto the corner of Amir's pillow. I can feel my left leg gently touching his right, his right arm brushing against my left. My phone is still on the table, lying dead. Sunlight has shot through the curtains, and we are still chatting.

55

Kind Stranger

(2022)

Meron Hadero

Addis Ababa was hardly recognizable, a city casting itself into a new mold: taller, more modern, more planned and plotted. I'd gotten used to crossing construction sites with big boulders and chiseled stone but nonetheless lost my footing and stumbled forward. Looking down, I saw a reclining man reaching for me. His head leaned toward his legs, his hands outstretched and clasping. He looked familiar, though it was unlikely that I actually knew him – I lived in the States now, and rarely made it back. It was hard to see him clearly in the long afternoon shadow of the cathedral. I knelt beside him to make sure he was okay.

'Are you hurt?' I asked, and tried to lift his head. I thought about calling for help, but he started talking without any introduction.

'Listen, my child.' His voice was barely a whisper so I had to bend down. 'One night near the end of the rainy season, I got caught in a storm. There was water – '

His voice cracked, so I reached into my shoulder bag to offer him some water, but he shook off the gesture and kept talking.

'I found myself jumping over the flooded gutters as I ran from the minibus toward home with my jacket over my head to keep myself a little drier, but you know how it is with the rainy season – a losing battle. The whole bus ride, I had to fight for space next to a boy and his damp, smelly goat; that boy showed no respect for his elders standing next to me like that. I was tired, and there was the boy and his soggy little beast, and the rain, and outside there were rows of yellow Mercedes, which I always thought I'd look quite good driving.'

I was surprised by this deluge of narrative coming from a stranger, and then tried to do what I thought I should: I felt his forehead, which wasn't hot. I checked his pulse, which didn't race. I rolled up my sleeves and sat down beside him. I tried telling him to take it easy, but he had more to say.

'So that night was – how do they say it in the movies? – a dark and stormy night,' he went on in English, adjusting his language for his audience.

'A dark and stormy night,' I repeated. 'That's what they say.'

'Besides the rain, the power outage made it hard to see except for the bursts of lightning that lit up the street, lit up the homes, lit the acacia trees on the hillside. The lightning flashed just as I was about to take out my keys and open the gate, and that's when I saw her: Marta Kebede standing under a big black umbrella, looking the same as the day she was arrested back in 1980. I hadn't heard of her or seen her since, though I'd thought of her often, of course.'

He said 'of course' like I knew him well, like none of this should come as a surprise to me, and on top of that, the way he leaned his head close and whispered into my ear felt intimate, as did the soft way he grasped my hand. The only thing I could think of worse than unrequited intimacy was mistaken intimacy.

'Sir, I think you have me confused with someone else,' I told the man. 'Just rest. I think you're hurt. Let me get you a car. I could give you some money.' When he declined, I looked again for a wound or sign of injury, but found none.

He didn't seem moved by my concern and just said, 'If you have a minute ... I just need to rest a minute. If you have a minute, I will take that.'

I didn't really have time to spare. This was a short visit to see relatives, and almost every moment was accounted for. Yet out of obligation, I felt like I should probably stay with him just a little longer.

He didn't wait for my response and simply continued his story: 'So I'd just seen Marta, the first time in decades, and there she was, caught in the middle of a storm. The lightning stopped for a moment and I could no longer see her silhouette. I tried to speak into the darkness, but thunder smothered my hello. I jogged toward where she had stood, moving with both excitement and hesitation, for the sight of her made me feel conflicting emotions: elation, dread, and also grief. Isn't that the way it is with grief, though? First we mourn the grief we bear, and then later we mourn the grief we've caused.'

As he said these words, the helplessness on his face that I'd taken for kindness seemed to vanish. I thought that this switch was strange – that his emotions could change so easily, so suddenly and completely.

'So that night on that dark street, I called out again to Marta, saying the only words I could think of: "Let's go for dinner." It was an awkward thing to say, but once I had said something, I started saying everything. "It's me, Gedeyon. Don't you remember? We were students in the same class at university – you were getting your degree in pharmacology, and I was studying chemistry. I asked you out on a date the first week, and you said no, and you made fun of my shoes, saying that they were farmer shoes, and that you wouldn't date a boy with farmer shoes because your father would kick you out of the house and your mother would drag you to the priest and drown you in holy water. I saved up a whole half year to buy new shoes, really nice ones, and I asked you out again, and you didn't know who I was. I told you I was going to be a professor and you said you wouldn't go out with me, but this time you didn't bother with a reason. I guess I must have loved you. How else could I explain the lengths I went to get your attention, your approval? I wish it hadn't happened that way, and I still wonder if we would have turned out differently if things happened some other way." Isn't that a lot to say into the darkness?' Now he gripped my arm and lifted himself onto the boulder to sit upright.

'Yes, it is a lot to say.' In any light, I thought.

'If she had acknowledged me, if things had gone a little differently between us, maybe I wouldn't have accused her. Did you ever live here during the Derg?' he asked, not giving me much time to consider what he'd just revealed. 'I think you didn't. I think you lived somewhere Western, some wealthy country with peace and freedom.'

'I know the Derg,' I replied. 'I was a child of the Derg, born of that era.'

Gedeyon shook his head. 'Those of you who left here when you were young or when the Derg was young, without more than a scratch, and had the luxury of living somewhere else don't know what some of us carry. You know what the Derg technically is, but you don't truly know. You know the Derg as a definition, a Cold War regime that lasted too long and did too much harm. But those of us who got to truly know the Derg over all those years, who knew it as an uninvited guest dropping in on each meal and in every interaction, well ...'

I felt my face flush, and now it was the grip of guilt that kept me there as he went on.

'I had been tortured by the Derg – that's how I got to know it. Some of the students avoided school back then to reduce the risk of being arrested and just stayed home. But I went to school every day, whether there was a demonstration or the threat of arrest or nothing at all because we got free lunch at the university, and if I didn't go, I didn't eat all day. It was a simple fact of life. So I went to school every day and was arrested, and who knows why back then. Maybe I had a friend or associate who was suspicious, or maybe my hair was too long or too short, or my fingernails were too clean or too dirty. Maybe it was on account of my nice new shoes – who knows? But when the Derg interrogated me, lashing my feet, asking me to name names to get myself free, I gave them Marta's name. She was wealthy, had power, and I thought she could escape, that she'd have a better chance of surviving it than I would. And it's not that I hated her, but she'd stung me. Marta had stung me. Those subtle stings to pride – they're worse than the big ego blows because they're not like some obvious pebble you can remove from your shoe. They are like shards that you know are there but can't find and can't get rid of. Oh, Marta, I wish she'd never made fun of my shoes.'

'So did Marta accept your dinner invitation during the thunderstorm?' I asked, trying to keep him awake since I was concerned at the exaggerated way his eyelids were beginning to droop.

'Well, I kept asking her to dinner, but she didn't say anything. I stood there waiting for another bolt of lightning, and when it came, I saw her far down the street talking to someone, but I didn't know who. The dark, the rain – everything was obscured. I approached her cautiously, ducking behind a tree, waiting for the right moment when I could finally go up to her and try to speak again. After another strike of lightning, she was alone at the minibus stop where I'd just come from. I walked over and stood next to her tall, illuminated figure. I just stared, hoping she would recognize me and start up a conversation. She eventually turned toward me, even smiled, and said, "Good evening."

She offered to share her umbrella, so I shifted closer to her. But she didn't seem to know who I was.'

'You said you last saw her in 1980? That's a long time ago,' I said.

'Not long enough to forget a friend.' The way Gedeyon twisted his lips with spite made me think this was a man of impossible expectations. 'She should have remembered,' he said. 'The thing is, she has always been on my mind. I wrapped all this guilt up around Marta, all this significance and longing; so much so that I could recognize her anywhere, even in the middle of a blackout with just a flash of lightning to reveal her face. It never occurred to me that her feelings wouldn't mirror mine, at least a little.'

'So what did you do then?' I asked, hoping he'd just wished her luck and walked away, but I already knew him well enough to be certain that he hadn't. And I couldn't walk away myself because his story now had a hold on me.

He continued: 'I responded to Marta, "Good evening to you as well," and added, "Don't I know you?" I thought that maybe she just hadn't given me a proper look yet, but when she turned and really examined me up and down with that judgment-filled face, she said, "No, I do not believe we have met."

'We began to talk. I didn't say much, just listened. She said she was going to stop by church to give thanks for how life had turned around for her. I realized this was my opportunity to ask about her life – maybe she would have a flash of recollection then. She told me some general details. She said there was a time she'd been in prison during the Derg, but that was then. I told her I had been thrown in prison, too, by mistake, and she said, "What a shame." She leaned a little closer to me, so I got the courage to ask why she'd been arrested, and she deflected, saying, "Oh, I don't remember, and besides, does it even matter?" "Of course it matters," I said. "Oh, I don't know," she replied. "They'd target you for the most absurd things." She shrugged as if she didn't want to give it much thought. I imagined exactly what they must have said to her anyway. They'd accused her of being a bourgeois princess, more interested in the state of her closet than the very state in which she lived, skipping rallies to do her hair and dodging speeches to read fashion magazines. That's what they might have said to her because that's what I'd told them. That she was a nonbeliever, a threat to the cause. Those were the words I'd used to trade her freedom for my own. It had to be done.'

I didn't know what to say to that.

'I'm sure you'd rather not be here.' He stared at me with despair. 'You left and avoided these difficult truths. You haven't had to see the heavy weight some of us carry around. Do you think I'm ashamed of having survived the way I did? Why should I be?'

I didn't defend myself from his misplaced accusation, which was softened by his fading voice.

'I never said I'm a good man,' he went on. 'I was just a regular man, but the Derg, it made me ... it made me and it unmade me. It heightened my worst instincts. It gave me permission to be worse than I was ever meant to be or would have been in another place, another time. It gave my sins a platform, gave them cover, gave them cause. And for whatever reason I still can't explain, I took the Derg up on this opportunity to abandon my good senses and do as I pleased. I believe – really believe – there was good in me once. I guess I don't know that for sure, but I think it's true. I think I was decent once. I could have been a regular kind of man. Maybe I didn't have the courage to be better, or didn't have the luxury to be better. I couldn't avoid the hard choices. I was here, made here, unmade here.'

He clasped my hand and held it closer, and the warmth of his breath on my skin began to repulse me. Why did I feel like I owed this stranger something? He seemed frail, and despite his bitterness, he needed me. I felt his forehead again, which was a bit hot. He put his cheek to my hand, pursing his dry lips.

'So the rain was just pouring down now, and the cars were whizzing by loudly, and Marta was almost shouting, telling me she'd not only survived the experience of prison, but that it also made her more self-reliant and tough. As awful as prison was, she had to invent ways to endure what she thought would be unbearable, what she thought would break her. She said she struggled but eventually created a space to be calm within herself. Gradually she was able to create a space to let joy enter her life as well, even there in prison – they were the most fleeting moments, but they were something. She found a way to make those fleeting moments last. She found a way to forget, which was the hardest accomplishment of her life. And when she learned how to do that, she found a way toward purpose. She hadn't cared about school before because she hadn't cared about much, she said. But she made a choice to get educated, and she was able to do it. The Derg loved to throw intellectuals in jail – the students, the professors, the writers – and the prisons during the Derg were the best schools in the country, as some say. Marta also met her husband there, and when they were both out – released or escaped or otherwise got free – they fled together to America, swept up in that wave of refugees, and landed safely on a shore called New England where they went back to school and started a family. She got a good job and didn't look back on that time except to acknowledge that she was lucky in the end.'

Gedeyon stopped to catch his breath, and I said, 'Well that's about as good an outcome as you could hope for.'

'You could say that.' He pressed his head to my hand once more. I could feel his fever now. He told me that he'd forgiven himself for the wrongs of the Derg, and damn anyone who judged him for that. 'Damn you, too, if you're judging,' he said. But he hadn't found a way to forgive himself for his other sins, and I saw then that he was making me his confessor.

'Is there someone I can take you to talk to?' I asked him.

'Would you rather me tell this to a friend? A friend who I want to respect and remember me well? Or tell my priest, who I have known all my life and who I respect? My family, who will carry forth my name? My colleagues in whose esteem I hope to remain? Would you rather me call it out from the rooftops and confess to the city? ... Or should I tell a stranger visiting from halfway across the world who looks like she doesn't make the return trip all that often? And who has managed to be a child of the Derg without carrying the same load, but who should shoulder it as well?'

And he paused, and I saw the evidence I'd been searching for all along, an empty bottle of pills falling from his pocket, and I couldn't tell if these had been to help him or if they were what made him sick. I couldn't even tell if he'd taken them.

When I asked him, he just said, 'Listen, child, to my last words.'

What could I do but hear him out and share the burden of his secret now? I knew if I said nothing, he'd continue, and he did.

'I asked Marta, "What was it like, being a refugee?" "It's not for the faint of heart," she said, sweeping her short curly hair off her face with her left hand. The strands caught the light and shined, and I thought I'd never seen her look so sophisticated, so strong, so completely out of reach. I was drawn to her, so I pulled in a little closer to listen.

'She told me, "Not even my mother knew where I'd gone when I fled Ethiopia, not at first, but eventually I was able to send a letter, and then we corresponded as much as we could. When my family finally saw me after thirty-five years, they told me how good I looked for someone who'd come back from the dead."

'I was gazing at Marta, clenching my fist so tight I felt my fingernails bending back, so I put my hands in my pockets and looked at the beams coming off the car headlights, circling her like she was encased in jewels, her body haloed by the glow of the streetlight behind her. She is still something, I thought. Not just someone who has reclaimed what's lost, but someone somehow ennobled by loss. I don't know how to explain this, but I looked at her like she was either my proudest creation or my most wretched punishment. I don't exactly know what I felt, but with false pride I told Marta about my own life, the basics: I was a chemistry and math professor, had a wife once, but it didn't last long. No children, my family mostly gone. I lived freely. Mine was what I called a content and unencumbered existence with routines, stability, and modest comforts, which was more than I'd been born with, and so I felt successful, for what was success if not to die with more than what you had coming into the world?

'Marta said I must be proud of all I was able to accomplish despite my time in prison. She added, "Sometimes, things even out in the end. Karma, justice, and all of that." "Like an equation," I replied. "That we're always balancing."

'She said something I couldn't hear over the rain, so I stepped a little closer, and when she craned her head to see if the minibus was on its way, I fixated again on the light glistening off her hair. I reached out to her by instinct. A car sped by and honked and I pulled myself back, which sent her umbrella out into the darkness, as if a strong gust of wind had caught it. Marta lost her step. She slipped on the muddy curb and fell onto the street, her ankle stuck in the gutter.

'She reached out, and I leaned toward her. She needed me – for once. So I reached for her, my hand nearly touching hers, and Marta whispered, "Kind stranger."

'And I froze, because even now, especially now, the Marta of my dreams and nightmares and fantasies, haunting Marta who had scolded me for wearing those old shoes, who had failed to recognize my achievement getting the new pair, who had talked to me for half an hour that very night and still had no idea who I was, now called me a stranger.

55 Kind Stranger

'I realized then, as she held her hand out to me, that she hadn't even introduced herself that night, hadn't told me her name, nor asked for mine. I was a stranger and always would be to her. I was frozen and the cars honked their horns, unable to stop, the beams of the headlights closing in, overtaking her, and she lunged desperately for my hand, almost a helping hand, almost a friend.

'When the ambulance came, there was really nothing left to do. I knew I could say with some degree of honesty that it had been an accident – a horn, the umbrella, Marta stumbling, me somehow not being able to get to her in time. I try to make sense of that moment. After all these years, I was given a chance to settle the past, but this wasn't the way, was it?'

He was posing a question, but not to me, whose name he'd never asked, a stranger who was there for him in his moment of need, something he didn't seem to recognize.

'Tell me what you think of my story,' he said, and I didn't speak, didn't move as he leaned forward and rubbed the dirt off his shoes, caring for them like they were his salvation.

Note

'Kind Stranger' was first published in 2020, and republished with minor amendments in 2022. The version of the story included in the present volume is the 2022 version.

56

Widows

(2023)

Margaret Atwood

Dear Stevie:

Thank you for your letter. I hope your health remains good.

It seems we must now begin a letter this way, with a Victorian tip of the hat to physical well-being: it's become a social prerequisite, as leaving calling cards once was. And we must end by saying, 'Keep safe.' What a ridiculous concept! There is no 'safe'. At any moment the fragile thread by which we dangle may break, and we may plummet into the unknown. 'Safe', the word, ought to be outlawed. It gives people false ideas.

Sorry. I'm becoming cranky about language, a thing you don't do unless you're past a certain age. For youngsters, things were always called what they are called right now, but for oldsters, not. We notice the gaps, the chasms. And the jokes of former decades have ceased to be jokes, while new jokes have arisen, jokes that are not always understood by us. Joking happens less frequently in the puritanical moment we are passing through – not that I wish to sound judgmental – but a few laughs are still permitted, it seems.

Though each generation's catchphrases die on the vine as a matter of course. What did 'twenty-three skidoo' mean? I said it as a child, but it was old even then and conveyed nothing to me except as part of a skipping rhyme. A sinister skipping rhyme, now that I think of it: a number of robbers have broken into a lady's house – grown-up women were called 'ladies' then – and are giving orders to her, such as turning around and touching the ground. No good would come of this: there were twenty-three of the robbers and only one of her. But 'skidoo' was this lady's exit line, so maybe she ran away.

What fun we used to make of death! Hallowe'en was a chance to put on a sheet and pretend to be a ghost, or to fill a bowl with peeled grapes, blindfold our little friends, and guide their hands to the bowl. 'Eyeballs,' we would say in sepulchral tones. 'Ewww!' was the expected reply. Next would come a chant about dying, being buried, becoming worm-infested, and turning green. All hilarious, to us, then. But how many of our once large basket of impish children are left? Not many. Gone, and with them the vestiges of the grape eyeballs and the green decaying bodies. A few old cronies clinging onto the cliff's edge, having tea and cookies in the sun and spilling crumbs and milk on their not entirely clean T-shirts, or distressing their neighbours by trying – slowly, ponderously, slipping dangerously on the ice – to shovel the snow off their walks. Here, let me do that for you. Oh no, I can manage, thank you. Beetles near the end of their life cycles, still gamely making their way up the once familiar flower stalk. Where am I and what am I doing here? the beetle might be wondering. How long can they go on? the neighbours muse. Surely not much longer.

Oh, don't suppose for an instant that we don't know what they're thinking. We thought it all ourselves, once. We still think it.

But none of this is happening to you, dear Stevie. You are much younger, although you don't think so now. If you live another thirty years – which I sincerely hope you will, and more, depending on your condition by then, of course – if you live another thirty years and are still enjoying it, or most of it – if anyone will be enjoying, or indeed living, considering the huge unknown wave that is already rolling toward us – I expect you will look at a picture of yourself as you are today, supposing your personal effects have survived flood, fire, famine, plague, insurrection, invasion, or whatever – and you will say, 'How young I was then!'

But that's a long digression. You asked me how I was doing, another social pleasantry. No one wants an honest answer to that one.

What you mean is how am I managing to cope, now that Tig has died. Am I lonely? Am I suffering? Is the house too empty? Am I checking all the boxes of the prescribed grieving process? Have I gone into the dark tunnel, dressed in mourning black with gloves and a veil, and come out the other end, all cheery and wearing bright colours and loaded for bear?

No. Because it's not a tunnel. There isn't any other end. Time has ceased to be linear, with life events and memories in a chronological row, like beads on a string. It's the strangest feeling, or experience, or rearrangement. I'm not sure I can explain it to you.

And it would alarm you unduly if I were to say to you, 'Tig isn't exactly gone.' You'd jump immediately to ghosts, or delusional states on my part, or dementia, but none of those would apply. You will understand it later, perhaps, this warping or folding of time. In some parts of this refolded time Tig still exists, as much as he ever did.

I don't intend to share any of this with you. I don't want you calling my younger friends and relatives in a state of concern and telling them something must be done about me. You were always a well-meaning busybody. I don't fault you for it – you have a kind heart, you are filled to the brim with good intentions, but I don't want any casseroles or oblique, probing questions, or visits from professionals, or nieces talking me into buying an assisted-care condo. And no, I do not wish to go on a cruise.

Meanwhile I'm hanging out with a clutch of other widows. Some of them are widowers: we have not yet got around to a gender-neutral term for those who have lost their life partners. Maybe TWHLTLP will appear shortly, but it hasn't yet. Some are women who have lost women or men who have lost men, but mostly they are women who have lost men. More fragile than we'd thought, those men: that much has made itself clear.

What do we talk about? The curious folding nature of time, the phenomenon I have just described to you: that has been experienced by all of us. The quirks and preferences of the lost ones. What they would have said – or are indeed still saying – on any given occasion.

The death scenes. We are a little obsessive about those: we share them, we revisit them, we edit them, arranging them to make them, perhaps, more tolerable. Which dwindling was the worst? Was it better to have witnessed a lingering fadeout, with pain but with lots of time to say goodbye, or on the other hand was a sudden stroke or heart failure preferable, easier for him, harder for you? *I could tell this was it. I left the room for five minutes and he was gone. We knew it was coming. Ten years? That must have been terrible.*

The tidying up. There's a lot of that. So much accumulates, year after year. Then there's a mini-explosion, and all the items that have been gathered together – the letters, the books, the passports, the photos, the favourite things kept in drawers and boxes or on shelves – all of this is strewn in the wake of the departing rocket or comet or wave of energy or silent breath, and the widows must sweep and sort and donate and bequeath and discard. Pieces of a soul, scattered here and there. The widows are thoroughly engaged by this task, and are being driven crazy by it in equal measure. We phone one another, all in a hand-wringing dither, and say, 'What am I possibly supposed to do with ... fill in the blank?' We offer lots of suggestions, none of which solves the central problem.

We talk about our regrets too; or some of them. *If only I had known. If only he had said. If only I had asked. I should have been more* ... fill in the blank. *If only we had* ... fill in the blank. There are a lot of blanks.

We're bad luck, of course, we widows. We know it. Awkward silences occur around us. People tiptoe. Should we be invited to dinner, or will we cast a pall? We certainly try not to cast palls: palls are unpleasant.

It used to be worse, in other places and in other eras. We'd get buried alive with the dead king, or we'd join him on his funeral pyre. If we escaped sharing his death, we'd have to wear black, or else white, forever. We had the evil eye. Black widow spiders, venomous enough to kill, were named after us. People crossed themselves and spat to avoid contamination by us. Or, if we were not decrepit – if we still had some blood left in us – we'd be merry widows, off the leash, looking for a little unbridled sexual action. An older man actually hinted at this to me at a party. (We do still go to parties. We paint our toenails red, though we put shoes on our feet so no one will see our flashy toes. We know this toe enhancement is absurd, but we do it anyway. A tiny dead-end pleasure.) I'd just met the man. No sooner were the introductions over than he gave the ghost of a leer and said, 'So, are you dating?' Meant as a joke, though possibly not. Widows are thought to be wealthy, and also susceptible.

I answered, a little sternly, 'I'm a widow. Tig just died.'

'So, you're hunting?'

It was a form of geriatric flirting on his part, I believe. People of our age can flirt like that without it being seriously inappropriate, because both parties know nothing will come of it. Or, more precisely, nothing *can* come of it. Flirtation Village, that's where we live. If I'd had an old-fashioned fan, I would have tapped him with it, archly, as in some grotesque Restoration comedy. *Oh, you are so naughty!*

I could not have said, 'Don't be silly. Tig is still here.' Instant gossip would have resulted: 'She's turned the corner into bonkersland.' 'Well, she was always a little odd.' And the like.

So we keep such notions to ourselves, we widows.

Needless to say, dear Stevie, I will not be sending you this letter. You are on the other side of the river. Over where you are, your beloved is still in tangible form. On this side, the widows. Between us flows the uncrossable. But I can wave to you, and wish you well, and that is what I will do. Thus:

Dear Stevie:

Thank you for your letter. I hope your health remains good. It's nice of you to ask how I'm doing. Quite well, I'm pleased to say. The winter dragged on, as it did for everyone, but now it's spring and I'm busy in the garden. Already there are snowdrops, and the daffodils are sending up their first shoots. I have my eye on some oriental lilies that I intend to plant in the front border. I used to have them years ago but the lily beetles got to them before I noticed. I'll be ready for those beetles this time: forewarned is forearmed.

The children are fine. The grandchildren are full of beans. I'm thinking of adopting a kitten. Not much other news. Let me know when you're coming this way and we'll grab lunch.

Stay safe.

Fondly,

Nell

Acknowledgements

The authors and publishers acknowledge the following sources of copyright material and are grateful for the permissions granted. While every effort has been made, it has not always been possible to identify the sources of all the material used, or to trace all copyright holders. If any omissions are brought to our notice, we will be happy to include the appropriate acknowledgements on reprinting.

'The Return' by Elizabeth Bowen, reproduced with permission of Curtis Brown Group Ltd, London, on behalf of the Literary Executors of the Estate of Elizabeth Bowen; 'Never' by H E Bates, reproduced with permission of Curtis Brown Group Ltd, London on behalf of The Estate of H E Bates. Copyright © H E Bates; 'A Lady's Beaded Bag' by Tennessee Williams, from the *Collected Stories of Tennessee Williams*, copyright © 1948 by The University of the South, reprinted by permission of New Directions Publishing Corp and *Collected Stories* copyright © 1930 by Tennessee Williams, © 1985 by the Estate of Tennessee Williams, reprinted by permission of Georges Borchardt, Inc. on behalf of the University of the South, all rights reserved; 'Like Mother Used to Make' from *The Lottery and Other Stories* by Shirley Jackson, Penguin Classics. Copyright © Shirley Jackson, 1948. Reprinted by permission of Penguin Books Limited and copyright © 1948, 1949 by Shirley Jackson. Copyright renewed 1976, 1977 by Laurence Hyman, Barry Hyman, Mrs Sarah Webster and Mrs Joanne Schnurer. Reprinted by permission of Farrar, Straus and Giroux, all rights reserved; 'The Lagoon' by Janet Frame. Copyright © Janet Frame Estate, 2004, used by permission of The Wylie Agency (UK) Limited; 'The Flying Machine' by Ray Bradbury, 1953, from *The Quickening Pulse 3*, Reprinted by permission of Don Congdon Associates, Inc. Copyright ©1953 by Ray Bradbury, renewed 1981 by Ray Bradbury; 'The Cricket Match' by Sam Selvon, 1957, from *Oxford Caribbean Short Stories*, Oxford University Press. Reproduced by permission of, and with thanks to, the Estate of Sam Selvon; 'The Blush' by Elizabeth Taylor from *The Complete Short Stories of Elizabeth Taylor* (Virago, 2012), reproduced with the permission of Johnson & Alcock; 'The Sacrificial Egg' by Chinua Achebe from *Girls at War and Other Stories* (Doubleday, 1973); 'Action Will Be Taken (An Action-Packed Story)' by Heinrich Boll, translated by Leila Vennewitz, from *18 Stories* (McGraw-Hill, 1966) used with permission of, Verlag Kiepenheuer & Witsch GmbH & Co. KG © 2024 and reproduced with the permission of Carla Reed, daughter of Leila Vennewitz; 'Woman from America' by Bessie Head, from *The Collector of Treasures* (Heinemann, 1992), reproduced with the permission of Johnson & Alcock; 'The Man Who Wouldn't Get Up' from *The Man Who Wouldn't Get Up and Other Stories* by David Lodge published by Vintage. Copyright © David Lodge, 2016. Reprinted by permission of The Random

House Group Limited and reproduced with permission of Curtis Brown Group Ltd, London on behalf of David Lodge, copyright © David Lodge 1998; 'A Very Desirable Residence' from *Sleep No More* by PD James, © P D James 1976, reproduced with the permission of Greene & Heaton, compilation copyright © 2017 by The Estate of P D James. Used by permission of Alfred A. Knopf, an imprint of the Knopf Doubleday Publishing Group, a division of Penguin Random House LLC., all rights reserved, and copyright © 2017 The Copyright Estate of P D James. Reprinted by permission of Alfred A. Knopf Canada, a division of Penguin Random House Canada Limited, all rights reserved; 'Sale' from *The Complete Stories* by Anita Desai published by Vintage. Copyright © Anita Desai, 2018. Reprinted by permission of Random House Limited and Copyright © Anita Desai. Reproduced by permission of the author c/o Rogers, Coleridge & White Ltd., 20 Powis Mews, London W11 1JN; 'Land Deal' from *Collected Fiction* by Gerald Murnane, reproduced with the permission of Giramondo Publishing Co, 2018; 'The Teddy-Bears' Picnic' from *The Stories of William Trevor* by William Trevor, reproduced with the permission of Johnson & Alcock; 'My Father Writes to My Mother' by Assia Djebar, translated by Dorothy S Blair, in *African Women's Writing* (Heinemann) reproduced with permission of Andrew Nurnberg Associates; 'Smoke' by Ila Mehta, translated from the original Gujarati by Sima Sharma, was first published in *Truth Tales: Contemporary Stories by Women Writers in India*, edited and published by Kali for women, New Delhi, 1986; 'Fishing' from *Electric City and Other Stories* © Patricia Grace, Penguin Random House NZ, 2002; 'The Fire Eater's Return' by Earl Lovelace, from *A Brief Conversation and Other Stories*, Persea Books, 2003, previously published by Heinemann, 1988, Copyright © Earl Lovelace 1988. Reproduced by permission of Earl Lovelace c/o Georgina Capel Associates Ltd and copyright © 1988 by Earl Lovelace. Used by permission of Persea Books, Inc (New York), www.perseabooks.com all rights reserved; 'The Secret of My Youth' by Mimoza Ahmeti translated from Albanian by Robert Elsie, first published in English in *Description of a Struggle: The Picador Book of Contemporary East European Prose* (Michael March, ed. London: Picador, 1994). The story was first published in its original language the periodical 'Nentori' Tirana, 1990; 'The Light on the Sea' by John Wickham, 1993, reprinted by permission of Francine Wickham on behalf of the Estate John Wickham; 'New York Day Women' from *Krik? Krak!*, copyright © 1991, 1995 by Edwidge Danticat reprinted by permission of Soho Press, Inc. All rights reserved; 'A Village After Dark' by Kazuo Ishiguro, published by The New Yorker, 2001. Copyright © Kazuo Ishiguro. Reproduced by permission of the author c/o Rogers, Coleridge & White Ltd., 20 Powis Mews, London W11 1JN; 'The Clean Slate' by Hilary Mantel (copyright © Tertius Enterprises, 2001) reproduced by permission of A M Heath on behalf of the Estate of Hilary Mantel and from *The Penguin Book of the Contemporary British Short Story* by Philip Hensher published by Penguin Press, reprinted by permission of Penguin Books Limited Copyright © Hilary Mantel, 2018; 'The American Embassy' from *The Thing Around Your Neck* by Chimamanda Ngozi Adichie, Copyright © 2009, Chimamanda Ngozi Adichie, used by permission of The Wylie Agency (UK) Limited, reprinted by permission of HarperCollins Publishers Ltd © 2009 and reprinted by permission of Vintage Canada/Alfred A Knopf Canada, a division of Penguin Random House Canada Limited. All rights reserved; 'Nietverloren' by J M Coetzee, published in *Three Stories* (Text Publishing), reprinted by permission of David Higham Associates; 'The Universal Story' from *The Penguin Book of the Contemporary British Short Story* by Philip Hensher published by Penguin Press, reprinted by permission of Penguin Books Limited, and from *The Whole Story and Other Stories* by Ali Smith, used by permission of Anchor Books, an imprint of the Knopf Doubleday Publishing Group, a division of Penguin Random House LLC., all rights reserved, copyright © 2003 by Ali Smith; 'Golden Boys' by Shih-li Know, reproduced with permission of the author. This story appears in the collection *Bone Weight and Other Stories* and was first published in Mud Season Review in 2008; 'Staying Behind' by Ken Liu, reprinted by permission of the author and author's agent, Scovil Galen Ghosh Literary Agency, 2020; 'My Father's Head' by Okwiri Oduor, Copyright © 2014, Okwiri Oduor, used by permission of The Wylie Agency (UK) Limited; 'The Nominee' from *You Think It, I'll Say It* by Curtis Sittenfeld published by Transworld. Copyright © Curtis Sittenfeld, 2018. Reprinted by permission of The Random House Group Limited and Copyright © 2018 by Curtis Sittenfeld; 'Hard to Say' from *Come On In* by Sharon Morse, published by Inkyard Press (2020), reproduced with permission from Talcott Notch Literary Services, LLC on behalf of the author, Sharon Morse; 'Reflection' from *Home of the Floating Lily* by Silmy Abdullah, Copyright © 2021, published by Dundurn Press Ltd; 'Kind Stranger' provided with permission of Meron Hadero © 2020 originally published in *Addis Ababa Noir*, edited for *A Down Home Meal for These Difficult Times*; 'Widows' from *Old Babes in the Wood* by Margaret Atwood, copyright © 2023 by O W Toad, Ltd. Used by permission of Doubleday, an imprint of the Knopf Doubleday Publishing Group, a division of Penguin Random House LLC., all rights reserved, and reprinted by permission of McClelland & Stewart, a division of Penguin Random House Canada Limited, all rights reserved.